C000155468

THE TOP 10 OF EVERYTHING 1992

RUSSELL ASH

Macdonald
Queen Anne Press

A QUEEN ANNE PRESS BOOK

© Queen Anne Press and Russell Ash 1991

First published in Great Britain in 1991 by
Queen Anne Press, a division of
Macdonald & Co (Publishers) Ltd
165 Great Dover Street
London SE1 4YA

A member of Maxwell Macmillan Publishing Corporation

All rights reserved. No part of this publication may be reproduced, stored in a
retrieval system, or transmitted, in any form or by any means, without the prior
permission in writing of the publisher, nor be otherwise circulated in any form of
binding or cover other than that in which it is published and without a similar
condition including this condition being imposed on the subsequent purchaser.

Design: Peter Champion and Michael Harris
Chapter title illustrations: Tom Saecker

A CIP catalogue record for this book is available from the British Library

ISBN 0-356-19607-0

Typeset by Tradespools Ltd, Frome, Somerset
Printed and bound in Great Britain by BPCC Hazell Books,
Aylesbury and Paulton

ABOUT THE AUTHOR

Photo by Susan Greenhill

Russell Ash was born in Surrey and went to school in Bedford. After obtaining a Joint Honours degree in Geography and Anthropology at the University of Durham, he worked briefly as an aviation insurance broker before his move into book publishing, which has occupied him for 22 years, latterly as a director of several major publishing companies. He has contributed to numerous publications, among them the *Sunday Times*, the *Observer*, *Punch* and the *Connoisseur*, and has a weekly column in the London magazine *Midweek*. He has written over 40 books in the diverse fields of art (particularly on the Impressionists and other late nineteenth-century painters including Sir Lawrence Alma-Tadema, van Gogh and Toulouse-Lautrec), animals real and fictitious (he is the author of *The Pig Book* and the official biographer of Paddington Bear), reference books including *The Londoner's Almanac*, as well as many humorous books, such as *The Cynic's Dictionary* and, as co-author, *Bizarre Books*. He compiles **THE TOP 10 OF EVERYTHING** with the indispensable help of his wife, Caroline, and using an Apple Macintosh computer – when his son Alexander lets him.

CONTENTS

INTRODUCTION

THE TOP 10 OF EVERYTHING is now in its third year, and is fast becoming a mini-industry: as well as the UK edition, it is now published in Australia, France, Germany, Italy and Japan. Additionally, two of the most popular categories featured in it – sport and music – are soon to become the subjects of special Top 10 books.

All this has been made possible by the growing support of **TOP 10** readers, and I am grateful to the many who have taken the trouble to write to me with their helpful suggestions. I have tried to answer everyone, but because the book has become such a major undertaking (I now start work on the new edition as soon as I've finished the current one!), this is not always possible, and if I haven't found the time to write back, please accept this as my acknowledgement of your contribution.

With each new edition I try to ring the changes as much as possible, juggling the balance between old favourites, updated lists and entirely new lists. Even lists that appear regularly have been closely monitored for changes: many of the music and film lists, for example, have been revised using even more accurate information. Just when I thought my 10 Deepest Caves list was definitive, the British Cave Research Association put me right. Even the list of the 10 Largest Dinosaurs has been revised in response to new data – so even something that's been around for 150 million years needs constant updating! A number of errors have also been corrected: big, bearded, butch astronaut Loren Acton was mistakenly included as one of the first 10 *women* in space! Perhaps his name caused the confusion, but my sincere apologies for this lapse, *Mr* Acton.

With annually changing lists there is, as always, an inevitable time lag before figures – especially official Government statistics – become available. In most instances figures are for 1990 unless otherwise stated. Published information on the two Germanys has not caught up since Unification and few statistics are available yet for the combined country.

Some sources are more reliable than others. I encountered this with lists such as that of the 10 Longest Seaside Piers: even the most recent and authoritative references included piers that had long since fallen into the sea, and the list was finally compiled after a great deal of communication with seaside resorts, pier owners and finally with the invaluable help of the National Pier Society. Just as with the lists of Most Valuable Jukeboxes, Most Expensive Photographs and Film Memorabilia, for instance, the only way to compile certain lists is to ask the experts – and, not for the first time, I was delighted that so many busy people were willing to find the time to provide information that would otherwise be unobtainable.

By slightly revising the design this year, we have managed to include more lists than ever. Many readers said they liked the quizzes, so there's a whole new batch. I have also added some short features giving extra information on a variety of subjects. As usual, in covering such a vast amount of ground, there are some odd juxtapositions: where else would you find the leading Nobel Prize winners and the most popular kissograms on the same page? I hope that this quirky range, and the many unexpected results thrown up by the lists, add to the book's continuing appeal.

Compiling **THE TOP 10 OF EVERYTHING** is not without its frustrations. Among them is the constant problem that it is often possible to start a list but not quite make it to 10. What also sometimes happens is that I get to 10 and then someone, perhaps a reader or an information source, says 'What about so-and-so?' Such a list is The 10 Tallest Free-standing Statues in the World (pages 98–99), which I referred to as a problem in the last edition. I feel sure that some well-travelled reader or statue-ologist will immediately tell me I have missed out some colossal statue in the heart of the USSR. For the list of 10 Longest Pub Names, I've been told that there is a pub called The Three Merry Companies in Bedlam Tavern (36 letters) – but does it still exist, and where is it?

As well as these 'problem' lists, there are certain lists about which no two sources agree and which seem almost impossible to compile – without your help. I am convinced from my readership response (especially from young readers) that there are many people who would be willing to share their specialist knowledge with the public. Here are some examples of lists which I am sure could be compiled, but for which I need your assistance:

What are The 10 Longest Book Titles? There are some pretty hefty science-fiction novel titles, among them: *Hot Wireless Sets, Aspirin Tablets, the Sandpaper Sides of Used Matchboxes, and Something that might have been Castor Oil*, and how about *The Mad Merger Meets the Gorn from Sucker at Some Indefinite Time in the Future When Things are in a Hell of a Mess but Everything Turns Out All Right in the End with the Death of the Hero*. But are these the longest ever?

What are The 10 Longest-lived Cats and Dogs – are there any that come close to the records of around 30 years?

Who are The 10 People with the Most First Names? The daughter of Sarah Jane and Arthur Pepper, born in Derby on 19 December 1882, was given one for every letter of the alphabet, starting with Ann and ending with Zeus – and there have since been many babies with far more than 26 names inflicted on them.

What are The 10 Most Valuable Stamps, The 10 Tallest Towers and The 10 Largest Domes in the World?

If you simply have one or more suggested entries for any of these categories, please send them in: if enough people do the same, it may be possible to build up a Top 10 list. If you are able to offer a complete Top 10, with reference sources, so much the better.

Russell Ash

If you have any comments or suggestions for
new Top 10 lists, please write to:

Russell Ash
c/o Queen Anne Press
165 Great Dover Street
London SE1 4YA

For Caroline, once again

THE UNIVERSE

THE 10 BRIGHTEST STARS

	Star	Constellation
1	Sun	Solar System
2	Sirius	Canis Major
3	Canopus	Carina
4	Alpha Centauri	Centaurus
5	Vega	Lyra
6	Capella	Auriga
7	Arcturus	Boötes
8	Rigel	Orion
9	Procyon	Canis Minor
10	Achernar	Eridanus

Based on apparent visual magnitude as viewed from Earth. At its brightest, the star Betelgeuse is brighter than some of these, but as it is variable its average brightness disqualifies it from the Top 10. If the Sun is excluded, the 10th brightest star is Beta Centauri in the constellation of Centaurus.

THE 10 STARS NEAREST TO EARTH

	Star	Light years	Distance km	miles
1	Proxima Centauri	4.22	33,923,310,000,000	24,805,160,000,000
2	Alpha Centauri	4.35	41,153,175,000,000	25,569,300,000,000
3	Barnard's Star	5.98	56,790,790,000,000	35,150,440,000,000
4	Wolf 359	7.75	73,318,875,000,000	45,554,500,000,000
5	Lalande 21185	8.22	77,765,310,000,000	48,317,160,000,000
6	Luyten 726–8	8.43	79,752,015,000,000	49,551,540,000,000
7	Sirius	8.65	81,833,325,000,000	50,844,700,000,000
8	Ross 154	9.45	89,401,725,000,000	55,547,100,000,000
9	Ross 248	10.40	98,389,200,000,000	61,131,200,000,000
10	Epsilon Eridani	10.80	102,173,400,000,000	63,482,400,000,000

A spaceship travelling at 56,327 kph/35,000 mph – which is faster than any human has yet reached in space – would take over 80 years to reach Earth's closest star, Proxima Centauri.

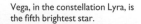

Vega, in the constellation Lyra, is the fifth brightest star.

QUIZ

STARS

1 With what theory of the universe is George Gamow associated: (a) Black Holes, (b) quarks, or (c) the Big Bang Theory?
2 What is the name given to the small dense stars first discovered by Jocelyn Bell in 1967?
3 From what film did Lee Marvin's Number One hit record *Wand'rin' Star* come?
4 How many stars were there on the original American 'Stars and Stripes' flag?
5 Early astronomers used an instrument to measure the position of the stars. Was it called (a) a planetoid, (b) an astrolabe, or (c) an orrery?
6 The motto of which organization is *Per Ardua ad Astra* – Through Adversity to the Stars?
7 Who ruled England when the supernova known as the Crab Nebula could be seen with the naked eye: (a) Julius Caesar, (b) Edward the Confessor, or (c) Queen Victoria?
8 After what animal is the constellation Cetus named?
9 Who had a 1981 Top 20 hit record with *Star*?
10 What is the origin of the word 'galaxy'?

THE 10 LARGEST PLANETARY MOONS

Moon	Planet	Diameter km	miles
1 Ganymede	Jupiter	5,262	3,270

Discovered by Galileo in 1609–10 and believed to be the largest moon in the Solar System, Ganymede – one of Jupiter's 16 satellites – is thought to have a surface of ice about 97 km/60 miles thick. The 1979 *Voyager 1* and 2 space probes failed to detect evidence of an atmosphere. NASA's *Galileo* probe is scheduled to investigate the Jovian moons Ganymede, Callisto, Io and Europa in November 1995.

2 Titan	Saturn	5,150	3,200

Titan, the largest of Saturn's 20 or more moons, is actually larger than two of the planets in the Solar System, Mercury and Pluto. It was discovered by the Dutch astronomer Christian Huygens in 1655. We have no idea what its surface looks like because it has a dense atmosphere containing nitrogen, ethane and other gases which shroud its surface – not unlike that of Earth 4 billion years ago – but data sent back by *Voyager 1* during 1980 and recent radio telescope observations suggest that it may have ethane 'oceans' and 'continents' of ice or other solid matter. NASA and the European Space Agency have announced plans to send a space probe to Titan as part of the Cassini Mission, to be launched in April 1996. It should touch down on Titan's surface in October 2002.

3 Callisto	Jupiter	4,820	2,995

Possessing a similar composition to Ganymede, Callisto is heavily pitted with craters, perhaps more so than any other body in the Solar System.

4 Io	Jupiter	3,632	2,257

Most of what we know about Io was reported back by the 1979 *Voyager* probe, which revealed a crust of solid sulphur with massive volcanic eruptions in progress, hurling sulphurous material 300 km/186 miles into space.

5 Moon	Earth	3,475	2,159

Our own satellite is a quarter of the size of the Earth, the 5th largest in the Solar System and, to date, the only one to have been explored by Man.

6 Europa	Jupiter	3,126	1,942

Although Europa's ice-covered surface is apparently smooth and crater-free, it is covered with mysterious black lines, some of them 64 km/40 miles wide and resembling canals.

7 Triton	Neptune	2,750	1,708

Discovered on 10 October 1846 by brewer and amateur astronomer William Lassell, 17 days after he had discovered Neptune itself, Triton is the only known satellite in the Solar System that revolves around its planet in the opposite direction to the planet's rotation. It is getting progressively closer to Neptune, and it is believed that in several million years the force of the planet's gravity may pull it apart, scattering it into a form like the rings of Saturn. Information sent back to Earth by *Voyager 2* during August 1989 revealed the presence of three or four rings and 'ring arcs', or incomplete rings, at distances of between 17,110 km/10,625 miles and 38,100 km/23,674 miles from the planet's cloud tops, as well as six previously undiscovered moons, which were given the temporary names of 1989N1–1989N6. These range in size from the 400 km/249 miles of 1989N1 (making it larger than Neptune's other previously known moon, Nereid, which was discovered in 1948, at 340 km/211 miles) down to 1989N6's 54 km/34 miles. The probe also showed that Triton has an atmosphere composed largely of methane and a surface covered with methane ice glaciers. Recent studies have more than halved Triton's estimated size, relegating it from 1st to 7th position in the Top 10 moons, and removing it altogether from its place in the 10 largest bodies in the Solar System.

8 Titania	Uranus	1,580	982

The largest of Uranus's 15 moons, Titania was discovered by William Herschel (who had discovered the planet six years earlier) in 1787 and has a snowball-like surface of ice. Its size estimate was revised by data from *Voyager 2*.

9 Rhea	Saturn	1,530	951

Saturn's second largest moon was discovered by seventeenth- century Italian-born French astronomer Giovanni Cassini. *Voyager 1*, which flew past Rhea in November 1980, confirmed that its icy surface is pitted with craters, one of them 225 km/140 miles in diameter.

10 Oberon	Uranus	1,516	942

Oberon was discovered by Herschel and given the name of the fairy king husband of Queen Titania, both characters in *A Midsummer Night's Dream*. New information from *Voyager 2* has relegated Oberon from 9th to 10th place in this list.

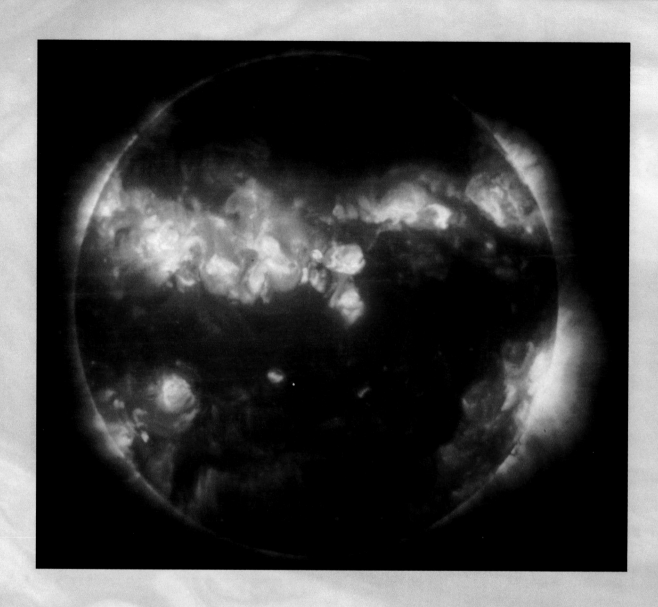

THE 10 LARGEST BODIES IN THE SOLAR SYSTEM

	Name	Maximum diameter	
		km	miles
1	Sun	1,392,140	865,036
2	Jupiter	142,984	88,846
3	Saturn	120,536	74,898
4	Uranus	51,118	31,763
5	Neptune	49,600	30,820
6	Earth	12,756	7,926
7	Venus	12,103	7,520
8	Mars	6,794	4,222
9	Ganymede	5,262	3,270
10	Titan	5,150	3,200

Ganymede is the largest of Jupiter's 16 satellites. Two planets do not quite make this Top 10 list: the diameter of Mercury is 4,880 km/3,032 miles, and that of Pluto, although uncertain, is thought to be approximately 2,284 km/1,419 miles. Triton, one of Neptune's two largest moons (the other is the much smaller Nereid), was formerly ranked 9th, but its diameter has recently been re-estimated (*see* The 10 Largest Planetary Moons).

ABOVE High-resolution x-ray of the Sun, the pre-eminent body in the Solar System.

BACKGROUND Jupiter, ranked second in size, with its satellite Ganymede in ninth place.

Asteroids are fragments of rock orbiting between Mars and Jupiter. There are perhaps 45,000 of them, but fewer than 10 per cent have been named. The first (and largest) to be discovered was Ceres, which was found by Giuseppi Piazzi (1746–1826), director of the observatory in Palermo, Sicily, on New Year's Day, 1801. All have been numbered according to the order in which they were discovered. Some have only code numbers, but most also have names: women's names are especially popular and include Hilda (No. 153), Bertha (No. 154), Marilyn (No. 1,486), Sabrina (No. 2,264) and Samantha (No. 3,147). Among asteroids named after men are Mark Twain (No. 2,362) and Brian (No. 3,254). Nos. 3,350–3,356 were named after the seven astronauts killed in the 1986 *Challenger* space shuttle disaster, No. 2,309 is called Mr Spock after the character in *Star Trek* and Nos. 453, 1,896 and 2,683 have the odd names, respectively, of Tea, Beer and Bus.

THE 10 LARGEST ASTEROIDS IN THE SOLAR SYSTEM

	Name	Year discovered	Diameter km	Diameter miles
1	Ceres	1801	936	582
2	Pallas	1802	607	377
3	Vesta	1807	519	322
4	Hygeia	1849	450	279
5	Euphrosyne	1854	370	229
6	Interamnia	1910	349	217
7	Davida	1903	322	200
8	Cybele	1861	308	192
9	Europa	1858	288	179
10	Patienta	1899	275	171

THE FIRST 10 ASTEROIDS

	Name	Year discovered
1	Ceres	1801
2	Pallas	1802
3	Juno	1804
4	Vesta	1807
5	Astraea	1845
6	Hebe	1847
7	Iris	1847
8	Flora	1847
9	Metis	1848
10	Hygeia	1849

BELOW The unusual elongated asteroid Hektor, largest of the Trojan asteroids (those following Jupiter's orbit).

THE 10 MOST FREQUENTLY SEEN COMETS

	Comet	Period (years)
1	Encke	3.30
2	Grigg-Skjellerup	4.91
3	Honda-Mrkós-Pajdusáková	5.21
4	Tempel 2	5.26
5	Neujmin 2	5.43
6	Tuttle-Giacobini-Kresák	5.48
7	Tempel-Swift	5.68
8	Tempel 1	5.98
9	Pons-Winnecke	6.30
10	de Vico Swift	6.31

Comets have been observed streaking across the heavens since ancient times, but it was not until 1682 that Edmund Halley, the Astronomer Royal, predicted that the comet observed that year was identical to the one recorded in 1531 and 1607, and that comets had an orbit or period that could be calculated and used to predict when they would return. 'Halley's Comet', as it became known, had, he declared, a period of about 76 years – and, sure enough, it was seen again in 1758 (although by then Halley himself was dead). Subsequently, it has been shown that Halley's Comet, which was last seen in 1986, had been widely observed during many of its previous visits without it being realized that it was the same comet: it was even seen in 1066 and was depicted in the Bayeux Tapestry. Since Halley's day, many comets have been observed with varying periods: those in the Top 10 and several others return with regularity (although with some notable variations), while others have such long periods that they may not be seen again for many thousands, or even millions, of years. The most frequent visitor is Encke's Comet, named after the German astronomer Johann Franz Encke, who in 1818 calculated the period of its elliptical orbit. It had been first observed shortly before his birth, but without its orbit being calculated, and has been seen on almost all its subsequent returns. Encke's Comet is becoming extremely faint (comets often disappear either through disintegration or changes in their orbits) and after its next expected return in 1994 it may well be 'lost'.

The portentous 1066 appearance of the comet we now know as Halley's is reported with alarm to King Harold in the Bayeux Tapestry.

ASTRONOMICAL NAMES

Space is certainly the 'final frontier' when it comes to naming new discoveries. Every new asteroid, star, moon and crater has to be given a designation, and it was not long into the history of astronomy before virtually every classical and mythological name had been used, causing astronomers to resort to ever stranger appellations.

In 1781 Sir William Herschel discovered the seventh planet and loyally decided to call it George, or 'the Georgian planet', after King George III. Other suggestions included Hypercronius and Herschel, but it was finally called after the Greek god Uranus. The features on one of Uranus's moons, Oberon, are all named after Shakespearean characters such as Hamlet, Romeo and Macbeth. Then there are moon craters called Hell (after Maximilian Hell, a Hungarian astronomer), and Billy, while Mercury's craters have an artistic ring – there are poets Milton, Byron and Coleridge, composers Beethoven, Chopin and Wagner, artists van Gogh, Gainsborough and Matisse and writers including Dickens, Shakespeare and Proust. There is an odd convention about naming the craters on Venus: large craters are called after mythological figures and small craters of 100 km/62 miles or less in diameter commemorate famous women, among them Florence Nightingale, the French novelist Colette, flier Amelia Earhart and dancer Anna Pavlova. When it was proposed to call one of them Eve, the American National Organization for Women objected because, they insisted, she was not a real woman.

Comets in particular attract strange names. When they are first discovered, they are simply called after the year and order in which they are found: 1977d, for example, is the fourth comet discovered in that year. When their orbits are fully calculated, they receive Roman numbers, but they are also often given the name – or names – of their discoverers. In this way we get names that roll less than trippingly off the tongue, such as Pons-Coggia-Winnecke-Forbes, Whipple-Fedtke-Tevzadze 1943 I, Schwassmann-Wachmann, or the one that sounds like a racing motorcycle – Tago-Honda-Yamamoto 1968 IV.

PLANET EARTH

ABOVE The 'meeting of the waters' of two great South American rivers, the Río Negro (black) and the Amazon (brown).

OPPOSITE The Zaïre, after the Nile the second longest river in the African continent.

THE 10 LONGEST RIVERS IN THE WORLD

	River	Countries	Length km	miles
1	Nile	Tanzania/Uganda/ Sudan/Egypt	6,670	4,145
2	Amazon	Peru/Brazil	6,448	4,007
3	Mississippi–Missouri– Red Rock	USA	5,971	3,710
4	Yenisey–Angara– Selenga	USSR	5,540	3,442
5	Yangtze Kiang	China	5,530	3,436
6	Ob'–Irtysh	USSR	5,410	3,362
7	Huang Ho (Yellow River)	China	4,830	3,001
8	Zaïre (Congo)	Angola/Zaïre	4,700	2,920
9	Lena–Kirenga	USSR	4,400	2,734
10	Amur–Argun	China/USSR	4,345	2,700

THE 10 LONGEST RIVERS IN SOUTH AMERICA

	River	Countries	Length km	miles
1	Amazon	Peru/Brazil	6,448	4,007
2	Plata–Paraná	Brazil/Paraguay/ Argentina/Uruguay	4,000	2,485
3	Madeira–Mamoré–Grande	Bolivia/Brazil	3,380	2,100
4	Purus	Peru/Brazil	3,207	1,993
5	São Francisco	Brazil	3,198	1,987
6	Orinoco	Colombia/Venezuela	2,736	1,700
7	Tocantins	Brazil	2,699	1,677
8	Paraguay	Paraguay/Brazil/ Argentina/Bolivia	2,549	1,584
9	Japurá–Caquetá	Colombia/Brazil	2,414	1,500
10	Negro	Colombia/Venezela/ Brazil	2,253	1,400

THE 10 LONGEST RIVERS IN NORTH AMERICA

	River	Country	km	Length miles
1	Mackenzie–Peace	Canada	4,241	2,635
2	Missouri–Red Rock	USA	4,088	2,540
3	Mississippi	USA	3,779	2,348
4	Missouri	USA	3,726	2,315
5	Yukon	USA	3,185	1,979
6	St Lawrence	Canada	3,130	1,945
7	Rio Grande	USA	2,832	1,760
8	Nelson	Canada	2,575	1,600
9	Arkansas	USA	2,348	1,459
10	Colorado	USA	2,334	1,450

The Mississippi, Missouri and Red Rock rivers are often combined, thus becoming the 3rd longest river in the world at 5,971 km/3,710 miles.

THE 10 LONGEST RIVERS IN AFRICA

	River	Countries	km	Length miles
1	Nile	Tanzania/Uganda/ Sudan/Egypt	6,670	4,145
2	Zaïre (Congo)	Angola/Zaïre	4,700	2,920
3	Niger	Guinea/Nigeria	4,100	2,550
4	Zambezi	Zambia/ Mozambique	2,650	1,650
5	Shebeli	Somalia	2,490	1,550
6	Ubangi	Zaïre	2,460	1,530
7	Orange	Namibia/ South Africa	2,250	1,400
8	Kasai	Zaïre	1,930	1,200
9	Senegal–Bafing	Mauritania/ Senegal	1,700	1,050
10	Blue Nile	Sudan	1,610	1,000

THE 10 LONGEST RIVERS IN THE UK

	River	km	Length miles
1	Severn	354	220
2	Thames	346	215
3	Trent	298	185
4	Aire	259	161
5	Great Ouse	230	143
6	Wye	217	135
7	Tay	188	117
8	Nene	161	100
9	Clyde	159	98.5
10	Spey	158	98

During their courses, some rivers change their names, for example, Trent/ Humber, Thames/Isis.

THE 10 LONGEST RIVERS IN EUROPE*

	River	Countries	Length km	miles
1	Danube	Germany/Austria/ Czechoslovakia/Hungary/ Yugoslavia/Romania/ Bulgaria	2,842	1,766
2	Rhine	Switzerland/Germany/ Holland	1,368	850
3	Elbe	Czechoslovakia/Germany	1,167	725
4	Loire	France	1,014	630
5	Tagus	Portugal	1,009	627
6	Meuse	France/Belgium/Holland	950	590
7	Ebro	Spain	933	580
8	Rhône	Switzerland/France	813	505
9	Guadiana	Spain/Portugal	805	500
10	Seine	France	776	482

*Excluding USSR.

Without excluding those rivers in the USSR in Europe, all 10 rivers would be Russian, with the 3,687-km/2,291-mile Volga heading the list.

THE 10 LONGEST RIVERS IN AUSTRALIA

	River	Length km	miles
1	Murray–Darling–Culgoa–Balonne– Condamine	3,750	2,330
2	Murray	1,754	1,090
3=	Barwon–Macintyre–Dumaresq–Severn	1,577	980
3=	Murrumbidgee	1,577	980
5	Lachlan	1,481	920
6	Fitzroy–Dawson	1,110	690
7	Macquarie	950	590
8	Namoi	853	530
9	Flinders	837	520
10	Bogan	724	450

THE 10 GREATEST* RIVERS IN THE WORLD

	River	Outflow	Average flow (m³/sec)
1	Amazon	Brazil	175,000
2	Zaïre	Angola/Zaïre	39,000
3	Negro	Brazil	35,000
4	Yangtze Kiang	China	32,190
5	Orinoco	Venezuela	25,200
6	Plata–Paraná–Grande	Uruguay	22,900
7	Madeira–Mamoré–Grande	Brazil	21,800
8	Yenisey–Angara–Selenga	USSR	18,000
9	Brahmaputra	Bangladesh	16,290
10	Lena–Kirenga	USSR	16,100

*Based on rate of discharge at source.

QUIZ

RIVERS

1 What river is popularly called 'Old Man River'?
2 What English river has the same name as the Egyptian goddess, the mother of Horus?
3 In American slang, why does to be 'sent up the river' mean 'sent to prison'?
4 What do the English rivers Witham, Welland, Nene and Great Ouse have in common?
5 What rivers were known to the Romans as the Sabrina, Sequana and Liger?
6 On what river does Moscow stand?
7 Who was the composer of *The Blue Danube*?
8 Where is the River Lethe?
9 On which river are Doggett's Coat and Badge race and the custom known as Swan-upping held annually?
10 Where is the Mad River?

THE 10 HIGHEST WATERFALLS IN THE WORLD

	Waterfall	River	Location/country	Drop m	ft
1	Angel	Carrao	Venezuela	979	3,212
2	Tugela	Tugela	South Africa	948	3,110
3	Utigård	Jostedal Glacier	Nesdale, Norway	800	2,625
4	Mongefossen	Monge	Mongebekk, Norway	774	2,540
5	Yosemite	Yosemite Creek	California, USA	739	2,425
6	Østre Mardøla Foss	Mardals	Eikisdal, Norway	657	2,154
7	Tyssestrengane	Tysso	Hardanger, Norway	646	2,120
8	Cuquenán	Arabopo	Venezuela	610	2,000
9	Sutherland	Arthur	South Island, New Zealand	580	1,904
10	Kjellfossen	Naero	Gudvangen, Norway	561	1,841

THE 10 HIGHEST WATERFALLS IN THE UK

	Waterfall	Country	Drop m	ft
1	Eas Coul Aulin	Scotland	201	658
2	Falls of Glomach	Scotland	113	370
3	Pystyll y Llyn	Wales	91	300
4	Pistyll Rhaeadr	Wales	73	240
5	Falls of Foyers	Scotland	62.5	205
6	Falls of Clyde	Scotland	62.2	204
7=	Falls of the Bruar	Scotland	61	200
7=	Caldron Snout	England	61	200
7=	Grey Mare's Tail	Scotland	61	200
10	Falls of Measach	Scotland	46	150

BELOW David Livingstone explores Africa. He was to discover and name the Victoria Falls.

THE MOUNTAIN OF CRYSTAL AND THE SMOKE THAT THUNDERS

In 1594 Sir Walter Raleigh journeyed up the Orinoco river in search of the legendary city of Eldorado. The climate, powerful currents and dwindling supplies forced him to abandon his quest, but before turning back he saw at a distance a waterfall that resembled a 'Mountain of Crystal...like a white church tower of an exceeding height'. What Raleigh had discovered was almost certainly the world's highest waterfall, which subsequent Spanish explorers – such as Ernesto Sanchez La Cruz in 1910 – also reported seeing, but without naming it. Giving the falls a name was left to the American adventurer James Angel, who was prospecting for gold in the Guiana Highlands. On 14 November 1933 he first spotted the falls from the air, later crash-landing his aeroplane on a nearby plateau. He survived and made his way back to civilization, and the Angel Falls were named in his honour.

★ ★ ★

From 1852 until 1856 Scottish missionary David Livingstone explored the heart of Africa. During his journey up the Zambezi river, he encountered one of the world's most spectacular waterfalls, writing in his diary on 17 November 1855:

'We came in sight for the first time of the columns of vapour appropriately called smoke, rising at a distance of five or six miles, exactly as when large tracts of grass are burned in Africa. Five columns now arose and, bending in the direction of the wind, they seemed placed against a low ridge covered with trees; the tops of the columns at this distance appeared to mingle with the clouds.'

Although the falls, known locally as Mosi-oa-tunya ('smoke that thunders'), were almost certainly known to Catholic missionaries who had visited the region more than 200 years earlier, Livingstone 'claimed' them for Britain, naming them Victoria Falls after Queen Victoria. Commemorating his discovery by carving his initials on a tree, Livingstone continued up the Zambezi.

THE 10 GREATEST* WATERFALLS IN THE WORLD

	Waterfall	Country	Average flow (m³/sec)
1	Boyoma	Zaïre	17,000
2	Guaíra	Brazil/Paraguay	13,000
3	Khône	Laos	11,500
4	Niagara	Canada/USA	6,000
5	Paulo Afonso	Brazil	2,800
6	Urubupungá	Brazil	2,700
7	Cataratas del Iguazú	Brazil/Paraguay	1,700
8	Patos–Maribondo	Brazil	1,500
9	Victoria	Zimbabwe	1,100
10	Churchill	Canada	1,000

*Based on volume of water.

In full flood, the rate of flow of the Guaíra has been calculated to reach a peak of 50,000 m³/sec. At 10.8 km/6.7 miles, the Khône Falls are the widest in the world.

THE 10 HIGHEST MOUNTAINS IN THE WORLD

	Mountain	Country	Height m	ft
1	Everest	Nepal/Tibet	8,848	29,029
2	K2 (Chogori or Godwin-Austen)	Kashmir/China	8,611	28,250
3	Kanchenjunga	Nepal/Sikkim	8,598	28,208
4	Lhotse	Nepal/Tibet	8,501	27,890
5	Makalu	Nepal/Tibet	8,470	27,790
6	Dhaulagiri I	Nepal	8,172	26,810
7	Manaslu	Nepal	8,156	26,760
8	Cho Oyu	Nepal	8,153	26,750
9	Nanga Parbat	Kashmir	8,126	26,660
10	Annapurna I	Nepal	8,078	26,504

LEFT The flow rate of the majestic Victoria Falls ranks them ninth greatest in the world.

RIGHT Scafell Pike (on the left). At 977m/3,206 ft it is England's highest mountain.

THE 10 HIGHEST MOUNTAINS IN ENGLAND

	Mountain	Height m	ft
1	Scafell Pike	977	3,206
2	Sca Fell	964	3,162
3	Helvellyn	949	3,113
4	Skiddaw	931	3,054
5	Bow Fell	902	2,960
6	Great Gable	899	2,949
7	Cross Fell	893	2,930
8	Pillar Fell	892	2,927
9	Esk Pike	885	2,903
10	Fairfield	873	2,863

All 10 of England's highest peaks are in Cumbria.

THE BATTLE FOR THE TOP

All 10 of the world's highest mountains are in the Himalayas, but the peak of Chimborazo in Ecuador, which is not even one of the Top 30 highest mountains in the world, is 2,151 m/7,057 ft further from the centre of the Earth than Everest's. This is because it is much nearer the Equator, where the Earth bulges more. No two sources agree on the precise heights of the world's tallest mountains, partly because of the inaccuracy of measuring instruments, which are affected by the gravitational attraction of the mountains, partly because the ice caps on their peaks vary in depth from season to season, and partly because many of them are inaccessible. Sir George Everest (1790–1866), the Surveyor-General of India, undertook the measurement of mountains in the Himalayas as part of a map-making programme that occupied him for more than 20 years during the early nineteenth century. Using theodolites, he and his colleagues took sightings on a number of peaks from observation points as far away as 100 miles, revealing that one of them rose to a height of over 29,000 feet – but only just: a height of 29,002 feet was assigned to it as a result of averaging out results from several triangulation stations. Since he was unaware of its Tibetan name (Chomolungma, or 'Goddess Mother of the World'), it was called after Everest himself. The calculation was extremely complicated, partly because it had to be based on height above sea level – and the nearest sea is almost 500 miles away. Recent surveys by Chinese surveyors using more precise equipment have shown that the calculations of the Everest team were out by the remarkably small margin of 0.09 per cent, and 27 feet 3 inches have been added to make the height of the world's tallest mountain 8,848 m/29,029 feet 3 inches. A recent and as yet not widely accepted satellite survey has gone further, putting its height at 8,863 m/29,078 ft. Another satellite survey suggested that K2 actually measured 8,859 m/29,064 ft, placing it some 11 m/35 ft higher than Everest – which was later refuted by the Chinese, who confirmed K2's height as 8,611 m/28,250 ft.

THE 10 HIGHEST MOUNTAINS IN IRELAND

	Mountain	Height m	ft
1	Carrauntual, Kerry	1,042	3,414
2	Beenkeraugh, Kerry	1,010	3,314
3=	Caher, Kerry	975	3,200
3=	Ridge of the Reeks, Kerry	975	3,200
5	Brandon, Kerry	953	3,127
6	Lugnaquilla, Wicklow	926	3,039
7	Galtymore, Tipperary	920	3,018
8=	Slieve Donard, Co Down	852	2,796
8=	Baurtregaum, Kerry	852	2,796
10	Mullaghcleevaun, Wicklow	850	2,788

Slieve Donard is the highest mountain in Northern Ireland. All the others are in the Irish Republic.

THE 10 HIGHEST MOUNTAINS IN SCOTLAND

	Mountain	Height m	ft
1	Ben Nevis, Highland	1,344	4,408
2	Ben Macdhui, Grampian	1,309	4,296
3	Braeriach, Grampian/ Highland	1,296	4,252
4	Cairn Toul, Grampian	1,293	4,241
5	Cairn Gorm, Grampian/ Highland	1,245	4,084
6	Aonach Beag, Highland	1,236	4,054
7	Carn Mór Dearg, Highland	1,223	4,012
8	Aonach Mór, Highland	1,219	3,999
9	Ben Lawers, Tayside	1,214	3,984
10	Beinn a' Bhùird, Grampian	1,196	3,924

THE 10 HIGHEST MOUNTAINS IN WALES

	Mountain	Height m	ft
1	Snowdon	1,085	3,560
2	Carnedd Llewelyn	1,062	3,484
3	Carnedd Dafydd	1,044	3,426
4	Glyder Fawr	999	3,279
5	Glyder Fâch	994	3,262
6	Y Garn	946	3,104
7	Foel Fras	942	3,091
8	Elidir Fawr	923	3,029
9	Tryfan	917	3,010
10	Aran Fawddwy	905	2,970

All the tallest Welsh peaks are in the Snowdonia region of the county of Gwynedd. Several also have sub-peaks that are similarly tall, but are not included as separate mountains.

LEFT Mount Foraker, Alaska, the sixth highest in North America.

OPPOSITE Striking rock formations in the Australian Desert.

THE 10 HIGHEST MOUNTAINS IN NORTH AMERICA

	Mountain	Country	Height m	ft
1	McKinley	USA	6,194	20,320
2	Logan	Canada	6,050	19,850
3	Citlaltépetl (Orizaba)	Mexico	5,700	18,700
4	St Elias	USA/Canada	5,489	18,008
5	Popocatépetl	Mexico	5,452	17,887
6	Foraker	USA	5,304	17,400
7	Ixtaccihuatl	Mexico	5,286	17,343
8	Lucania	Canada	5,226	17,147
9	King	Canada	5,173	16,971
10	Steele	Canada	5,073	16,644

Includes only the tallest peak of each mountain.

THE 10 LARGEST OCEANS AND SEAS IN THE WORLD

	Ocean/sea	Approx. area	
		sq km	sq miles
1	Pacific Ocean		
	(with adjacent seas)	181,343,000	70,017,000
	(without adjacent seas)	166,241,000	64,186,000
2	Atlantic Ocean		
	(with adjacent seas)	94,314,000	36,415,000
	(without adjacent seas)	86,557,000	33,420,000
3	Indian Ocean		
	(with adjacent seas)	74,118,000	28,617,000
	(without adjacent seas)	73,426,000	28,350,000
4	Arctic Ocean		
	(with adjacent seas)	12,256,000	4,732,000
	(without adjacent seas)	9,485,000	3,662,000
5	Coral Sea	4,791,000	1,850,000
6	Arabian Sea	3,864,000	1,492,000
7	South China Sea	3,686,000	1,423,000
8	Caribbean Sea	2,753,000	1,063,000
9	Mediterranean Sea	2,515,000	971,000
10	Bering Sea	2,305,000	890,000

THE 10 LARGEST LAKES IN THE WORLD

	Lake	Countries	Approx. area	
			sq km	sq miles
1	Caspian Sea	Iran/USSR	371,800	143,552
2	Superior	Canada/USA	82,350	31,795
3	Victoria	Kenya/Tanzania/ Uganda	69,500	26,834
4	Aral Sea	USSR	65,500	25,290
5	Huron	Canada/USA	59,600	23,012
6	Michigan	USA	58,000	22,394
7	Tanganyika	Burundi/Tanzania/ Zaïre/Zambia	32,900	12,703
8	Great Bear	Canada	31,800	12,278
9	Baikal	USSR	30,500	11,776
10	Nyasa (Malawi)	Malawi/Mozambique/ Tanzania	29,600	11,429

Lake Superior is the world's largest freshwater lake. Lake Baikal (or Baykal) in Siberia, with a depth of as much as 1.94 km/1.2 miles in parts, is the world's deepest.

THE 10 LARGEST DESERTS IN THE WORLD

	Desert	Location	Approx. area	
			sq km	sq miles
1	Sahara	North Africa	9,000,000	3,474,920
2	Australian	Australia	3,830,000	1,478,771
3	Arabian	Southwest Asia	1,300,000	501,933
4	Gobi	Central Asia	1,295,000	500,002
5	Kalahari	Southern Africa	520,000	200,772
6	Turkestan	Central Asia	450,000	173,745
7	Takla Makan	China	327,000	126,255
8=	Sonoran	USA/Mexico	310,000	119,691
8=	Namib	Southwest Africa	310,000	119,691
10=	Thar	Northwest India/ Pakistan	260,000	100,386
10=	Somali	Somalia	260,000	100,386

A satellite photograph of Great Britain, largest island in Europe and eighth largest in the world.

THE 10 LARGEST ISLANDS IN EUROPE

	Island	Location	Approx. area sq km	sq miles
1	Great Britain	North Atlantic	218,041	84,186
2	Iceland	North Atlantic	103,000	39,769
3	Ireland	North Atlantic	83,766	32,342
4	West Spitsbergen (Vestspitzbergen)	Arctic Ocean	39,368	15,200
5	Sicily	Mediterranean Sea	25,400	9,807
6	Sardinia	Mediterranean Sea	23,800	9,189
7	North East Land (Nordaustlandet)	Barents Sea	15,000	5,792
8	Cyprus	Mediterranean Sea	9,251	3,572
9	Corsica	Mediterranean Sea	8,720	3,367
10	Crete	Mediterranean Sea	8,260	3,189

THE 10 LARGEST ISLANDS IN THE WORLD

	Island	Location	Approx. area* sq km	sq miles
1	Greenland (Kalaatdlit Nunaat), Denmark	Arctic Ocean	2,175,590	840,000
2	New Guinea	West Pacific	789,900	304,980
3	Borneo	Indian Ocean	751,000	289,961
4	Madagascar (Malagasy Republic)	Indian Ocean	587,041	226,657
5	Baffin Island, Canada	Arctic Ocean	507,451	195,926
6	Sumatra, Indonesia	Indian Ocean	422,200	163,011
7	Honshu, Japan	Northwest Pacific	230,092	88,839
8	Great Britain	North Atlantic	218,041	84,186
9	Victoria Island, Canada	Arctic Ocean	217,290	83,896
10	Ellesmere Island, Canada	Arctic Ocean	196,236	75,767

Mainlands, including areas of inland water, but excluding offshore islands.

Australia is regarded as a continental land mass rather than an island; otherwise it would rank 1st, at 7,618,493 sq km/2,941,517 sq miles, or 35 times the size of Great Britain.

THE 10 DEEPEST CAVES IN THE WORLD

	Cave system	Location	Depth m	ft
1	Réseau Jean Bernard	France	1,602	5,262
2	Shakta Pantjukhina	USSR	1,508	4,948
3	Sistema del Trave	Spain	1,441	4,728
4	Puerta de Illamina	Spain	1,408	4,619
5	Cueva Cheve	Mexico	1,386	4,547
6	Sneznaja – Mezonnogo	USSR	1,370	4,495
7	Sistema Huautla	Mexico	1,353	4,439
8	Réseau de la Pierre Saint-Martin	France	1,342	4,403
9	Boj Bulok	USSR	1,340	4,396
10	Sistema Cuicateca	Mexico	1,243	4,078

The deepest cave in the UK is the 308 m/1,010 ft Ogof Ffynnon Ddu in Wales. The most extensive cave system in the world is that of the limestone Mammoth Cave System, Kentucky, which extends some 560 km/348 miles.

PLANTS & CROPS

THE 10 TALLEST TREES IN THE UK*

	Tree	Location	Height m	ft
1	Grand Fir	Strone House, Argyll, Strathclyde	63.4	208
2	Douglas Fir	The Hermitage, Dunkeld, Tayside	62.5	205
3	Sitka Spruce	Private estate, Strath Earn, Tayside	61.6	202
4=	Giant Sequoia	Castle Leod, Strathpeffer, Highland	53.0	174
4=	Low's Fir	Diana's Grove, Blair Castle, Strathclyde	53.0	174
6	Norway Spruce	Moniack Glenn, Highland	51.8	170
7=	Western Hemlock	Benmore Younger Botanic Gardens, Argyll, Strathclyde	50.9	167
7=	Noble Fir	Ardkinglas House, Argyll, Strathclyde	50.9	167
9	European Silver Fir	Armadale Castle, Skye, Highland	50.0	164
10	London Plane	Bryanston School, Blandford, Dorset	47.6	156

By species (i.e. the tallest known example of each of the 10 tallest species).

THE 10 BIGGEST TREES IN THE USA BY SPECIES

	Species	State	Points
1	General Sherman Giant Sequoia	Sequoia National Park, California	1,300
2	Coast Redwood	Humboldt Redwoods State Park, California	1,010
3	Western Redcedar	Forks, Washington	924
4	Sitka Spruce	Olympic National Forest, Washington	922
5	Coast Douglas Fir	Olympic National Park, Washington	762
6	Common Baldcypress	Cat Island, Louisiana	748
7	Sycamore	Jeromesville, Ohio	737
8	Port-Orford Cedar	Siskiyou National Forest, Oregon	680
9	Incense Cedar	Marble Mountains Wilderness, California	626
10	Bluegum Eucalyptus	Fort Ross State Historic Park, California	622

The American Forestry Association operates a National Register of Big Trees which is constantly updated as new 'champion trees' are nominated. Their method of measurement, which gives this Top 10 by species, is based not solely on height, but also takes account of the thickness of the trunk and spread of the upper branches and leaves, or crown. The formula adds the circumference in inches of the tree at breast height (4½ feet above the ground) to the total height of the tree in feet and to one-quarter of the average crown spread in feet. The General Sherman Giant Sequoia is 998 inches in circumference, 275 feet tall and with an average crown spread of 107 feet, hence 998 + 275 + 27 = 1,300 points. However it is measured, it comes out not only at the top of this list, but is also the largest tree – and the largest living object – on the planet.

THE 10 MOST FORESTED COUNTRIES IN THE WORLD

	Country	% forest cover
1	Surinam	92
2	Solomon Islands	91
3	Papua New Guinea	84
4	Guyana	83
5	French Guiana	82
6	Gabon	78
7	Finland	76
8	Kampuchea	75
9	North Korea	74
10	Bhutan	70

These are the 10 countries with the greatest area of forest and woodland as a percentage of their total land area. The world average is 31 per cent, and that of the UK less than 10 per cent, with Ireland just 4 per cent. The least forested large countries in the world are the desert lands of the Middle East and North Africa, such as Libya with under 0.4 per cent.

OPPOSITE TOP The hybrid larch covers some six per cent of the total UK forest area.

OPPOSITE BOTTOM The Kielder Forest, Northumberland, is the largest in Great Britain.

THE 10 COUNTRIES WITH THE LARGEST AREAS OF FOREST

	Country	Hectares	Acres
1	USSR	945,000,000	2,335,142,250
2	Brazil	555,560,000	1,372,816,538
3	Canada	356,000,000	879,693,800
4	USA	265,188,000	655,292,807
5	Zaïre	174,970,000	432,359,618
6	China	117,115,000	289,397,021
7	Indonesia	113,433,000	280,298,615
8	Australia	106,000,000	261,931,300
9	Peru	68,900,000	170,255,345
10	India	66,600,000	164,571,930
	UK	*2,364,000*	*5,841,562*
	World total	*4,049,041,000*	*10,005,382,760*

THE 10 LARGEST FORESTS IN GREAT BRITAIN

	Forest	Area hectares	acres
1	Kielder	39,380	97,310
2	Newton Stewart	35,275	87,166
3	Dornoch	35,180	86,932
4	Ayrshire and Arran	29,189	72,127
5	Castle Douglas	27,415	67,774
6	Kintyre	26,287	64,956
7	Loch Awe	25,202	62,275
8	Aberfoyle	24,431	60,370
9	Easter Ross	23,795	58,799
10	Cowal	23,521	58,122

The Kielder Forest is in Northumberland, but the other nine largest forests under the aegis of the Forestry Commission are all located in Scotland. The total area of forest in Great Britain is 2,135,000 hectares/5,275,692 acres.

THE 10 COMMONEST TREES IN GREAT BRITAIN

	Tree	% forest area
1	Sitka Spruce	28
2	Scots Pine	13
3	Oak	9
4	Lodgepole Pine	7
5=	Hybrid Larch	6
5=	Norway Spruce	6
7=	Ash	4
7=	Beech	4
7=	Birch	4
10=	Douglas Fir	2
10=	Larch	2

THE TOP 10 TEA, COFFEE AND SUGAR PRODUCERS

RIGHT Sugar cane harvest in Australia, ninth among the world's sugar producers.

	TEA		COFFEE		SUGAR	
	Country	Annual production (tonnes)	Country	Annual production (tonnes)	Country	Annual production (tonnes)
1	India	686,000	Brazil	1,510,000	India	10,200,000
2	China	591,000	Colombia	664,000	USSR	9,565,000
3	Sri Lanka	207,000	Indonesia	390,000	Cuba	8,188,000
4	Kenya	181,000	Mexico	312,000	Brazil	7,409,000
5	USSR	160,000	Côte d'Ivoire	265,000	USA	6,464,000
6	Indonesia	135,000	Guatemala	220,000	China	5,634,000
7	Turkey	124,000	India	215,000	France	4,130,000
8	Japan	90,000	Ethiopia	200,000	Thailand	4,052,000
9	Iran	46,000	Uganda	180,000	Australia	3,679,000
10	Bangladesh	42,000	Philippines	155,000	Mexico	3,678,000
	World total	2,475,000		5,775,000		105,649,000

The top three tea producers are responsible for 60 per cent and the Top 10 for over 90 per cent of the world's total tea production. Perhaps surprisingly, Kenya does not appear in the Top 10 coffee producers as its annual total is 119,000 tonnes, ranking it in 13th place, after Costa Rica and Ecuador. Although the UK's sugar production does not qualify it for a place in the Top 10, it is in the Top 20 at 1,304,000 tonnes.

THE TOP 10 POTATO, RICE AND WHEAT PRODUCERS

	POTATOES		RICE		WHEAT	
	Country	Annual production (tonnes)	Country	Annual production (tonnes)	Country	Annual production (tonnes)
1	USSR	72,000,000	China	179,403,000	China	91,002,000
2	Poland	34,390,000	India	107,500,000	USSR	90,500,000
3	China	30,045,000	Indonesia	43,566,000	USA	55,407,000
4	USA	16,659,000	Bangladesh	26,600,000	India	53,995,000
5	India	14,500,000	Thailand	22,300,000	France	31,817,000
6	East Germany	9,167,000	Vietnam	18,100,000	Canada	24,383,000
7	West Germany	7,811,000	Myanmar (Burma)	13,581,000	Turkey	15,729,000
8	Romania	7,200,000	Japan	12,934,000	Pakistan	14,419,000
9	Netherlands	6,856,000	Brazil	11,107,000	Australia	14,200,000
10	UK	6,369,000	Philippines	9,459,000	UK	13,900,000
	World total	276,740,000		506,291,000		538,056,000

It should be noted that dividing a country's population by the weight of potatoes grown will not reveal who eats the most, since a great deal of the world's potato harvest is used in the manufacture of alcohol and other products.

RIGHT Rice harvest in the Punjab. India is second only to China as a rice producer.

QUIZ

CROPS

1 What do King Tonkin, Duchess of Oldenburg, Simpson Starking and Rambo have in common?
2 What grain crops have the scientific names *Oryza sativa* and *Avena sativa*?
3 What country is Europe's largest producer of strawberries?
4 Where would you find the largest vine in England?
5 What agricultural machine did Cyrus Hall McCormick patent on 21 June 1834?
6 What fruit is the title of a 1971 Woody Allen film?
7 How many times is the potato mentioned in Shakespeare's works?
8 What is 'mummy wheat'?
9 What plant, known in French as *pomme d'amour* or 'love apple', was first introduced into Europe from the New World in the sixteenth century?
10 What do British people call what Americans know as an alligator pear, zucchini, endive and eggplant?

THE TOP 10 BANANA, ORANGE AND APPLE PRODUCERS

	BANANAS Country	Annual production (tonnes)	ORANGES Country	Annual production (tonnes)	APPLES Country	Annual production (tonnes)
1	Brazil	5,558,000	Brazil	16,807,000	USSR	6,000,000
2	India	4,750,000	USA	8,149,000	USA	4,367,000
3	Philippines	3,190,000	China	3,715,000	China	4,316,000
4	China	2,430,000	Spain	2,629,000	France	2,339,000
5	Ecuador	2,376,000	Mexico	2,269,000	Italy	1,940,000
6	Indonesia	2,350,000	Italy	2,100,000	Turkey	1,900,000
7	Thailand	1,610,000	India	1,800,000	West Germany	1,767,000
8	Mexico	1,600,000	Egypt	1,370,000	Poland	1,312,000
9	Burundi	1,490,000	Pakistan	1,100,000	Japan	1,075,000
10	Vietnam	1,480,000	Morocco	994,000	Iran	1,010,000
	World total	43,685,000		50,630,000		40,226,000

During the 1980s, orange production progressively increased from a world total of less than 40,000,000 tonnes. China's, in particular, has rocketed up almost fivefold from under 800,000 tonnes to its present 3rd position in the world league table. The UK's production of apples steadily declined during the 1980s in the face of cheap imports (although it has recently increased somewhat), and is now estimated at about 298,000 tonnes.

Over 10 per cent of the world's bananas now come from India.

THE TOP 10 TOBACCO PRODUCERS

	Country	Annual production (tonnes)
1	China	2,871,000
2	USA	671,000
3=	Brazil	445,000
3=	India	445,000
5	USSR	342,000
6	Turkey	253,000
7	Italy	175,000
8	Indonesia	145,000
9	Bulgaria	125,000
10	Greece	124,000
	World total	7,293,000

RIGHT Cigarette-smoking became fashionable among members of Victorian High Society.

THE STORY OF TOBACCO

The practice of smoking tobacco was observed by the earliest travellers to North and South America – one of the first uses of the word 'tobacco' was by a visitor to Haiti as early as 1535 – but the first tobacco to reach Europe was taken from Brazil to France by André Thevet in 1556. Three years later, Jean Nicot, a young French scholar and diplomat, was sent to Portugal to negotiate the marriage of six-year-old Princess Marguerite de Valois to the five-year-old King Sebastian of Portugal. Although his mission failed, he sent back tobacco plants that had recently arrived from Florida. In this period it was principally valued as a medicinal plant, many claiming it could cure virtually all known ills, and was also powdered and taken as snuff (in 1561 Nicot sent tobacco to queen Catherine De' Medici to soothe her migraine). By the year of his death in 1600, Nicot's name was attached to the plant, which was called *Nicotiana*, but later 'nicotine' was assigned specifically to the deadly poisonous active ingredient of the tobacco plant.

It is often said that tobacco was first taken to England in 1586 by Sir Walter Raleigh (although there are rival claimants, among them Sir Ralph Lane, the first Governor of Virginia, and Welsh sea captain Thomas Price). However, one of the earliest descriptions of pipe-smoking in England was that given by the Elizabethan writer William Harrison in 1573, six years *before* Raleigh had even returned from his first voyage to America, by which time it had clearly already become fashionable:

'In these days the taking in of the smoke of the Indian herb called tobacco by an instrument formed like a little ladle, whereby it passeth from the mouth into the head and stomach, is greatly taken up and used in England against rheums [colds] and some other diseases engendered in the lungs and inward parts, and not without effect.'

By 1612 tobacco was cultivated in Virginia by the English settler John Rolfe. He married red Indian princess Pocahontas and in 1616 sailed with her to England (where she died), together with a cargo of Virginian tobacco. For over two hundred years pipe-smoking was the norm, but cigars became increasingly popular from the eighteenth century. Earlier and alternative origins have been claimed for cigarettes, but one account suggests that they were invented in 1799 by Turkish soldiers while Acre was under siege by the French under Napoleon. When the hookah in which they usually smoked their tobacco was smashed, they rolled tobacco in the touchpapers they used for firing their cannon. Cigarettes became fashionable among both men and women in France in the early 1840s, and it was also in France in 1843 that cigarettes were first commercially manufactured, soon followed by Britain during the 1850s. It is also probable that cigarette-smoking was introduced into England by troops who had seen Turks smoking them during the Crimean War (1853–56).

Although tobacco had its critics from the earliest period (King James I of England wrote *A Counterblaste To Tobacco* in 1604), it was not until the twentieth century that a health lobby actively sought to publicize the hazards of smoking and to have smoking restricted or banned in public locations – in spite of which, world tobacco production has almost doubled since the 1970s.

THE 10 MOST POPULAR FLOWERS AS GIFTS IN THE UK

1	Carnation
2	Chrysanthemum
3	Rose
4	Daffodil/narcissus
5	Freesia
6	Lily
7	Tulip
8	Gypsophila
9	Gerbera
10	Alstroemeria

A message of love: Valentine's Day flowers by Interflora.

SAYING IT WITH FLOWERS

The Flower Telegraphic Delivery Association was established in the USA to arrange the delivery of flowers ordered by telegraph within the USA. In 1923 17 British florists, all associate members of the FTDA, established Interflora, the international flower relay service, which took as its logo Mercury, the Roman winged messenger of the gods. The idea soon caught on and today there are 2,900 member companies within the UK and 55,000 worldwide in a total of 136 countries. The world is divided between groups affiliated to the British unit, based in Sleaford, Lincolnshire, with associates in other countries including Australia and South Africa, and close affiliation with the original American organization (which was renamed The Florists Transworld Delivery Association and is based in Michigan) and Fleurop, the European group based in Zurich. To overcome the problems of converting currencies between the various members, a special unit of currency based on the Swiss franc and known as the Fleurin is used within Interflora. In the UK Interflora's members, all of whom are independent retailers, conduct business by phone that is today worth over £50,000,000 per annum.

ANIMALS & BIRDS

THE 10 MOST POPULAR TYPES OF PET IN GREAT BRITAIN

1	Dog
2	Cat
3	Goldfish
4	Budgerigar
5	Rabbit
6	Tropical fish
7	Hamster
8	Guinea pig
9	Canary
10	Horse/pony/donkey

THE 10 MOST POPULAR DOG BREEDS IN THE USA

	Breed	No. registered by American Kennel Club
1	Cocker Spaniel	111,636
2	Labrador Retriever	91,107
3	Poodle	78,600
4	Golden Retriever	64,269
5	German Shepherd (Alsatian)	58,422
6	Rottweiler	51,291
7	Chow Chow	50,150
8	Dachshund	44,305
9	Beagle	43,314
10	Miniature Schnauzer	42,175

THE 10 MOST POPULAR DOG BREEDS IN GREAT BRITAIN

	Breed	No. registered by Kennel Club
1	Yorkshire Terrier	25,665
2	Labrador Retriever	24,456
3	German Shepherd (Alsatian)	18,908
4	West Highland White Terrier	18,688
5	Cavalier King Charles Spaniel	16,823
6	Golden Retriever	15,983
7	Cocker Spaniel	12,866
8	English Springer Spaniel	11,349
9	Staffordshire Bull Terrier	7,609
10	Boxer	6,949

The number of dogs registered by the Kennel Club increased substantially in 1990, although the principal breeds remain in the Top 10, with some adjustments to the order. Yorkshire and West Highland White Terriers rose considerably in popularity and Boxers entered at No. 10. The fashion for large and potentially dangerous dogs appears to be waning, perhaps in response to press reports of attacks by certain animals: as with Dobermans two years earlier, Rottweilers dropped out of the list, falling to 16th place.

An alternative Top 10 is that produced by the Gallup National Dog Survey:

1	Labrador Retriever
2	German Shepherd (Alsatian)
3	Jack Russell
4	Border Collie
5	Golden Retriever
6	Yorkshire Terrier
7	English Springer Spaniel
8	Cocker Spaniel
9	Poodle
10	Cavalier King Charles Spaniel

ABOVE Guinea pigs are among Britain's most popular pets.

RIGHT The ever popular Cavalier King Charles spaniel.

THE 10 MOST POPULAR DOGS' NAMES IN GREAT BRITAIN

Female		Male
Penny	1	Sam
Gemma	2	Patch
Sally	3	Ben
Bella	4	Max
Bess	5	Jamie
Sasha	6	Charlie
Bea	7	Barney
Kim	8	Roly
Holly	9	Prince
Meg	10	Toby

In the 1980s there was a noticeable move away from traditional dogs' names. At the beginning of the decade the Top 10 list included such evergreen (and specifically canine) names as Shep, Brandy, Whisky, Patch, Butch, Rex, Lassie and, of course, Rover, although among names given to bitches there was a tendency to use names that might be given to girls: Sally, Rosie, Mandy and Tessa, for example. Nowadays, virtually any of the names could equally be those of people.

QUIZ

FAMOUS ANIMALS

Who were the owners of the following real and fictitious animals?

1 The dog Snowy.
2 The chestnut stallion Copenhagen.
3 The Berkshire pig Empress of Blandings.
4 The cat Foss.
5 The horse Silver.
6 The cocker spaniel Flush.
7 The parrot Captain Flint.
8 The King Charles spaniel Dash.
9 The black stallion Bucephalus.
10 The little black dog Toto.

THE 10 MOST POPULAR DOGS' NAMES IN THE USA

1	Lady
2	King
3	Duke
4	Peppy
5	Prince
6	Pepper
7	Snoopy
8	Princess
9	Heidi
10=	Sam
10=	Coco

A recent study of names appearing on dog licences in the USA produced a list that has only 'Prince' and 'Sam' in common with the British Top 10. The same American list also exposed a number of bizarre dogs' names, including Beowulf, Bikini, Fag, Rembrandt and Twit.

The Abyssinian, in Britain's Top 10 of pedigree cats by a whisker but No. 3 in the USA.

THE 10 MOST POPULAR PEDIGREE CAT BREEDS IN THE USA

	Breed	Total registered
1	Persian	56,847
2	Siamese	3,743
3	Abyssinian	2,669
4	Maine Coon	2,449
5	Burmese	1,206
6	Oriental Shorthair	1,179
7	Exotic Shorthair	1,124
8	American Shorthair	1,104
9	Scottish Fold	983
10	Birman	918

The Cat Fanciers' Association of the USA is the world's largest pedigree cat registry. In 1989 it registered 79,145 cats of 35 different breeds, of which Traditional, Pointed Pattern and Colorpoint Carrier Persians were by far the most popular breed, with Oriental Longhair the rarest (just 14 registrations). Of the total, females outnumbered males (46,487 compared with 32,558).

THE 10 MOST POPULAR PEDIGREE CAT BREEDS IN GREAT BRITAIN

	Breed
1	Persian
2	Siamese
3	British Blue
4	Burman
5	Maine Coon
6	Somali
7	Devon Rex
8	Burmese
9	Abyssinian
10	Ragdoll

THE 10 MOST POPULAR CATS' NAMES IN THE USA

Female		Male
Samantha	1	Tiger/Tigger
Misty	2	Smokey
Patches	3	Pepper
Cali/Calico	4	Max/Maxwell
Muffin	5	Simon
Angel/Angela	6	Snoopy
Ginger	7	Morris
Tiger/Tigger	8	Mickey
Princess	9	Rusty/Rusti
Punkin/Pumpkin	10	Boots/Bootsie

THE 10 MOST POPULAR CATS' NAMES IN GREAT BRITAIN

1	Sooty
2	Tiger
3	Smokey/Smoky
4	Tigger
5	Whiskey/Whisky
6	Kitty
7	Lucky
8	Susie
9	Fluffy
10	Snowy

A Gallup Survey commissioned by Kattomeat asked 4,000 owners about their pets and revealed this list, with Suky, Thomas and Tabby in equal 11th place.

THE FIRST 10 DINOSAURS TO BE NAMED

	Name	Year
1	Megalosaurus	1824
2	Iguanodon	1825
3	Hylaeosaurus	1833
4	Macrodontophion	1834
5	Thecodontosaurus	1836
6	Pelosaurus	1850
7=	Deinodon	1856
7=	Palaeoscinus	1856
7=	Thespesius	1856
7=	Trachodon	1856
7=	Troodon	1856

The name Megalosaurus ('great lizard'), the first to be given to a dinosaur, was proposed by William Buckland (1784–1856), an English geologist. (He was also Dean of Westminster and a noted eccentric who, out of scientific curiosity, once ate the mummified heart of the French King, Louis XIV!) Although suggested by the Rev William Daniel Conybeare, another geologist, the Iguanodon – along with the Hylaeosaurus and Pelosaurus – was named by Sussex geologist Gideon Algernon Mantell (1790–1852). A Polish nobleman, Count Zborzewski, named Macrodontophion; Samuel Stutchbury and H. Riley named Thecodontosaurus, while all the others received their names from Joseph Leidy (1823–91), an American paleontologist (though some of his discoveries, known only from fossilized teeth, are of dubious authenticity). After the 1850s, the hunting, identifying and naming of dinosaurs became highly competitive, with dinosaurologists vying with each other to discover and assign names to every new find.

LEFT The Crystal Palace model of Hylaeosaurus, the third-named dinosaur.

DINING IN A DINOSAUR

On New Year's Eve 1853, a number of eminent British scientists received a bizarre invitation to a dinner party. Not only was the invitation itself a strange object, being printed on a replica of the wing of a Pterodactyl (a huge extinct flying reptile), but the venue was unique – *inside* an Iguanodon. This was one of 29 life-sized stucco-covered brick and iron models of prehistoric monsters being designed and built by animal sculptor Benjamin Waterhouse Hawkins for display at the Crystal Palace, the gigantic building that had been the home of the 1851 Great Exhibition and which was afterwards dismantled and moved to Sydenham, on the outskirts of London. The 22 guests (including Sir Richard Owen, the zoologist who in 1841 had coined the word 'dinosaur') who attended the dinner found themselves seated inside the creature's body. There they were served a sumptuous meal by a team of waiters who clambered to the dining table across a scaffolding platform. After the banquet, according to the *Illustrated London News*, the party returned to London by train, 'well pleased with the modern hospitality of the Iguanodon, whose ancient sides there is no reason to suppose had ever before been shaken with philosophic mirth'. The Iguanodon and the rest of Hawkins' monster models were completed soon afterwards and can still be seen at Crystal Palace.

ABOVE 'Dinner is served' – one of London's most bizarre dinner parties takes place inside a model Iguanodon.

THE 10 LARGEST DINOSAURS

1 'Seismosaurus'
Length: 30–36 m/98–119 ft   Estimated weight: 50–80 tonnes

A single skeleton of this colossal plant-eater was
excavated in 1985 near Albuquerque, New Mexico, by US
paleontologist David Gillette and given an unofficial name
(i.e. one that is not yet an established scientific name) that
means 'earth-shaking lizard'. It is currently being studied
by the New Mexico Museum of Natural History, which
may confirm its position as the largest dinosaur yet
discovered.

2 Supersaurus
Length: 24–30 m/80–100 ft   Height: 16 m/54 ft
Estimated weight: 50 tonnes

The remains of Supersaurus were found in Colorado in
1972 (like those of Ultrasaurus, by James A. Jensen). Some
scientists have suggested a length of up to 42 m/138 ft and
a weight of 75–100 tonnes.

3 Antarctosaurus
Length: 18–30 m/60–98 ft   Estimated weight: 40–50 tonnes

Named Antarctosaurus ('southern lizard') by German
paleontologist Friedrich von Huene in 1929, this creature's
thigh bone alone measures 2.3 m/7½ ft.

4 Barosaurus
Length: 23–27.5 m/75–90 ft   Height and weight uncertain

Barosaurus (meaning 'heavy lizard', so-named by US
paleontologist Othniel C. Marsh in 1890) has been found in
both North America and Africa, thus proving the existence
of a land link in Jurassic times (205–140 million years ago).

5 Mamenchisaurus
Length: 27 m/89 ft   Height and weight uncertain

An almost complete skeleton discovered in 1972 showed it
had the longest neck of any known animal, comprising
more than half its total body length – perhaps up to 15 m/
49 ft. It was named by Chinese paleontologist Young
Chung Chien after the place in China where it was found.

6 Diplodocus
Length: 23–27 m/75–89 ft   Estimated weight: 12 tonnes

As it was long and thin, Diplodocus was a relative
lightweight in the dinosaur world. It was also probably
one of the most stupid dinosaurs, having the smallest
brain in relation to its body size. Diplodocus was given its
name (which means 'double beam') in 1878 by Marsh. One
skeleton was named *Diplodocus carnegii*, in honour of
Scottish-American millionaire Andrew Carnegie, who
financed the excavations that discovered it.

7 'Ultrasaurus'
Length: Over 25 m/82 ft   Height: 16 m/52 ft
Estimated weight: 50 tonnes

Ultrasaurus was discovered by US paleontologist James A.
Jensen in Colorado in 1979 but has not yet been fully
studied. Some authorities have claimed its weight as an
unlikely 100–140 tonnes. Confusingly, although its
informal name (which means 'ultra lizard') was widely
recognized, another, smaller dinosaur has been given the
same official name.

8 Brachiosaurus
Length: 25 m/82 ft   Height: 16 m/52 ft
Estimated weight: 50 tonnes

Its name (given to it in 1903 by US paleontologist Elmer S.
Riggs) means 'arm lizard'. Some paleontologists have put
the weight of Brachiosaurus as high as 190 tonnes, but this
seems improbable (if not impossible, in the light of
theories of the maximum possible weight of terrestrial
animals).

9 Pelorosaurus
Length: 24 m/80 ft   Height and weight uncertain

The first fragments of Pelorosaurus ('monstrous lizard')
were found in Sussex and named by British doctor Gideon
A. Mantell as early as 1850.

10 Apatosaurus
Length: 20–21 m/66–70 ft   Estimated weight: 20–30 tonnes

Apatosaurus (its name, coined by Marsh, means
'deceptive lizard') is better known by its former name of
Brontosaurus ('thunder reptile'). The bones of the first one
ever found, in Colorado in 1879, caused great confusion
for many years because its discoverer attached a head
from a different species to the rest of the skeleton.

The first dinosaur bones were found in Sussex in 1822. The
name 'dinosaur' was given to them by the naturalist Sir
Richard Owen, and first appeared in print in 1841. It
comes from two Greek words, *deinos*, fearful, and *sauros*,
lizard.

The Top 10 is based on the most reliable recent evidence
of their lengths and indicates the probable ranges; as more
and more information is assembled, these are undergoing
constant revision. Lengths have often been estimated from
only a few surviving fossilized bones, and there is much
dispute even among experts about these and even more
about the weights of most dinosaurs. Some, such as
Diplodocus, had squat bodies but extended necks, which
made them extremely long but not necessarily immensely
heavy.

Everyone's favourite dinosaur, *Tyrannosaurus rex*
('tyrant lizard'), does not appear in the Top 10 list because
although it was one of the fiercest flesh-eating dinosaurs, it
was not as large as many of the herbivorous ones.
However, measuring a probable 12 m/39 ft and weighing
more than six tonnes it certainly ranks as one of the largest

A Brachiosaurus skeleton in the Natural History Museum, Berlin.

flesh-eating animals yet discovered. Bones of an earlier dinosaur called Epanterias were found in Colorado in 1877 and 1934, but incorrectly identified until recently, when studies suggested that this creature was possibly larger than Tyrannosaurus.

To compare these sizes with living animals, note that the largest recorded crocodile measured 6.2 m/20.3 ft and the largest elephant 10.7 m/35 ft from trunk to tail and weighed about 12 tonnes. The largest living creature ever measured is the blue whale at 33.6 m/110 ft – slightly smaller than the size claimed for Seismosaurus.

THE 10 FASTEST FISH IN THE WORLD

	Fish	Maximum recorded speed	
		kph	mph
1	Sailfish	110	68
2	Marlin	80	50
3	Wahoo	78	48
4	Tunny	74	46
5	Bluefish tuna	70	44
6	Great blue shark	69	43
7=	Bonefish	64	40
7=	Swordfish	64	40
9=	Four-winged flying fish	56	35
9=	Tarpon	56	35

THE 10 FASTEST MAMMALS IN THE WORLD

	Mammal	Maximum recorded speed	
		kph	mph
1	Cheetah	105	65
2	Pronghorn antelope	89	55
3=	Mongolian gazelle	80	50
3=	Springbok	80	50
5=	Grant's gazelle	76	47
5=	Thomson's gazelle	76	47
7	Brown hare	72	45
8	Horse	69	43
9=	Greyhound	68	42
9=	Red deer	68	42

Although some authorities have alleged higher speeds, this list is based on data from reliable sources using accurate methods of measurement. In addition to these speeds, estimated over distances of up to 0.4 km/¼ mile, charging lions can achieve 80 kph/50 mph over very short distances, while various members of the antelope family, wildebeests, elks, dogs, coyotes, foxes, hyenas, zebras and Mongolian wild asses, have all been credited with unsustained spurts of 64 kph/40 mph or more.

THE 10 FASTEST BIRDS IN THE WORLD

	Bird	Maximum recorded speed	
		kph	mph
1	Spine-tailed swift	171	106
2	Frigate bird	153	95
3	Spur-winged goose	142	88
4	Red-breasted merganser	129	80
5	White-rumped swift	124	77
6	Canvasback duck	116	72
7	Eider duck	113	70
8	Teal	109	68
9=	Mallard	105	65
9=	Pintail	105	65

This does not include the speeds obtained by certain birds of prey in gravity-aided dives (such as the 362 kph/225 mph claimed for a peregrine falcon), or other exceptional circumstances, such as wind-assisted flight.

THE 10 COMMONEST BIRDS IN THE UK

1	Starling
2	House sparrow
3	Blue tit
4	Blackbird
5	Chaffinch
6	Greenfinch
7	Robin
8	Great tit
9	Hedge sparrow
10	Collared dove

THE 10 MOST INTELLIGENT MAMMALS

1	Man
2	Chimpanzee
3	Gorilla
4	Orang-utan
5	Baboon
6	Gibbon
7	Monkey
8	Smaller toothed whale
9	Dolphin
10	Elephant

This list is based on research conducted by Edward O. Wilson, Professor of Zoology at Harvard University, who defined intelligence as speed and extent of learning performance over a wide range of tasks, also taking account of the ratio of the animal's brain size to its body bulk. Perhaps surprisingly, the dog does not make the Top 10, and if Man is excluded, No. 10 becomes the pig.

THE 10 DEADLIEST SNAKES

Species	Native region
1= Taipan Mortality is nearly 100% unless antivenin is administered promptly.	Australia and New Guinea
1= Black mamba Mortality nearly 100% without antivenin.	Southern and Central Africa
3 Tiger snake Very high mortality without antivenin.	Australia
4 Common krait Up to 50% mortality even with antivenin.	South Asia
5 Death adder Over 50% mortality without antivenin.	Australia
6 Saw-scaled or carpet viper High mortality and, as it is relatively common, perhaps the cause of more deaths than any other snake.	Africa and Asia
7 Yellow or Cape cobra The most dangerous type of cobra; high mortality.	Southern Africa
8= Boomslang High mortality.	Africa
8= Bushmaster High mortality.	Central and South America
8= Coral snake High mortality.	North and South America

Measuring the strength of the venom of snakes is scientifically possible, but this does not indicate how dangerous they may be: the Australian smooth-scaled snake, for example, is believed to be the most venomous land snake, but no human victims have ever been recorded. The Top 10 takes account of the degree of threat posed by those snakes that have a record of causing fatalities – although it can only be approximate, since circumstances such as the amount of venom injected, speed of administering antivenin (an antitoxin that counteracts the venom), age and health of victim and so on, can vary enormously.

The boomslang, eighth deadliest, but nonetheless menacing.

Diversity is the constant glory of the animal world, and even within a single species of animal there can be immense variations in size. Since any Top 10 of large animals would inevitably be dominated by members of the whale family, an attempt has been made to indicate the range of 'largeness' across a broad spectrum of animals. Even here there are practical problems that make measurement difficult – in the wild it is virtually impossible to weigh an elephant, for example. Similarly, in the area of longevity, there are problems of assessing age: other than in captivity, few animals have their birth dates accurately recorded, so life spans are not simply measured. The following lists, therefore, represent 'likely averages' based on informed observations, rather than one-off assessments or extreme record-breaking cases.

The 480-day gestation of the walrus includes a delay of up to five months while the fertilized embryo is held as a blastocyst (a sphere of cells) but does not embed in the wall of the uterus, enabling it to produce its offspring at a more favourable time of the year. Human gestation, which ranges from 253 to 303 days, is exceeded not only by those mammals appearing in the Top 10, but also by various others, including the porpoise, horse and water buffalo.

THE 10 MAMMALS WITH THE LONGEST GESTATION PERIODS

	Animal	Average gestation (days)
1	African elephant	660
2	Asiatic elephant	600
3	Baird's beaked whale	520
4	White rhinoceros	490
5	Walrus	480
6	Giraffe	460
7	Tapir	400
8	Arabian camel (dromedary)	390
9	Fin whale	370
10	Llama	360

THE 10 MAMMALS WITH THE SHORTEST GESTATION PERIODS

	Animal	Average gestation (days)
1	Short-nosed bandicoot*	12
2	Opossum*	13
3	Shrew	14
4	Golden hamster	15
5=	Lemming	20
5=	Mouse	20
7	Rat	21
8	Gerbil	24
9=	Mole	28
9=	Rabbit	28

These animals are marsupials. Their young are not fully developed when born and are transferred into a 'pouch' to continue their development.

BACKGROUND African elephant mother with offspring – after nature's longest wait.

THE 10 HEAVIEST ANIMALS IN THE WORLD

	Animal	Weight kg	lb
1	Blue whale	190,000	418,878
2	African elephant	5,000	11,023
3	Indian elephant	4,000	8,818
4	White rhinoceros	2,200	4,850
5	Hippopotamus	2,000	4,409
6	Giraffe	1,200	2,646
7	Crocodile	1,100	2,425
8	Asian gaur	900	1,984
9=	Bison	800	1,764
9=	Kodiak bear	800	1,764
9=	Yak	800	1,764
9=	Giant eland	800	1,764
9=	Alaskan moose	800	1,764

Weights are for large, but not extreme specimens (there are rare examples of African elephants of more than double the weight given). This list could be devoted entirely to large marine animals including whales and the 3,000 kg/6,614 lb giant ray, but by restricting them to a single representative – the largest of the whale family – the relative sizes of terrestrial heavyweights are put into perspective.

THE 10 LONGEST ANIMALS IN THE WORLD

	Animal	Length m	ft	in
1	Blue whale	33.5	109	11
2=	Reticulated python	10.0	32	10
2=	Tapeworm	10.0	32	10
4	Whale shark	9.8	32	2
5	African elephant	7.2*	23	7
6	Crocodile	5.9	19	5
7	Giraffe	5.8	19	0
8	Hippopotamus	4.9	16	1
9	Arabian camel (dromedary)	4.1	13	6
10=	Indian bison	3.4	11	2
10=	African lion	3.4	11	2
10=	White rhinoceros	3.4	11	2

Trunk to tail.

The 'Lion's mane' jellyfish, which lives in the Arctic Ocean, has tentacles as long as 40 m/131 ft trailing behind it, but its 'body' is relatively small, and it has thus not been included. Only one fish (the whale shark is a fish, not a true whale) and one snake have been included. Although the South American anaconda is sometimes claimed to be the longest snake, this has not been verified and it seems that the python remains entitled to claim pre-eminence.

THE 10 LONGEST-LIVED ANIMALS*

	Animal	Maximum age (years)
1	Quahog (marine clam)	up to 200
2	Giant tortoise	150
3	Greek tortoise	110
4	Killer whale	90
5	European eel	88
6	Lake sturgeon	82
7	Sea anemone	80
8	Elephant	78
9	Freshwater mussel	75
10	Andean condor	70

*Excluding humans.

The ages of animals in the wild are difficult to determine with accuracy as the precise birth and death dates of relatively few long-lived animals have ever been recorded. In some instances there are secondary clues, such as annual growth of shells and teeth; in the case of whales, even measurements of ear wax are used to estimate age. The Top 10 represents only documented maximum ages of animals where more than one example has attained it or come close – although there may well be extreme cases of animals exceeding these life spans. Although there are alleged instances of parrots living to ages of 80 years or more, few stand up to scrutiny, and the Andean condor's 70 years is a more plausible example of longevity among birds.

OPPOSITE The crocodile can measure almost 6m/20ft long.

ABOVE A giant tortoise, longest-lived of all terrestrial animals.

BELOW A family of wild boar, among the most prolific of all mammals.

THE 10 MOST PROLIFIC MAMMALS IN THE WORLD

	Animal	Average litter
1	Tailless tenrec	21
2	Golden hamster	11
3	Ermine	10
4	Coypu	8.5
5=	European hedgehog	7
5=	African hunting dog	7
7=	Meadow vole	6.5
7=	Wild boar	6.5
9=	Wolf	6
9=	Black-backed jackal	6

These are *averages* – extreme examples, for example, of pigs with litters of 30 or more, are recorded. Although the tiny tenrec from Madagascar has similarly produced as many as 31 in a single litter, average mammalian litter sizes are minute when compared with those of other animals. Fish, for example, commonly lay more than 10,000 eggs at a time and many amphibians more than 1,000. The most staggeringly prolific creature of all is probably the Ocean sunfish, which lays as many as 300,000,000 eggs.

THE 10 MOST ENDANGERED MAMMALS IN THE WORLD

	Mammal	Number
1=	Tasmanian wolf	?
1=	Halcon fruit bat	?
1=	Ghana fat mouse	?
4	Kouprey	10
5	Javan rhinoceros	50
6	Iriomote cat	60
7	Black lion tamarin	130
8	Pygmy hog	150
9	Tamaraw	200
10	Indus dolphin	400

The first three mammals on the list have not been seen for many years and may well be extinct, but zoologists are hopeful of the possibility of their survival: the Tasmanian wolf, for example, has been technically extinct since the last specimen died in a zoo in 1936, but occasional unconfirmed sightings suggest that there may still be animals in the wild, and a 648,000-hectare/1,601,240-acre nature reserve has been set aside for it in Tasmania in the expectation that it will be found again. The only Halcon fruit bat that has ever been seen is one that was discovered in the Philippines in 1937 (another bat, the Tanzanian woolly bat, was discovered in the 1870s but has not been observed since, and is assumed to be extinct).

All the species on this list, which is ranked in order of rarity, face global extinction – unlike many species which may be at serious risk in one area but flourishing elsewhere. Some species that would once have been on the 'most endangered' list, such as the Arabian oryx, were 'extinct' in the wild, but have successfully been bred in captivity and reintroduced into their natural habitats.

ABOVE The ostrich, largest of all living birds, so powerful it can even run carrying a man.

TOP Lone wolf? The Tasmanian wolf is exceedingly rare, if not totally extinct.

THE 10 HEAVIEST BIRDS IN THE WORLD

	Bird	Weight kg	lb
1	Ostrich	156.5	345
2	Two-wattled cassowary	81.7	180
3	Emu	49.9	110
4	Emperor penguin	30.8	68
5	Greater rhea	25.0	55
6	Kori bustard	18.1	40
7	Trumpeter swan	16.8	37
8	Mute swan	16.3	36
9=	Wandering albatross	15.9	35
9=	Great bustard	15.9	35

The first five birds in the Top 10 are flightless. The theoretical maximum weight for a bird that can fly has been calculated to be about 18.1 kg/40 lb. Although some outsize examples of certain flighted birds have been observed, including swans weighing almost 22.7 kg/50 lb, it was not established whether they were able to take off.

HUMAN BODY & HEALTH

HEALTH SPENDING: THE 10 LEADING COUNTRIES

	Country	Average annual health spending per person (US$)
1	USA	2,051
2	Canada	1,483
3	Iceland	1,241
4	Sweden	1,233
5	Switzerland	1,225
6	Norway	1,149
7	France	1,105
8	West Germany	1,093
9	Luxembourg	1,050
10	Netherlands	1,041
	UK	758

The USA not only spends the most per head on health care, but also the most as a percentage of gross domestic product (11.2 per cent, compared with the UK's 6.1 per cent). Among European countries, Turkey spends the least – just $148 per capita.

ABOVE RIGHT Early porcelain dentures pegged into a bone base, and their creator, Claudius Ash.

THE 10 COUNTRIES WITH THE MOST DENTISTS

	Country	Patients per dentist	Dentists
1	USA	1,805	137,817
2	Brazil	1,390	106,000
3	USSR	2,722	105,000
4	Japan	1,909	68,499
5	France	1,483	37,836
6	Germany	2,148	36,608
7	Italy	1,870	30,767
8	UK	2,570	22,255
9	Argentina	1,597	20,000
10	Mexico	4,970	17,000

OPPOSITE Blood pressure problems are the fourth commonest reason for visits to GPs.

FALSE TEETH

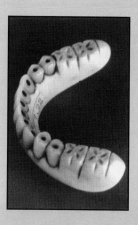

Although regarded as a subject that no one talks about, false teeth have been around for centuries. Dentures of a sort existed in ancient times, and have been found in skeletons dating from the fifteenth century, but until modern improvements they seldom fitted properly and often flew out while their owners were talking. Few even achieved the purpose for which they were designed – they were so uncomfortable to use for eating that it was once regarded as good form to remove one's dentures before starting and place them beside the plate until the meal was over. It was not until the eighteenth century that a Frenchman, Pierre Fauchard, tackled the problem of making them stay in place by attaching springs to teeth carved out of ivory or walrus tusks. Another method of the time was to make dentures out of the teeth taken from dead bodies – 'Waterloo teeth' was one euphemism for dentures made from the teeth extracted from corpses on the field after the Battle of Waterloo.

Perhaps the most famous victim of primitive dentures was America's first President, George Washington. Every picture of him shows him with his mouth firmly shut, and studies of his portraits – including that on the US one-dollar bill – have revealed how his face changed shape as his teeth disappeared and were replaced by a succession of odd and often painful gadgets, including false teeth made of lead and ivory, as well teeth taken from assorted animals (including an elk) and dead people, held together with springs so powerful that his jaw snapped shut like a trap.

One man who contributed to the improvement of these horrors was Claudius Ash. A London goldsmith of the early nineteenth century, he was approached by a dentist who asked him to make false teeth. But Claudius was somewhat squeamish about handling dead men's teeth, and so experimented with imitation teeth made of durable porcelain, pioneering dental manufacturing and establishing a business that continues today.

THE 10 COMMONEST REASONS FOR VISITS TO THE DOCTOR

	Condition	Consulting rate per 2,500 patients
1	Upper respiratory tract infections	600
2	Non-specific 'symptoms'	375
3	Skin disorders	350
4=	Psychoemotional problems	250
4=	High blood pressure	250
4=	Minor accidents	250
7	Gastro-intestinal conditions	200
8	Rheumatic aches and pains	150
9=	Chronic rheumatism	100
9=	Acute throat infections	100
9=	Acute bronchitis	100
9=	Lacerations	100
9=	Eczema/dermatitis	100

The Royal College of General Practitioners considers that these statistics represent the average number of consultations per condition that a doctor with a typical practice of 2,500 patients might expect to deal with in a year. These relatively common complaints contrast with others that are extremely rare, so that on average a doctor might expect to see a person with a dislocated hip only once every 20 years, or a patient with phenylketonuria (a metabolic disorder) just once in 200 years.

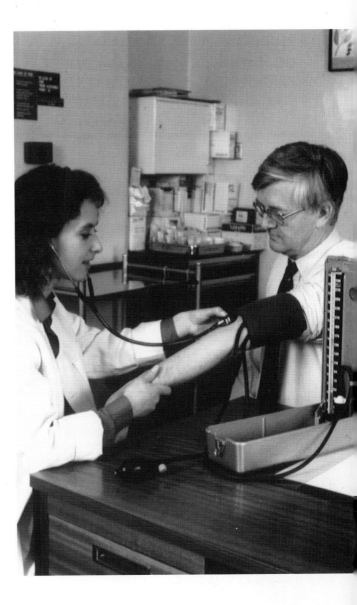

QUIZ

TOP DOCS

Link these doctors with their correct achievements:

1	Christian Barnard.	**A**	The first woman doctor in the USA.
2	Alexander Fleming.	**B**	The first use of antiseptics in surgery.
3	Arthur Conan Doyle.	**C**	The founder of homeopathic medicine.
4	Ronald Ross.	**D**	The discovery of penicillin.
5	Karl Landsteiner.	**E**	The first heart transplant.
6	Elizabeth Blackwell.	**F**	The pioneer of vaccination.
7	Edward Jenner.	**G**	The discovery of blood groups.
8	Samuel Hahnemann.	**H**	The author of the *Sherlock Holmes* stories.
9	Joseph Lister.	**I**	The first woman doctor in England.
10	Elizabeth Garrett Anderson.	**J**	The discovery of the cause of malaria.

THE 10 MOST COMMONLY PERFORMED SURGICAL OPERATIONS

1 Appendectomy (removal of appendix)

2 Inguinal (groin) hernia repair

3 Tonsil and adenoid removal

4 Cholecystectomy (removal of gall bladder)

5 Hysterectomy (removal of womb)

6 Cataract removal (eye operation)

7 Prostatectomy (removal of prostate gland)

8 Hip replacement

9 Cystoscopy (bladder operation)

10 Myringotomy (eardrum operation)

THE 10 COMMONEST HOSPITAL CASUALTY COMPLAINTS

1 Cuts

2 Bruises

3 Dog bites

4 Sprained ankles

5 Eye injuries

6 Head injuries

7 Minor burns

8 Fractures

9 Upper respiratory tract infections

10 Gastroenteritis

The ratio of casualties varies considerably according to such factors as the time of the year – people suffer from more chest infections in the winter, and trip and injure themselves more frequently during icy weather, for example. The nature of the local community is also significant: in certain areas patients are more likely to consult their general practitioners for minor complaints, whereas in others they turn to the hospital casualty department first for treatment of anything from toothache to a nosebleed.

THE 10 MOST POPULAR NON-PRESCRIPTION MEDICINES IN GREAT BRITAIN

	Medicine	Sales (£)
1	Analgesics (painkillers such as aspirin)	145,000,000
2	Food supplements	128,000,000
3	Vitamins	81,000,000
4	Sore throat remedies	71,000,000
5	Cough remedies	56,000,000
6	Cold remedies	49,000,000
7	Indigestion remedies	42,000,000
8	Skin treatments (other than acne products)	32,000,000
9	Acne skin products	25,000,000
10	Laxatives	17,000,000

In 1990 we spent a total of £650,000,000 on non-prescription or 'over-the-counter' home remedies, or £778,000,000 with the category of 'Food supplements', which was included for the first time in that year (this excludes vitamins, but encompasses such substances as evening primrose oil, garlic and fish oil, indicative of an observable trend towards preventative measures rather than cures for existing symptoms).

In 1988, after a BBC Television *QED* programme suggested that vitamins contributed to increased intelligence among children, sales of vitamins generally went up by 12 per cent and those of children's vitamins soared by 25 per cent, making this the No. 1 item on the list. In 1989 sales declined again from their £144,000,000 record, and analgesics once again became the country's favourite home remedy, remaining so in 1990. Another *QED* programme on the relationship of vitamins to intelligence was screened early in 1991, and it will be interesting to assess whether this has a similar effect on sales.

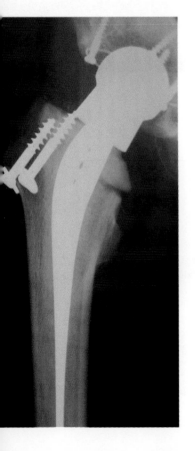

LEFT Hip replacement is the eighth commonest operation.

RIGHT A range of perennially popular over-the-counter medicines.

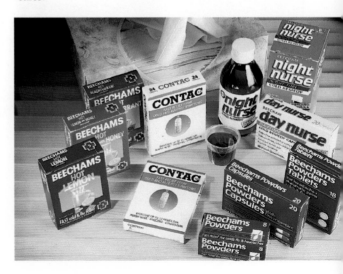

THE 10 LONGEST BONES IN THE HUMAN BODY

		Average length	
	Bone	cm	in
1	Femur (thighbone – upper leg)	50.50	19.88
2	Tibia (shinbone – inner lower leg)	43.03	16.94
3	Fibula (outer lower leg)	40.50	15.94
4	Humerus (upper arm)	36.46	14.35
5	Ulna (inner lower arm)	28.20	11.10
6	Radius (outer lower arm)	26.42	10.40
7	7th rib	24.00	9.45
8	8th rib	23.00	9.06
9	Innominate bone (hipbone – half pelvis)	18.50	7.28
10	Sternum (breastbone)	17.00	6.69

These are average dimensions of the bones of an adult male measured from their extremities (ribs are curved, and the pelvis measurement is taken diagonally). The same bones in the female skeleton are usually 6 to 13 per cent smaller, with the exception of the sternum which is virtually identical.

THE 10 LARGEST HUMAN ORGANS

			Average weight	
	Organ		g	oz
1	Liver		1,560	55.0
2	Brain	male	1,408	49.7
		female	1,263	44.6
3	Lungs	right	580	20.5
		left	510	18.0
		total	1,090	38.5
4	Heart	male	315	11.1
		female	265	9.3
5	Kidneys	left	150	5.3
		right	140	4.9
		total	290	10.2
6	Spleen		170	6.0
7	Pancreas		98	3.5
8	Thyroid		35	1.2
9	Prostate	male only	20	0.7
10	Adrenals	left	6	0.2
		right	6	0.2
		total	12	0.4

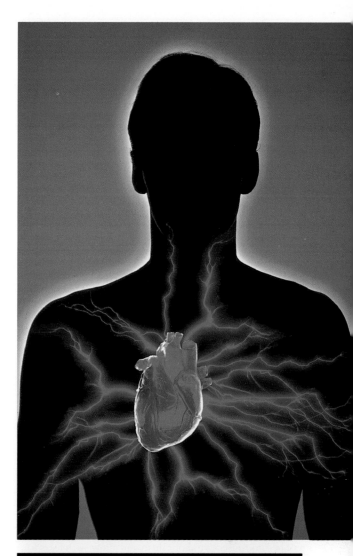

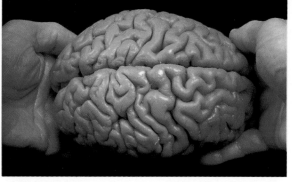

Based on average immediate post-mortem weights, as recorded by St Bartholemew's Hospital, London, and other sources during the past 10 years. Various instances of organs far in excess of the average have been recorded, including male brains of over 2,000 g/ 70.6 oz.

TOP Big hearted: in reality the heart is the fourth largest organ in the human body.

ABOVE Brain power: the brain weighs more than four times as much as the average heart.

THE 10 COMMONEST PHOBIAS

	Object of phobia	Medical term
1	Spiders	Arachnephobia or arachnophobia
2	People and social situations	Anthropophobia or sociophobia
3	Flying	Aerophobia or aviatophobia
4	Open spaces	Agoraphobia, cenophobia or kenophobia
5	Confined spaces	Claustrophobia, cleisiophobia, cleithrophobia or clithrophobia
6	Heights	Acrophobia, altophobia, hypsophobia or hypsiphobia
7	Cancer	Carcinomaphobia, carcinophobia, carcinomatophobia, cancerphobia or cancerophobia
8	Thunderstorms	Brontophobia or keraunophobia; related phobias are those associated with lightning (astraphobia), cyclones (anemophobia) and hurricanes and tornadoes (lilapsophobia)
9	Death	Necrophobia or thanatophobia
10	Heart disease	Cardiophobia

A phobia is a morbid fear that is out of all proportion to the object of the fear. Many people would admit to being uncomfortable about these principal phobias, as well as others, such as snakes (ophiophobia), injections (trypanophobia) or ghosts (phasmophobia), but most do not become obsessive about them and allow such fears to rule their lives. True phobias often arise from some incident in childhood when a person has been afraid of some object and has developed an irrational fear that persists into adulthood. Nowadays, as well as the valuable work done by the Phobics Society and other organizations, phobias can be cured by taking special desensitization courses, for example, to conquer one's fear of flying.

There are many phobias that are much less common than those appearing in the Top 10. Even if only one person has ever been observed with a specific phobia, psychologists have often given it a name – some more bizarre than others:

Beards	Pogonophobia
Chickens	Alektorophobia
Chins	Geniophobia
Eggshells	No medical term
Everything	Pantophobia, panophobia, panphobia or pamphobia
Opening one's eyes	Optophobia
Gravity	Barophobia

The fear of heights is a common phobia and featured as the theme of Hitchcock's 1958 thriller *Vertigo*.

Hair	Chaetophobia
Mirrors	Eisoptrophobia
Money	Chrometophobia
Satellites plunging to Earth	Keraunothnetophobia
Slime	Blennophobia or myxophobia
String	Linonophobia
Teeth	Odontophobia
The number thirteen	Terdekaphobia, tridecaphobia, triakaidekaphobia or triskaidekaphobia

THE 10 COMMONEST ALLERGENS*

Food		Environmental
Wheat	1	House dust mites
Milk	2	House dust
Yeast	3	Mould
Eggs	4	Grass pollen
Corn	5	Domestic gas
Chocolate	6	Formaldehyde
Coffee	7	Petrol fumes
Cheese	8	Animal fur and danders†
Beef	9	Perfume
Oranges	10	Aerosols

Substances that cause allergies.
†*Small particles of hair or feathers.*

The words 'allergy' and 'allergen' date back only about 80 years. Dr Keith Mumby, founder of the Food and Environmental Allergy Clinic and author of *The Allergy Handbook*, defines an allergy as 'an unpleasant reaction to foreign matter, specific to that substance, which is altered from the normal response and peculiar to the individual concerned'. The allergens that cause these reactions are commonly foods but also environmental agents, pollen as a cause of hay-fever being perhaps one of the best known. Reactions to them can result in a huge variety of symptoms ranging from severe mental or physical disability to more minor irritations – mild headache in the presence of fresh paint, for example. 'Elimination dieting' to identify and dispense with food allergens and the identification and avoidance of environmental allergens can result in complete cures from a wide variety of allergies.

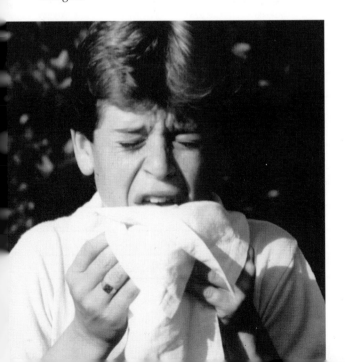

THE 10 HEAVIEST-SMOKING NATIONS IN THE WORLD

	Country	Cigarettes per adult per annum
1	Cuba	3,920.0
2	Cyprus	3,736.9
3	Greece	3,216.5
4	Iceland	3,100.0
5	Kuwait	2,773.0
6	Poland	2,652.0
7	Hungary	2,549.8
8	Japan	2,537.0
9	Yugoslavia	2,453.8
10	China	2,265.0
	UK	*1,694.9*

In the Top 10 the *average* consumption of manufactured cigarettes by adults aged 15 and over ranges from the equivalent of almost 11 to just over 6 cigarettes per day. As each country's population also includes many non-smokers, light and occasional smokers, there must be large numbers of extremely heavy smokers to bring the average up to these levels. In Western countries, there has been an increasing trend towards non-smoking: in the UK, for example, smokers are now outnumbered by non-smokers, and since the World Health Organization last compiled these statistics, the average has probably declined in most countries – although it may even have increased in certain Third World territories.

THE TOP 10 CAUSES OF STRESS-RELATED ILLNESS

	Event	Value
1	Death of spouse	100
2	Divorce	73
3	Marital separation	65
4=	Detention in prison or other institution	63
4=	Death of close family member	63
6	Major personal injury or illness	53
7	Marriage	50
8	Losing one's job	47
9=	Marital reconciliation	45
9=	Retirement	45

Psychiatrists Dr Thomas Holmes and Dr Richard Rahe devised what they called the 'Social Readjustment Rating Scale' to place a value on the likelihood of illness occurring as a result of stress caused by various 'life events'. Even agreeable occasions such as weddings, promotion at work and Christmas have been evaluated for their stress value on this scale. The cumulative effect of several incidents increases the risk factor – if an individual's points total over 300 in a given year, he is reckoned to have a 79 per cent chance of major illness.

LEFT Bless you! Hay-fever caused by grass pollen is one of many reactions to environmental agents.

THE 10 COUNTRIES WITH THE HIGHEST FEMALE LIFE EXPECTANCY

	Country	Life expectancy (years)
1	Japan	82.1
2	Switzerland	81.0
3	Sweden	80.2
4	France	80.0
5=	Canada	79.9
5=	Norway	79.9
7=	Netherlands	79.8
7=	Spain	79.8
9	Australia	79.6
10	Iceland	79.0
	USA	*78.5*
	UK	*78.1*

THE 10 COUNTRIES WITH THE HIGHEST MALE LIFE EXPECTANCY

	Country	Life expectancy (years)
1	Japan	75.9
2	Iceland	74.9
3	Greece	74.1
4=	Sweden	74.0
4=	Switzerland	74.0
6	Israel	73.4
7	Spain	73.2
8=	Canada	73.1
8=	Netherlands	73.1
10	Australia	73.0
	UK	*72.4*
	USA	*71.8*

The 10 principal causes of death remain the same and in approximately the same order from year to year, with only slight fluctuations in total numbers. Total UK deaths in 1989 were 8,555 (1.3 per cent) higher than in the previous year. In category 1, heart attacks are the principal killer (a UK total of 173,409), and in category 2, lung cancer killed the most – 39,646 in 1989. In category 5, motor vehicle accidents accounted for most deaths (5,624).

ABOVE Motor vehicle crashes cause more than a quarter of all deaths by accidents and violence.

THE 10 COMMONEST CAUSES OF DEATH IN THE UK

	Cause	England & Wales	Scotland	Northern Ireland	Total
1	Diseases of circulatory system	264,600	31,223	7,422	303,245
2	Cancer	145,120	15,054	3,571	163,745
3	Diseases of respiratory system	66,712	8,668	2,886	78,266
4	Diseases of digestive system	18,679	1,961	380	21,020
5	Accidents and violence	17,500	2,811	693	21,004
6	Diseases of nervous system	13,718	887	178	14,783
7	Mental disorders	13,234	1,105	45	14,384
8	Endocrine, nutritional and metabolic diseases and immunity disorders	10,153	765	83	11,001
9	Diseases of genito-urinary system	7,772	834	243	8,849
10	Diseases of musculo-skeletal system	5,374	98	45	5,517
	*Total deaths from all causes**	*576,872*	*65,017*	*15,844*	*657,733*

Including some that do not appear in the Top 10.

HUMAN ACTIVITIES & ACHIEVEMENTS

THE WORLD'S 10 LONGEST-REIGNING MONARCHS

	Monarch	Country	Reign	Age at accession	Reign years
1	Louis XIV	France	1643–1715	5	72
2	John II	Liechtenstein	1858–1929	18	71
3	Franz-Josef	Austria–Hungary	1848–1916	18	67
4	Victoria	Great Britain	1837–1901	18	63
5	Hirohito	Japan	1926–89	25	62
6	George III	Great Britain	1760–1820	22	59
7	Louis XV	France	1715–74	5	59
8	Pedro II	Brazil	1831–89	6	58
9	Wilhelmina	Netherlands	1890–1948	10	58
10	Henry III	England	1216–72	9	56

Some authorities have claimed a 73-year reign for Alfonso I of Portugal, but his father, Henry of Burgundy, who conquered Portugal, ruled as Count, and it was this title that Alfonso inherited on 30 April 1112, at the age of two. His mother, Theresa of Castile, ruled until he took power in 1128, but he did not assume the title of king until 25 July 1139, during the Battle of Ourique at which he vanquished the Moors. He thus ruled as king for 46 years until his death on 6 December 1185. Even more extravagant claims are sometimes made for long-reigning monarchs in the ancient world, such as the alleged 94 years of Phiops II, a Sixth Dynasty Egyptian pharaoh, but since it is uncertain when he was either born or died, he has not been included.

THE 10 LONGEST-REIGNING BRITISH MONARCHS

	Monarch	Reign	Age at accession	Age at death	Reign years
1	Victoria	1837–1901	18	81	63
2	George III	1760–1820	22	81	59
3	Henry III	1216–72	9	64	56
4	Edward III	1327–77	14	64	50
5	Elizabeth I	1558–1603	25	69	44
6	Elizabeth II	1952–	25	–	39
7	Henry VI	1422–61 (deposed; d.1471)	8 months	49	38
8	Henry VIII	1509–47	17	55	37
9	Charles II	1649–85	19	54	36
10	Henry I	1100–35	31/32*	66/67*	35

Henry I's birthdate is unknown, so his age at accession and death are uncertain.

This list excludes the reigns of monarchs before 1066, so omits such rulers as Ethelred II who reigned for 37 years. Queen Elizabeth II overtook Henry VI's 38 years and 185 days reign in August 1990. If she is still on the throne on 11 September 2015, she will have beaten Queen Victoria's record by one day. She will then be 89 years old.

THE 10 SHORTEST-REIGNING BRITISH MONARCHS

	Monarch	Reign	Duration
1	Jane	1553	14 days
2	Edward V	1483	75 days
3	Edward VIII	1936	325 days
4	Richard III	1483–85	2 years
5	James II	1685–88	3 years
6	Mary I	1553–58	5 years
7	Mary II	1689–94	5 years
8	Edward VI	1547–53	6 years
9	William IV	1830–37	7 years
10	Edward VII	1901–10	9 years

Queen Victoria in 1896, the year she overtook George III's record 59 years on the throne.

THE 10 LONGEST-LIVED BRITISH MONARCHS

	Monarch	Born	Reign	Age at death
1	Victoria	1819	1837–1901	81
2	George III	1738	1760–1820	81
3	Edward VIII	1894	1936 (abdicated; d.1972)	77
4	George II	1683	1727–60	76
5	William IV	1765	1830–37	71
6	George V	1865	1910–36	70
7	Elizabeth I	1533	1558–1603	69
8	Edward VII	1841	1901–10	68
9	Edward I	1239	1272–1307	68
10	James II	1633	1685–88	67

Queen Victoria and George III are close rivals for the title of longest-lived British monarch, and George's dates might suggest that he lived slightly longer than Victoria. However, during his lifetime, in 1752, the Gregorian Calendar was adopted in Great Britain, as a result of which 11 days were lost. Taking this into account, Queen Victoria lived for 81 years 243 days and George III for 81 years 239 days. The difference between the lifetimes of Edward VII and Edward I is also very slight, with Edward VII the winner by just six months; in fact, there is just a two-month difference between the life spans of Edward I and James II, who ranks 10th.

Edward I's 16 children place him at the head of the list of Britain's most prolific monarchs.

THE 10 BRITISH MONARCHS WITH MOST LEGITIMATE CHILDREN

	Monarch	Sons	Daughters	Total
1	Edward I	6	10	16
2=	James II	6	9	15
2=	George III	9	6	15
4	Edward III	7	5	12
5	Edward IV	3	7	10
6=	William I	4	5	9
6=	Charles I	4	5	9
6=	Victoria	4	5	9
9=	Henry II	5	3	8
9=	George II	3	5	8

Although Edward I tops this list, the claim that he had as many as 18 legitimate children cannot be substantiated. By his first wife, Eleanor, he had four sons (John and Henry, who died in infancy; Alfonso, who died at the age of 12; and Edward II, who succeeded him) and nine daughters (Eleanor, Joanna, Margaret, Mary and Elizabeth and four others who died young), and by his second wife, Margaret, he had two sons (Thomas and Edward) and a daughter who died in childhood. James II had the greatest total of legitimate and illegitimate offspring – 19 (eight by Lady Anne Hyde, seven by Mary of Modena and four illegitimate). If all of his daughter Queen Anne's pregnancies had been successful, she would have held the record. Between 1684 and 1700 she was pregnant 17 times, but she had 12 miscarriages and six confinements, only one of which produced a child who survived infancy – William, Duke of Gloucester, although he died at the age of 11. Henry I may have had as many as 22 illegitimate children, as well as one or two legitimate sons and one daughter; Charles II had no legitimate offspring, and an uncertain number of illegitimate children by several mistresses.

THE 10 OLDEST MONARCHS TO ASCEND THE BRITISH THRONE

	Monarch	Reign	Age at accession
1	William IV	1830–37	64
2	Edward VII	1901–10	59
3	George IV	1820–30	57
4	George I	1714–27	54
5	James II	1685–88	51
6	George V	1910–36	44
7	George II	1727–60	43
8	Edward VIII	1936	41
9	George VI	1936–52	40
10	William I	1066–87	39

THE TOP 10 IN LINE TO THE BRITISH THRONE

1	HRH The Prince of Wales (Prince Charles Philip Arthur George) b. 14 November 1948	*then his elder son:*
2	HRH Prince William of Wales (Prince William Arthur Philip Louis) b. 21 June 1982	*then his younger brother:*
3	HRH Prince Henry of Wales (Prince Henry Charles Albert David) b. 15 September 1984	*then his uncle:*
4	HRH The Duke of York (Prince Andrew Albert Christian Edward) b. 19 February 1960	*then his elder daughter:*
5	HRH Princess Beatrice of York (Princess Beatrice Elizabeth Mary) b. 8 August 1988	*then her younger sister:*
6	HRH Princess Eugenie of York (Princess Eugenie Victoria Helena) b. 23 March 1990	*then her uncle:*
7	HRH Prince Edward (Prince Edward Antony Richard Louis) b. 10 March 1964	*then his sister:*
8	HRH The Princess Royal (Princess Anne Elizabeth Alice Louise) b. 15 August 1950	*then her son:*
9	Master Peter Mark Andrew Phillips b. 15 November 1977	*then his sister:*
10	Miss Zara Anne Elizabeth Phillips b. 15 May 1981	

THE 10 YOUNGEST BRITISH MONARCHS

	Monarch	Reign	Age at accession years	months
1	Henry VI	1422–61	0	8
2	Henry III	1216–72	9	1
3	Edward VI	1547–53	9	3
4	Richard II	1377–99	10	5
5	Edward V	1483	12	5
6	Edward III	1327–77	14	2
7	Jane	1553	15	8
8	Henry VIII	1509–47	17	10
9	Victoria	1837–1901	18	1
10	Charles II	1649–85	18	8

Henry VI was born on 6 December 1421 and became King of England on 1 September 1422, the day after the death of his father, Henry V. At the age of 10 months (following the death of his grandfather, Charles VI, on 21 October 1422), he also became King of France. Before the Norman Conquest, Edward the Martyr became king in 975 when aged about 12 and Ethelred II ('The Unready') in 978 at the age of about 10.

The birth in 1988 of Princess Beatrice altered the order of succession, ousting David Albert Charles Armstrong-Jones, Viscount Linley (b. 3 November 1961), from the No. 10 position, while the birth in 1990 of her sister, Princess Eugenie, evicted HRH Princess Margaret, Countess of Snowdon (Princess Margaret Rose, b. 21 August 1930) from the Top 10.

THE TOP 10 GIRLS' AND BOYS' NAMES IN THE USA

| | GIRLS | | | BOYS | |
White	Ethnic		White		Ethnic
Ashley	Ashley	1	Michael		Michael
Jessica	Brittany	2	Matthew		Christopher
Amanda	Jessica	3	Christopher		Brandon
Sarah	Sierra	4	Joshua		Anthony
Megan	Danielle	5	Andrew		James
Jennifer	Tiffany	6	Justin		Joshua
Katherine	Erica	7	Daniel		Steven
Rachel	Crystal	8	Ryan		Charles
Stephanie	Jasmine	9	James		Darryl
Heather	Tanisha	10	David		Brian/Kevin/ Robert/William

American name fashions are even more volatile than those in England and Wales, and vary considerably according to the child's ethnic background. Back in 1984, Ashley, which now tops the girls' lists, was already being noted as *the* girl's name of the year, just as Angela had been 10 years earlier. Heather has surprisingly maintained its momentum and has actually grown in popularity since the 1970s, despite the decline of other names derived from flowers, such as Daisy, Violet and Lily. It has been claimed that Jennifer (recently overtaken by Jessica) rose to prominence after the heroine of the book and film *Love Story*, and that Tiffany entered the Top 10 in 1980, influenced by the character Tiffany Welles in the TV series, *Charlie's Angels*. Among boys' names, Joshua appeared in the Top 10 for the first time in 1983, while Richard plummeted out of the Top 10 after Richard Nixon's disgrace during the Watergate scandal. Michael has topped every US list since 1964.

OPPOSITE William IV, at the age of 64 the oldest monarch to ascend the British throne.

BELOW Jennifer (Ali MacGraw), the name of the heroine of the 1971 film *Love Story*, achieved a surge of popularity in the 1970s.

THE TOP 10 GIRLS' AND BOYS' NAMES IN ENGLAND AND WALES

Girls		Boys
Rebecca	1	Daniel
Sarah	2	Christopher
Emma	3	Michael
Laura	4	James
Rachel	5	Matthew
Samantha	6	Andrew
Charlotte	7	Adam
Kirsty	8	Thomas
Nicola	9	David
Amy	10	Richard

A survey of first names registered in England and Wales reveals that only two girls' names – Charlotte and Emma – and three boys' names – James, Thomas and David – also make an appearance in the Top 10 *Times* names lists (*see* p.58). Other popular names on the *Times* list are placed much lower in the national Top 10, with 'traditional' names such as Alice, Olivia, Charles and Henry, which are perennial favourites among *Times* readers, not even appearing in the England and Wales Top 50. Kylie is moving up the British list but has some way to go to make the Top 10 – as it did in Australia.

QUIZ
NAMES

Connect the real names with those by which the following famous men are better known:

1 William Henry Pratt.
2 Robert Davies.
3 Allen Stewart Konigsberg.
4 Maurice Micklewhite.
5 Leslie Lynch King.
6 David John Moore Cornwell.
7 Bernard Schwartz.
8 William Perks.
9 Charles Lutwidge Dodgson.
10 Steveland Morris.

A British comedian Jasper Carrott.
B US President Gerald Ford.
C British horror film actor Boris Karloff.
D *Alice in Wonderland* author Lewis Carroll.
E Rolling Stone Bill Wyman.
F American actor Tony Curtis.
G British spy novelist John Le Carré.
H American singer Stevie Wonder.
I British actor Michael Caine.
J American comedian and film-maker Woody Allen.

THE TOP 10 GIRLS' AND BOYS' NAMES ANNOUNCED IN THE BIRTHS COLUMN OF *THE TIMES*

FIRST NAME ONLY

	Girls	No.		Boys	No.
1	(1) Charlotte	84	1	(1) James	180
2	(3) Sophie	82	2	(2) Thomas	170
3	(8) Lucy	75	3	(3) Alexander	153
4	(2) Emily	70	4	(4) William	123
5=	(7) Alexandra	67	5	(7) Oliver	94
5=	(5) Alice	67	6	(6) Charles	92
7	(4) Emma	61	7	(5) Edward	90
8	(–) Jessica	60	8	(8) George	68
9	(6) Olivia	59	9	(9=) Henry	62
10	(–) Georgina	55	10	(–) Samuel	55

ALL NAMES (INCLUDING MIDDLE NAMES)

	Girls	No.		Boys	No.
1	(1) Elizabeth	232	1	(1) James	431
2	(2) Charlotte	135	2	(2) William	281
3	(3) Alice	126	3	(3) Alexander	267
4	(8) Alexandra	117	4	(5) Thomas	232
5	(6=) Sophie	109	5	(7) John	195
6	(10) Lucy	105	6	(4) Edward	191
7	(4) Emily	103	7	(6) Charles	184
8	(5) Victoria	99	8	(8) George	145
9	(–) Katherine	80	9	(9) David	143
10	(6=) Emma	79	10	(–) Henry	134

Last year's position given in brackets.

Since 1947, various people have monitored the Births column of *The Times* and listed the frequency of given names, a task now carried out by the paper's own Social Editor. In 1947, the most popular names were Ann(e) and John. In 1990 a total of 5,847 births were recorded – 2,856 girls and 2,991 boys (in 1989 it was 5,425: 2,645 girls and 2,780 boys). James has been the most popular boy's name since 1964, while the order of the other names has fluctuated a good deal, George and Olivia, for example, both entering the first name list for the first time in 1989, with Samuel, Georgina and Jessica joining them in 1990. The name William, which has maintained its resurgence in recent years, revives a tradition of very long standing, as research in sixteenth-century parish registers has revealed that more than one in five of all boys were baptized with that name.

THE TOP 10 YOUTH ORGANIZATIONS IN THE UK

	Organization	Members
1	YMCA	1,616,000*
2	Youth Clubs UK	567,624
3	Brownie Guides	376,217
4	Cub Scouts	244,000
5	Girl Guides	232,453
6	National Association of Boys' Clubs	170,000
7	Boy Scouts	160,000
8	Boys' Brigade	106,250
9	Girls' Brigade	91,480
10	Combined Cadet Force	39,559

Includes 886,000 male, 730,000 female members aged under 21.

With 232,453 members in the UK, the new-look Girl Guides now outnumber the Boy Scouts.

THE TOP 10 ENVIRONMENTAL ORGANIZATIONS IN THE UK

	Organization	Membership
1	National Trust	2,031,743
2	Royal Society for the Protection of Birds	820,000*
3	Greenpeace	385,000
4	Civic Trust	304,000
5	Royal Society for Nature Conservation	262,000**
6	World Wide Fund for Nature†	261,000
7	English Heritage	235,837
8	National Trust for Scotland	218,000
9	Friends of the Earth	200,000
10	Ramblers Association	81,500‡

Includes 127,000 members of the Young Ornithologists Club.
**Includes junior body, WATCH, with 50,000 members.*
†Formerly the World Wildlife Fund.
‡Includes membership in the Republic of Ireland.

THE TOP 10 TRADE ('LABOR') UNIONS IN THE USA

	Union	Members
1	National Education Association	2,000,000
2	International Brotherhood of Teamsters, Chauffeurs, Warehousemen and Helpers of America	1,600,000
3	United Food and Commercial Workers' International Union	1,235,000
4	American Federation of State, County and Municipal Employees	1,200,000
5	International Union of Automobile, Aerospace and Agricultural Implement Workers of America	944,000
6	International Union of Service Employees	850,000
7	International Brotherhood of Electrical Workers	845,000
8	International Association of Machinists and Aerospace Workers	767,000
9	American Federation of Teachers	715,000
10	Communications Workers of America	700,000

THE TOP 10 TRADE UNIONS IN GREAT BRITAIN

	Union	Members
1	Transport & General Workers' Union (TGWU)	1,270,766
2	GMB (Formerly General, Municipal Boilermakers and Allied Trades Union)	823,176
3	National & Local Government Officers' Association (NALGO)	750,000
4	Amalgamated Engineering Union (AEU)	741,647
5	Manufacturing, Science & Finance Union (MSF)	668,901
6	National Union of Public Employees (NUPE)	604,912
7	Union of Shop, Distributive & Allied Workers (USDAW)	375,891
8	Electrical, Electronic, Telecommunications & Plumbing Union (EETPU)	360,000
9	Royal College of Nursing (RCN)	283,713
10	Union of Construction, Allied Trades & Technicians (UCATT)	258,616

Total trade union membership is around 8,500,000, but numbers have steadily declined and there are fewer than half the number of unions affiliated to the Trades Union Congress (TUC) that there were 30 years ago, when there were still unions serving such bygone trades as glass bevelling and felt hat making – though some still retain splendid descriptive names evoking highly specialized industries, among them the Card Setting Machine Tenters' Society and the Amalgamated Association of Beamers, Twisters and Drawers (Hand and Machine). Many of the smaller unions have been disbanded in recent years – the Spring Trapmakers' Society, for example, was dissolved in 1988 – although in marked contrast to the unions in the Top 10 there are some tiny survivors, such as the Military and Orchestral Musical Instrument Makers' Trade Society (35 members), the Society of Shuttlemakers (30) and the Sheffield Wool Shearers' Union (15).

THE TOP 10 WOMEN'S ORGANIZATIONS IN THE UK

	Organization	Approx. membership
1	National Alliance of Women's Organizations	4,729,100
2	Trades Union Congress Women's Committee	2,800,000
3	Conservative Women's National Committee	500,000
4	National Federation of Women's Institutes	330,000
5	National Equal Rights Advisory Committee of GMB (Formerly General, Municipal Boilermakers and Allied Trades Union)	300,000
6	Transport and General Workers Union Women's Committee	220,000
7	The Mothers' Union	180,000
8	Townswomen's Guilds	125,000
9	National Association of Schoolmasters & Union of Women Teachers	59,000
10	National Childbirth Trust	54,000

The TUC Women's Committee is one of the largest women's organizations in the UK.

THE FIRST 10 PRESIDENTS OF THE USA

	President (dates)	Period in office
1	George Washington (1732–99)	1789–97
2	John Adams (1735–1826)	1797–1801
3	Thomas Jefferson (1743–1826)	1801–09
4	James Madison (1751–1836)	1809–17
5	James Monroe (1758–1831)	1817–25
6	John Quincy Adams (1767–1848)	1825–29
7	Andrew Jackson (1767–1845)	1829–37
8	Martin Van Buren (1782–1862)	1837–41
9	William Henry Harrison (1773–1841)	1841
10	John Tyler (1790–1862)	1841–45

THE WORLD'S FIRST 10 FEMALE PRIME MINISTERS AND PRESIDENTS

	Name	Country	Period in office
1	Sirimavo Bandaranaike (PM)	Ceylon (Sri Lanka)	1960–64 1970–77
2	Indira Gandhi (PM)	India	1966–84
3	Golda Meir (PM)	Israel	1969–74
4	Maria Estela Perón (President)	Argentina	1974–75
5	Elisabeth Domitien (PM)	Central African Republic	1975
6	Margaret Thatcher (PM)	UK	May 1979–Nov 1990
7	Dr Maria Lurdes Pintasilgo (PM)	Portugal	Aug–Nov 1979
8	Vigdís Finnbogadóttir (President)	Iceland	Jun 1980–
9	Mary Eugenia Charles (PM)	Dominica	Jul 1980–
10	Gro Harlem Brundtland (PM)	Norway	Feb–Oct 1981 May 1986–Oct 1989

Mrs Bandaranaike of Sri Lanka (Ceylon) became the world's first female prime minister on 21 July 1960. Mrs Thatcher became Britain's first on 4 May 1979. The first 10 have been followed by Corazón Aquino, who became President of the Philippines in 1986, by Benazir Bhutto, Prime Minister of Pakistan (1988–90), Violeta Barrios de Chamorro, President of Nicaragua (1990–), Ertha Pascal-Trouillot, President of Haiti (1990–), Mary Robinson, President of the Irish Republic (1990–) and Edith Cresson, Prime Minister of France (1991–).

THE FIRST 10 COUNTRIES TO GIVE WOMEN THE VOTE

	Country	Year
1	New Zealand	1893
2	Australia (South Australia 1894; Western Australia 1898; Australia was united in 1901)	1902
3	Finland (then a Grand Duchy under the Russian Crown)	1906
4	Norway (restricted franchise; all women over 25 in 1913)	1907
5	Denmark and Iceland (a Danish dependency until 1918)	1915
6=	Netherlands	1917
6=	USSR	1917
8=	Austria	1918
8=	Canada	1918
8=	Germany	1918
8=	Great Britain and Ireland (Ireland part of the United Kingdom until 1921; women over 30 only – lowered to 21 in 1928)	1918
8=	Poland	1918

Although not a country, the Isle of Man was the first place to give women the vote, in 1880. Until 1920 the only other European countries to enfranchise women were Sweden in 1919 and Czechoslovakia in 1920. Certain states of the USA gave women the vote at earlier dates (Wyoming in 1869, Colorado in 1894, Utah in 1895 and Idaho in 1896), but it was not granted nationally until 1920. A number of countries, such as France and Italy, did not give women the vote until 1945. Switzerland did not allow women to vote in elections to the Federal Council until 1971, and Liechtenstein was one of the last to relent, in 1984. In certain countries, such as Saudi Arabia, women are not allowed to vote at all – but neither can men.

THE 10 LONGEST-SERVING BRITISH PRIME MINISTERS

	Prime minister (dates)	Periods in office	Total duration years	months*
1	Sir Robert Walpole (1676–1745)	3 Apr 1721–8 Feb 1742	20	10
2	William Pitt the Younger (1759–1806)	19 Dec 1783–14 Mar 1801 10 May 1804–23 Jan 1806	18	11
3	Earl of Liverpool (1770–1828)	7 Jun 1812–17 Feb 1827	14	8
4	Marquess of Salisbury (1830–1903)	23 Jun 1885–28 Jan 1886 26 Jul 1886–11 Aug 1892 25 Jun 1895–22 Jan 1901 23 Jan 1901–11 Jul 1902	13	9
5	William Gladstone (1809–1898)	4 Dec 1868–17 Feb 1874 23 Apr 1880–9 Jun 1885 1 Feb 1886–20 Jul 1886 15 Aug 1892–2 Mar 1894	12	4
6	Lord North (1732–1779)	28 Jan 1770–20 Mar 1782	12	2
7	Margaret Thatcher (b.1925)	4 May 1979–9 Jun 1983 10 Jun 1983–4 May 1987 12 Jun 1987–29 Nov 1990	11	6
8	Viscount Palmerston (1784–1865)	6 Feb 1855–21 Feb 1858 12 Jun 1859–18 Oct 1865	9	5
9	Herbert Asquith (1852–1928)	5 Apr 1908–7 May 1910 8 May 1910–5 Dec 1916 (coalition 25 May 1915–)	8	8
10	Winston Churchill (1874–1965)	10 May 1940–26 Jul 1945 (coalition–23 May 1945) 26 Oct 1951–6 Feb 1952 7 Feb 1952–5 Apr 1955	8	8

*To nearest month.

Sir Robert Walpole is usually regarded as the first prime minister, although the office was not officially recognized until 1905, most earlier prime ministers deriving their authority from their position as First Lords of the Treasury. It is arguable whether Walpole's ministry should be dated from the time he became First Lord of the Treasury and Chancellor of the Exchequer in 1721 or from 15 May 1730 when his brother-in-law, Lord Townshend, resigned as Secretary of State (in order to devote the remainder of his life to turnip farming!), leaving Walpole in sole control of the Cabinet. Even if, on this basis, he is disqualified from the No. 1 position, his ministry from 1730 until 1742 still entitles him to 6th position.

OPPOSITE TOP Indira Gandhi became the second woman prime minister in the world in 1966.

OPPOSITE BOTTOM Gladstone's total service as British prime minister places him fifth in the all-time list.

THE 10 YOUNGEST BRITISH PRIME MINISTERS

	Prime minister (dates)	Appointment year	age
1	William Pitt (1759–1806)	1783	24
2	Duke of Grafton (1735–1811)	1768	33
3	Marquess of Rockingham (1730–82)	1765	35
4	Duke of Devonshire (1720–64)	1756	36
5	Lord North (1732–92)	1770	38
6	Lord Liverpool (1770–1828)	1812	42
7	Henry Addington (1757–1844)	1801	43
8	Sir Robert Walpole (1676–1745)	1721	44
9	Viscount Goderich (1782–1859)	1827	44
10	Duke of Portland (1738–1809)	1783	44

Although the last three on this list all became prime minister at the age of 44, Sir Robert Walpole was Viscount Goderich's senior by less than three months, while there were just 50 days between the ages of Viscount Goderich and the Duke of Portland.

THE 10 BRITISH GOVERNMENTS WITH THE GREATEST GENERAL ELECTION MAJORITIES*

	Year	Ruling party	PM/party	Majority
1	1931	National Government	Ramsay Macdonald (Lab.)	492
2	1918	Coalition	David Lloyd-George (Lib.)	283
3	1935	National Government	Stanley Baldwin (Con.)	242
4	1832	Whig/Liberal	Earl Grey (Whig)	225
5	1924	Conservative	Stanley Baldwin (Lib.)	210
6	1895	Conservative	Lord Salisbury (Con.)	153
7	1945	Labour	Clement Attlee (Lab.)	147
8	1983	Conservative	Margaret Thatcher (Con.)	144
9	1900	Conservative	Lord Salisbury (Con.)	135
10	1906	Liberal	Henry Campbell Bannerman (Lib.)	129

*Since 1832.

Two further postwar General Elections also resulted in high majorities – that of the Conservatives under Margaret Thatcher in 1987 (a majority of 102) and Labour under Harold Wilson in 1966 (97).

THE 10 LONGEST-SERVING MEMBERS OF PARLIAMENT

	Member of Parliament/ periods in office	Constituency	Total years in office
1	Sir Francis Knollys 1572–1588 1597–1648	Oxfordshire Berkshire	67
2	Rt Hon Charles Pelham Villiers 1835–1898	Wolverhampton	63
3	Sir Winston Churchill 1900–1906 1906–1922 1924–1945 1945–1964	Oldham NW Manchester Epping Woodford	62
4=	William Aislabie 1721–1781	Ripon	60
4=	Christopher R. M. Talbot 1830–1890	Mid-Glamorganshire	60
6	Sir John Aubrey 1768–1826	(Seven different constituencies)	58
7	Sir Charles Burrell 1806–1862	Shoreham	56
8=	Philips Gybbon 1707–1762	Rye, Sussex	55
8=	Hon Henry Lowther 1812–1867	Westmorland	55
10=	Sir John Rushout 1713–1768	Malmesbury	54
10=	David Lloyd George 1890–1945	Caernarvon	54
10=	Clement Tudway 1761–1815	Wells	54

THE FIRST 10 MOUNTAINEERS TO CLIMB EVEREST

	Mountaineer	Nationality	Date
1	Edmund Hillary	New Zealander	29 May 1953
2	Tenzing Norgay	Nepalese	29 May 1953
3	Jürg Marmet	Swiss	23 May 1956
4	Ernst Schmied	Swiss	23 May 1956
5	Hans-Rudolf von Gunten	Swiss	24 May 1956
6	Adolf Reist	Swiss	24 May 1956
7	Wang Fu-chou	Chinese	25 May 1960
8	Chu Ying-hua	Chinese	25 May 1960
9	Konbu	Tibetan	25 May 1960
10=	James Whittaker	American	1 May 1963
10=	Nawang Gombu	Indian	1 May 1963

James Whittaker and Nawang Gombu are 10th equal because, neither wishing to deny the other the privilege of being first, they ascended the last feet to the summit side by side.

THE FIRST 10 CROSS-CHANNEL SWIMMERS

			Time		
	Swimmer	Nationality	hr	min	Date
1	Matthew Webb	British	21	45	24–25 Aug 1875
2	Thomas Burgess	British	22	35	5–6 Sep 1911
3	Henry Sullivan	American	26	50	5–6 Aug 1923
4	Enrico Tiraboschi	Italian	16	33	12 Aug 1923
5	Charles Toth	American	16	58	8–9 Sep 1923
6	Gertrude Ederle*	American	14	39	6 Aug 1926
7	Millie Corson	American	15	29	27–28 Aug 1926
8	Arnst Wierkotter	German	12	40	30 Aug 1926
9	Edward Temme**	British	14	29	5 Aug 1927
10	Mercedes Gleitze	British	15	15	7 Oct 1927

*The first woman to swim the Channel.
**In 1934 Temme also swam from England to France, thus becoming the first person successfully to cross in both directions.

The first three crossings were from England to France, the rest from France to England.

CAPTAIN WEBB AND THE FIRST CROSS-CHANNEL SWIM

THE 10 FASTEST CROSS-CHANNEL SWIMMERS

	Swimmer	Nationality	Year	Time hr	min
1	Penny Lee Dean	American	1978	7	40
2	Philip Rush	New Zealander	1987	7	55
3	Richard Davey	British	1988	8	05
4	Irene van der Laan	Dutch	1982	8	06
5	Paul Asmuth	American	1985	8	12
6	Anita Sood	Indian	1987	8	15
7	Monique Wildschutt	Dutch	1984	8	19
8	Eric Johnson	American	1985	8	20
9	Susie Maroney	Australian	1990	8	29
10	Lyndon Dunsbee	British	1984	8	34

Captain Matthew Webb photographed in 1875, the year of his celebrated first Channel swim.

Captain Matthew Webb (1848–83) was one of the most celebrated men in Victorian England. The son of a Shropshire doctor and one of 12 children, he went to sea at the age of 12 and soon became renowned for his strength and stamina in the water, saving the lives of swimmers – including one of his brothers – and winning medals for bravery. Yet his fame derived largely from a single exploit, when he became the first person to swim the English Channel.

It may be difficult to imagine today why this was once regarded as a great achievement, as the Channel has subsequently been swum underwater (by Fred Baldasare on 10–11 July 1962), both ways (and even three times non-stop), and by children as young as 11 – indeed the record was once held by a 16-year-old American girl, Lynne Cox, and has been held since 1978 by another American, Penny Dean, who was aged 23 at the time of her 7 hr 40 min swim on 29 July 1978. But in 1875, the year of Webb's triumph, the feat was regarded as virtually impossible, with bookmakers offering huge odds against his succeeding.

Crossings with artificial aids had previously been made, including one in 1862 by a sailor called William Hoskins, sitting on a bale of straw, and one just prior to Webb by Captain Paul Boyton, an American, in a buoyant life-saving suit. Having given up an earlier attempt on 12 August, Webb set off again from Dover 12 days later, greased with porpoise oil as protection against the cold and followed by a small flotilla of boats. He was sustained by beef-tea, beer, coffee and an omelette, and after being stung by a starfish

he also took some brandy. During the last hours, within sight of the French coast, he had to battle against a strong sea and tide. As a contemporary report put it, 'nothing but unflinching bulldog pluck kept the man going'. He landed at Calais after 21 hours 44 minutes 55 seconds in the water.

After his epic Channel swim, Webb was hailed as a hero, fêted all over the world, depicted in ceramic effigies and on such unlikely media as the label of Bryant and May's *Captain Webb* matches. He was also responsible for making swimming a respectable and popular sport. His life, however, went downhill: virtually unemployable, he turned his attention to creating bizarre inventions, including a flying machine, but without success, and he earned a modest living from giving swimming demonstrations. What he needed was a fresh challenge, and so, with his wife and children, he set off to America with the intention of swimming the rapids and whirlpool below Niagara Falls. Like his Channel swim eight years earlier, the feat was said to be impossible, but on this occasion Captain Webb failed to confound his critics and he was drowned in the attempt.

During the next 36 years no fewer than 71 people, 22 of them women, tried to emulate Webb's cross-Channel swim, but it was not until 1911 that 37-year-old Thomas William Burgess of Rotherham, Yorkshire, finally succeeded in becoming the second man to swim the Channel. It was to be a further 16 years before the tally reached 10, three of them women.

THE TOP 10 NOBEL PRIZE WINNING COUNTRIES

	Country	Phy	Che	Phy/Med	Lit	Pce	Eco	Total
1	USA	54	36	66	9	17	16	198
2	UK	20	23	22	8	9	5	87
3	Germany	19	27	12	7	4	–	69
4	France	9	7	7	12	9	1	45
5	Sweden	4	4	7	7	5	2	29
6=	Switzerland	2	4	5	2	3	–	16
6=	USSR	7	1	2	3	2	1	16
8	Italy	3	1	3	5	1	–	13
9=	Denmark	3	–	5	3	1	–	12
9=	Netherlands	6	2	2	–	1	1	12

Key: Phy – Physics; Che – Chemistry; Phy/Med – Physiology or Medicine; Lit – Literature; Pce – Peace; Eco – Economic Sciences. Germany includes the united country before 1948 and West Germany to 1990.

At his death in 1896, the Swedish scientist Alfred Nobel left his fortune of some £1,750,000, amassed through his invention of dynamite, to establish a trust fund, which is now estimated to be worth over £150,000,000. Interest earned from this has enabled annual prizes to be awarded since 1901 to those who have achieved the greatest common good in the fields of Physics, Chemistry, Physiology or Medicine, Literature, Peace and, since 1969, Economic Sciences. All the award ceremonies take place in Stockholm, Sweden, with the exception of the Peace Prize, which is awarded in Oslo, Norway. The list includes all winners up to 1990, when the prizes were each worth over £400,000. In that year, the USSR doubled its total of Peace Prizes when the award went to President Mikhail Gorbachev. Two other countries – Belgium and Austria – have each produced nine Nobel Prize laureates, and some 29 other countries between one and eight winners. However, it should be noted that the prizes are won by individuals, and not the countries from which they come, and that, in addition to these winners, various stateless institutions such as the Red Cross have won the Peace Prize a total of 16 times.

THE 10 MOST POPULAR KISSOGRAMS

1	Policeman/policewoman
2	Schoolgirl
3	French maid
4	Leathergirl
5	Rolypoly (20-stone woman)
6	Vicar
7	Tarzan
8	Gorilla
9	Nurse
10	Chat-up gram

'Me Tarzan, you embarrassed' – a Tarzanogram swings into action.

TOWN & COUNTRY

THE 10 LARGEST CITIES IN THE WORLD

	City	Country	1990	Population estimate for AD 2000 [projected position]
1	Tokyo/Yokohama	Japan	26,952,000	29,971,000 [1]
2	Mexico City	Mexico	20,207,000	27,872,000 [2]
3	São Paulo	Brazil	18,052,000	25,354,000 [3]
4	Seoul	South Korea	16,268,000	21,976,000 [4]
5	New York	USA	14,622,000	14,648,000 [6]
6	Osaka/Kobe/Kyoto	Japan	13,826,000	14,287,000 [7]
7	Bombay	India	11,777,000	15,357,000 [5]
8	Calcutta	India	11,663,000	14,088,000 [10]
9	Buenos Aires	Argentina	11,518,000	12,911,000 [11]
10	Rio de Janeiro	Brazil	11,428,000	14,169,000 [9]
16	*London*	*UK*	*9,170,000*	*8,574,000* [23]

Calculating the populations of the world's cities is fraught with difficulties, not least that of determining whether the city is defined by its administrative boundaries or by its continuously built-up areas or conurbations. Since different countries adopt different schemes, and some have populations concentrated in city centres while others are spread out in suburbs sprawling over hundreds of square miles, it has been impossible to compare them meaningfully. In order to resolve this problem, the US Bureau of the Census has adopted the method of defining cities as population clusters or 'urban agglomerations' with densities of more than 5,000 inhabitants per square mile. It should be stressed that totals based on this system will differ considerably from those based on other methods: by it, for example, the hugely spread-out city of Shanghai is reckoned to have a population of 6,873,000, compared with the total of 12,620,000 estimated for its administrative area and which appears in the list of The 10 Largest Non-Capital Cities.

London was once the most populous city in the world, reaching its peak (though calculated on a different basis) of almost 9,000,000 in 1939. It has been in decline ever since, and fell behind Tokyo in 1957. By 2000 its continuing fall will relegate it to 23rd place in the world league, while Tehran, 17th in the 1990 assessment, will have risen to occupy 8th position with its population increasing from 9,354,000 to 14,251,000.

THE 10 LARGEST CITIES IN THE WORLD 100 YEARS AGO

	City	Population
1	London	4,231,431
2	Paris	2,423,946
3	Peking	1,648,814
4	Canton (Kwangchow)	1,600,000
5	Berlin	1,579,244
6	Tokyo	1,552,457
7	New York	1,515,301
8	Vienna	1,364,548
9	Chicago	1,099,850
10	Philadelphia	1,046,964

In 1890, Nanking in China was the only other city in the world with a population of more than 1,000,000, with another Chinese city, Tien-tsing, close behind. Several other cities, including Constantinople (called Istanbul since 1930), St Petersburg (Leningrad since 1924) and Moscow, all had populations in excess of 750,000. However, it is remarkable to consider that, as a result of the rapid growth of American cities in the second half of the nineteenth century, Brooklyn, with a population in 1890 of 806,343, was marginally larger than Bombay (804,470 in 1891). Today, Bombay's population of 11,777,000 makes it more than five times the size of Brooklyn, while Calcutta (840,130 in 1891) is even bigger.

RIGHT By far the world's greatest metropolis: London 100 years ago.

THE 10 LARGEST CITIES IN THE UK

	City	Area sq km	Area sq miles	Population density per sq km	Total population
1	London	1,579	609.7	4,291	6,735,400
2	Birmingham	264	102.0	3,803	1,004,100
3	Glasgow	198	76.3	3,662	725,100
4	Leeds	562	217.0	1,265	710,900
5	Sheffield	368	141.9	1,452	534,300
6	Liverpool	113	43.6	4,274	483,000
7	Bradford	370	142.9	1,252	463,100
8	Manchester	116	44.9	3,891	451,400
9	Edinburgh	261	100.6	1,679	438,232
10	Bristol	110	42.3	3,559	391,500

THE 10 OLDEST CITIES IN GREAT BRITAIN

	City	Original charter granted
1	Ripon	886
2	London	1066
3	Edinburgh	1124
4	Chichester	1135
5=	Lincoln	1154
5=	Oxford	1154
5=	Derby	1154
8=	Nottingham	1155
8=	Winchester	1155
10	Exeter	1156

Although most of the 58 British cities were settled in earlier times, some as far back as the first century BC, their status as cities is dated from when their charters, issued by the Crown and establishing certain privileges, such as the power to enact local laws or collect taxes, were granted.

THE 10 LARGEST CITIES IN THE UK IN 1801

	City	Population
1	London	864,845
2	Manchester	94,876
3	Edinburgh	82,560
4	Liverpool	79,722
5	Glasgow	77,385
6	Birmingham	73,670
7	Portsmouth	43,461
8	Plymouth	43,194
9	Newcastle-upon-Tyne	36,963
10	Norwich	36,832

Early estimates of the population of England suggest that it first exceeded 5,000,000 early in the seventeenth century and had reached 6,000,000 by 1700. Britain's first Census was held in 1801 and indicated a total population of 10,500,956 for England, Wales and Scotland. Ireland was not included. Censuses have been held every 10 years since 1801, except for 1941.

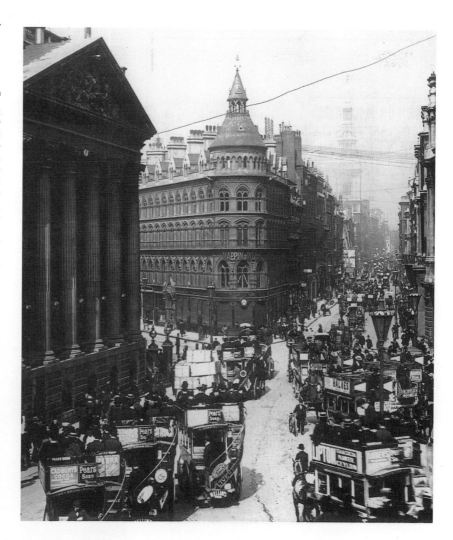

ABOVE By 1901 London's population was rapidly approaching 5,000,000.

OPPOSITE A familiar sight: a traffic jam in London's Oxford Street in 1951.

THE 10 LARGEST CITIES IN THE UK IN 1851

	City	Population
1	London	2,362,236
2	Manchester	404,465
3	Liverpool	375,955
4	Glasgow	340,653
5	Birmingham	232,841
6	Edinburgh	193,929
7	Leeds	172,270
8	Bristol	137,328
9	Sheffield	135,310
10	Plymouth	102,380

The total population of England, Wales and Scotland as shown by the 1851 Census was 20,816,351.

THE 10 LARGEST CITIES IN THE UK IN 1901

	City	Population
1	London	4,613,812
2	Glasgow	786,897
3	Liverpool	716,810
4	Manchester	553,486
5	Birmingham	533,039
6	Leeds	443,559
7	Sheffield	425,528
8	Dublin	375,350
9	Belfast	349,180
10	Bristol	338,895

Dublin is included as the whole of Ireland was part of the United Kingdom until the Partition of 1921. If only the cities of the current UK are included, however, Belfast and Bristol move up to 8th and 9th positions and Edinburgh becomes the new No. 10 with a population of 327,441 at the time of the 1901 Census. By this year, the total population of the United Kingdom was 38,237,000.

THE 10 LARGEST CITIES IN THE UK IN 1951

	City	Population
1	London	8,346,137
2	Birmingham	1,112,340
3	Glasgow	1,093,337
4	Liverpool	789,532
5	Manchester	703,175
6	Sheffield	512,834
7	Leeds	504,954
8	Edinburgh	466,770
9	Bradford	462,500
10	Belfast	443,143

By 1951 the total population of the United Kingdom had exceeded 50,000,000.

THE 10 LARGEST CITIES IN EUROPE

	City	Population
1	Moscow*	8,879,000
2	Paris*	8,706,963
3	London*	6,735,400
4	Leningrad	4,948,000
5	Istanbul	4,870,747
6	Madrid*	4,731,224
7	Barcelona	4,597,429
8	Berlin	3,300,635
9	Athens*	3,027,331
10	Rome*	2,821,420

*Capital city.

The problem of defining a city's boundaries means that population figures generally relate to 'urban agglomerations', which often include suburbs sprawling over very large areas. In addition to the Top 10, Lisbon, Valencia, Kiev and Budapest all have populations in excess of 2,000,000, and many other European cities have populations of more than 1,000,000.

The population of Paris today places it between Moscow and London in the European table.

QUIZ

CAPITAL CITIES

1 In what year did Brasília replace Rio de Janeiro as the capital of Brazil – 1940, 1950 or 1960?
2 Of what country is Suva the capital?
3 The French soldier Jean Parisot de La Valette gave his name to what capital city?
4 What capital city's name means, literally, 'good winds'?
5 Angora goats, rabbits and cats all derive their names from the former name of what capital city?
6 What is the capital of Mongolia?
7 What Oceanian capital city was named after a famous British soldier?
8 Harare, the capital of Zimbabwe, was previously named after which British prime minister?
9 The capitals of which of these European countries is *not* a sea port – Spain, Sweden, Portugal, Ireland or Finland?
10 Why was Kinshasa, the capital of Zaïre, originally called Léopoldville?

THE 10 LARGEST NON-CAPITAL CITIES IN THE WORLD

	City	Country	Population	(Capital/population)
1	Shanghai	China	12,620,000	(Peking 10,810,000)
2	Calcutta	India	9,166,000	(Delhi 6,220,000)
3	São Paulo	Brazil	8,490,763	(Brasília 1,576,657)
4	Bombay	India	8,202,000	(Delhi 6,220,000)
5	New York	USA	7,352,700	(Washington DC 617,000)
6	Karachi*	Pakistan	6,500,000	(Islamabad 350,000)
7	Tien-tsing (Tianjin)	China	5,620,000	(Peking 10,810,000)
8	Rio de Janeiro*	Brazil	5,094,396	(Brasília 1,576,657)
9	Alexandria	Egypt	5,000,000	(Cairo 14,000,000)
10	Leningrad*	USSR	4,948,000	(Moscow 8,879,000)

*Former capital.

Based on comparison of population within administrative boundaries – hence not comparable with the list of 10 Largest Cities in the World.

THE 10 LARGEST CITIES IN THE USA

	City	State	Population
1	New York	New York	7,352,700
2	Los Angeles	California	3,352,710
3	Chicago	Illinois	2,977,520
4	Houston	Texas	1,698,090
5	Philadelphia	Pennsylvania	1,647,000
6	San Diego	California	1,070,310
7	Detroit	Michigan	1,035,920
8	Dallas	Texas	987,360
9	San Antonio	Texas	941,150
10	Phoenix	Arizona	923,750

These are estimates for central city areas only, not for the total metropolitan areas that surround them, which may be several times as large.

THE 10 LARGEST CITIES IN THE USA IN 1900

	(Position now)	City	Population
1	(1)	New York	3,437,202
2	(3)	Chicago	1,698,575
3	(5)	Philadelphia	1,293,697
4	(34)	St Louis	575,238
5	(19)	Boston	560,892
6	(11)	Baltimore	508,957
7	(22)	Cleveland	381,768
8	(50)	Buffalo	352,387
9	(13)	San Francisco	342,782
10	(40)	Cincinnati	325,902

Only the first three cities are in the present Top 10, the rest having been overtaken by seven others that had relatively small populations at the turn of the century: Los Angeles (102,479 in 1900), Houston (44,633), San Diego (17,700), Detroit (285,704), Dallas (42,638), San Antonio (53,321) and Phoenix (5,444). The population of Buffalo has actually declined from 352,387 in 1900 to 313,570 today.

THE 10 MOST HIGHLY POPULATED COUNTRIES IN THE WORLD

	Country	Population
1	China	1,119,700,000
2	India	811,820,000
3	USSR	285,860,000
4	USA	248,760,000
5	Indonesia	179,140,000
6	Brazil	147,400,000
7	Japan	123,120,000
8	Nigeria	109,170,000
9	Pakistan	106,680,000
10	Bangladesh	106,510,000
	UK	*57,200,000*

These figures, based on latest United Nations estimates, show that the population of China is more than 19 times that of the UK and represents almost 22 per cent of the total population of the world (in 1990 estimated to be more than 5,200,000,000), proving the commonly stated statistic that 'one person in five is Chinese'. The members of the Top 10 remain largely the same from year to year, although differential rates of population increase result in changes in the order: in 1990, for example, the population of Nigeria overtook that of Pakistan.

THE 10 MOST HIGHLY POPULATED COUNTRIES 100 YEARS AGO

	Country	Population
1	China	360,250,000
2	India	286,696,960
3	Russia	108,843,192
4	USA	62,981,000
5	Germany	49,421,803
6	Austria	41,345,329
7	Japan	40,072,020
8	France	38,343,192
9	UK	37,888,153
10	Turkey	32,978,100

In the 1890s many national boundaries were quite different from their present form: for example, India encompassed what are now Pakistan and Bangladesh, Poland was part of Russia and Austria and Turkey were extensive empires that included all their territories in their censuses. The 1891 Census of the UK indicated that the population of England and Wales was 29,001,018, Scotland 4,033,103 and Ireland (then part of the UK) 4,706,162, with the populations of the Channel Islands, Isle of Man, etc, accounting for a further 147,870. The estimated total population of the entire British Empire at this time was 340,220,000, making it second only to China's.

THE 10 COUNTRIES WITH THE HIGHEST ESTIMATED POPULATION IN THE YEAR 2000

	Country	Population
1	China	1,255,656,000
2	India	961,531,000
3	USSR	314,818,000
4	USA	268,079,000
5	Indonesia	204,486,000
6	Brazil	179,487,000
7	Nigeria	161,930,000
8	Bangladesh	145,800,000
9	Pakistan	142,554,000
10	Japan	127,683,000
	UK	56,235,000

The estimates for the population of the Top 10 countries all assume increases, while that of the UK predicts a decrease as a result of the trend towards smaller families.

THE 10 MOST DENSELY POPULATED COUNTRIES AND COLONIES IN THE WORLD

	Country/ colony	Area sq km	sq miles	Population total	per sq mile
1	Macau	16.06	6.2	450,000	72,581
2	Monaco	1.81	0.7	27,063	38,661
3	Hong Kong	1,037.29	400.5	5,760,000	14,382
4	Gibraltar	6.47	2.5	30,689	12,276
5	Singapore	619.01	239.0	2,680,000	11,213
6	Vatican City	0.44	0.17	1,000	5,882
7	Bermuda	53.35	20.6	60,000	2,913
8	Malta	313.39	121.0	350,000	2,893
9	Bangladesh	143,998.15	55,598.0	106,510,000	1,916
10	Bahrein	675.99	261.0	490,000	1,877
	UK	244,046.79	94,227.0	57,200,000	607
	USA	9,372,614.90	3,618,787.0	248,760,000	69
	World total	135,597,770.00	52,509,600.0	5,292,178,000	average 96

Among the *least* densely populated countries in the world are the Falkland Islands, an area of 12,168 sq km/4,698 sq miles with a population of 1,916, or 0.41 of a person per sq mile, and Greenland (2,175,590 sq km/840,000 sq miles) with a population of 60,000, equivalent to 0.07 of a person per sq mile.

THE 10 MOST HIGHLY POPULATED COUNTRIES IN EUROPE

	Country	Population
1	USSR (in Europe)	218,607,000
2	Germany	78,674,000
3	Italy	57,441,000
4	UK	57,200,000
5	France	55,873,000
6	Spain	39,054,000
7	Poland	37,862,000
8	Yugoslavia	23,559,000
9	Romania	23,112,000
10	Czechoslovakia	15,608,000

The unification of West and East Germany on 24 September 1990 has created an enlarged country with a total population that is 27 per cent greater than that of West Germany alone, while the elimination of East Germany as a separate entity elevates Czechoslovakia into 10th place in the list.

LEFT Even with birth control measures, India's population growth is set to take it towards the billion mark by the end of the twentieth century.

THE 10 MOST HIGHLY POPULATED COUNTRIES IN ASIA

	Country	Population
1	China	1,119,700,000
2	India	811,820,000
3	Indonesia	179,140,000
4	Japan	123,120,000
5	Pakistan	106,680,000
6	Bangladesh	106,510,000
7	USSR (in Asia)	67,253,000
8	Vietnam	65,680,000
9	Philippines	60,100,000
10	Thailand	55,560,000

THE 10 MOST HIGHLY POPULATED COUNTRIES IN OCEANIA

	Country	Population
1	Australia	16,810,000
2	Papua New Guinea	3,590,000
3	New Zealand	3,310,000
4	Fiji	740,000
5	Solomon Islands	320,000
6	Samoa (US & Western)	205,200
7	French Polynesia	190,000
8	New Caledonia	160,000
9	Vanuatu	150,000
10	Guam	138,089

THE 10 MOST HIGHLY POPULATED COUNTRIES IN SOUTH AMERICA

	Country	Population
1	Brazil	147,400,000
2	Argentina	31,930,000
3	Colombia	31,190,000
4	Peru	21,790,000
5	Venezuela	19,250,000
6	Chile	12,960,000
7	Ecuador	10,490,000
8	Bolivia	7,190,000
9	Paraguay	4,160,000
10	Uruguay	3,080,000

Rush hour in Calcutta. India is the second most populous country in Asia.

THE 10 MOST HIGHLY POPULATED COUNTRIES IN AFRICA

	Country	Population
1	Nigeria	109,170,000
2	Egypt	53,080,000
3	Ethiopia	49,510,000
4=	South Africa	34,490,000
4=	Zaïre	34,490,000
6	Kenya	24,870,000
7	Algeria	24,600,000
8	Morocco	24,520,000
9	Sudan	23,480,000
10	Tanzania	23,174,000

Worlds apart: the Nigerian throng (**RIGHT**) contrasts dramatically with the minuscule resident population of the Vatican.

THE 10 LEAST POPULATED COUNTRIES IN THE WORLD

	Country	Population
1	Vatican City	1,000
2	Falkland Islands	1,916
3	Nauru	8,100
4	Tuvalu	8,229
5	Wallis and Fortuna	14,800
6	Cook Islands	17,185
7	San Marino	22,361
8	Monaco	27,063
9	Liechtenstein	28,181
10	Gibraltar	30,689

THE 10 LEAST POPULATED COUNTRIES IN EUROPE

	Country	Population
1	Vatican City	1,000
2	San Marino	22,361
3	Monaco	27,063
4	Liechtenstein	28,181
5	Gibraltar	30,689
6	Andorra	49,000
7	Iceland	253,482
8	Malta	350,000
9	Luxembourg	377,100
10	Cyprus	698,300

WORLD POPULATION

Year	Estimated total
1000	254,000,000
1500	460,000,000
1600	579,000,000
1700	679,000,000
1800	954,000,000
1850	1,094,000,000
1900	1,633,000,000
1950	2,515,312,000
1960	3,019,376,000
1970	3,697,918,000
1980	4,450,210,000
1985	4,853,848,000
1990	5,292,178,000

World population is believed to have exceeded 5,000,000 before 8000 BC, and surpassed 5,000,000,000 in 1987. The United Nations has estimated the future growth of world population within three ranges – 'low', 'medium' and 'high', depending on the extent of birth control measures and other factors during the coming decades. The high scenario, which assumes that few additional checks are placed on population expansion, implies a 78 per cent global increase by the year 2025.

Year	Low	Medium	High
1995	5,679,685,000	5,765,861,000	5,854,986,000
2000	6,088,506,000	6,251,055,000	6,410,707,000
2005	6,463,211,000	6,728,574,000	6,978,754,000
2010	6,805,064,000	7,190,762,000	7,561,301,000
2015	7,109,736,000	7,639,547,000	8,167,357,000
2020	7,368,995,000	8,062,274,000	8,791,432,000
2025	7,589,731,000	8,466,516,000	9,422,749,000

THE 10 COUNTRIES WITH THE LONGEST OFFICIAL NAMES

	Official name	Common English name	Number of letters
1	al-Jamāhīrīyah al-'Arabīya al-Lībīyah ash-Sha'biyah al-Ishtirākīyah	Libya	56
2	al-Jumhūrīyah al-Jazā'irīyah ad-Dīmuqrāṭīyah ash-Sha'biyah	Algeria	49
3=	United Kingdom of Great Britain and Northern Ireland	United Kingdom	45
3=	Socijalistička Federativna Republika Jugoslavija	Yugoslavia	45
5=	Soyuz Sovetskikh Sotsialisticheskikh Respublik	USSR	43
5=	Sri Lankā Prajathanthrika Samajavadi Janarajaya	Sri Lanka	43
7	Jumhūrīyat al-Yaman ad-Dimuqrāṭī-yah ash-Sha'bīyah	People's Democratic Republic of Yemen	42
8=	Republika Popullore Socialiste e Shqipërisë	Albania	39
8=	YeĒtiyop'iya Hezbawi Dimokrasīyawī Republēk	Ethiopia	39
10	République Fédérale Islamique des Comores	The Comores	37

Since many official names have to be transliterated from languages that do not use the Roman alphabet, their length may vary according to the method used. Fortunately, most have a short version, otherwise considerable problems could arise – not least that of fitting their names onto stamps . . .

THE 10 COMMONEST PLACE NAMES IN GREAT BRITAIN

	Name	Number of occurrences
1	Newton	150
2	Blackhill/Black Hill	141
3	Mountpleasant/Mount Pleasant	130
4	Castlehill/Castle Hill	127
5	Woodside/Wood Side	116
6	Newtown/New Town	111
7	Greenhill/Green Hill	108
8	Woodend/Wood End	106
9	Burnside	105
10	Beacon Hill	94

Research undertaken specially for *The Top 10 of Everything* by Adrian Room (the author of *A Concise Dictionary of Modern Place-names in Great Britain and Ireland*) reveals the place names most frequently encountered in Great Britain. These include the names of towns and villages, as well as woods, hills and other named locations, but exclude combinations of these names with others (Newton Abbot and Newton-le-Willows, for example, are not counted with the Newtons). A further study of the 250,000 names appearing on the Ordnance Survey 1:50,000 scale 'Landranger' maps shows that certain names of farms and houses appear even more frequently than the general names in this list:

	Name	Number of occurrences
1	Manor Farm	590
2	Park Farm	357
3	Hill Farm	355
4	Home Farm	341
5	Manor House	288
6=	Grange Farm	265
6=	Lodge Farm	265
8	The Grange	202
9	Hall Farm	182
10	Glebe Farm	171

THE 10 COMMONEST STREET NAMES IN GREAT BRITAIN

1 High Street
2 Station Road
3 Church Road
4 Park Road
5 The Drive
6 Station Approach
7 Green Lane
8 The Avenue
9 London Road
10 Church Lane

Based on research undertaken by Adrian Room.

The list of commonest street names in the USA continues with Oak, Eighth, Elm, Lincoln, Ninth, Pine, Walnut, Tenth and Cedar.

THE 10 COMMONEST PLACE NAMES IN THE USA

Name	Number of occurrences
1 Fairview	104
2 Midway	90
3 Centerville	72
4 Oak Grove	68
5 Riverside	67
6 Five Points	65
7 Mount Pleasant	56
8= Oakland	54
8= Pleasant Hill	54
10 Georgetown	49

THE 10 COMMONEST STREET NAMES IN THE USA

1 Second Street
2 Park Street
3 Third Street
4 Fourth Street
5 Fifth Street
6 First Street
7 Sixth Street
8 Seventh Street
9 Washington Street
10 Maple Street

'A single to Gor ... that place in Wales, please.'

THE 10 LONGEST PLACE NAMES IN THE UK

	Place name	Letters
1	Gorsafawddachaidraigddanheddogleddollônpenrhyn-areurdraethceredigion (*see* World List, No. 3)	67
2	Llanfairpwllgwyngyllgogerychwyrndrobwllllantysilio-gogogoch (*see* World List, No. 4)	58
3	Sutton-under-Whitestonecliffe, North Yorkshire	27
4	Llanfihangel-yng-Ngwynfa, Powys	22
5=	Llanfihangel-y-Creuddyn, Dyfed	21
5=	Llanfihangel-y-traethau, Gwynedd	21
7	Cottonshopeburnfoot, Northumberland	19
8=	Blakehopeburnhaugh, Northumberland	18
8=	Coignafeuinternich, Inverness-shire	18
10=	Claddochknockline, North Uist, Outer Hebrides	17
10=	Claddochbaleshare, North Uist, Outer Hebrides	17

These are all single and hyphenated names. The longest multiple name in England is North Leverton with Habblesthorpe, Nottinghamshire (30 letters), followed by Skidbrooke cum Saltfeet Haven, Lincolnshire (26) and Preston upon the Weald Moors, Shropshire (24). In Wales it is Lower Llanfihangel-y-Creuddyn, Dyfed (26) followed by Llansantffraid Cwmdeuddwr, Powys (24), and in Scotland Huntingtower and Ruthvenfield (27) – although there is also a loch on the island of Lewis called Loch Airidh Mhic Fhionnlaidh Dhuibh (31) (*see* World List, No. 10).

If the parameters are extended to encompass Ireland, the single word Muckanaghederdauhaulia (22) is scooped into the net. Runners-up include Doddiscombsleigh, Moretonhampstead, Woolfardisworthy (pronounced 'Woolsery'), Combe-in-Teignhead and Stoke-in-Teignhead, all of which are in Devon and have 16 letters.

The longest parish name in the UK was for many years Saint Andrew, Holborn above the Bars, with Saint George the Martyr (54) in London, until the formation on 5 April 1971 of Saint Mary le More and All Hallows with Saint Leonard and Saint Peter, Wallingford (68).

THE 10 LONGEST PLACE NAMES IN THE WORLD

	Place name	Letters
1	Krung Thep Mahanakhon Bovorn Ratanakosin Mahintharayutthaya Mahadilok pop Noparatratchathani Burirom Udomratchanivetmahasathan Amornpiman Avatarnsathit Sakkathattiyavisnukarmprasit	167

When the poetic name of Bangkok, capital of Thailand, is used, it is usually abbreviated to 'Krung Thep' (city of angels).

2	Taumatawhakatangihangakoauauotamateaturipuk-akapikimaungahoronukupokaiwhenuakitanatahu	85

This is the longer version (the other has only 83 letters) of the Maori name of a hill in New Zealand. It translates as 'The place where Tamatea, the man with the big knees, who slid, climbed and swallowed mountains, known as land-eater, played on the flute to his loved one'.

3	Gorsafawddachaidraigddanheddogleddollônpenrhyn-areurdraethceredigion	67

A name contrived by the Fairbourne Steam Railway, Gwynedd, North Wales, for publicity purposes and in order to outdo No. 4.

4	Llanfairpwllgwyngyllgogerychwyrndrobwllllantysilio-gogogoch	58

This is the place in Gwynedd famed especially for the length of its railway tickets. It means 'St Mary's Church by the pool of the white hazel trees, near the rapid whirlpool, by the red cave of the church of St Tysilio'. Its official name comprises only the first 20 letters.

5	El Pueblo de Nuestra Señora la Reina de los Angeles de la Porciuncula	57

The site of a Franciscan mission and the full Spanish name of Los Angeles; it means 'the town of Our Lady the Queen of the Angels of the Little Portion'. Nowadays it is customarily known by its initial letters, 'LA', making it also one of the shortest-named cities in the world.

6	Chargoggagoggmanchauggagoggchaubunagungamaugg	45

America's longest place name, a lake near Webster, Massachusetts. Its Indian name, loosely translated, means 'You fish on your side, I'll fish on mine, and no one fishes in the middle'. It is pronounced 'Char-gogg-a-gogg (pause) man-chaugg-a-gogg (pause) chau-bun-a-gung-a-maugg'.

7=	Lower North Branch Little Southwest Miramichi	40

Canada's longest place name – a short river in New Brunswick.

Krung Thep – city of angels. The 167-letter version of Bangkok's name puts it at the top of the world list.

7=	Villa Real de la Santa Fe de San Francisco de Asis	40

The full Spanish name of Santa Fe, New Mexico, translates as, 'Royal city of the holy faith of St Francis of Assisi'.

9	Te Whakatakanga-o-te-ngarehu-o-te-ahi-a-Tamatea	38

The Maori name of Hammer Springs, New Zealand; like the second name in this list, it refers to a legend of Tamatea, explaining how the springs were warmed by 'the falling of the cinders of the fire of Tamatea'.

10	Loch Airidh Mhic Fhionnlaidh Dhuibh	31

This is the name of a loch on the island of Lewis, Scotland.

THE 10 SMALLEST COUNTRIES IN THE WORLD

	Country	Area sq km	sq miles
1	Vatican City	0.44	0.17
2	Monaco	1.81	0.7
3	Gibraltar	6.47	2.5
4	Macau	16.06	6.2
5	Nauru	21.23	8.2
6	Tuvalu	25.90	10.0
7	Bermuda	53.35	20.6
8	San Marino	59.57	23.0
9	Liechtenstein	157.99	61.0
10	Antigua	279.72	108.0

OPPOSITE Brazil, the largest country in South America and fifth largest in the world.

BELOW Gibraltar, one of the smallest countries in the world.

THE 10 LARGEST COUNTRIES IN THE WORLD

	Country	Area sq km	sq miles
1	USSR	22,402,000	8,649,461
2	Canada	9,970,537	3,849,646
3	China	9,596,961	3,705,408
4	USA	9,372,614	3,618,787
5	Brazil	8,511,965	3,286,488
6	Australia	7,686,848	2,967,909
7	India	3,287,590	1,269,346
8	Argentina	2,766,889	1,068,302
9	Sudan	2,505,813	967,500
10	Algeria	2,381,741	919,595
75	UK	244,046	94,227
	World total	136,597,770	52,509,600

The 10 largest countries comprise some 57.7 per cent of the total Earth's surface. The USSR alone occupies approximately 16.5 per cent and has an area 92 times greater than the UK.

THE 10 LARGEST COUNTRIES IN OCEANIA

	Country	Area sq km	sq miles
1	Australia	7,686,848	2,967,909
2	Papua New Guinea	461,691	178,260
3	New Zealand	268,676	103,736
4	Solomon Islands	28,446	10,983
5	New Caledonia	19,058	7,358
6	Fiji	18,274	7,055
7	Vanuatu	14,763	5,700
8	French Polynesia	4,000	1,544
9	Samoa	3,039	1,173
10	Kiribati	728	281

Australia is over nine times as large as the rest of the Top 10 Oceanian countries put together. The virtually uninhabited Ross Dependency which comes under New Zealand's control is actually larger than New Zealand itself (750,310 sq km/286,696 sq miles, including permanent ice shelf).

THE 10 LARGEST COUNTRIES IN AFRICA

	Country	Area sq km	Area sq miles
1	Sudan	2,505,813	967,500
2	Algeria	2,381,741	919,595
3	Zaïre	2,345,409	905,567
4	Libya	1,759,540	679,362
5	Chad	1,284,000	495,755
6	Niger	1,267,080	489,191
7	Angola	1,246,700	481,354
8	Mali	1,240,000	478,791
9	Ethiopia	1,221,900	471,778
10	South Africa	1,221,031	471,445

Sudan, the largest country in Africa, has an area 10 times that of the UK.

THE 10 LARGEST COUNTRIES IN ASIA

	Country	Area sq km	Area sq miles
1	USSR (in Asia)	16,831,000	6,498,486
2	China	9,596,961	3,705,408
3	India	3,287,590	1,269,346
4	Saudi Arabia	2,149,640	830,000
5	Indonesia	1,904,569	735,358
6	Iran	1,648,000	636,296
7	Mongolia	1,565,000	604,250
8	Pakistan	803,936	310,401
9	Turkey (in Asia)	756,953	292,261
10	Burma	676,552	261,218

THE 10 LARGEST COUNTRIES IN SOUTH AMERICA

	Country	Area sq km	Area sq miles
1	Brazil	8,511,965	3,286,488
2	Argentina	2,766,889	1,068,302
3	Peru	1,285,216	496,225
4	Colombia	1,138,914	439,737
5	Bolivia	1,098,581	424,165
6	Venezuela	912,050	352,144
7	Chile	756,945	292,258
8	Paraguay	406,752	157,048
9	Ecuador	283,561	109,484
10	Guyana	214,969	83,000

The size of the Top 10 South American countries ranges from Brazil, the 5th largest in the world, down to Guyana, which is smaller than the UK.

THE 10 LARGEST COUNTRIES IN EUROPE

	Country	Area sq km	sq miles
1	USSR (in Europe)	5,571,000	2,150,975
2	France	547,026	211,208
3	Spain	504,782	194,897
4	Sweden	449,964	173,732
5	Germany	356,367	137,594
6	Finland	337,007	130,119
7	Norway	324,219	125,182
8	Poland	312,677	120,725
9	Italy	301,225	116,304
10	Yugoslavia	255,808	98,768
11	UK	244,046	94,227

THE 10 LONGEST FRONTIERS IN THE WORLD

	Country	Frontiers km	miles
1	China	24,000	14,913
2	USSR	20,619	12,812
3	Brazil	13,076	8,125
4	India	12,700	7,891
5	USA	12,002	7,458
6	Zaïre	9,902	6,153
7	Argentina	9,414	5,850
8	Canada	9,010	5,599
9	Mongolia	8,000	4,971
10	Sudan	7,805	4,850

This list represents the *total* length of frontiers, compiled by adding together the lengths of individual borders. The 12,002 km/7,458 miles of the USA's frontiers include those shared with Canada (6,416 km/3,987 miles – the longest *continuous* frontier in the world), with Alaska (2,475 km/1,538 miles) and with Mexico (3,111 km/1,933 miles).

OPPOSITE Navajo Indians, the largest tribal group in the USA.

BELOW Italy is the ninth largest country in Europe.

THE TOP 10 COUNTRIES OF ORIGIN OF UK IMMIGRANTS

	Country	Total
1	India	5,020
2	Pakistan	4,280
3	USA	3,750
4	Australia	3,520
5	Bangladesh	2,890
6	New Zealand	2,680
7	Iran	1,500
8	Japan	1,340
9	Canada	1,190
10	Ghana	1,180

Although this list is based on immigration to the UK in a single year (1988), it remains fairly constant, as does the total number of immigrants accepted for settlement, which averages at around 50,000 per annum.

THE 10 LARGEST AMERICAN INDIAN RESERVATIONS

	Reservation	State	Population
1	Navajo	Arizona/New Mexico/ Utah	173,018
2	Cherokee	Oklahoma	58,232
3	Creek	Oklahoma	54,606
4	Choctaw	Oklahoma	21,858
5	Pine Ridge	South Dakota	19,246
6	Southern Pueblo	New Mexico	17,079
7	Chickasaw	Oklahoma	11,780
8	Rosebud	South Dakota	11,685
9	Gila River	Arizona	10,688
10	Papago-Sells	Arizona	10,138

Of the total American Indian population of over 1,500,000, about 861,500 live on reservations.

THE TOP 10 COUNTRIES OF ORIGIN OF USA IMMIGRANTS, 1820–1989

	Country	Number
1	Germany	7,053,918
2	Italy	5,335,187
3	Great Britain	5,084,974
4	Ireland	4,715,478
5	Austria/ Hungary*	4,329,800
6	Canada	4,239,506
7	USSR**	3,444,467
8	Mexico	2,868,341
9	West Indies	2,598,894
10	Sweden†	1,390,188

*Combined before 1905; Austria included with Germany 1938–45.
**Russia before 1917.
†Figures combined with Norway during 1820–68.

Emma Lazarus's poem, *The New Colossus*, which is inscribed on the Statue of Liberty, contains the lines, 'Give me your tired, your poor/Your huddled masses yearning to breathe free', and for many years the United States was the magnet that attracted vast numbers of immigrants: in 1903–15, for example, an average of 982,655 arrived every year. From 1820, when detailed records were first kept, until 1989, the total numbered 54,978,717. In 1989, the last year for which complete statistics are available, the US Immigration and Naturalization Service recorded 612,110 immigrants, and a further 478,814 illegal aliens.

THE 10 LARGEST STATES IN THE USA

	State	Area	
		sq km	sq miles
1	Alaska	1,478,425	570,823
2	Texas	678,924	262,134
3	California	404,973	156,361
4	Montana	377,069	145,587
5	New Mexico	314,456	121,412
6	Arizona	293,749	113,417
7	Nevada	284,611	109,889
8	Colorado	268,753	103,766
9	Wyoming	251,288	97,023
10	Oregon	249,115	96,184

Alaska, the largest state, has the second smallest population (524,000; Wyoming is the smallest with 479,000), equivalent to one person per square mile. The smallest US state is Rhode Island (2,717 sq km/1,049 sq miles); the District of Columbia covers 174 sq km/67 sq miles.

By comparison, the UK (244,046 sq km/94,227 sq miles) is smaller than the 10th largest state, and the area of England (130,440 sq km/50,363 sq miles) slightly smaller than that of Alabama (131,333 sq km/50,708 sq miles).

THE FIRST 10 STATES OF THE USA

	State	Entered Union
1	Delaware	7 Dec 1787
2	Pennsylvania	12 Dec 1787
3	New Jersey	18 Dec 1787
4	Georgia	2 Jan 1788
5	Connecticut	9 Jan 1788
6	Massachusetts	6 Feb 1788
7	Maryland	28 Apr 1788
8	South Carolina	23 May 1788
9	New Hampshire	21 Jun 1788
10	Virginia	25 Jun 1788

NAMING THE FIRST 10 STATES

The names of two of the first 10 American states commemorate early colonists. Delaware Bay (and hence the river and later the state) was named after Thomas West, Lord De La Warr, a governor of Virginia. Pennsylvania was called 'Pensilvania', or 'Penn's woodland', in its original charter, issued in 1681 to the Quaker leader William Penn. He had acquired the territory as part settlement of a debt of £16,000 owed to his father, Admiral William Penn, by King Charles II. Two states were named after places with which their founders had associations: New Jersey was the subject of a deed issued in 1644 by the Duke of York to John Berkeley and Sir George Cartaret, who came from Jersey in the Channel Islands, and New Hampshire was called after the English county by settler Captain John Mason. Two names are of American Indian origin: Connecticut after the Algonquin Indian name 'kuenihtekot', meaning 'long river at' (the extra syllable 'c' was probably added by a writer who had 'connect' in mind); and Massachusetts, which is believed to be Indian for 'high hill, little plain', the name of a place and of a tribe. The remaining four states' names have royal connections: Virginia after Queen Elizabeth I, the 'Virgin Queen', and Georgia, so-called by English soldier and politician James Oglethorpe in honour of King George II, who in 1723 issued a charter allowing him to colonize the area. The colony of Maryland, named after Queen Henrietta Maria, wife of Charles I, was projected by George Calvert, Baron Baltimore, but he died two months before the charter was signed and it was his son Cecilius who established it. South Carolina was originally a French settlement called La Caroline after the French king Charles IX, but the tract of land was issued in 1619 to Sir Robert Heath, who renamed it Carolana after the English king Charles I.

THE 10 MOST EXPENSIVE COUNTRIES IN THE WORLD

	Country	Index
1	Finland	210.3
2	Japan	201.7
3	Zaïre	200.1
4	Côte d'Ivoire	196.8
5	Sweden	186.1
6=	Libya	186.0
6=	Norway	186.0
8	Denmark	177.5
9	Switzerland	175.8
10	Austria	146.6
	UK	*100.0*

Living costs in each country (as calculated by the organization Employment Conditions Abroad) are compared with those in the UK. The cost of living index includes a range of consumer goods and services such as food, drink, tobacco, household durables, services, entertainment, clothing and motoring. Rates of exchange and each country's level of inflation have a considerable effect on the results.

A price to pay: Japan's powerful economy makes it the second most expensive country in the world.

BUILDINGS & STRUCTURES

THE WORLD'S 10 TALLEST BUILDINGS BEFORE THE AGE OF SKYSCRAPERS

	Building	Location	Year completed	Height m	ft
1	Eiffel Tower	Paris, France	1889	300	984
2	Washington Memorial	Washington DC, USA	1885	169	555
3	Ulm Cathedral	Ulm, Germany	1890	161	528
4	Lincoln Cathedral	Lincoln, England	c1307 (destroyed 1548)	160	525
5	Cologne Cathedral	Cologne, Germany	1880	156.4	513
6	Notre-Dame	Rouen, France	1530	156	512
7	St Pierre Church	Beauvais, France	1568 (collapsed 1573)	153	502
8	St Paul's Cathedral	London, England	1315 (destroyed 1561)	149	489
9	Rouen Cathedral	Rouen, France	1876	148	485
10	Great Pyramid	Giza, Egypt	c2580BC	146.5	480.9

The first tall office buildings of 10 storeys or more were constructed in Chicago and New York in the 1880s, with the Eiffel Tower following at the end of the decade. It was not until 1913 that the first true 'skyscraper' – a secular building exceeding the height of the great medieval cathedrals – was built: the Woolworth Building, New York. At 241 m/792 ft it remained the tallest habitable building in the world until 1930, when the Chrysler Building (*see* The 10 Tallest Habitable Buildings in the World) overtook both it *and* the Eiffel Tower. A year later the Empire State Building topped them all, and remained the world's tallest for 40 years.

The height of the Washington Memorial is less than it was when it was erected, as it has steadily sunk into the ground. Lincoln Cathedral was the tallest building in the world for over 200 years, but fell in a storm. St Pierre at Beauvais collapsed in 1573. 'Old St Paul's' was destroyed by lightning on 4 June 1561; the present St Paul's Cathedral is only 112 m/366 ft high. The Great Pyramid stood as the world's tallest building for nearly 4,000 years, and was numbered among the Seven Wonders of the World. The loss of its topstone reduced its height to 137 m/449 ft.

THE 10 TALLEST MASTS IN THE UK

	Mast	Height m	ft
1	TV, Belmont, Lincs*	388	1,272
2	TV, Durris, Grampian	345	1,132
3	TV, Emley Moor, West Yorks	336	1,102
4	TV, Waltham on the Wolds, Leics	314	1,031
5	TV, Bilsdale, West Moor	312	1,022
6	TV, Mendip	305	1,001
7	British Telecom, Rugby	250	820
8	TV, Sutton Coldfield	242	794
9	British Telecom, Anthorn, Carlisle	226	740
10	TV, Crystal Palace	222	728

ABOVE RIGHT Just in the Top 10: the 222 m/728 ft BBC TV mast at Crystal Palace.

Tallest mast built 1967; no taller structure in UK.

SKYSCRAPERS THAT NEVER WERE

After an unsuccessful attempt to build a Channel tunnel as early as 1869, visionary railway pioneer Sir Edward Watkin turned his attention in 1890 to a new scheme, launching a competition to build a 'Great Tower of London' to rival the Eiffel Tower, which had been opened the previous year. Many extraordinary plans were submitted, with designs ranging from Gothic cathedrals to huge helter-skelters scaled by railway locomotives. One entry, by Albert Brunel, was for a Great Tower of London 700 m/2,296 ft high (vastly exceeding the Eiffel Tower's 300 m/984 ft). The winning entry was remarkably similar in appearance to the Eiffel Tower, and at 351 m/1,150 ft would have been the tallest building in the world until the Empire State Building of 1931. Work started on it in 1891, but construction progressed slowly, and three years later it had reached only 47 m/155 ft – one-seventh of its proposed height. Watkin's company experienced financial difficulties and work halted. It lay rusting for years and was eventually blown up. The ground was cleared and Wembley Stadium was built on the site of the ill-fated Great Tower.

At the same time as Watkin's Great Tower was failing to get off the ground in England, Alberto di Palicio's Columbus monument was being planned to commemorate the 400th anniversary of the discovery of America. To be erected on the island of San Salvador, where Columbus first landed, it was to comprise a globe 305 m/1,000 ft in diameter on a 250 ft high concrete base, with a statue of Columbus on the top. Inside the globe were to be coffee houses, hotels, restaurants and fairs, with museums, lecture halls and a planetarium in the base. Communication with this Victorian Disneyland was by an elaborate electric tramway. Its total estimated cost of $8,000,000 ensured, however, that it never got beyond di Palicio's drawing board.

In 1894 a company ironically named 'Castle in the Air Ltd' was formed by a Mr Tobianski of Antwerp. Planned as the focal point of a forthcoming exhibition, it resembled a castle with a theatre, restaurant and gardens. Its exceptional feature was that it was to be suspended in the air by balloons containing 150,000 cu ft of hydrogen. Up to 200 visitors at a time would be accommodated, and ascended by means of lifts raised and lowered by 19 powerful steam engines. So seriously was the project taken that half a million francs were invested in it and a committee established to mastermind it – before the Belgian Government stepped in and refused to sanction it.

In 1919–20 avant garde Russian architect Vladimir E. Tatlin designed his 'Monument to the Third International'. Intended to be 305 m/1,000 ft high, it comprised two intertwining spirals with huge glass meeting halls suspended inside, rotating at different speeds: the outer one turned once a year, the next one once a month, the next once a day and the inner one hourly. It never got beyond a model. In 1934 another Russian architect, B. M. Iofan, planned a gigantic 'Palace of the Soviets' for Moscow. Some 457 m/1,500 ft tall (76 m/250 ft taller than the Empire State Building), its massive wedding-cake structure was to be surmounted by a colossal statue of Lenin. It was repeatedly redesigned, but like the rest of these extraordinary structures, was never built.

Heights are of buildings less their TV and radio antennae and uninhabited extensions – the Empire State Building, for example, has a 50 m/164 ft TV tower. The introduction of the Atlanta, Georgia, C & S Plaza building means that for the first time all those in the Top 10 are more than 1,000 feet tall.

THE 10 TALLEST HABITABLE BUILDINGS IN THE WORLD

	Building	Location	Year completed	Storeys	Height m	ft
1	Sears Tower	Chicago, USA	1974	110	443	1,454
2	World Trade Center*	New York City, USA	1972	110	417	1,368
3	Empire State Building	New York City, USA	1931	102	381	1,250
4	Bank of China	Hong Kong	1989	72	368	1,209
5	Standard Oil Building	Chicago, USA	1971	80	346	1,136
6	John Hancock Center	Chicago, USA	1967	100	344	1,127
7	Chrysler Building	New York City, USA	1930	77	319	1,046
8	C & S Plaza	Atlanta, USA	uc**	55	312	1,024
9	First Interstate World Center	Los Angeles, USA	1989	73	310	1,017
10	Texas Commerce Tower	Houston, USA	1981	75	305	1,002

*Twin towers; the second tower, completed in 1973, has the same number of storeys but is slightly smaller at 415 m/1,362 ft.
**Under construction.

THE 10 TALLEST HABITABLE* BUILDINGS IN THE UK

	Building	Year completed	Height m	ft
1	Canary Wharf Tower, London E14	1991	244	800
2	National Westminster Tower, London EC2	1979	183	600
3	Post Office Tower, London W1	1966	177	580
4	Blackpool Tower	1894	158	519
5	Barbican, London EC2:			
	Shakespeare Tower	1971	128	419
	Cromwell Tower	1973	128	419
	Lauderdale Tower	1974	128	419
6	Euston Centre, Euston Road, London NW1	1969	124	408
7	Cooperative Insurance Society Building, Miller Street, Manchester	1962	122	399
8	Centrepoint, New Oxford Street, London WC1	1966	121	398
9	Britannic House, Moor Lane, London EC2	1967	120	395
10=	Commercial Union, Undershaft, London EC3	1969	118	387
10=	Millbank Tower, Millbank, London SW1	1963	118	387

Excludes radio masts, chimneys and church spires.

The 244 m/800 ft Canary Wharf Tower is not only now the tallest habitable building in the UK, but also the second tallest in Europe, after the Frankfurt Messeturm (331 m/1,086 ft). On a global scale, however, it does not even appear in the Top 30, and is only 2.4 m/8 ft taller than the Woolworth Building, New York, which was built in 1913. The Barbican towers are the tallest blocks of flats in the UK. Property developers Don and Roy Richardson recently unveiled plans to build their 610 m/2,000 ft Merry Hill Tower in Dudley, West Midlands.

QUIZ

LONDON BUILDINGS

In what famous London buildings would you find the following?

1 Little Ease.
2 The King's Library.
3 A floor mosaic depicting Greta Garbo and Sir Winston Churchill.
4 Lord Nelson's tomb.
5 The Stone of Scone.
6 The Lord Mayor's Coach.
7 The Lutine Bell.
8 The Domesday Book.
9 Airy's Transit Circle.
10 A statue of the engineer Robert Stephenson.

THE 10 TALLEST CHURCHES IN THE WORLD

	Church	Year completed	Height m	ft
1	Chicago Methodist Temple	1924	173	568
2	Ulm Cathedral	1890	161	528
3	Cologne Cathedral	1880	156.4	513
4	Rouen Cathedral	1876	148	485
5	St Nicholas, Hamburg	1847	145	475
6	Notre Dame, Strasbourg	1439	142	465
7	St Peter's, Rome	1612	140	458
8	St Stephen's Cathedral, Vienna	1433	136	446
9	St Joseph's Oratory, Montreal	1922	126	412
10	Antwerp Cathedral	1525	124	406
	Salisbury Cathedral	*1375*	*123*	*404*

THE 10 LARGEST CEMETERIES IN LONDON

	Cemetery	Founded	Area (acres)
1	St Pancras and Islington, N2	1854	182
2	City of London, E12	1856	130*
3	Kensal Green, NW19	1832	77
4=	Battersea New, Morden	1891	70
4=	Streatham Park, SW16	1909	70
6	Lee, SE6	1873	65
7	Camberwell New, SE23	1927	61
8	Great Northern, N11	1861	60
9	Merton and Sutton, Morden	1947	57.5**
10	Tottenham, N17	1856	56

Plus 46 in reserve.
**22 in use.*

Despite the appalling overcrowding of inner-city church graveyards, public cemeteries such as Père-Lachaise, Paris, which opened in 1804, were much longer in becoming established in England. In 1832 Kensal Green became the first to open in London, and was gradually followed by some 100 more serving London's needs. Today, though many are neglected and overgrown, they are worth visiting for their often remarkable last resting places of both the famous and unknown – some, such as Highgate Cemetery, even organize guided tours. Among the interesting tombs in the 10 largest are those of Henry Croft, the original 'Pearly King', and Ford Madox-Brown, the Pre-Raphaelite painter, both at St Pancras and Islington; Winston Churchill's nanny, Elizabeth Everest, at the City of London; the comedian Will Hay and numerous other variety artists at Streatham Park; and world light-heavyweight boxing champion Freddie Mills at Camberwell New Cemetery. Kensal Green, perhaps the finest of all London cemeteries, contains the tombs of numerous eminent Victorians, including the engineer Isambard Kingdom Brunel, Blondin the tightrope walker, novelists Wilkie Collins, William Thackeray and Anthony Trollope (who also invented the pillarbox), and Major Walter Wingfield, the inventor of lawn tennis. 'James' Barry, who was buried there in 1865, was actually a woman who posed as a man all her adult life and became the first qualified female doctor in Britain.

LEFT Cologne Cathedral, the world's tallest during the 1880s, but overtaken by Ulm in 1890.

OPPOSITE Elevated status: Canary Wharf is now the UK's tallest habitable building.

THE 10 LARGEST NATIONAL TRUST PROPERTIES IN THE UK

	Property	Rooms
1	**Knole, Kent** Originally a medieval palace of the Archbishops of Canterbury. It is known as the 'Calendar House' because it has 365 rooms, 52 towers and seven courtyards.	365
2	**Penrhyn Castle, Gwynned** A 'Norman' castle with keep and walls built in the early nineteenth century. If corridors are included, it has almost 400 rooms, most of them open to the public.	321
3	**Nostell Priory, Yorkshire** A splendid Palladian house with one of England's finest collections of Chippendale furniture, made especially for it.	150
4	**Dunham Massey, Cheshire** An eighteenth-century mansion with 30 of its 121 rooms (including eight staircases) open to the public.	121
5	**Castle Coole, County Fermanagh** A magnificent eighteenth-century house recently restored by the National Trust.	116
6	**Petworth, Sussex** A treasure house with an important collection of paintings including several by Turner. Only 18 rooms are open to the public.	109
7	**Tatton Park, Cheshire** A nineteenth-century house by Samuel Wyatt, with 30 rooms open to visitors.	105
8	**Lanhydrock, Cornwall** A lovely seventeenth-century house that was substantially rebuilt after a disastrous fire over 100 years ago. Forty of its rooms are open to the public.	97
9	**Cliveden, Buckinghamshire** The former home of the Astor family is now a luxury hotel.	87
10	**Blickling Hall, Norfolk** A romantic Jacobean house set in beautiful grounds.	80

Cliveden is leased from the National Trust and open only to hotel residents. If it is thus discounted as unavailable to the public, the next largest Trust property in the UK is Saltram, Devon, a Georgian house designed by Robert Adam, which has 75 rooms. Knole is the largest private house in the UK, although Buckingham Palace is the largest residential building, containing some 600 rooms.

RIGHT The Kariba dam holds back the second largest man-made lake in the world.

BELOW The library at Nostell Priory, the National Trust's third largest property.

THE TOP 10 HOUSE NAMES IN THE UK

1	The Bungalow
2	The Cottage
3	Rose Cottage
4	The School House
5	The White House
6	Hillcrest
7	The Lodge
8	Woodlands
9	The Coach House
10	Hillside

THE 10 LONGEST SEASIDE PIERS IN THE UK

	Pier	Length m	ft
1	Southend, Essex	2,158	7,080
2	Southport, Merseyside	1,107	3,633
3	Walton-on-the-Naze	1,097	3,600
4	Ryde, Isle of Wight	805	2,640
5	Llandudno, Gwynedd	700	2,295
6	Ramsay, Isle of Man	692	2,270
7=	Clacton, Essex	640	2,100
7=	Hythe, Hampshire	640	2,100
9	Brighton (Palace Pier), East Sussex	536	1,760
10	Bangor (Garth Pier), Gwynedd	472	1,550

THE 10 LARGEST MAN-MADE LAKES IN THE WORLD*

	Dam/lake	Location	Year completed	Volume (m²)
1	Owen Falls	Uganda	1954	204,800,000,000
2	Kariba	Zimbabwe	1959	181,592,000,000
3	Bratsk	USSR	1964	169,270,000,000
4	High Aswan	Egypt	1970	168,000,000,000
5	Akosombo	Ghana	1965	148,000,000,000
6	Daniel Johnson	Canada	1968	141,852,000,000
7	Guri	Venezuela	1986	136,000,000,000
8	Krasnoyarsk	USSR	1967	73,000,000,000
9	Bennett	Canada	1967	70,309,000,000
10	Zeya	USSR	1978	68,400,000,000

*Includes only those formed as a result of dam construction.

ART

THE 10 MOST EXPENSIVE OLD MASTER PAINTINGS EVER SOLD AT AUCTION

	Painting	Price (£)
1	Jacopo da Carucci (Pontormo), *Portrait of Duke Cosimo I de Medici* Christie's, New York, 31 May 1989 ($35,200,000)	22,370,511
2	Francesco Guardi, *View of the Giudecca and the Zattere, Venice* Sotheby's, Monaco, 1 December 1989 (FF89,250,000)	9,384,858
3	Andrea Mantegna, *Adoration of the Magi* Christie's, London, 18 April 1985	8,100,000
4	Rembrandt, *Portrait of a Girl Wearing a Gold-trimmed Cloak* Sotheby's, London, 10 December 1986	7,260,000
5	Canaletto, *View of Molo from Bacino di San Marco, Venice* and *View of the Grand Canal Facing East from Campo di Santi, Venice* (pair) Sotheby's, New York, 1 June 1990 ($11,000,000)	6,586,826
6	Bartolomeo di Giovanni, *Argonauts in Colchis* Sotheby's, London, 6 December 1989	5,060,000
7	Lucas Cranach the Elder, *Portraits of Kurfurst Herzog Johann von Sachsen and his son Johann Friedrich* (pair) Christie's, London, 6 July 1990	4,840,000
8	Master of 1487, *Departure of the Argonauts* Sotheby's, London, 6 December 1989	4,620,000
9	Jan Davidsz de Heem, *Banquet Still Life* Christie's, New York, 15 January 1988 ($6,600,000)	3,728,814
10	Leonardo da Vinci, *Studies of Drapery, Kneeling Figure, etc* Sotheby's, Monaco, 1 December 1989 (FF33,600,000)	3,533,123

THE 10 MOST EXPENSIVE BRITISH PAINTINGS EVER SOLD AT AUCTION

	Painting	Price (£)
1	John Constable, *The Lock* Sotheby's, London, 25 November 1990	10,780,000
2	J. M. W. Turner, *Seascape, Folkestone* Sotheby's, London, 5 July 1984	7,370,000
3	J. M. W. Turner, *Juliet and her Nurse* Sotheby's, New York, 29 May 1980 ($7,040,000)	3,128,884*
4	Francis Bacon, *Triptych May–June* Sotheby's, New York, 2 May 1989 ($6,270,000)	3,777,109
5	Francis Bacon, *Study for Portrait of van Gogh II* Sotheby's, New York, 2 May 1989 ($5,830,000)	3,512,048*
6	Francis Bacon, *Study for Pope* Christie's, New York, 7 November 1989 ($5,720,000)	3,620,253*
7	Francis Bacon, *Study for Portrait* Sotheby's, New York, 8 May 1989 ($5,500,000)	3,273,810
8	Johann Zoffany, *Group Portrait of John, 14th Lord Willoughby de Broke, and his Family* Christie's, London, 17 November 1989	3,080,000
9	John Constable, *Flatford Lock and Mill* Christie's, London, 21 November 1986	2,640,000
10	Francis Bacon, *Portrait of Lucien Freud* Sotheby's, New York, 8 May 1990 ($3,300,000)	2,160,715

Ranked by price at location of auction; as a result of exchange rate variations between sales, converting into sterling alters the order.

All prices include buyer's premium; $/£ conversion at rate then prevailing.

Mantegna's *Adoration of the Magi* held the record price for an Old Master for only four years.

THE 10 MOST EXPENSIVE PAINTINGS EVER SOLD AT AUCTION

Painting	Price (£)
1　Vincent van Gogh, *Portrait of Dr Gachet* Christie's, New York, 15 May 1990 ($82,500,000)	49,107,142

Bought by Ryoei Saito, chairman of the Japanese firm Daishowa Paper Manufacturing.

2　Pierre-Auguste Renoir, *Au Moulin de la Galette* Sotheby's, New York, 17 May 1990 ($78,100,000)	46,488,095

Also purchased by Ryoei Saito.

3　Vincent van Gogh, *Irises* Sotheby's, New York, 11 November 1987 ($53,900,000)	30,187,623

After much speculation, its mystery purchaser was eventually confirmed as Australian businessman Alan Bond. However, as he was unable to pay for it in full, its former status as the world's most expensive work of art has been disputed and regarded by some as 'artificial'. Early in 1990 it was revealed that it had been sold privately to the J. Paul Getty Museum, Malibu, for an undisclosed sum, with speculation ranging from $60,000,000 to as little as $35,000,000.

4　Pablo Picasso, *Les Noces de Pierrette* Binoche et Godeau, Paris, 30 November 1989 (FF315,000,000/$51,895,000)	33,083,023

Is this the third or fourth most expensive painting ever sold at auction? The answer depends on whether the 315,000,000 French francs paid for it is converted into pounds or US dollars. As a result of exchange rate fluctuations, if converted into sterling it breaks the record set by *Irises*. However, if the price is converted into dollars, it falls short by over $2,000,000. Another consideration is that the price includes a five per cent buyer's premium, whereas the prices of paintings sold in New York and London are inflated by a 10 per cent premium. If this is deducted, *Les Noces de Pierrette* becomes the more expensive by $424,000. Whatever its place in the league table, it is the most expensive twentieth-century work of art. It was sold by Swedish financier Fredrik Roos and bought by Tomonori Tsurumaki, a Japanese property developer, bidding from Tokyo by telephone. He has exhibited it in an art gallery which opened in 1991 at 'Autopolis', a motor racing circuit he has built near Mount Aso, some 700 miles south of Tokyo.

5　Pablo Picasso, *Self Portrait: Yo Picasso* Sotheby's, New York, 9 May 1989 ($47,850,000)	28,825,301

The purchaser has remained anonymous but unconfirmed reports have identified him as Stavros Niarchos, the Greek shipping magnate.

6　Pablo Picasso, *Au Lapin Agile* Sotheby's, New York, 15 November 1989 ($40,700,000)	25,710,675

The painting depicts Picasso as a harlequin at the bar of the café Lapin Agile. The owner of the café acquired the picture in exchange for food and drink at a time when Picasso was hard up. In 1989 it was bought by the Walter Annenberg Foundation.

7　Vincent van Gogh, *Sunflowers* Christie's, London, 30 March 1987	24,750,000

At the time, the most expensive picture ever sold, it was bought by the Yasuda Fire and Marine Insurance Company of Tokyo.

8　Jacopo da Carucci (Pontormo), *Portrait of Duke Cosimo I de Medici* Christie's, New York, 31 May 1989 ($35,200,000)	22,370,511

The world record price for an Old Master – and the only one in the Top 10 – it was bought by the J. Paul Getty Museum, Malibu. The previous record for an Old Master was held by Andrea Mantegna's *Adoration of the Magi*, sold at Christie's, London, on 18 April 1985 for £8,100,000.

9　Pablo Picasso, *Acrobate et Jeune Arlequin* Christie's, London, 28 November 1988	20,900,000

Until the sale of *Yo Picasso*, this held the world record for a twentieth-century painting. It was bought by Mitsukoshi, a Japanese department store.

10　Edouard Manet, *La rue Mosnier aux drapeaux* Christie's, New York, 14 November 1989 ($26,400,000)	16,708,860

Until the sale of Renoir's *Au Moulin de la Galette*, this held the world record price for a French Impressionist painting. Few top quality Impressionist works were auctioned during the art boom period of the late 1980s, with the result that van Gogh (a Post-Impressionist) and Picasso have dominated the scene. When the same painting was previously sold in 1958, it held the then record price for a Manet of £113,000.

All prices include buyer's premium; $/£ conversion at rate then prevailing.

THE 10 MOST EXPENSIVE PAINTINGS BY TWENTIETH-CENTURY ARTISTS EXCLUDING PICASSO

	Painting	Price (£)
1	Wassily Kandinsky (1866–1944), *Fugue* Sotheby's, New York, 17 May 1990 ($20,900,000)	12,440,476†
2	Willem de Kooning (b.1904), *Interchange* Sotheby's, New York, 8 November 1989 ($20,680,000)	13,039,092*†
3	Jasper Johns (b.1930), *False Start* Sotheby's, New York, 10 November 1988 ($17,050,000)	9,406,896**
4	Fernand Léger (1881–1955), *Contrastes de Formes* Christie's, London, 27 November 1989	9,350,000
5	Marc Chagall (1887–1985), *Anniversaire* Sotheby's, New York, 17 May 1990 ($14,850,000)	8,839,286
6	Jasper Johns, *Two Flags* Sotheby's, New York, 8 November 1989 ($12,100,000)	7,658,228
7	Jackson Pollock (1912–56), *Number 8 1950* Sotheby's, New York, 2 May 1989 ($11,550,000)	7,289,157
8	Amedeo Modigliani (1884–1920), *Garçon à la Veste Bleue* Sotheby's, New York, 17 May 1990 ($11,550,000)	6,875,000
9	Georges Braque (1883–1963), *Femme Lisant* Sotheby's, London, 2 December 1986	6,600,000
10	André Derain (1880–1954), *Bateaux dans le Port, Collioure* Christie's, London, 26 June 1986	6,160,000

Currently the world record for a painting by a living artist.
**In 1960, the same painting was sold for $3,150.*
†*Ranked by price at location of auction; as a result of exchange rate variations between sales, converting into sterling alters the order.*

All prices include buyer's premium; $/£ conversion at rate then prevailing.

In addition to those in the Top 10, prices in excess of $4,000,000 have been paid in New York for works by twentieth-century artists including Piet Mondrian, Joan Miró, Robert Rauschenberg, Francis Bacon, Roy Lichtenstein, Frank Stella and Andy Warhol.

QUIZ

FAMOUS PAINTINGS

1 What is the better known title of Leonardo da Vinci's painting sometimes called *La Gioconda*?
2 Where can you see Edouard Manet's painting, *The Bar at the Folies-Bergère*?
3 The title of which 1967 painting by David Hockney was also used as the title of a film?
4 What is the haywain doing in John Constable's famous painting of this title?
5 What is depicted in J. M. W. Turner's painting, *Rain, Steam and Speed*?
6 Who was the painter of the series of paintings known as *The Rake's Progress*?
7 Sir Edwin Landseer's painting of a stag was intended for the House of Lords but is now owned by John Dewar & Sons, the whisky distillers. What is its title?
8 What was the subject of Claude Monet's series of paintings designed to hang in the Orangerie, Paris?
9 What painting by Pablo Picasso arrived in Spain on 10 September 1981 after spending 40 years in the USA, and why?
10 A Shakespearean character who met a watery end is the subject of what painting by the Pre-Raphaelite artist Sir John Everett Millais?

Léger's *Contrastes de Formes*, fourth most expensive twentieth-century painting at £9,350,000.

THE 10 MOST EXPENSIVE PAINTINGS BY PABLO PICASSO

	Painting	Price (£)
1	*Les Noces de Pierrette* Binoche et Godeau, Paris, 30 November 1989 (FF315,000,000)	33,083,023
2	*Self Portrait: Yo Picasso* Sotheby's, New York, 9 May 1989 ($47,850,000)	28,825,301
3	*Au Lapin Agile* Sotheby's, New York, 15 November 1989 ($40,700,000)	25,710,675
4	*Acrobate et Jeune Arlequin* Christie's, London, 28 November 1988	20,900,000
5	*Le Miroir* Sotheby's, New York, 15 November 1989 ($26,400,000)	16,677,195
6	*Maternité* Christie's, New York, 14 June 1988 ($24,750,000)	13,026,315
7	*Mère et Enfant* Sotheby's, New York, 15 November 1989 ($18,700,000)	11,813,013
8	*Famille de l'Arlequin* Christie's, New York, 14 November 1989 ($15,400,000)*	9,728,364
9	*La Cage d'Oiseaux* Sotheby's, New York, 10 November 1988 ($15,400,000)*	8,496,552
10	*La Maternité* Christie's, London, 27 November 1989	7,150,000

*8= if ranked by price at location of auction; as a result of exchange rate variations between 1988 and 1989, converting into sterling alters the order.

Picasso's *La Maternité*, his 10th costliest painting.

THE 10 MOST EXPENSIVE PAINTINGS BY IMPRESSIONISTS AND POST-IMPRESSIONISTS*

	Painting	Price (£)
1	Pierre-Auguste Renoir, *Au Moulin de la Galette* Sotheby's, New York, 17 May 1990 ($78,100,000)	46,488,095
2	Edouard Manet, *La rue Mosnier aux drapeaux* Christie's, New York, 14 November 1989 ($26,400,000)	16,708,860
3	Claude Monet, *Dans La Prairie* (*Camille in the Meadow*) Sotheby's, London, 28 June 1988	14,300,000**
4	Paul Gauguin, *Mata Mua* (*In Olden Times*) Sotheby's, New York, 9 May 1989 ($24,200,000)	14,578,313**
5	Paul Cézanne, *Pommes et Serviette* Christie's, London, 27 November 1989	11,000,000
6	Pierre-Auguste Renoir, *La Promenade* Sotheby's, London, 4 April 1989	10,340,000
7	Edouard Manet, *Le Banc* (*Le Jardin de Versailles*) Christie's, New York, 15 May 1990 ($16,500,000)	9,821,429
8	Edouard Manet, *La Promenade* Sotheby's, New York, 15 November 1989 ($14,850,000)	9,380,922
9=	Claude Monet, *Le Parlement, coucher de soleil* Christie's, New York, 10 May 1989 ($14,300,000)	8,614,753**
9=	Pierre-Auguste Renoir, *La Liseuse* Christie's, New York, 14 November 1989 ($14,300,000)	9,033,480**

*Excluding Vincent van Gogh.
**Ranked by price at location of auction; as a result of exchange rate variations between sales, converting into sterling alters the order.

THE 10 MOST EXPENSIVE PAINTINGS BY VINCENT VAN GOGH

	Painting	Price (£)
1	*Portrait of Dr Gachet* Christie's, New York, 15 May 1990 ($82,500,000)	49,107,142
2	*Irises* Sotheby's, New York, 11 November 1987 ($53,900,000)	30,187,623
3	*Sunflowers* Christie's, London, 30 March 1987	24,750,000
4	*Self Portrait* Christie's, New York, 15 May 1990 ($26,400,000)	15,714,285
5	*Le Vieil If* Christie's, New York, 14 November 1989 ($20,350,000)	12,798,742
6	*Le Pont de Trinquetaille* Christie's, London, 29 June 1987	12,650,000
7	*Paysage au Soleil Levant* Sotheby's, New York, 24 April 1985 ($9,900,000)	7,920,000
8	*Portrait of Adeline Ravoux* Christie's, New York, 11 May 1988 ($13,750,000)	7,325,519
9	*Carriera près de Saint-Rémy* Sotheby's, New York, 15 November 1989 ($11,550,000)	7,296,272
10	*Romans Parisiens (Les Livres Jaunes)* Christie's, London, 27 June 1988	7,150,000

THE RISE AND RISE OF ART PRICES

Before the nineteenth century the highest ever price for a painting was the £8,500 paid in 1759 by Friedrich Augustus II of Saxony for Raphael's *The Sistine Madonna*. In 1852 Murillo's *The Immaculate Conception* became the world's most expensive work of art when it was bought at auction by the Louvre Museum for £24,600. The growing number of wealthy collectors in the Victorian era, however, meant that higher and higher prices were progressively achieved, especially for Old Masters. It was many years before the Impressionists were similarly appreciated: at the turn of the century, when the £100,000 level was reached for another work by Raphael, it was still possible to buy a painting by Vincent van Gogh for about £40, a Cézanne for £200, a Manet for £400, a Monet for less than £1,000 and a Renoir for £2,000. Even allowing for inflation during the intervening period, these prices represent a tiny fraction of what paintings by these same artists were to reach in modern times.

The American millionaire Henry Huntingdon bought Thomas Gainsborough's *The Blue Boy* for $620,000 in 1913 – then equivalent to £148,000 – and the following year Leonardo da Vinci's *Benois Madonna* was sold to Tsar Nicholas II of Russia for £310,400. It held the record as the world's most expensive painting for nearly 50 years.

In the 1950s, works by Impressionist and modern artists were fetching increasingly high prices: a Cézanne, *Garçon au Gilet Rouge*, made £220,000 in 1948, and by the late 1950s paintings by Picasso, few of which had previously attained more than £2,000, were being sold for over £50,000. At the same time, after a steady climb in the price of his works, van Gogh's *Public Garden in Arles* achieved a new record for the artist of £132,000.

In 1961 Rembrandt's *Aristotle Contemplating the Bust of Homer* was bought by the Metropolitan Museum, New York, for £821,429. The £1,000,000 barrier was passed in 1967 with a Leonardo da Vinci and £2,000,000 in 1970 with a Velazquez. By 1970, works by Impressionists including van Gogh, Monet and Renoir had all achieved prices of more than £500,000. In the same year George Stubbs' *A Cheetah with Two Indians* broke the record for a British painting when it was sold for £220,000.

Despite short-lived art market recessions in 1974–75 and 1981–82, prices rose dramatically during the 1970s and 1980s. In 1980 J. M. W. Turner briefly held the world record not only for a British painting but for any work of art when his *Juliet and Her Nurse* was sold in New York for £3,128,884. In the same year van Gogh's *Le Jardin de Poète, Arles* was sold for £2,270,000 and in 1981 Picasso's *Self Portrait: Yo Picasso* made £2,950,000. In 1984 another Turner, *Seascape, Folkestone*, astonished the art world when it reached £7,370,000 at auction. In 1985 Mantegna's *The Adoration of the Magi* overtook it at £8,100,000 and soon afterwards van Gogh's *Paysage au Soleil Levant* made £7,920,000.

No one anticipated the colossal price spiral that followed. It began in 1987 with the sale of van Gogh's *Sunflowers* for an astonishing £24,750,000 (almost trebling the previous record for a van Gogh), a figure soon overtaken by his *Irises* which went for £30,187,623. Both sums have since been exceeded (see The 10 Most Expensive Paintings Ever Sold at Auction). Japanese corporate buyers dominated the art market in the late 1980s and 1990: many large Japanese companies have museums of Western art, largely bought as investments, and paintings are commonly exhibited in department stores as a lure to customers. A number of wealthy purchasers followed the fashionable trend of buying works by the Impressionists, whose paintings tend to be visually appealing and easy on the eye, if not the pocket. There are also relatively large numbers of their works available compared with other categories of paintings. There are signs now, however, that the incredible price boom is over and it seems unlikely that the prices of any of the Top 10 paintings will be exceeded for many years.

THE 10 MOST EXPENSIVE PHOTOGRAPHS EVER SOLD AT AUCTION

	Photograph	Price ($)
1	Tina Modotti, *Roses, Mexico*, 1925 Sotheby's, New York, 18 April 1991	165,000
2	Edward Weston, *Palm Trunk, Cuernavaca*, 1925 Sotheby's, New York, 18 April 1991	154,000
3	El Lissitzky, *Photomontage* Christie's, New York, 16 April 1991	132,000
4	Man Ray, Untitled (rayograph) Christie's, New York, 17 October 1990	126,500
5	Man Ray, *The Primacy of Matter over Thought* Sotheby's, New York, 3 November 1990	121,000
6	Edward Weston, *Nautilus Shell*, 1927 Sotheby's, New York, 26–27 April 1989	115,000
7	Edward Steichen, *George F. Watts* Christie's, New York, 30 October 1989	110,000
8	Man Ray, Untitled (rayograph) Christie's, New York, 16 April 1991	104,500
9=	Paul Outerbridge, *Self Portrait* Sotheby's, New York, 26–27 April 1989	99,000
9=	Alfred Stieglitz, *Georgia O'Keeffe* Sotheby's, New York, 16–17 October 1990	99,000

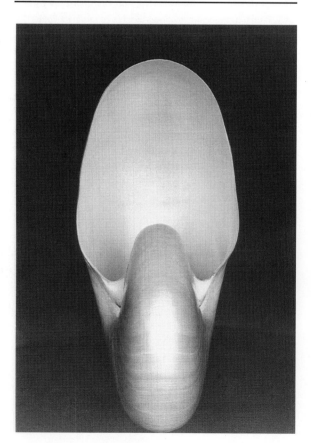

The prices paid for works by the master-photographers of the twentieth century have escalated rapidly in recent years, yet even higher prices than those in the Top 10 have been paid privately for photographs. The highest known is the $190,000 paid by a Californian collector in 1990 for a print of Edward Weston's *Nautilus Shell*, one of only 16 in existence (*see also* No. 6 in the Top 10). In 1985 a Paul Strand photograph, *Wall Street* (1915), was sold to the Canadian Center for Architecture for $170,000, and other works by the same photographer have been reputedly sold for similarly high prices. Graham Nash, the British member of the rock groups the Hollies and Crosby, Stills and Nash, an avid collector of rare photographs, was reported in 1990 to have equalled the current auction record by paying $165,000 for Edward Steichen's *Self Portrait with Clara on their Honeymoon* (1903). Photographs by other photographers represented in the Top 10, including Man Ray and Paul Outerbridge, have been sold for more than $100,000, as have prints by André Kertész and Charles Sheeler (the latter's *Wheels*, a photograph of a railway locomotive's wheels, was purchased in 1988 by the Getty Museum for about $130,000). A photograph by Anthony Berger of Abraham Lincoln and his son Tad (1864) was sold at Sotheby's, New York, on 27 March 1985 for $104,500, but its high value derived less from the photograph itself than from the fact that it was autographed by Lincoln. It is now in the Forbes Magazine Collection, New York.

THE 10 TALLEST FREE-STANDING STATUES IN THE WORLD

	Statue	Height m	ft
1	Chief Crazy Horse Thunderhead Mountain, South Dakota, USA	172	563

Started in 1948 by Polish-American sculptor Korczak Ziolkowski (d.1982) and continued by his widow and eight of his children, this gigantic equestrian statue is even longer than it is high (195 m/641 ft). It is being carved out of the granite mountain by dynamiting and drilling more than 5,000,000 tonnes of rock in total, and is not expected to be completed until the next century.

	Statue	Height m	ft
2	The Indian Rope Trick Riddersberg Säteri, Jönköping, Sweden	103	337

Sculptor Calle Örnemark's 144-tonne wooden sculpture depicts a long strand of 'rope' held by a fakir, while another figure ascends.

	Statue	Height m	ft
3	Motherland, 1967 Volgograd, USSR	82	270

Unveiled in 1967, this concrete statue of a woman with raised sword, designed by Yevgeniy Vuchetich, commemorates the Soviet victory at the Battle of Stalingrad (1942–43).

4	Buddha	53	173
	Bamian, Afghanistan		

Near this third–fourth century AD statue lie the remains of the even taller Sakya Buddha, said to have measured 305 m/1,000 ft.

5	Kannon	52	170
	Otsubo-yama, near Tokyo, Japan		

The immense statue of the goddess of mercy was unveiled in 1961 in honour of the dead of the Second World War.

6	Statue of Liberty	46	151
	New York, USA		

Designed by Auguste Bartholdi and presented to the USA by the people of France, the statue was shipped in sections to Liberty (formerly Bedloes) Island where it was assembled. It was unveiled on 28 October 1886, and restored and reinaugurated on 4 July 1986. It consists of sheets of copper on an iron frame, which weighs 229 tonnes in total. The height of the statue itself is 46 m/151 ft from the base to the top of the torch, and 34 m/111 ft from the heel to the tip of the crown. It stands on a massive pedestal which more than doubles the overall height to 93 m/305 ft from the base to the torch.

7	Christ	38	125
	Rio de Janeiro, Brazil		

The work of sculptor Paul Landowski and engineer Heitor da Silva Costa, the figure of Christ weighs 1,163 tonnes. It was unveiled in 1931 and has recently been restored.

8	Colossi of Memnon	21	70
	Karnak, Egypt		

Two seated sandstone figures of Pharaoh Amenhotep III.

9	Sphinx	20	66
	Giza, Egypt		

The huge body of a lion, with the face of fourth-dynasty Pharaoh Chepren, was carved from limestone and measures 73 m/240 ft in length.

10	Hermanns-Denkmal	19	62
	Teutoburger Forest, Lower Saxony, Germany		

Unveiled in 1875, this copper statue of a figure holding a 7 m/23 ft sword has an additional 29 m/95 ft base. There are many other heroic figures of heights approaching this elsewhere in Germany and Eastern Europe, among them a massive stone figure of Bismarck in Hamburg.

Two of the Seven Wonders of the World were giant free-standing statues: the Colossus of Rhodes, a 36-m/117-ft bronze of the sun-god Helios or Apollo by the sculptor Chares of Lindus, which fell in an earthquake in 224BC and the 12-m/40-ft statue of Zeus in the temple at Olympia, created by Phidias in 457BC.

The tallest statue in the United Kingdom is the 4 m/18 ft (9 m/30 ft with base), 34-tonne bronze Achilles (1822) in Hyde Park, London. The stone statue of Nelson on Nelson's Column (1843) measures 5 m/17 ft, but stands at an elevation of 44 m/145 ft. What is less well known is that there is an even higher statue in London – a 3.7 m/12 ft figure of George I incongruously surmounting the steeple of St George's Church, Bloomsbury Way, London, at a height of 44.8 m/147 ft.

In addition to these free-standing statues, there are many large relief carvings in the sides of hills and mountains, some of which date back to ancient times, among them the 20-m/65-ft effigies of Pharaoh Rameses II cut into the cliffs at Abu Simbel. In modern times the heads of US Presidents Washington, Jefferson, Lincoln and Theodore Roosevelt at Mount Rushmore, South Dakota, were sculpted between 1927 and 1941 by John Gutzon de la Mothe Borglum (1858–1941) and his son Lincoln. Washington's head is 18 m/60 ft high. The Stone Mountain Confederate Memorial, unveiled in 1970 near Atlanta, Georgia, is also not free-standing, but measures a colossal 58 x 93 m/190 x 305 ft. Among other tall monuments (though not strictly statues) are the 174-m/570-ft memorial commemorating the 1836 Battle of San Jacinto, near Houston, Texas, and the Portuguese National Thanksgiving Memorial, Lisbon, unveiled on 17 May 1957. Its total height of 109 m/357 ft includes a 28-m/91-ft figure of Christ.

OPPOSITE Edward Weston's $115,000 photograph, *Nautilus Shell*.

ABOVE RIGHT Lend a hand: Liberty's arm in progress in sculptor Auguste Bartholdi's workshop, 1882.

THE TOP 10 ARTS COUNCIL GRANTS*

	Recipient	Total
1	Royal Opera House	15,200,000
2	South Bank Centre	11,500,000
3	National Theatre	8,900,000
4	English National Opera	7,800,000
5	Royal Shakespeare Company	6,040,000
6	Opera North	2,900,000
7	Welsh National Opera**	2,700,000
8	English National Ballet	1,500,000
9	Western Orchestral Society Ltd	1,200,000
10	Royal Liverpool Philharmonia	1,100,000

*1990-91.
**For touring to England only; core funding supplied by Welsh Arts Council.

Robert Doisneau's bestselling poster, *Baiser, Hôtel de Ville*.

HALLMARK CARDS' 10 BESTSELLING GREETINGS CARDS IN THE UK

	Subject	Occasion
1	Barrow of pansies	General
2	'God's Masterpiece' (new-born baby, cupids and flowers)	Birth congratulations
3	Three angels	Christmas
4	Pink roses and other flowers	Mother's birthday
5	Cute animals	Grandson's birthday
6	Delicate flowers, pearlized, embossed finish	Wedding congratulations
7	Champagne and glasses	Golden (50th) wedding anniversary
8	Teddy bear and hearts	Boyfriend's birthday
9	Black flocked	General
10	Cute centipede	2-year-old's birthday

POSTER SHOPS' 10 BESTSELLING POSTERS IN THE UK

	Poster	Artist/photographer
1	*Baiser, Hôtel de Ville*	Robert Doisneau
2	*Irises* (J. Paul Getty Museum, Malibu)	Vincent van Gogh
3	*Bis*	Pamela Hanson
4	*The Garden Path*	Claude Monet
5	*Fred with Tyres*	Herb Ritts
6	*Accident*	Anon.
7	*Irises* (Metropolitan Museum, New York)	Vincent van Gogh
8	*Penguin Pete & Pat*	Marcus Pfister
9	*Penguin Family*	Marcus Pfister
10	*Parc Monceau*	Claude Monet

THE 10 BESTSELLING POSTCARDS IN THE NATIONAL PORTRAIT GALLERY, LONDON

1	The Brontë Sisters
2	Charlotte Brontë
3	Virginia Woolf
4	Oscar Wilde
5	Elizabeth I
6	Emily Brontë
7	Anne Boleyn
8	William Shakespeare
9	Ellen Terry
10	Henry VIII

LE BAISER DE L'HÔTEL DE VILLE, PARIS 1950

ROBERT DOISNEAU

Kansas City-based Hallmark is the world's largest manufacturer of greetings cards. Founded in 1910 by Joyce Clyde Hall (a man, despite his name!), it remains a family firm with diverse interests that include television, property development and the manufacture of Crayola crayons. Today the business has annual sales of $2,500,000,000, producing more than 11,000,000 cards a day in 20 languages for sale in 100 countries. The company has operated in the UK since the late 1950s.

CULTURE & LEARNING

THE 10 MOST EXPENSIVE PUBLIC SCHOOLS* IN GREAT BRITAIN

	School	Boarding fees per annum (£)
1	Harrow School, Middlesex	10,200
2	Winchester College, Hampshire	9,900
3	Charterhouse, Surrey	9,795
4=	Bryanston School, Dorset	9,750
4=	Uppingham School, Leicestershire	9,750
6	Rugby School, Warwickshire	9,660
7=	Cranleigh School, Surrey	9,585
7=	Haileybury School, Hertfordshire	9,585
7=	Roedean School, Brighton	9,585
10	Marlborough College, Wiltshire	9,495

*Excluding specialist schools for the disabled, music schools, etc, some of which are more expensive than these.

Perhaps surprisingly, Eton College, Buckinghamshire, with annual fees of £9,396, does not make the Top 10. Roedean is the only girls' school in the Top 10.

THE 10 OLDEST SCHOOLS IN THE UK

	School	Year founded
1	King's School, Canterbury	c600
2	King's School, Rochester	604
3	St Peter's School, York	627
4	Warwick School	914
5	King's School, Ely	970
6	Wells Cathedral School	1180
7	Dundee High School	1239
8	Norwich School	1250
9	Abingdon School	1256
10	Winchester College	1382

All are boys' schools. The oldest girls' school in England is Christ's Hospital, Hertford, founded in 1552, and in Scotland, Mary Erskine School, Edinburgh (1694).

THE 10 MOST POPULAR OPEN UNIVERSITY COURSES

1. Fundamentals of Computing
2. Introduction to Psychology
3. The Enlightenment
4. Culture and Belief in Europe
5. The Nineteenth-century Novel and its Legacy
6. Introduction to Information Technology: Social and Technological Issues
7. Social Problems and Social Welfare
8. Health and Disease
9. Mathematical Models and Methods
10. Analogue and Digital Electronics

The Open University was established in 1969 and has grown to become the UK's largest single teaching institution. At any one time there are some 200,000 students, of whom about half use study packs to follow non-degree courses while the rest are registered for a wide variety of 'distance-teaching' courses which use radio and television broadcasts in place of the lecture hall, enabling students to work at home. The largest single group of Open University students are those studying for a Bachelor of Arts (BA) degree (72,000 in 1990). On average, it takes five or six years to gain the six credits needed for a degree – another two credits are required to gain honours. Some nine per cent of all first degrees in the UK are now OU degrees.

OPPOSITE Top of the Top 10: boys at Harrow, Britain's most expensive public school.

THE 10 LARGEST UNIVERSITIES IN THE UK

	University	Full-time students
1	London	47,806*
2	Manchester	18,207
3	Oxford	13,950
4	Cambridge	13,553
5	Leeds	12,393
6	Glasgow	12,247
7	Edinburgh	11,500
8	Birmingham	10,104
9	Ulster	9,205
10	Liverpool	9,039

Internal only; London University also has approximately 24,500 external students.

BELOW The University of Paris is the fourth largest in the world.

THE 10 LARGEST UNIVERSITIES IN THE WORLD

	University	Students
1	State University of New York, USA	369,318
2	University of Mexico, Mexico	327,000
3	University of Buenos Aires, Argentina	248,453
4	University of Paris, France	244,096
5	University of Calcutta, India	235,162
6	University of Guadalajara, Mexico	217,022
7	University of Rajasthan, India	192,039
8	University of Rome, Italy	180,000
9	University of Bombay, India	162,000
10	University of California, USA	145,727

Several other universities in the USA, India, Egypt and Italy have more than 100,000 students. It should be noted that certain universities listed, such as the State University of New York and the University of Paris, are divided into numerous separate centres and that figures are for the totals of all centres.

THE 10 BRITISH UNIVERSITIES AWARDING THE MOST FIRST CLASS DEGREES

	University	% of first class degrees (1990)
1	Cambridge	21.4
2	Oxford	14.2
3	Bath	13.4
4	Aston	12.2
5	Salford	11.4
6	Loughborough	11.3
7	Strathclyde	9.8
8	London	9.6
9	University of Manchester Institute of Science and Technology	9.5
10	Bristol	9.2

Contrasting with the universities with high proportions of first class degrees are those awarding the least: two universities in Northern Ireland, Queen's University, Belfast (4.7 per cent) and the University of Ulster (3.1); and two Welsh universities, Aberystwyth (3.3) and St David's, Lampeter, the lowest at 1.9 per cent.

THE 10 OLDEST UNIVERSITIES AND COLLEGES IN THE USA

	University/college	Location	Founded
1	Harvard University	Cambridge, Massachusetts	1636
2	College of William and Mary	Williamsburg, Virginia	1693
3	Yale University	New Haven, Connecticut	1701
4	University of Pennsylvania	Philadelphia, Pennsylvania	1740
5	Moravian College	Bethlehem, Pennsylvania	1742
6	Princeton University	Princeton, New Jersey	1746
7	Washington and Lee University	Lexington, Virginia	1749*
8	Columbia University	New York, New York	1754
9	Brown University	Providence, Rhode Island	1764
10	University of Delaware	Newark, Delaware	1765**

*Founded as Augusta Academy 1749, name changed to Liberty Hall Academy 1782, Washington Academy 1798, Washington College 1813, present name 1871.
**Founded as Newark Academy 1765, chartered 1769, name changed 1833.

JOHN HARVARD – THE BRITISH FOUNDER OF AMERICA'S FIRST UNIVERSITY

John Harvard, the founder of Harvard University, was born in Southwark, London, not far from London Bridge, in 1607, the son of a butcher who died of the plague. He studied at Emmanuel College, Cambridge, and graduated in 1631. His mother, who had remarried, inherited property including an inn, the Queen's Head, which she bequeathed to John in 1635. Two years later John Harvard married Ann Sadler, a clergyman's daughter, sold the inn and sailed to America, where they established themselves in Charlestown, Massachusetts. In 1636 the settlement had decided to set up a college in New Town, later called Cambridge, and had voted to endow it with a sum of £400. In 1638 Harvard died of consumption and in his will presented half his estate, comprising £779 17s 2d and 320 books, to the proposed college. Work soon began on America's first university, which, it was decided, should be called after its principal benefactor. A fire in 1764 destroyed Harvard's original library except for a single book, but he is commemorated in England by a plaque at his old college and by the Harvard Chapel in Southwark Cathedral, paid for by the members of Harvard University and opened in 1907 on the 300th anniversary of his birth.

Harvard, the USA's oldest university, celebrates its 350th anniversary.

Although Newcastle was founded in 1852, it was a college of Durham University until 1963. If only universities that were established as such are included, No. 10 becomes the University of Wales (1893). No other British universities date from before 1900, but several educational establishments founded during the nineteenth century have since acquired university status.

THE 10 OLDEST UNIVERSITIES IN GREAT BRITAIN

	University	Founded
1	Oxford	1249
2	Cambridge	1284
3	St Andrews	1411
4	Glasgow	1451
5	Aberdeen	1495
6	Edinburgh	1583
7	Durham	1832
8	London	1836
9	Manchester	1851
10	Newcastle	1852

THE 10 OLDEST CAMBRIDGE COLLEGES

	College	Founded
1	Peterhouse	1284
2	Clare	1326
3	Pembroke	1347
4	Gonville & Caius	1348
5	Trinity Hall	1350
6	Corpus Christi	1352
7	King's	1441
8	Queens'	1448
9	St Catharine's	1473
10	Jesus	1496

THE 10 OLDEST OXFORD COLLEGES

	College	Founded
1	University	1249
2	Balliol	1263
3	Merton	1264
4	St Edmund Hall	1278
5	Exeter	1314
6	Oriel	1326
7	Queen's	1340
8	New	1379
9	Lincoln	1427
10	All Souls	1438

THE TOP 10 COUNTRIES OF ORIGIN OF FOREIGN STUDENTS IN FULL-TIME EDUCATION IN THE UK

	Country	Number
1	Hong Kong	7,386
2	Malaysia	6,517
3	USA	5,358
4	Germany	3,493
5	Irish Republic	3,460
6	France	3,206
7	Greece	2,866
8	Singapore	2,052
9	Spain	1,746
10	Cyprus	1,558

King's College, Cambridge, founded 550 years ago.

Rivalries between Eastern European libraries and the West seem to have been responsible for the hugely inflated figures claimed for the State M.E. Saltykov-Shchedrin (28,500,000) and State V.I. Lenin Libraries (39,000,000). As these appear to include individual copies of newspapers and periodicals, they cannot be compared with the holdings of bound books in Western libraries. It is also known that a very large number of books were recently destroyed in a disastrous fire at the Saltykov-Shchedrin. The figures for books in such vast collections as those of the British Library represent only the tip of a cultural iceberg which encompasses millions of additional items, including manuscripts, microfilms, maps, prints and records. The Library of Congress has perhaps 60,000,000 and the New York Public Library 20,000,000 catalogued items other than books.

THE 10 LARGEST LIBRARIES IN THE WORLD

	Library	Location	Founded	Books
1	Library of Congress	Washington, DC, USA	1800	26,000,000
2	British Library	London, UK	1753*	18,000,000
3	Harvard University Library	Cambridge, MA, USA	1638	11,781,270
4	State V.I. Lenin Library of the USSR	Moscow, USSR	1862	11,750,000
5	New York Public Library	New York, NY, USA	1848	9,834,933**
6	Biblioteca Academiei Republicii Socialiste Romania	Bucharest, Romania	1867	9,255,556
7	Bibliothèque Nationale	Paris, France	1480	9,000,000
8	Yale University Library	New Haven, CT, USA	1701	8,718,619
9	State M.E. Saltykov-Shchedrin State Public Library	Leningrad, USSR	1795	8,000,000
10	University of Illinois	Urbana, IL, USA	1867	7,561,615

*Founded as part of the British Museum, 1753; became an independent body, 1973.
**Reference holdings only; a further 15,000,000 books are held in the various NYPL lending library branches.

The Library of Congress, the world's largest library.

THE 10 LARGEST LIBRARIES IN THE UK

	Library	Location	Founded	Books
1	British Library	London	1753	18,000,000
2	Bodleian Library	Oxford	1602	>5,000,000
3	National Library of Scotland	Edinburgh	1682	5,000,000
4	University of Cambridge	Cambridge	c1400	4,530,000
5	Lancashire County Library	Preston	1924	3,562,484
6	Hampshire County Library	Winchester	1925	3,500,000
7	John Rylands Library*	Manchester	1851	3,400,000
8	Kent County Library	Maidstone	1921	3,300,000
9	Birmingham Public Library	Birmingham	1861	2,600,000
10	National Library of Wales	Aberystwyth	1907	2,500,000

In 1972 the John Rylands Library (founded 1900) was amalgamated with Manchester University Library (1851).

In addition to the books held by these libraries, many have substantial holdings of manuscripts, periodicals and other printed material: the Bodleian Library, for example, has almost 1,000,000 maps.

THE 10 LARGEST LIBRARIES IN THE USA

	Library	Location	Founded	Books
1	Library of Congress	Washington, DC	1800	26,000,000
2	Harvard University Library	Cambridge, MA	1638	11,781,270
3	New York Public Library	New York, NY	1848	9,834,933
4	Yale University Library	New Haven, CT	1701	8,718,619
5	University of Illinois	Urbana, IL	1867	7,561,615
6	University of California	Berkeley, CA	1868	7,366,672
7	University of Michigan	Ann Arbor, MI	1817	6,237,521
8	University of Texas	Austin, TX	1883	6,066,136
9	University of California	Los Angeles, CA	1919	5,976,588
10	Columbia University	New York, NY	1754	5,894,135

THE 10 MOST STUDIED FOREIGN LANGUAGES

1	English	6	Arabic
2	French	7	German
3	Spanish	8	Chinese
4	Italian	9	Japanese
5	Russian	10	Turkish

Based on total number of hours studied per language by students at the Polytechnic of Central London, the largest provider of language teaching in the state sector in the whole of Europe, which offers courses in 28 different languages. If English is excluded (although it is a 'foreign' language to many who study it), the 10th most studied language is Dutch.

Students at the Polytechnic of Central London, which offers courses in a total of 28 different languages.

THE 10 COMMONEST WORDS IN WRITTEN ENGLISH

1	The	6	In
2	Of	7	Is
3	And	8	You
4	A	9	That
5	To	10	It

THE 10 LONGEST WORDS IN THE ENGLISH LANGUAGE

Word	Letters
1 Acetylseryltyrosylserylisoleucylthreonylserylprolylserylglutaminylphenylalanylvalylphenylalanylleucylserylserylvalyltryptophylalanylaspartylprolylisoleucylglutamylleucyllleucyllasparaginylvalylcysteinylthreonylserylserylleucylglyclclasparaginylglutaminylphenylalanylglutaminylthreonylglutaminylglutaminylalanylarginylthreonylthreonylglutaminylvalylglutaminylglutaminylphenylalanylserylglutaminylvalyltryptophyllysylprolylphenylalanylprolylglutaminylserylthreonylvalylarginylphenylalanylprolylglycylaspartylvalyltyrosyllsyslvalyltyrosylarginyltyrosylasparaginylalanylvalylleucylaspartylprolylleucylisoleucylthreonylalanylleucylleucylglycylthreonylphenylalanylaspartylthreonylarginylasparaginylarginylisoleucylisoleucylglutamylvalylglutamylasparaginylglutaminylglutaminylserylprolylthreonylthreonylalanylglutamylthreonylleucylaspartylalanylthreonylarginylarginylvalylaspartylaspartylalanylthreonylvalylalanylisoleucylarginylserylalanylasparaginylisoleucylasparaginylleucylvallasparaginylglutamylleucylvalylarginylglycylthreonylglycylleucyltyrosylasparaginylglutaminylasparaginylthreonylphenylalanylglutamylserylmethionylserylglycylleucylvalyltryptophylthreonylserylalanylprolylalanylserine	1,185

The word for the Tobacco Mosaic Virus, Dahlemense Strain, qualifies as the longest word in English because it has actually been used in print (in the American Chemical Society's *Chemical Abstracts*) whereas certain even longer words for chemical compounds, which have been cited in such sources as the *Guinness Book of Records*, are bogus in the sense that they have never been used by scientists or appeared in print. Long words for chemical compounds may be regarded by purists as cheating, since such words as trinitrophenylmethylnitramine (29 letters) – a type of explosive – can be created by linking together the scientific names of their components. Other words that are also discounted are those that have been invented with the sole intention of being long words, such as James Joyce's 100-letter examples in *Finnegans Wake*.

2 Aopadotenachoselachogaleokranioleipsanodrimhipotrimmatosilphioparaomelitokatakechymenokichlepikossyphophattoperisteralektryonoptekephalliokigklopeleiolagoiosiraiobaphetraganopterygon	182

The English transliteration of a 170-letter Greek word that appears in *The Ecclesiazusae* (a comedy on government by women) by the Greek playwright, Aristophanes (c448–380BC). It is used as a description of a 17-ingredient dish.

3 Aequeosalinocalcalinosetaceoaluminosocupreovitriolic	52

Invented by a medical writer, Dr Edward Strother (1675–1737), to describe the spa waters at Bath.

4 Asseocarnisanguineoviscericartilaginonervomedullary	51

Coined by writer and East India Company official Thomas Love Peacock (1785–1866), and used in his satire *Headlong Hall* (1816) as a description of the structure of the human body.

5 Pneumonoultramicroscopicsilicovolcanoconiosis	45

It first appeared in print (though ending in '-koniosis') in F. Scully's *Bedside Manna* [sic] (1936), then found its way into *Webster's Dictionary* and is now in the *Oxford English Dictionary* – but with the note that it occurs 'chiefly as an instance of a very long word'. It is said to mean a lung disease caused by breathing fine dust.

6 Hepaticocholangiocholecystenterostomies	39

A surgical operation to create channels of communication between gall bladders and hepatic ducts or intestines.

7= Pseudoantidisestablishmentarianism	34

A word meaning 'false opposition to the withdrawal of state support from a Church', derived from that perennial favourite long word, antidisestablishmentarianism (a mere 28 letters). Another composite made from it (though usually hyphenated) is ultra-antidisestablishmentarianism, which means 'extreme opposition to the withdrawal of state support from a Church' (33 letters).

7= Supercalifragilisticexpialidocious	34

An invented word, but perhaps now eligible since it has appeared in the *Oxford English Dictionary*. It was popularized by the song of this title in the film *Mary Poppins* (1964) where it is used to mean 'wonderful', but it was originally written in 1949 in an unpublished song by Parker and Young who spelt it 'supercalafajalistickespialadojus' (32 letters). In 1965–66, Parker and Young unsuccessfully sued the makers of *Mary Poppins*, claiming infringement of copyright. In summarizing the case, the US Court decided against repeating this mouthful, stating that 'All variants of this tongue-twister will hereinafter be referred to collectively as "the word".'

9= Encephalomyeloradiculoneuritis	30

A syndrome caused by a virus associated with encephalitis.

9= Hippopotomonstrosesquipedalian	30

Appropriately, the word that means 'pertaining to an extremely long word'.

9=	Pseudopseudohypoparathyroidism	30

First used (hyphenated) in the USA in 1952 and (unhyphenated) in Great Britain in *The Lancet* in 1962 to describe a medical case in which a patient appeared to have symptoms of pseudohypoparathyroidism, but with 'no manifestations suggesting hypoparathyroidism'.

If the rules are changed and No. 1 is disqualified as a compound chemical name, and No. 2 because it is a transliteration from Greek, the next longest word is:

Floccinaucinihilipilification	29

Alternatively spelt 'Flocci-nauci-nihili-pilification' or, by Sir Walter Scott, in his *Journal* (18 March 1829), 'Floccipaucinihilipilification', it means the action of estimating as worthless. Until supercalifragilistic-expialidocious, floccinaucinihilipilification was the longest word in the *Oxford English Dictionary*.

THE 10 EUROPEAN COUNTRIES WHERE ENGLISH IS UNDERSTOOD BY MOST PEOPLE

	Country	% understanding English
1	Sweden	73
2	Netherlands	72
3	Denmark	61
4	Norway	58
5	Finland	48
6=	Luxembourg	44
6=	West Germany	44
8	Austria	42
9	Switzerland	40
10	Belgium	34

Based on Reader's Digest's *Eurodata Report*, a survey of the lifestyles, consumer spending habits and attitudes of people in 17 European countries (12 EC and five EFTA). The country where English is least understood is Spain (12 per cent).

Never be at a loss for words: the complete *Oxford English Dictionary*.

THE OXFORD ENGLISH DICTIONARY

Although conceived earlier, work on the *Oxford English Dictionary* started in earnest in 1879 under the editorship of James Murray. The first part covering A–Ant was published in 1884 and other sections followed at intervals. Murray died in 1915, but the work continued until 1928 when the first edition was complete. In 12 volumes, it defined 414,825 words and phrases, with about 2,000,000 quotations providing information on the first recorded use, continuing usage and later variations in the use of each word. Supplements were added over the ensuing years until it was decided to computerize all the material, work on which commenced in 1984. The original *Dictionary*, *Supplements* and new entries were incorporated onto a gigantic database occupying 540 megabytes of storage. Over 120 keyboard operators keyed in more than 350,000,000 characters, their work checked by over 50 proof-readers. The complete second edition, costing about £10,000,000 to produce, was published in 1989. Its 20 volumes, currently priced at £1,650, contain 21,728 pages with about 60,000,000 words of text defining some 557,889 words (over 34 per cent more than the first edition), together with 2,435,671 quotations. Work is now in hand for putting the entire dictionary onto CD-ROM (a single compact disc).

THE 10 MOST-QUOTED SOURCES IN THE OXFORD ENGLISH DICTIONARY

	Source	Approximate number of references*
1	The Times	19,098
2	Cursor Mundi**	11,035
3	Encyclopaedia Britannica	10,102
4	Daily News	9,650
5	Nature	9,150
6	Transactions of the Philological Society	8,972
7	Chronicle	8,550
8	Westminster Gazette	7,478
9	History of England	7,180
10	Listener	7,139

*These figures may not be absolutely precise because of variations in the way in which source books and journals are quoted, where there is more than one example from the same source, etc.

**Cursor Mundi is a long fourteenth-century Northumbrian poem which is extensively cited for early uses of English words.

References to Daily News, Chronicle and History of England may include several different works with similar titles.

THE 10 MOST-QUOTED AUTHORS IN THE OXFORD ENGLISH DICTIONARY

	Author	Dates	Approximate number of references*
1	William Shakespeare	1564–1616	29,142
2	Sir Walter Scott	1771–1832	15,732
3	John Milton	1608–74	12,000
4	Geoffrey Chaucer	c1343–1400	11,013
5	John Wyclif	c1330–84	10,776
6	William Caxton	c1422–91	9,553
7	John Dryden	1631–1700	8,777
8	Charles Dickens	1812–70	8,189
9	Philemon Holland	1552–1637	7,947
10	Alfred, Lord Tennyson	1809–92	6,680

*These figures may not be absolutely precise because of variations in the way in which sources are quoted, where there is more than one example from the same author, etc.

THE 10 WORDS WITH MOST MEANINGS IN THE OXFORD ENGLISH DICTIONARY

	Word	Meanings
1	Set	464
2	Run	396
3	Go	368
4	Take	343
5	Stand	334
6	Get	289
7	Turn	288
8	Put	268
9	Fall	264
10	Strike	250

THE 10 LETTERS OF THE ALPHABET WITH FEWEST ENTRIES IN THE OXFORD ENGLISH DICTIONARY

	Letter	Entries
1	X	152
2	Z	733
3	Q	1,824
4	Y	2,298
5	J	2,326
6	K	3,491
7	V	5,430
8	N	5,933
9	O	7,737
10	W	8,804

THE 10 LETTERS OF THE ALPHABET WITH MOST ENTRIES IN THE OXFORD ENGLISH DICTIONARY

	Letter	Entries
1	S	34,556
2	C	26,239
3	P	24,980
4	M	17,495
5	A	15,880
6	T	15,497
7	R	15,483
8	B	14,633
9	D	14,519
10	U	12,943

This list of the 10 commonest *first* letters does not correspond with the list of the 10 most frequently *used* letters in written English, which is generally held to be ETAOINSHRD. If the alphabet were restricted to just these letters, among the useful phrases that could be created – without repeating any letters – are 'the inroads', 'note radish', 'date rhinos' and 'hot sardine'.

OPPOSITE Tennyson (left) and Dickens (right), two authors extensively quoted in the *Oxford English Dictionary*.

THE 10 LONGEST WORDS IN THE OXFORD ENGLISH DICTIONARY

	Word	Letters
1	Pneumonoultramicroscopicsilicovolcanoconiosis	45
2	Supercalifragilisticexpialidocious	34
3	Pseudopseudohypoparathyroidism	30
4=	Floccinaucinihilipilification	29
4=	Triethylsulphonemethylmethane	29
6=	Antidisestablishmentarianism	28
6=	Octamethylcyclotetrasiloxane	28
6=	Tetrachlorodibenzoparadioxin	28
9	Hepaticocholangiogastronomy	27
10=	Radioimmunoelectrophoresis	26
10=	Radioimmunoelectrophoretic	26

Words that are hyphenated, including such compound words as 'transformational-generative' and 'tristhio-dimethyl-benzaldehyde', have not been included. Only one unhyphenated word did not quite make it into the Top 10, the 25-letter psychophysicotherapeutics. After this, there is a surprisingly large number of words containing 20–24 letters (pneumonoencephalographic, pneumonoventriculography, psychoneuroendocrinology, radioimmunoprecipitation, spectrophotofluorometric, thyroparathyroidectomize, hypergammaglobulinaemia, hypergammaglobulinaemic, roentgenkymographically, tribothermoluminescence, photomorphogenetically, honorificabilitudinity and immunosympathectomized, for example) – few of which are ever used by anyone except scientists and crossword compilers.

THE 10 EARLIEST DATED WORDS IN THE OXFORD ENGLISH DICTIONARY

	Word	Source	Date
1=	Town	Laws of Ethelbert	601–4
1=	Priest	Laws of Ethelbert	601–4
3	Earl	Laws of Ethelbert	616
4	This	Bewcastle Column	c670
5	Streale	Ruthwell Cross	c680
6	Ward	Caedmon, *Hymn*	680
7	Thing	Laws of Hlothaer and Eadric	685–6
8	Theft	Laws of Ine	688–95
9	Worth	Laws of Ine	695
10	Then	Laws of King Wihtraed	695–6

The 10 earliest citations in the *OED* come from seventh-century Anglo-Saxon documents and stone inscriptions. All have survived as commonly used English words, with the exception of 'streale', which is another name for an arrow. A few other English words can be definitely dated to before 700, among them 'church' which, like 'then', appears in a law of King Wihtraed.

THE 10 MOST TRANSLATED AUTHORS IN THE WORLD

1	V. I. Lenin
2	Agatha Christie
3	Jules Verne
4	William Shakespeare
5	Enid Blyton
6	Leo Tolstoy
7	Charles Perrault
8	Georges Simenon
9	Karl Marx
10	Fyodor Dostoevski

Based on the total numbers of translations of books in the postwar period, Lenin leads the field by a long margin, followed by Agatha Christie, the world's most successful novelist. Just outside the Top 10 are such popular children's authors as Hans Christian Andersen and the Brothers Grimm, followed by Mark Twain, Charles Dickens and Arthur Conan Doyle, with Barbara Cartland, the world's most popular romantic novelist, just behind them.

Agatha Christie, the second most translated author in the world.

THE 10 BOOKS WITH MOST APPEARANCES AT NO. 1 IN THE UK

	Title	Author	Pub.	Appearances at No. 1
1	The Country Diary of an Edwardian Lady	Edith Holden	1977	66
2	Life on Earth	David Attenborough	1979	40*
3	The Growing Pains of Adrian Mole	Sue Townsend	1984	39**
4	Watership Down	Richard Adams	1974	30
5=	The Silmarillion	J. R. R. Tolkien	1977	26
5=	The Secret Diary of Adrian Mole, Aged 13¾	Sue Townsend	1983	26†
7	A Brief History of Time	Stephen Hawking	1988	23
8	Chronicle of the 20th Century	Derrik Mercer (ed.)	1988	22
9=	The Ascent of Man	Jacob Bronowski	1974	19
9=	The Human Factor	Graham Greene	1978	19

*Collins edition; the Reader's Digest version also had two appearances at No. 1.
**Hardback edition.
†Paperback edition.

This Top 10 list is based on the total number of appearances at No. 1 since the *Sunday Times* bestseller lists were first published in April 1974.

THE 10 BESTSELLING HARDBACK BOOKS OF 1990 IN THE UK

	Title	Author	Estimated sales*
1	The Guinness Book of Records	Donald McFarlan (ed.)	240,000
2	Delia Smith's Christmas	Delia Smith	210,000
3	The Trials of Life	David Attenborough	111,000
4	Around the World in 80 Days	Michael Palin	90,000
5	Hugh Johnson's Pocket Wine Book	Hugh Johnson	80,000
6	A Brief History of Time	Stephen Hawking	75,000
7	Longshot	Dick Francis	70,000
8	The RHS Gardeners' Encyclopedia of Plants and Flowers	Christopher Brickell (ed.)	65,000
9	Michelin Red Guide: France	Michelin	60,000
10	Delia Smith's Complete Illustrated Cookery Course	Delia Smith	55,000

*Excluding book club sales.

Nos. 1, 4, 5 and 6 were also in the Top 10 Hardbacks of 1989.

THE 10 BESTSELLING PAPERBACK BOOKS OF 1990 IN THE UK

	Title	Author	Estimated sales*
1	*The Negotiator*	Frederick Forsyth	350,000
2	*The Shell Seekers*	Rosamunde Pilcher	243,000
3	*A Time to Die*	Wilbur Smith	240,000
4	*The Russia House*	John le Carré	215,000
5	*Devices and Desires*	P. D. James	210,000
6	*The Harrogate Secret*	Catherine Cookson	200,000
7	*A History of the World in 10½ Chapters*	Julian Barnes	195,000
8	*Rosemary Conley's Inch Loss Plan*	Rosemary Conley	175,000
9	*Rosemary Conley's Hip and Thigh Diet*	Rosemary Conley	170,000
10	*The Remains of the Day*	Kazuo Ishiguro	145,000

*Excluding book club sales.

Nos. 2 and 9 were also in the Top 10 Paperbacks of 1989.

THE 10 BESTSELLING COOKERY BOOKS IN THE UK

	Title	Author	Estimated sales*
1	*Delia Smith's Complete Illustrated Cookery Course*	Delia Smith	2,100,000**
2	*Madhur Jaffrey's Indian Cookery*	Madhur Jaffrey	700,000
3	*Ken Hom's Chinese Cookery*	Ken Hom	600,000
4	*Sarah Brown's Vegetarian Kitchen*	Sarah Brown	550,000
5	*Crank's Recipe Book*	Kay Canter	432,500
6	*Floyd on France*	Keith Floyd	275,000
7	*Hamlyn's New All-Colour Cookbook*	Hamlyn (pub.)	263,000
8	*Delia Smith's Christmas*	Delia Smith	210,000
9	*Food Aid Cookery Book*	Delia Smith (ed.)	200,000
10	*Good Housekeeping Cookery Book*	Good Housekeeping	112,000

*Excluding book club sales.
**Total sale, including paperback editions of each of the three volumes, plus hardback and illustrated editions of the three-volume compendium.

TOP Dick Francis's *Longshot* was one of the bestsellers of 1990.

ABOVE Keith Floyd, author of the bestselling *Floyd on France*.

THE 10 BESTSELLING PENGUIN CLASSICS

	Author	Book	First published*
1	Emily Brontë	*Wuthering Heights*	1847
2	Charles Dickens	*Hard Times*	1854
3	Jane Austen	*Pride and Prejudice*	1813
4	Charlotte Brontë	*Jane Eyre*	1847
5	Charles Dickens	*Great Expectations*	1862
6	Thomas Hardy	*Tess of the D'Urbervilles*	1891
7	Thomas Hardy	*The Mayor of Casterbridge*	1886
8	Thomas Hardy	*Far from the Madding Crowd*	1874
9	Jane Austen	*Emma*	1816
10	Jane Austen	*Mansfield Park*	1814

In book form (some nineteenth-century novels were originally issued in weekly parts before appearing as books).

The Penguin Classics series was started in 1944 by E. V. Rieu, whose own translation of Homer's *Odyssey*, the first title published, has sold over 1,000,000 copies. The Top 10 of the now huge list of books in print is dominated by nineteenth-century novels – to some extent reflecting their use as 'set books' in English literature courses – but the same authors, with others such as Joseph Conrad and E. M. Forster, also predominate in the Top 50, with only a few earlier writers making an appearance, among them Geoffrey Chaucer, Jonathan Swift, John Bunyan and Daniel Defoe. The Top 10 represents the all-time bestsellers, which corresponds closely to current sales with only slight changes of order: the first nine titles all appeared in the bestsellers of 1990, with Thomas Hardy's *Jude the Obscure* (1895) replacing *Mansfield Park* at No. 10.

QUIZ

BOOKS

1 What is meant by a 'Grangerized' book?
2 What is the name given to books published before 1500 – imprimatur, infundibular or incunabula?
3 What did Isaac Bickerstaff, Lemuel Gulliver and T. Fribble have in common?
4 What is a 'Bowdlerized' book?
5 In what year were the first Penguin paperback books published?
6 What name is given to a booklover – biblioclast, bibliophile or bibliomancer?
7 Why should a booklover beware of *Trogium pulsatorium*?
8 What is the name given to a book measuring 191 x 127mm/7½ x 5 inches?
9 What did Thomas Carlyle's *History of the French Revolution*, Lord Byron's *Memoirs* and T. E. Lawrence's *The Seven Pillars of Wisdom* have in common?
10 What would a book collector understand by the initials 't.e.g.'?

THE FIRST 10 WINNERS OF THE 'ODDEST TITLE AT THE FRANKFURT BOOK FAIR' COMPETITION

	Title	Year
1	*Proceedings of the Second International Workshop on Nude Mice*	1978
2	*The Madam as Entrepreneur: Career Management in House Prostitution*	1979
3	*The Joy of Chickens*	1980
4	*Last Chance at Love – Terminal Romances*	1981
5	Judges split between *Population and Other Problems* and *Braces Owners Manual*	1982
6	*The Theory of Lengthwise Rolling*	1983
7	*The Book of Marmalade: Its Antecedents, Its History and Its Role in the World Today*	1984
8	*Natural Bust Enlargement with Total Mind Power: How to Use the Other 90 Per Cent of Your Mind to Increase the Size of Your Breasts*	1985
9	*Oral Sadism and the Vegetarian Personality*	1986
10	*Versailles: The View from Sweden*	1988

Every year since 1978 the Diagram Group and *The Bookseller* have organized a competition for the book title spotted at the Frankfurt Book Fair that 'most outrageously exceeds all bounds of credibility'. In 1987 the judges did not consider that the standard was sufficiently high, and no award was presented. In other years, however, many of the runners-up were as extraordinary as the winning entries, among them: *Entertaining with Insects: The Original Guide to Insect Cookery*; *Scurvy Past and Present*; *Big and Very Big Hole Drilling*; *The Winged Bean*; *The Potatoes of Bolivia: Their Breeding, Value and Evolutionary Relationship*; *The Social History of Gas Masks*; *Knifethrowing: A Practical Guide*.

OPPOSITE Something to smile about: Thomas Keneally's novel is the bestselling Booker Prize winner of all time.

THE 10 BESTSELLING BOOKER PRIZE WINNERS IN THE UK

	Title	Author	Prize year	Estimated sales*
1	Schindler's Ark	Thomas Keneally	1982	90,000
2	The Old Devils	Kingsley Amis	1986	80,000
3	Oscar and Lucinda	Peter Carey	1988	70,000
4	The Remains of the Day	Kazuo Ishiguro	1989	65,000
5	Hotel du Lac	Anita Brookner	1984	62,000
6	Rites of Passage	William Golding	1980	60,000
7	Moon Tiger	Penelope Lively	1987	59,000
8	Possession	A. S. Byatt	1990	50,000
9	Life and Times of Michael K	J. M. Coetzee	1983	45,000
10	Midnight's Children	Salman Rushdie	1981	40,000

*Hardback only, excluding book club sales.

THE 10 MOST EXPENSIVE BOOKS AND MANUSCRIPTS EVER SOLD AT AUCTION

	Book/manuscript	Price (£)
1	The Gospels of Henry the Lion, c1173–75 Sotheby's, London, 6 December 1983	7,400,000

The most expensive manuscript, book or work of art other than a painting ever sold.

2	The Gutenberg Bible, 1455 Christie's, New York, 22 October 1987	2,934,131

One of the first books ever printed, by Johann Gutenberg and Johann Fust in 1455, it holds the record for the most expensive printed book.

3	The Northumberland Bestiary, c1250–60 Sotheby's, London, 29 November 1990	2,700,000

The highest price ever paid for an English manuscript.

4	Autograph manuscript of nine symphonies by Wolfgang Amadeus Mozart, c1773–74 Sotheby's, London, 22 May 1987	2,350,000

The record for a music manuscript and for any post-medieval manuscript.

5	John James Audubon's The Birds of America, 1827–38 Sotheby's, New York, 6 June 1989	2,292,993

The record for any natural history book.

6	The Bible in Hebrew, a manuscript written in Iraq, Syria or Babylon in the 9th or 10th century Sotheby's, London, 5 December 1989	1,850,000

The record for any Hebrew manuscript.

7	The Monypenny Breviary, illuminated manuscript, c1490–95 Sotheby's, London, 19 June 1989	1,700,000

The record for any French manuscript.

8	The Hours and Psalter of Elizabeth de Bohun, Countess of Northampton, c1340–45 Sotheby's, London, 21 June 1988	1,400,000
9	The Gospels of St Hubert, c860–80 Sotheby's, London, 26 November 1985	1,300,000
10	Life of Thomas Becket, attributed to Matthew Paris, c1230–40 Sotheby's, London, 24 June 1986	1,250,000

The record for any 13th-century manuscript.

Franz Kafka's manuscript of The Trial, sold at Sotheby's, London, on 17 November 1988 for £1,000,000, holds the record for any modern literary manuscript.

THE TOP 10 DAILY NEWSPAPER PUBLISHERS

	Country	No. of daily newspapers	Average daily circulation
1	USSR*	723	122,982,000
2	Japan	124	68,653,000
3	USA	1,657	62,502,000
4	China	73	37,860,000
5	UK	105	23,913,000
6	India	1,978	21,857,000
7	West Germany	318	20,987,000
8	France	92	10,670,000
9	Mexico	308	10,356,000
10	East Germany	39	9,467,000

This list ranks the Top 10 countries according to average total daily circulation. However, if the table is arranged by total sales of daily newspapers per 1,000 inhabitants, the result is somewhat different:

	Country	Sales per 1,000 inhabitants
1	East Germany	570
2	Japan	566
3	Finland	543
4	Sweden	534
5	Norway	530
6	Switzerland	500
7	Liechtenstein	486
8	Iceland	469
9	USSR*	442
10	UK	421

*Excluding Byelorussian SSR and Ukrainian SSR.

One curious anomaly is that of the Vatican City's one newspaper, *l'Osservatore Romano*, an average of 70,000 of which are printed. Since the population of the Vatican is only about 1,000, it implies a daily sale of 70,000 per 1,000, or 70 copies per head! In fact, of course, most of them are sent outside the Holy See.

THE TOP 10 DAILY NEWSPAPERS IN THE WORLD*

	Newspaper	Country	Average daily circulation
1	*Pravda*	USSR	10,700,000
2	*Yomiuri Shimbun*	Japan	8,700,000
3	*Asahi Shimbun*	Japan	7,400,000
4	*People's Daily*	China	6,000,000
5	*Bild Zeitung*	Germany	5,900,000
6	*Wall Street Journal*	USA	1,935,866**
7	*USA Today*	USA	1,387,233
8	*Los Angeles Times*	USA	1,210,077†
9	*New York Daily News*	USA	1,180,139
10	*New York Times*	USA	1,149,683‡

*Excluding the UK – see The Top 10 British National Daily Newspapers.
**National edition; Eastern edition average 805,089.
†Daily; Sunday 1,504,540.
‡Daily; Sunday 1,706,013.

THE TOP 10 CONSUMERS OF NEWSPRINT

	Country	Consumption per inhabitant kg	lb	oz
1	USA	54.043	119	2
2	Denmark	44.928	99	1
3	New Zealand	44.475	98	1
4	Switzerland	44.041	97	1
5	Finland	38.790	85	8
6	Australia	36.828	81	3
7	Canada	34.920	77	0
8	Austria	33.022	72	13
9	Netherlands	31.979	70	8
10	UK	30.031	66	3

National consumption of newsprint – the cheap wood-pulp paper used for printing newspapers – provides a measure of the extent of newspaper sales in the Top 10 countries.

THE TOP 10 BRITISH NATIONAL DAILY NEWSPAPERS

	Newspaper	Average daily sale (Jul to Dec 1990)
1	*Daily Mirror/ Daily Record* (Scotland)	3,860,822
2	*The Sun*	3,854,694
3	*Daily Mail*	1,723,385
4	*Daily Express*	1,708,280
5	*Daily Telegraph*	1,075,980
6	*Daily Star*	911,761
7	*Today*	539,690
8	*The Guardian*	424,124
9	*The Times*	420,127
10	*The Independent*	411,378

The 11th bestselling daily newspaper in Great Britain is the *Financial Times*, with total average worldwide daily sales during this period of 289,726 copies (including editions published in Frankfurt and New York). The combined sales of all the 'quality' daily newspapers (*Daily Telegraph, Guardian, The Times, Independent* and *Financial Times*) are more than 1,000,000 less than the *Daily Mirror*.

THE TOP 10 BRITISH NATIONAL SUNDAY NEWSPAPERS

	Newspaper	Average sales per issue (Jul to Dec 1990)
1	*News of the World*	5,046,315
2	*Sunday Mirror*	2,893,868
3	*The People*	2,565,687
4	*Mail on Sunday*	1,902,706
5	*Sunday Express*	1,663,922
6	*Sunday Times*	1,165,474
7	*Sunday Telegraph*	594,223
8	*Observer*	551,475
9	*Sunday Sport*	401,911
10	*Independent on Sunday*	352,335

During this period the *Sunday Correspondent*, which formerly occupied 10th place, ceased publication, and sales of the *Sunday Telegraph* overtook those of the *Observer*.

THE TOP 10 UK REGIONAL NEWSPAPERS

	Newspaper	Average sales per issue
1	*London Standard*	501,624
2	*Manchester Evening News*	267,400*
3	*Wolverhampton Express & Star*	241,478
4	*Birmingham Evening Mail*	227,174
5	*Liverpool Echo*	202,236**
6	*Glasgow Evening Times*	171,909†
7	*Birmingham Sunday Mercury*	151,983
8	*Newcastle Evening Chronicle*	144,275‡
9	*Belfast Telegraph* (Evening)	141,310
10	*Leicester Mercury*	141,297

*Monday to Friday (Saturday 251,368).
**Monday to Friday (Saturday 177,277).
†Monday to Friday (Saturday 117,399).
‡Monday to Friday (Saturday 126,056).

The *Observer*, founded 4 December 1791, is Britain's oldest Sunday newspaper.

THE TOP 10 MAGAZINES IN THE UK

	Magazine	Average sale per issue
1	Radio Times	2,771,617
2	TV Times	2,669,943
3	Reader's Digest	1,605,741
4	Woman's Weekly	1,128,690
5	Viz	1,018,752
6	Woman's Own	889,534
7	Me	871,677
8	Woman	857,861
9	Best	791,607
10	Prima	672,741

Radio Times, the top UK magazine.

THE 10 BESTSELLING BRITISH COMICS OF ALL TIME

1 Beano (1938–)

2 Comic Cuts (1890–1953)

3 Dandy (1937–)

4 Eagle (1950–69; revived 1982)

5 Film Fun (1920–62)

6 Illustrated Chips (1890–1953)

7 Mickey Mouse Weekly (1936–57)

8 Radio Fun (1938–61)

9 Rainbow (1914–56)

10 School Friend (1950–65)

Accurate circulation figures for British comics are hard to come by, but information supplied by the Association of Comics Enthusiasts indicates that all 10 comics listed (in alphabetical order) achieved very high circulation figures – Eagle, Film Fun, Rainbow and School Friend all hitting 1,000,000 at peak.

THE 10 BESTSELLING BRITISH CHILDREN'S COMICS AND MAGAZINES

1 Beano

2 Dandy

3 Fast Forward

4 Look In

5 2000 AD

6 Roy of the Rovers

7 Thomas the Tank Engine and Friends

8 Hi

9 My Little Pony

10 My Little Pony and Friends

This list is based on certified figures. If they were verified, reported print orders for such publications as Teenage Mutant Hero Turtles, Playdays, Duckula, Fantastic Max and Monty the Dragon would place them all in the middle of the Top 10.

Pleasures from times past: bestselling British comics.

THE TOP 10 D.C. THOMSON CHILDREN'S COMICS AND MAGAZINES

	Comic	First issue
1	Beano	30 July 1938
2	Dandy	4 December 1937
3	Jackie	11 January 1964
4	Bunty	14 January 1958
5	Beezer and Topper	21 January 1956/ 7 February 1953*
6	Hi	4 December 1988
7	Twinkle	27 January 1968
8	Victor	25 February 1961
9	Mandy	21 January 1967
10	Judy	16 January 1960

*Amalgamated 22 September 1990.

After the long-established *Beano* and *Dandy*, *Jackie* and *Bunty* are D. C. Thomson's bestsellers.

D. C. Thomson & Co of Dundee began publishing comics in the 1920s. Their boys' adventure papers, *Rover* (1922–61), *Wizard* (1922–63) and *Hotspur* (1933–59), presented footballers and other working-class heroes with whom their audiences could identify more readily than the public school chaps featured in rival publications such as *The Boy's Own Paper* (1879–1967) and *Magnet* (1908–40), but by the early 1960s changing fashions and the rise of popular culture based on television and pop music ousted this style of publication. D. C. Thomson's old-established humour favourites are still going strong, however, and their two pre-war comics are still their bestsellers: *Dandy*, first published in 1937 and featuring Desperate Dan and Korky the Cat, and *Beano*, dating from 1938, which introduced its best-known character, Dennis the Menace, in 1951.

THE 10 MOST VALUABLE BRITISH COMICS*

	Comic	Issue no.	Value (£)
1	Beano	1	1,000
2	Dandy	1	900
3	Beano	2	500
4	Dandy	2	450
5=	Beano	3	400
5=	Dandy	3	400
7=	Dandy	4	300
7=	Beano	4	300
9	Viz	1	250
10=	Viz	2	200
10=	Knockout	1	200
10=	The Magic Comic	1	200

*Since 1938.

Based on information supplied by Stateside Comics plc.

All prices are for copies in 'Very Fine' condition. Rare copies of early comics in 'Mint' condition may command even higher prices, but unlike the huge prices encountered in the collectors' market in the USA, few British comics outside the Top 10 attain values of more than £100 – a price of £125 is reckoned for a copy of the first-ever *Eagle* and for further early issues of *Dandy*, while *Film Fun* No. 1 and *Viz* No. 3 are rated at £100.

THE 10 OLDEST PERIODICALS IN PRINT IN THE UK

	Periodical	Founded
1	Philosophical Transactions of the Royal Society	1665
2	Archaeologia (Journal of the Society of Antiquaries)	1770
3	Curtis's Botanical Magazine	1787
4	The Lancet	1823
5	The Spectator	1828
6	Royal Society of Edinburgh Proceedings	1832
7	Gospel Standard	1835
8	British Medical Journal	1840
9=	Punch	1841
9=	Jewish Chronicle	1841

Includes only those continuously published under their original titles.

MUSIC

THE TOP 10 BEATLES SINGLES OF ALL TIME IN THE UK

	Song	Year
1	*She Loves You*	1963
2	*I Want to Hold Your Hand*	1963
3	*Can't Buy Me Love*	1964
4	*I Feel Fine*	1964
5	*We Can Work it Out*	1965
6	*Help!*	1965
7	*Hey Jude*	1968
8	*A Hard Day's Night*	1964
9	*From Me to You*	1963
10	*Hello Goodbye*	1967

UK sales of Beatles singles range from almost 2,000,000 for *She Loves You* to less than 700,000 for *Hello Goodbye*. The UK-only list differs in some respects from the global list published in the first edition of *The Top 10 of Everything*, which itself may be subject to revision, with *I Want to Hold Your Hand* now considered to be the Beatles' bestselling single worldwide.

THE TOP 10 ELVIS PRESLEY SINGLES OF ALL TIME IN THE UK

	Song	Year
1	*It's Now or Never*	1960
2	*Jailhouse Rock*	1958
3	*Are You Lonesome Tonight?*	1961
4	*Wooden Heart*	1961
5	*Return to Sender*	1962
6	*Can't Help Falling in Love*	1962
7	*The Wonder of You*	1970
8	*Surrender*	1961
9	*Way Down*	1977
10	*All Shook Up*	1957

Elvis Presley attained his peak sales in the UK not in his 1950s heyday, but shortly after he left the army (5 March 1960). *It's Now or Never* was his only 1,000,000-seller in the UK, although all the singles in the Top 10 registered sales in excess of 600,000 and between them accounted for a total of 46 weeks at the top of the UK singles chart.

THE TOP 10 CLIFF RICHARD SINGLES OF ALL TIME WORLDWIDE

	Song	Year
1	*We Don't Talk Anymore*	1979
2	*The Young Ones*	1962
3	*Devil Woman*	1976
4	*Congratulations*	1968
5	*The Next Time / Bachelor Boy*	1962
6	*Living Doll*	1959
7	*Summer Holiday*	1963
8	*Lucky Lips*	1963
9	*Dreamin'*	1980
10	*Daddy's Home*	1981

Cliff Richard (born 14 October 1940, Lucknow, India, real name Harry Roger Webb) had his first chart hit in 1958 with *Move It*. Since then, he has habitually achieved several hits virtually every year, the five most successful of which have sold in excess of 2,000,000 records with *We Don't Talk Anymore* clocking up sales of 2,500,000.

THE TOP 10 ROLLING STONES SINGLES OF ALL TIME IN THE UK

	Song	Year
1	*The Last Time*	1965
2	*(I Can't Get No) Satisfaction*	1965
3	*Honky Tonk Women*	1969
4	*It's All Over Now*	1964
5	*Get Off Of My Cloud*	1965
6	*Paint It Black*	1966
7	*Jumpin' Jack Flash*	1968
8	*Little Red Rooster*	1964
9	*Miss You*	1978
10	*Brown Sugar*	1971

All these were Number One hits except *Miss You* (highest chart position 3) and *Brown Sugar* (2).

ABOVE Rocking on, Rolling Stones Mick Jagger and Ronnie Wood.

LEFT The 'Fab Four', unrivalled Sixties hitmakers.

Quiz

POP GROUPS

Put the singers with their correct groups:

1	Brian Poole	and the Pips	A
2	Reparata	and the Pacemakers	B
3	Frankie Lymon	and the Union Gap	C
4	Gladys Knight	and the Teenagers	D
5	Smokey Robinson	and the Muffins	E
6	Ian Dury	and the Tremeloes	F
7	Martha Reeves	and the Delrons	G
8	Gary Puckett	and the Miracles	H
9	Gerry	and the Vandellas	I
10	Martha	and the Blockheads	J

THE 10 FEMALE SINGERS WITH THE MOST TOP 20 HITS IN THE UK

	Singer	Hits
1	Madonna	22
2=	Diana Ross (including one duet with Marvin Gaye, one with Lionel Richie)	17
2=	Petula Clark (excluding the remixed reissue of *Downtown*)	17
2=	Connie Francis	17
5	Donna Summer (including one duet with Barbra Streisand)	15
6=	Dusty Springfield (including one duet with the Pet Shop Boys)	14
6=	Winifred Atwell	14
6=	Cilla Black	14
9=	Shirley Bassey	12
9=	Brenda Lee	12

Runners-up include Whitney Houston (11 Top 20 hits) and Kate Bush (also 11, including one duet with Peter Gabriel), both of which could replace Shirley Bassey and Brenda Lee in the list by next year. They are followed by Olivia Newton-John (10, including two duets with John Travolta, one with ELO, one with Cliff Richard) and Doris Day (10, including two duets with Johnnie Ray and one with Frankie Laine).

OPPOSITE TOP Supreme Supremes, with a record 17 Top 20 hits.

RIGHT Connie Francis, one of the most successful female singers of all time.

THE 10 FEMALE SINGERS WITH THE MOST TOP 20 HITS IN THE USA AND UK*

	Singer	Hits
1=	Connie Francis	28
1=	Aretha Franklin (including one duet with George Michael)	28
1=	Diana Ross (including three duets with Marvin Gaye, one with Lionel Richie and one with Julio Iglesias)	28
4	Madonna	27
5	Olivia Newton-John (including two duets with John Travolta and one each with Andy Gibb, Cliff Richard and ELO)	26
6	Brenda Lee	24
7	Donna Summer (including one duet with Barbra Streisand)	23
8	Petula Clark	21
9	Dionne Warwick (including one duet with the Detroit Spinners and one with 'Friends': Stevie Wonder, Gladys Knight and Elton John)	19
10	Dusty Springfield (including one duet with the Pet Shop Boys)	17

*To 28 February 1991.

This covers USA and/or UK Top 20 hits, including the listed duets with other acts, but not those achieved as a member of a group – Diana Ross's successes with the Supremes are therefore not counted. The only change to the Top 10 in the past year is that Madonna has moved up from 6= position to 4th by increasing her tally of hits from 23 to 27.

THE 10 MOST EXPENSIVE ITEMS OF POP MEMORABILIA

	Item	Price (£)
1	John Lennon's 1965 Rolls-Royce Phantom V touring limousine, finished in psychedelic paintwork Sotheby's, New York, 29 June 1985 ($2,299,000)	1,768,462
2	Jimi Hendrix's Fender Stratocaster guitar Sotheby's, London, 25 April 1990	198,000
3	Gibson acoustic guitar, c1945, owned by Buddy Holly, in a tooled leather case made by him Sotheby's, New York, 23 June 1990 ($242,000)	139,658
4	John Lennon's 1970 Mercedes-Benz 600 Pullman four-door limousine Christie's, London, 27 April 1989	137,500
5	Elvis Presley's 1963 Rolls-Royce Phantom V touring limousine Sotheby's, London, 28 August 1986	110,000
6	Buddy Holly's Fender Stratocaster guitar, 1958 Sotheby's, New York, 23 June 1990 ($110,000)	63,481
7	Elvis Presley's one-piece 'Shooting Star' stage outfit, 1972 Phillips, London, 24 August 1988	28,600
8	Buddy Holly's spectacles, 1958 Sotheby's, New York, 23 June 1990 ($45,100)	26,027
9	An unreleased 8 mm film of the Beatles in America, 1965 Christie's, London, 29 August 1986	24,000
10	Tape recorded interview with John Lennon, 1968 Sotheby's, London, 5 August 1987	23,650

Pioneered particularly by Sotheby's in London, pop memorabilia has become big business – especially if it involves personal association with mega-stars such as the Beatles and, latterly, Buddy Holly. In addition to the Top 10, high prices have also been paid for a guitar belonging to John Entwistle of the Who and pianos that were once owned by Paul McCartney and John Lennon.

THE TOP 10 FEMALE GROUPS OF ALL TIME IN THE UK*

	Group	No. 1	Top 10	Top 20
1	Supremes	1	13	17
2	Bananarama	–	9	14
3	Three Degrees	1	5	7
4	Sister Sledge	1	4	7
5	Nolans	–	3	7
6	Bangles	1	3	5
7	Mel and Kim	–	4	4
8	Pointer Sisters	–	2	5
9	Beverley Sisters	–	2	4
10	Crystals	–	2	3

To 28 February 1991. Ranked according to total number of hits.

The Supremes also had three other Top 20 hits which have not been included because they were recorded in partnership with Motown male groups Four Tops and Temptations. However, Bananarama's charity revival of *Help!*, shared with comediennes Dawn French and Jennifer Saunders, has been included since all the participants are female.

Jimi Hendrix's £198,000 Fender Stratocaster, which he played at Woodstock in 1969.

THE FIRST TOP 10 SINGLES IN THE UK

	Song	Singer
1	*Here in My Heart*	Al Martino
2	*You Belong to Me*	Jo Stafford
3	*Somewhere Along the Way*	Nat 'King' Cole
4	*Isle of Innisfree*	Bing Crosby
5	*Feet Up*	Guy Mitchell
6	*Half as Much*	Rosemary Clooney
7	*High Noon*	Frankie Laine
8	*Sugar Bush*	Doris Day and Frankie Laine
9	*Homing Waltz*	Vera Lynn
10	*Auf Wiedersehen*	Vera Lynn

'An authentic weekly survey of the best-selling "pop" records', is how the *New Musical Express* heralded the first-ever British singles chart, which it published on Friday, 14 November 1952. Before it was instituted, charts were based only on sheet music sales. In subsequent weeks, *You Belong to Me* also reached Number One, *Feet Up* rose to Number Two and *Half as Much* to Number Three.

THE TOP 10 SINGLES OF ALL TIME IN THE UK

	Song	Artist	Release
1	*Do They Know it's Christmas?*	Band Aid	1984
2	*Mull of Kintyre*	Wings	1977
3	*Rivers of Babylon / Brown Girl in the Ring*	Boney M	1978
4	*She Loves You*	Beatles	1963
5	*You're the One that I Want*	John Travolta and Olivia Newton-John	1978
6	*Relax!*	Frankie Goes to Hollywood	1983
7	*Mary's Boy Child / Oh My Lord*	Boney M	1978
8	*I Just Called to Say I Love You*	Stevie Wonder	1984
9	*I Want to Hold Your Hand*	Beatles	1963
10	*Tears*	Ken Dodd	1965

Sales of singles have steadily declined over the years and now account for only about nine per cent of the record market. As a result, unless there are further exceptional records such as Band Aid's colossal hit (with sales in the UK of almost 3,000,000 and more than 7,000,000 globally), it seems unlikely that this Top 10 will change much over the coming years.

THE TOP 10 SINGLES OF ALL TIME WORLDWIDE

	Song	Artist	Sales exceed
1	*White Christmas*	Bing Crosby	30,000,000
2	*Rock Around the Clock*	Bill Haley and his Comets	17,000,000
3	*I Want to Hold Your Hand*	Beatles	12,000,000
4	*It's Now or Never*	Elvis Presley	10,000,000
5=	*Hound Dog/Don't Be Cruel*	Elvis Presley	9,000,000
5=	*Diana*	Paul Anka	9,000,000
7=	*Hey Jude*	Beatles	8,000,000
7=	*I'm A Believer*	Monkees	8,000,000
9=	*Can't Buy Me Love*	Beatles	7,000,000
9=	*Do They Know it's Christmas?*	Band Aid	7,000,000
9=	*We Are the World*	USA for Africa	7,000,000

Global sales are notoriously difficult to calculate, particularly in countries outside the UK and USA and especially in the Far East. 'Worldwide' is thus usually taken to mean the known minimum 'western world' sales. Bing Crosby's 1942 record, *White Christmas*, is indisputably the all-time bestselling single, and the *song*, recorded by others and sold as sheet music, has also achieved such enormous sales that it would additionally appear in the No. 1 position in any list of bestselling songs.

THE 10 SINGLES THAT STAYED LONGEST IN THE UK CHARTS

	Song	Artist	First chart entry	Weeks in charts
1	*My Way*	Frank Sinatra	1969	122
2	*Amazing Grace*	Judy Collins	1970	67
3	*Rock Around the Clock*	Bill Haley and his Comets	1955	57
4	*Release Me*	Engelbert Humperdinck	1967	56
5	*Stranger on the Shore*	Mr Acker Bilk	1961	55
6	*Relax!*	Frankie Goes to Hollywood	1983	52
7	*Blue Monday*	New Order	1983	49
8	*I Love You Because*	Jim Reeves	1964	47
9	*Let's Twist Again*	Chubby Checker	1961	44
10	*White Lines (Don't Do It)*	Grandmaster Flash and Melle Mel	1983	43

THE 10 YOUNGEST SINGERS OF ALL TIME IN THE UK SINGLES CHARTS

	Singer	Song	Year	Highest chart position	Age yrs	mths
1	Microbe (Ian Doody)	*Groovy Baby*	1969	29	3	
2	Natalie Casey	*Chick Chick Chicken*	1984	72	3	
3	Little Jimmy Osmond	*Long Haired Lover From Liverpool*	1974	2	9	7
4	Lena Zavaroni	*Ma He's Making Eyes at Me*	1974	10	10	4
5	Neil Reid	*Mother of Mine*	1972	2	11	
6	Michael Jackson	*Got To Be There*	1972	5	13	5
7	Laurie London	*He's Got the Whole World in His Hands*	1957	12	13	9
8	Jimmy Boyd	*I Saw Mommy Kissing Santa Claus*	1953	3	13	10
9	Marie Osmond	*Paper Roses*	1973	2	14	1
10	Helen Shapiro	*Don't Treat Me Like a Child*	1961	3	14	5

ABOVE Lena Zavaroni achieved her first UK chart hit at the age of 10.

TOP Judy Collins' *Amazing Grace* scored an amazing 67 weeks in the UK charts.

OPPOSITE Wings perform *Mull of Kintyre*, the second most successful single of all time in the UK.

The ages given are those reached by these artists during their first-ever week in the UK singles chart. Since this is a chart of solo acts, assorted hitmaking children's choirs are not included, nor is Michael Jackson's initial impact with the Jackson Five, made when he was only 10. With a few honourable exceptions, most of these precocious stars never achieved a follow-up chart success.

THE 10 OLDEST SINGERS OF ALL TIME IN THE UK SINGLES CHARTS

	Singer	Song	Year	Highest chart position	Age yrs	mths
1	Bing Crosby	*That's What Life is All About*	1975	41	73	3
2	Frank Sinatra	*New York, New York*	1986	4	70	4
3	Louis Armstrong	*Sunshine of Love*	1968	41	68	1
4	Walter Brennan	*Old Rivers*	1962	38	67	11
5	Max Bygraves	*White Christmas*	1989	71	67	2
6	Doris Day	*Move Over Darling*	1987	45	63	1
7	Perry Como	*I Want to Give*	1974	31	62	1
8	Gracie Fields	*Little Donkey*	1959	20	61	11
9	Eartha Kitt	*This is My Life*	1986	73	58	2
10	Petula Clark	*Downtown '88*	1988	10	56	2

Septuagenarian Frank Sinatra, still hitmaking after all these years.

The ages given are those of the artists concerned during the final chart week of their last UK hit single – discounting any posthumous hits. Not far behind are Andy Stewart, James Brown, Bobby Vinton, Tom Jones and Cliff Richard, all of whom have had UK chart hits since their 50th birthday.

ABOVE The Shadows' impressive tally of hits includes two out of the Top 10 instrumental singles.

OPPOSITE MC Hammer's *You Can't Touch This* is a Kiss 100 FM listeners' favourite.

THE TOP 10 INSTRUMENTAL SINGLES OF ALL TIME IN THE UK

	Song	Year	Artist
1	*Stranger on the Shore*	1961	Mr Acker Bilk
2	*Eye Level*	1972/74	Simon Park Orchestra
3	*Telstar*	1962	Tornados
4	*The Birdie Song*	1981	Tweets
5	*Amazing Grace*	1972	Royal Scots Dragoon Guards Band
6	*Albatross*	1968	Fleetwood Mac
7	*Wonderful Land*	1962	Shadows
8	*Apache*	1960	Shadows
9	*Floral Dance*	1977	Brighouse and Rastrick Brass Band
10	*Fanfare for the Common Man*	1977	Emerson, Lake and Palmer

Although it never made Number One, *Stranger on the Shore* spent over a year in the British charts. The Simon Park Orchestra, Brighouse and Rastrick Brass Band, Emerson, Lake and Palmer and Tweets never had another single in the charts, before or after. *Eye Level* was the last instrumental Number One record.

THE TOP 10 MOTOWN SINGLES OF ALL TIME IN THE UK

	Song	Artist	Release
1	I Just Called to Say I Love You	Stevie Wonder	1984
2	I Heard it Through the Grapevine	Marvin Gaye	1969
3	Hello	Lionel Richie	1984
4	Three Times a Lady	Commodores	1978
5	Reach Out, I'll Be There	Four Tops	1966
6	One Day in Your Life	Michael Jackson	1981
7	I'm Still Waiting	Diana Ross	1971
8	Baby Love	Supremes	1964
9	I Want You Back	Jackson Five	1970
10	Tears of a Clown	Smokey Robinson and the Miracles	1970

Stevie Wonder's song, *I Just Called to Say I Love You*, came from the film *The Woman in Red*, and won an Academy Award for Best Song. The single sold almost 1,800,000 copies in the UK, making it one of the UK's all-time bestselling singles. Michael Jackson's *One Day in Your Life* was recorded on the Motown label and not released until long after he had left, when it became his biggest-selling Motown single in the UK.

CAPITAL FM LISTENERS' TOP 10 SINGLES OF ALL TIME

	Song	Artist
1	Careless Whisper	George Michael
2	Against All Odds	Phil Collins
3	Vogue	Madonna
4	Bohemian Rhapsody	Queen
5	Stairway to Heaven	Led Zeppelin
6	Money for Nothing	Dire Straits
7	Imagine	John Lennon
8	Ride on Time	Black Box
9	Unchained Melody	Righteous Brothers
10	The Power	Snap

The independent London radio station Capital FM has been conducting its 'Hall of Fame' poll for several years, compiling a Top 500 based on listeners' nominations for their three all-time favourite records. A large number of recent releases appear alongside long-established favourites both in the Top 10 and throughout the Top 500, hinting at the relative youthfulness of most of the voters.

KISS 100 FM LISTENERS' TOP 10 DANCE RECORDS OF ALL TIME

	Record	Artist
1	Hold On	En Vogue
2	Keep On Movin'	Soul II Soul
3	The Power	Snap
4	Back to Life	Soul II Soul
5	You Can't Touch This	MC Hammer
6	Expansions	Lonnie Liston Smith
7	Tears	Frankie Knuckles (featuring Satoshi Tomie)
8	Rebel Without A Plause	Public Enemy
9	Poison	Bell Biv Devoe
10	The Masterplan	Diana Brown and Barrie K. Sharpe

This Top 10 is derived from a poll conducted at the time of their launch by London dance music radio station Kiss 100 FM. A former pirate radio station established in 1985, it attracted a wide following among young Londoners. It applied for a licence and went 'legit' on 1 September 1990, and has rapidly achieved substantial success as a commercial station.

Bill Haley and his Comets' *Rock Around the Clock* has been a jukebox smash for 36 years.

hand-operated Edison phonograph with coinbox and four listening tubes, was unveiled at the Palais Royal Saloon, San Francisco, on 23 November 1889. No choice of recordings was offered, the listener hearing whatever cylinder happened to be in the machine. The first in which records could be selected in advance, the 'Multiphone', patented in 1905 by John C. Dunton of Grand Rapids, Michigan, gave a choice of 24 recordings. The first all-electric model was made in 1927 by the Automatic Musical Instrument Co. The word jukebox first appeared in print in *Time* magazine of 27 November 1939, which noted that 'Glenn Miller attributes his crescendo to the "juke-box", which retails recorded music at 5¢ a shot in bars, restaurants and roadside dance joints'. Wurlitzer, the best-known manufacturer of jukeboxes, dominated the market in the postwar period, the Wurlitzer 1015 selling 56,000 models in 1946.

THE 10 MOST VALUABLE JUKEBOXES

Jukebox	Value (£)*
1 Wurlitzer 950 (1942)	35,000

Made in 1942 when wartime restrictions were imposed on the supply of plastic and nickel (two crucial design elements), the result is a testament to the resourcefulness of Wurlitzer's chief designer, Paul Fuller. A combination of its aesthetic appeal and rarity – only 3,497 were made – makes it by far the most valuable jukebox.

2 Wurlitzer 850 (1941)	20,000

Known as the 'Peacock', this was the most spectacular jukebox designed by Paul Fuller. Its central feature was a silkscreened peacock illuminated from behind by polarized coloured filters that presented an ever-changing display of iridescent colour. Wurlitzer's last full production model before the Second World War, a total of 10,002 were made in 1941.

3 Elton John's Wurlitzer 750 (1941)	17,600

Sold at Sotheby's in London on 6 September 1988 with an estimate of £10,000, bidding reached a surprising £16,000 (£17,600 with the 10 per cent buyer's premium).

4 Rockola Commando (1942–45)	14,000

In response to wartime restrictions on materials, Rockola came up with a highly creative design which looked more like a sculpture than a conventional jukebox. Its uniqueness and rarity contribute to its high market value.

5 Wurlitzer 81 (1940)	12,000

As well as full-sized jukeboxes, Wurlitzer also manufactured small 'tabletop' machines which played only one side of a dozen 78-rpm discs. Of all the tabletop

THE TOP 10 JUKEBOX HITS OF ALL TIME

	Song	Artist	Year
1	*Hound Dog/Don't Be Cruel*	Elvis Presley	1956
2	*Crazy*	Patsy Cline	1961
3	*Rock Around the Clock*	Bill Haley and his Comets	1955
4	*Dock of the Bay*	Otis Redding	1968
5	*I Heard it Through the Grapevine*	Marvin Gaye	1968
6	*Mack the Knife*	Bobby Darin	1959
7	*Light My Fire*	Doors	1967
8	*Blueberry Hill*	Fats Domino	1956
9	*Old Time Rock 'n' Roll*	Bob Seger	1979
10	*My Girl*	Temptations	1965

The list is based on a survey by the USA Amusement and Music Operators' Association, and is of most-played records in the USA – the home of the jukebox. The first, a models the 81 is regarded as the most desirable, partly because only 1,100 were made and also because its design incorporated marbled plastics not found in any other model. The countertops came with a stand almost as valuable as the machine itself – hence the high price of the two together.

6	Wurlitzer 1015 (1946–47)	11,000

Arguably *the* archetypal jukebox, this postwar machine evokes the spirit of Rock and Roll. Wurlitzer manufactured 56,000 of this model and launched a massive advertising campaign to link the 1015 with every festival in American life, from Christmas to Thanksgiving. Mechanically reliable, numerous examples remained in use well into the 1950s. Its visual appeal, deriving from its rotating colour cylinders and streaming bubble tubes, and its associations with a nostalgic era account for the 1015's value, despite the relatively large numbers available.

7	Wurlitzer 1080 (1947)	10,000

Made in 1947 and known as the 'Colonial', this model was designed for elegant sites, although many regard its bizarre eighteenth-century styling as verging on the kitsch.

8	Wurlitzer 'Victory' Model (1943–45)	9,500

A wartime model in which glass replaced plastic, the Victory was essentially a cabinet that could be placed over any earlier Wurlitzer in order to keep the company name in the public consciousness.

9	Wurlitzer 800 (1940)	9,000

A large jukebox made in 1940, the 800 was the first to use bubble tubes. Enormous illuminated pilasters on each side featured rotating colour cylinders that projected a moving zebra stripe pattern.

10	Wurlitzer 1100 (1948)	8,000

Paul Fuller's last jukebox before his retirement, it featured a state-of-the-art sound system for 78-rpm records, with a lightweight tone arm and pre-amp. Although the most colourful 1940s jukebox when lit up, it was not well received in its day, perhaps because stylistically it harked back to wartime design (its dome was even compared with that of a bomber!), but by the time it was manufactured in 1948, America was looking forward to the 1950s and so the 1100 marks the end of an era.

Based on average market price in the UK of a model in fine condition – with the exception of No. 3, the value of which was inflated by its connection with a celebrity owner.

The jukeboxes made in the 1940s, which usually played one side of 20 or 24 78-rpm records, represent the most desirable, and hence valuable among collectors, although 1950s examples are also becoming more widely

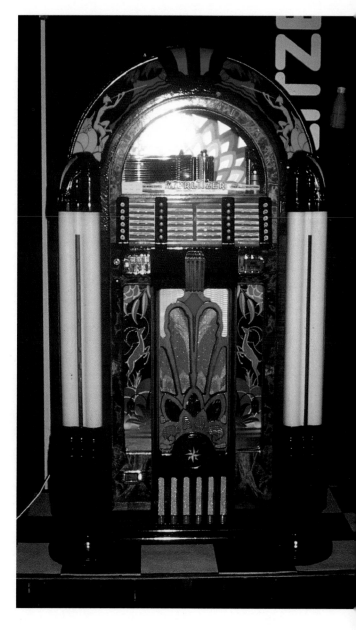

The Wurlitzer 950, most desirable of all classic jukeboxes.

appreciated. Good original or sympathetically-restored machines command the highest prices, but jukeboxes are generally bought for their visual appeal, nostalgic associations – and because they will also play one's favourite records. Additionally, in recent years, as prices have escalated, they have also become acknowledged as a sound investment. All but one of the 10 most valuable jukeboxes were made by the same company, Wurlitzer, all of these created by the same designer, Paul Fuller, during the 1930s and 1940s. Regarded as the doyen of jukebox cabinet designers, Fuller was responsible for 13 full-size jukeboxes and five tabletop models. His importance was such that some collectors bid only for his machines.

Data supplied by Ian Brown, Co-editor of Jukebox Journal *(PO Box 545, Brighton, BN1 4HU), and the Chicago Sound Co.*

THE 10 BESTSELLING EUROVISION SONG CONTEST WINNERS IN THE UK

	Song	Artist	Country represented	Year
1	Save Your Kisses for Me	Brotherhood of Man	UK	1976
2	Puppet on a String	Sandie Shaw	UK	1967
3	Making Your Mind Up	Bucks Fizz	UK	1981
4	Waterloo	Abba	Sweden	1974
5	All Kinds of Everything	Dana	Ireland	1970
6	What's Another Year	Johnny Logan	Ireland	1980
7	A Little Peace	Nicole	Germany	1982
8	Boom Bang-A-Bang	Lulu	UK	1969
9	Come What May	Vicky Leandros	Luxembourg	1972
10	Hold Me Now	Johnny Logan	Ireland	1987

The top seven records all reached Number One, as did *Congratulations* by Cliff Richard, runner-up in the 1968 contest.

THE 10 LEAST SUCCESSFUL UK EUROVISION SONG CONTEST ENTRIES IN THE UK CHARTS

	Song	Artist	Highest chart position	Year
1=	All	Patricia Bredin	–	1957
1=	I Love the Little Things	Matt Monro	–	1964
1=	Runner in the Night	Ryder	–	1986
1=	Only the Light	Rikki	–	1987
5	Why Do I Always Get it Wrong?	Live Report	73	1989
6	Go	Scott Fitzgerald	52	1988
7	Love Is	Vikki	49	1983
8	Love Enough for Two	Prima Donna	48	1980
9	Ring-a-Ding Girl	Ronnie Carroll	46	1962
10	Mary Ann	Black Lace	42	1979

While attempting to appeal to the Euro-masses, especially in the 1980s, a number of the UK's Eurovision Song Contest entries were revealed to be totally out of touch with record-buying taste. No fewer than six entries from the decade appear in this list, including two that failed to appear in the charts at all – even though by this period the UK charts encompassed the Top 75 singles, whereas in 1957 only the Top 30 were listed. Perversely, Matt Monro's song came second in the 1964 contest and Prima Donna were third in 1980. Half the artists – Patricia Bredin, Ryder, Rikki, Live Report and Scott Fitzgerald – never again had a chart record. Black Lace have fared considerably better since *Mary Ann*, however, becoming major UK hitmakers with songs such as *Superman* (1983, Number Nine) and *Agadoo* (1984, Number Two).

THE TOP 10 FOREIGN-LANGUAGE SINGLES OF ALL TIME IN THE UK*

	Song	Artist	Year	Language
1	Je T'Aime... Moi Non Plus	Jane Birkin and Serge Gainsbourg	1969	French
2	Rock Me Amadeus	Falco	1986	German
3	Begin the Beguine	Julio Iglesias	1981	Spanish
4	Sadness	Enigma	1990/91	Latin/French
5	Chanson d'Amour	Manhattan Transfer	1977	French
6	La Bamba	Los Lobos	1987	Spanish
7	Come Prima/Volare	Marino Marini	1958	Italian
8	Nessun Dorma	Luciano Pavarotti	1990	Italian
9	Joe Le Taxi	Vanessa Paradis	1988	French
10	Lambada	Kaoma	1989	Portuguese

*To 28 February 1991.

Although foreign-language hits are fairly rare in the UK, as in most English-speaking markets, the top six in this list all reached Number One in the UK singles chart, and the rest made the Top 10. French is by far the most familiar foreign language to infiltrate the UK market. The success in 1990 of the new Nos. 4 and 8 evicted two French songs from this Top 10 – *Dominique* by the Singing Nun (Soeur Sourire) (1963) and *Voyage Voyage by* Desireless (1987/88). There are also several other notable chart hits containing passages sung in French, such as the Overlanders' cover version of the Beatles' *Michelle* (Number One in 1966) and Bill Wyman's 'Franglais' *(Si Si) Je Suis un Rock Star* (Number 14 in 1981).

OPPOSITE Brotherhood of Man's 1976 Number One hit *Save Your Kisses for Me* remains the bestselling UK Eurovision winner of all time.

THE TOP 10 ON CD JUKEBOXES

	CD	Artist
1	*Now 17*	Various
2	*Now 18*	Various
3	*Labour of Love II*	UB40
4	*The Immaculate Collection*	Madonna
5	*…But Seriously*	Phil Collins
6	*Changes*	David Bowie
7	*Now Dance 902*	Various
8	*Foreign Affair*	Tina Turner
9	*Compact Snap*	Jam
10	*I Do Not Want*	Sinead O'Connor

Information supplied by BLMS.

The Top 10 is based on the most-played compact discs on Arbiter Discmaster CD Jukeboxes. Approximately 3,000 have been installed in the UK and offer listeners the opportunity to select individual tracks from a range of popular CDs.

THE TOP 10 ALBUMS OF ALL TIME IN THE UK

	Album	Artist
1	*Brothers in Arms*	Dire Straits
2	*Sgt Pepper's Lonely Hearts Club Band*	Beatles
3	*Bad*	Michael Jackson
4	*Thriller*	Michael Jackson
5	*…But Seriously*	Phil Collins
6	*Bridge over Troubled Water*	Simon and Garfunkel
7	*Greatest Hits*	Simon and Garfunkel
8	*Rumours*	Fleetwood Mac
9	*The Sound of Music*	Original Soundtrack
10	*Dark Side of the Moon*	Pink Floyd

Dire Straits' masterwork has sold more than 3,000,000 copies in the UK, while Nos. 2, 3 and 4 on the list have achieved sales of over 2,700,000. Still selling strongly at the beginning of 1991 was Phil Collins' *…But Seriously*, now approaching sales of 2,500,000 and almost certain to exceed this figure during the year.

THE TOP 10 ALBUMS OF ALL TIME WORLDWIDE

	Album	Artist
1	*Thriller*	Michael Jackson
2	*Saturday Night Fever*	Original Soundtrack
3	*Grease*	Original Soundtrack
4	*Sgt Pepper's Lonely Hearts Club Band*	Beatles
5	*Bridge over Troubled Water*	Simon and Garfunkel
6	*Born in the USA*	Bruce Springsteen
7	*The Sound of Music*	Original Soundtrack
8	*Abbey Road*	Beatles
9	*Rumours*	Fleetwood Mac
10	*Brothers in Arms*	Dire Straits

THE TOP 10 WOMEN IN THE UK ALBUM CHARTS

1	Madonna
2	Barbra Streisand
3	Diana Ross
4	Tina Turner
5	Kate Bush
6	Shirley Bassey
7	Whitney Houston
8=	Elkie Brooks
8=	Nana Mouskouri
10	Donna Summer

Based on total number of weeks their albums have stayed in the UK charts. Madonna leads the field by a long margin, her seven albums having spent a total of more than 450 weeks in the UK charts.

THE TOP 10 POP CDs OF ALL TIME IN THE UK

	CD	Artist
1	*Brothers in Arms*	Dire Straits
2	*Bad*	Michael Jackson
3	*Thriller*	Michael Jackson
4	*…But Seriously*	Phil Collins
5	*Greatest Hits*	Queen
6	*Whitney*	Whitney Houston
7	*Tango in the Night*	Fleetwood Mac
8	*No Jacket Required*	Phil Collins
9	*The Joshua Tree*	U2
10	*Graceland*	Paul Simon

Compact discs were the music marketing success story of the 1980s, overtaking vinyl's share of the album market by the end of the decade. Generally, albums appealing to the 20–30 age group tend to have the greater percentage of their sales on CD, but among the Top 10 there are close parallels with the bestselling albums of recent years.

THE 10 ALBUMS THAT STAYED LONGEST IN THE UK CHARTS

	Album	Artist	First year in chart
1	*Rumours*	Fleetwood Mac	1977
2	*Bat out of Hell*	Meatloaf	1978
3	*The Sound of Music*	Original Cast	1965
4	*Greatest Hits*	Queen	1981
5	*Bridge over Troubled Water*	Simon and Garfunkel	1970
6	*Dark Side of the Moon*	Pink Floyd	1973
7	*South Pacific*	Original Cast	1958
8	*Greatest Hits*	Simon and Garfunkel	1972
9	*Face Value*	Phil Collins	1981
10	*Tubular Bells*	Mike Oldfield	1973

The 10 longest-staying records virtually took up residence in the album charts (the Top 50, 75 or 100, depending on the years during which the charts were compiled), remaining there for periods ranging from over five years for *Tubular Bells* to the astonishing eight-and-a-half-year occupation of Fleetwood Mac's *Rumours*.

ABOVE LEFT Meatloaf in action: his *Bat out of Hell* is the second longest stayer in the UK album charts.

THE TOP 10 ORIGINAL SOUNDTRACK ALBUMS OF ALL TIME IN THE UK

1	*The Sound of Music*
2	*Grease*
3	*Saturday Night Fever*
4	*Dirty Dancing*
5	*South Pacific*
6	*West Side Story*
7	*Top Gun*
8	*A Star is Born*
9	*That'll be the Day*
10	*Fame*

THE TOP 10 COUNTRY ALBUMS OF 1990 IN THE UK

	Album	Artist
1	*The Hard Way*	Stevie Earle and the Dukes
2	*Heroes and Friends*	Randy Travis
3	*Storms*	Nanci Griffith
4	*Country's Greatest Hits*	Various
5	*Greatest Hits*	Dolly Parton
6	*Greatest Hits*	Glen Campbell
7	*Duets*	Emmylou Harris
8	*No Holdin' Back*	Randy Travis
9	*Love Can Build a Bridge*	Judds
10	*The Kenny Rogers Story*	Kenny Rogers

THE TOP 10 HEAVY METAL ALBUMS OF 1990 IN THE UK

	Album	Artist
1	*No Prayer for the Dying*	Iron Maiden
2	*The Razors Edge*	AC/DC
3	*Rocking All Over the Years*	Status Quo
4	*Soul Provider*	Michael Bolton
5	*Blaze of Glory / Young Guns II*	Jon Bon Jovi
6	*Still Got the Blues*	Gary Moore
7	*Heart of Stone*	Cher
8	*Alannah Myles*	Alannah Myles
9	*Brigade*	Heart
10	*A Bit of What You Fancy*	Quireboys

THE TOP 10 JAZZ ALBUMS OF 1990 IN THE UK

	Album	Artist
1	*We Are In Love*	Harry Connick Jr
2	*Music from the Motion Picture Soundtrack When Harry Met Sally...*	Harry Connick Jr
3	*Montage*	Kenny G.
4	*Visions Tale*	Courtney Pine
5	*Blue Note Sampler*	Various
6	*Soft on the Inside*	Andy Shephard
7	*Question and Answer*	Pat Metheny, Dave Holland, Roy Haynes
8	*Big Boss Band*	George Benson and Count Basie Orchestra
9	*The Fabulous Baker Boys* Original Soundtrack	Dave Gruisin
10	*Aura*	Miles Davis

ABOVE RIGHT Harry Connick Jnr achieved the double with No. 1 and 2 in the top jazz albums of 1990.

RIGHT Status Quo's *Rocking All Over the Years* was a heavy metal album hit of 1990.

LEFT Madonna, top woman artiste in the UK album charts.

THE 10 OPERAS MOST FREQUENTLY PERFORMED AT THE ROYAL OPERA HOUSE, COVENT GARDEN, 1946–90

	Opera	Composer	First performance	Total
1	La Bohème	Puccini	15 Oct 1948	267
2	Aïda	Verdi	29 Sep 1948	253
3	Carmen	Bizet	14 Jan 1947	248
4	Tosca	Puccini	18 Nov 1950	207
5	Le Nozze di Figaro	Mozart	22 Jan 1949	185
6	Rigoletto	Verdi	31 Oct 1947	184
7	Die Zauberflöte	Mozart	20 Mar 1947	178
8	La Traviata	Verdi	6 Apr 1948	173
9	Madama Butterfly	Puccini	17 Jan 1950	164
10	Der Rosenkavalier	Richard Strauss	22 Apr 1947	161

In the first edition of *The Top 10 of Everything* we published a list of the 10 most-performed operas of all time at the Royal Opera House, some of which were first staged as early as the 1830s. This new list covers only performances from 1946 to 1990 and gives a better view of the relative popularity of operas in modern times. During this period *La Bohème* has risen from 2nd to 1st place and *Carmen* has fallen from 1st to 3rd. *Le Nozze di Figaro*, *Die Zauberflöte* and *Der Rosenkavalier* did not appear at all in the previous list. Mozart's *Don Giovanni* has left the Top 10 altogether, slipping from 6th to 16th place, while Charles Gounod's *Faust*, No. 4 in the all-time list with 428 performances, and Vincenzo Bellini's *Norma*, No. 7 with 353, do not even feature in the postwar Top 20.

La Bohème has attained a record-breaking 267 postwar performances at the Royal Opera House.

THE TOP 10 CLASSICAL ALBUMS OF 1990 IN THE UK

	Album	Artist
1	Carreras, Domingo, Pavarotti – *In Concert*	José Carreras, Placido Domingo, Luciano Pavarotti, Zubin Mehta
2	*The Essential Pavarotti*	Luciano Pavarotti
3	Vivaldi: *Four Seasons*	Nigel Kennedy/English Chamber Orchestra
4	Mendelssohn: *Violin Concerto in E Minor*/Bruch: *Violin Concerto No. 1 in G Minor*/ Schubert: *Rondo in A*	Nigel Kennedy, Jeffrey Tate/ English Chamber Orchestra
5	*Classic Experience II*	Various
6	Beethoven: *Symphony No. 9 Ode to Freedom, Bernstein in Berlin*	Leonard Bernstein/Berlin Philharmonic Orchestra
7	*Essential Classics*	Various
8	*Music for the Last Night of the Proms*	Sir Charles Groves/ Royal Philharmonic Orchestra
9	*A Night at the Opera*	Various
10	Elgar: *Cello Concerto/Sea Pictures*	Sir John Barbirolli/London Symphony Orchestra Jacqueline du Pré, Dame Janet Baker

THE TOP 10 OF 'YOUR HUNDRED BEST TUNES'

	'Tune'	Composer
1	*In the Depths of the Temple* (from *The Pearl Fishers*)	Georges Bizet
2	*Chorus of the Hebrew Slaves* (from *Nabucco*)	Giuseppi Verdi
3	*Miserere*	Gregorio Allegri
4	*Violin Concerto No. 1 in G Minor* (*Adagio*)	Max Bruch
5	*Canon in D*	Johann Pachelbel
6	*Symphony No. 6* ('*Pastoral*') (last movement)	Ludwig van Beethoven
7	*Piano Concerto No. 21* (*Andante*)	Wolfgang Amadeus Mozart
8	*Lament: What is Life?* (from *Orfeo ed Euridice*)	Christoph Willibald von Gluck
9	*The Holy City*	Stephen Adams
10	*Nimrod* (from *Enigma Variations*)	Sir Edward Elgar

BBC Radio 2's *Your Hundred Best Tunes* first went on the air as *The Hundred Best Tunes in the World* on 22 November 1959, and is still broadcast every Sunday night by its original presenter, Alan Keith. The Top 10 comes from the programme's listeners' poll of all-time favourites.

THE TOP 10 CLASSICAL COMPOSERS IN PERFORMANCE

	Composer	Performances
1	Mozart	56
2	Beethoven	55¾
3	Brahms	27
4	Mahler	20⅖
5=	Haydn	20
5=	Schubert	20
7	Shostakovich	18
8	Sibelius	14
9	Tchaikovsky	13
10	Bruckner	12

David Chesterman has been writing to *The Times* every year since 1952, reporting on the 10 composers whose symphonies have been most performed at the Royal Albert, Royal Festival, Barbican and Queen Elizabeth Halls and at St John's, Smith Square, London. His analysis is based on the number of times each composer's work is played, with individual movements counted as fractions of the whole symphony. In 1990 Mozart beat Beethoven for only the third time in almost 40 years, and the celebration of the bicentenary of his death in 1991 is certain to guarantee his continued supremacy. Also in 1990, Brahms moved up from 10th position in 1989 to 3rd, while Dvořák (5th in 1989), with 11-1/2 performances, failed for the first time to attain the Top 10.

THEATRE

THE 10 LONGEST-RUNNING COMEDIES OF ALL TIME IN THE UK

	Show	Performances
1	*No Sex, Please – We're British*	6,761
2	*Run for Your Wife*	2,638
3	*There's a Girl in My Soup*	2,547
4	*Pyjama Tops*	2,498
5	*Boeing Boeing*	2,035
6	*Blithe Spirit*	1,997
7	*Worm's Eye View*	1,745
8	*Dirty Linen*	1,667
9	*Reluctant Heroes*	1,610
10	*Seagulls Over Sorrento*	1,551

THE 10 LONGEST-RUNNING SHOWS OF ALL TIME IN THE UK

	Show	Performances
1	*The Mousetrap*	15,952*
2	*No Sex, Please – We're British*	6,761
3	*The Black and White Minstrel Show*	6,464
4	*Me and My Girl*	4,779*
5	*Cats*	4,139*
6	*Oliver*	4,125
7	*Oh! Calcutta!*	3,918
8	*Jesus Christ, Superstar*	3,357
9	*Life with Father*	3,213
10	*Starlight Express*	2,912*

Still running; total at 31 March 1991.

All the longest-running shows in the UK have been London productions. *The Mousetrap* opened on 25 November 1952 at the Ambassadors Theatre. After 8,862 performances it transferred to St Martin's Theatre where it re-opened on 25 March 1974. It is not the only play in the world to have run continuously since the 1950s – Eugène Ionesco's *The Bald Prima Donna* has been on in Paris since 1953.

LEFT *Me and My Girl*, 4,779 performances and still going strong.

ABOVE Long runner: *Run for Your Wife* clocked up 2,638 performances to make No. 2 in the comedy stakes.

THE 10 LONGEST-RUNNING MUSICALS OF ALL TIME IN THE UK

	Show	Performances
1	The Black and White Minstrel Show	6,464
2	Me and My Girl	4,779*
3	Cats	4,139*
4	Oliver	4,125
5	Jesus Christ, Superstar	3,357
6	Starlight Express	2,912*
7	Evita	2,900
8	The Sound of Music	2,386
9	Salad Days	2,283
10	My Fair Lady	2,281

*Still running; total at 31 March 1991.

The Black and White Minstrel Show total includes both the original 10-year run (1962–72) and the 1973 revival. Me and My Girl opened at the Victoria Palace on 16 December 1937 and, apart from a brief closure when war was declared in 1939, ran until 29 June 1940, by which time it had achieved 1,646 performances. Revivals in 1941, 1945–46, 1949–50 and 1985– have boosted the total to the present figure, making it the UK's longest-running musical comedy of all time. Total performances of Oliver include runs at different theatres from 1960–66, 1967–68, 1977–80 and 1983–84. On 12 May 1989 Cats, which opened in 1981, became the longest continuously running musical in British theatre history.

THE 10 LONGEST-RUNNING NON-MUSICALS OF ALL TIME IN THE UK

	Show	Performances
1	The Mousetrap	15,952*
2	No Sex, Please – We're British	6,761
3	Oh! Calcutta!	3,918
4	Run for Your Wife	2,638
5	There's a Girl in My Soup	2,547
6	Pyjama Tops	2,498
7	Sleuth	2,359
8	Boeing Boeing	2,035
9	Blithe Spirit	1,997
10	Worm's Eye View	1,745

*Still running; total at 31 March 1991.

Oh! Calcutta! is included here as it is regarded as a revue with music, rather than a musical.

Andrew Lloyd Webber's musical, Cats, a huge and sustained hit on both sides of the Atlantic.

THE 10 LONGEST-RUNNING SHOWS OF ALL TIME ON BROADWAY

	Show	Performances
1	A Chorus Line	6,137
2	Oh! Calcutta!	5,959
3	Cats	3,541*
4	42nd Street	3,486
5	Grease	3,388
6	Fiddler on the Roof	3,242
7	Life with Father	3,224
8	Tobacco Road	3,182
9	Hello Dolly!	2,844
10	My Fair Lady	2,717

*Still running; total at 31 March 1991.

A Chorus Line ran from 1974–90; Cats opened in 1982 and between 1990 and 1991 rose from 8th to 3rd place in the Top 10.

THE 10 LONGEST-RUNNING MUSICALS OF ALL TIME ON BROADWAY

	Show	Performances
1	A Chorus Line	6,137
2	Cats	3,541*
3	42nd Street	3,486
4	Grease	3,388
5	Fiddler on the Roof	3,242
6	Hello Dolly!	2,844
7	My Fair Lady	2,717
8	Annie	2,377
9	Man of La Mancha	2,328
10	Oklahoma!	2,212

*Still running; total at 31 March 1991.

THE 10 LONGEST-RUNNING NON-MUSICALS OF ALL TIME ON BROADWAY

	Show	Performances
1	Oh! Calcutta!	5,959
2	Life with Father	3,224
3	Tobacco Road	3,182
4	Abie's Irish Rose	2,327
5	Deathtrap	1,792
6	Gemini	1,788
7	Harvey	1,775
8	Born Yesterday	1,642
9	Mary, Mary	1,572
10	Voice of the Turtle	1,557

More than half the longest-running non-musical shows on Broadway began their runs before the Second World War – in the case of *Abie's Irish Rose*, in 1922. The others all date from the period up to the 1970s, before the long-running musical completely dominated the Broadway stage.

SHAKESPEARE'S 10 LONGEST PLAYS

	Play	Lines
1	Hamlet	3,901
2	Richard III	3,886
3	Coriolanus	3,820
4	Cymbeline	3,813
5	Othello	3,672
6	Antony and Cleopatra	3,630
7	Troilus and Cressida	3,576
8	Henry VIII	3,450
9	Henry V	3,368
10	The Winter's Tale	3,354

Albert Finney as Hamlet, one of Shakespeare's most talkative characters.

SHAKESPEARE'S 10 MOST DEMANDING ROLES

	Role	Play	Lines
1	Hamlet	Hamlet	1,422
2	Falstaff	Henry IV, Parts I and II	1,178
3	Richard III	Richard III	1,124
4	Iago	Othello	1,097
5	Henry V	Henry V	1,025
6	Othello	Othello	860
7	Vincentio	Measure for Measure	820
8	Coriolanus	Coriolanus	809
9	Timon	Timon of Athens	795
10	Antony	Antony and Cleopatra	766

Hamlet's role comprises 11,610 words – over 36 per cent of the total number of lines spoken in the play, but he is beaten by Falstaff who, as well as appearing in *Henry IV*, Parts I and II, also appears in *The Merry Wives of Windsor* where he has 436 lines. His total of 1,614 lines thus makes him the most talkative of all Shakespeare's characters.

FILM

TOP 10 FILM LISTS

Films that appear in the various lists of '10 Most Successful' and Top 10s of films in which various stars have appeared are ranked according to the total rental fees paid to distributors by cinemas in North America (USA and Canada). This is regarded by the film industry as a reliable guide to what a film has earned in those markets, while as a rough rule of thumb – also used by the industry itself – doubling the North American rental receipts gives a very approximate world total.

It should be noted that rental income is not the same as 'box office gross', which is another commonly-used way of comparing the success of films. While the latter method is certainly valid over a short period – for example, to compare films released in the same year – it indicates what the cinemas rather than the films themselves earned and, of course, varies according to ticket price.

Inflation is a key factor in calculating 'success', whichever method of assessment is used: as cinema ticket prices go up, so do box office income *and* the rental fees charged by distributors. This means that the biggest earners tend to be among the most recent releases. If inflation is taken into account, the most successful film ever would be *Gone With the Wind*; while it has earned actual rental fees of almost $80,000,000, inflation since the film's release in 1939 makes this worth over $500,000,000 in today's money.

Attempts have been made to compile precise comparative lists by building in factors for increases in ticket prices and inflation, but with such changes taking place so frequently in recent years, and with a total lack of uniformity in box office prices even in one country, it is virtually impossible to achieve consistent or meaningful results, and rental fees remain the most satisfactory index for comparing the success of one film against another. However, even the dollar rental amounts are extremely volatile, with new information constantly emerging about not only newly-released films but also many older ones. The order of those in the various Top 10 lists should therefore be taken only as a guide based on the best evidence currently available. Actual amounts are given only for the 'All-Time Film Rental Blockbusters' category, as an indication of the exceptional earning power of this élite group of films – only 12 films have made more than $100,000,000, while of all the films ever made fewer than 75 have earned total rental fees of more than $50,000,000.

It must not be forgotten that over recent years additional income has been derived by distributors from sales of video recordings and TV broadcasting rights. As this is not generally included in rental fees, it may alter the overall earnings of certain films, and hence their order in the Top 10 lists.

Especially in recent years, some films that were enormously expensive to make have also been among the highest earners, while others have failed disastrously at the box office; conversely, certain films that were produced with relatively low budgets have gone on to earn huge sums. It is ultimately the differential between the cost of making a film and its income – which is notoriously difficult to estimate – that determines whether it has been a success or a 'flop'.

THE TOP 10 FILMS RELEASED IN THE 1920s

	Film	Year
1	*The Big Parade*	1925
2	*Ben Hur*	1926
3	*The Ten Commandments*	1923
4=	*What Price Glory?*	1926
4=	*The Covered Wagon*	1923
6	*Way Down East*	1921
7	*The Singing Fool*	1928
8=	*Wings*	1927
8=	*The Four Horsemen of the Apocalypse*	1921
10	*The Jazz Singer*	1927

All the films in this list were black and white, with the exception of *Ben Hur*, which, despite its early date, contains a colour sequence, and all were silent, apart from *The Jazz Singer*, which is hailed – not entirely accurately – as 'the first talkie'. Curiously, an even earlier film, *The Birth of a Nation* (1915), has earned almost twice as much as *The Big Parade*, making it the most successful film made before 1937.

The 'anti-war war film', *The Big Parade*, the top moneymaker of the 1920s.

THE TOP 10 FILMS RELEASED IN THE 1930s

	Film	Year
1	Gone With the Wind	1939
2	Snow White and the Seven Dwarfs	1937
3	King Kong	1933
4	The Wizard of Oz	1939
5	San Francisco	1936
6=	Mr Smith Goes to Washington	1939
6=	Lost Horizon	1937
6=	Cavalcade	1933
6=	Hell's Angels	1930
10	Maytime	1937

THE TOP 10 FILMS RELEASED IN THE 1940s

	Film	Year
1	Bambi	1942
2	Fantasia	1940
3	Cinderella	1949
4	Pinocchio	1940
5	Song of the South	1946
6	Mom and Dad	1944
7	Samson and Delilah	1949
8=	Duel in the Sun	1946
8=	The Best Years of Our Lives	1946
10	This is the Army	1943

THE TOP 10 FILMS RELEASED IN THE 1950s

	Film	Year
1	The Ten Commandments	1956
2	Lady and the Tramp	1955
3	Peter Pan	1953
4	Ben Hur	1959
5	Around the World in Eighty Days	1957
6	Sleeping Beauty	1959
7=	South Pacific	1958
7=	The Robe	1953
9	The Bridge on the River Kwai	1957
10	This is Cinerama	1952

THE TOP 10 FILMS RELEASED IN THE 1960s

	Film	Year
1	The Sound of Music	1965
2	Jungle Book	1967
3	Dr Zhivago	1965
4	Butch Cassidy and the Sundance Kid	1969
5	Mary Poppins	1964
6	The Graduate	1968
7	One Hundred and One Dalmatians	1961
8	Thunderball	1965
9	Funny Girl	1968
10	Cleopatra	1963

Gone With the Wind and Snow White and the Seven Dwarfs have generated far more income than any other pre-war films, none of which has earned more than $10,000,000. If the almost $80,000,000 income of Gone With the Wind is adjusted for inflation, it may be regarded as the most successful film of all time. Gone With the Wind and The Wizard of Oz both celebrated their 50th anniversaries in 1989, the extra publicity generated by these events further enhancing their rental income.

RIGHT Up and away: David Niven and Cantiflas in *Around the World in Eighty Days*, one of the most successful films of the 1950s.

OPPOSITE *Jaws*, a box office blockbuster of the 1970s.

THE TOP 10 FILMS RELEASED IN THE 1970s

	Film	Year
1	Star Wars	1977
2	Jaws	1975
3	Grease	1978
4	The Exorcist	1973
5	The Godfather	1972
6	Superman	1978
7	Close Encounters of the Third Kind	1977*
8	The Sting	1973
9	Saturday Night Fever	1977
10	National Lampoon's Animal House	1978

*Close Encounters' place in the Top 10 derives from the success of its original release and the 1980 'Special Edition'.

THE TOP 10 FILMS RELEASED IN THE 1980s

	Film	Year
1	E.T.	1982
2	Return of the Jedi	1983
3	Batman	1989
4	The Empire Strikes Back	1980
5	Ghostbusters	1984
6	Raiders of the Lost Ark	1981
7	Indiana Jones and the Last Crusade	1989
8	Indiana Jones and the Temple of Doom	1984
9	Beverly Hills Cop	1984
10	Back to the Future	1985

THE MOST-FILMED STORIES OF ALL TIME

Such is the variety of treatments of many popular stories that it would be almost impossible to compile a list of the Top 10 Remakes. The *Cinderella* story is claimed to be the most frequently featured, with at least 70 versions that encompass straightforward retellings of the traditional fairy story and adaptations set in modern times, as well as all-black, musical, animated and puppet Cinderellas. There have also been more than 50 versions of such stories as *Carmen* and of Shakespeare's *Hamlet* (together with numerous films of *Romeo and Juliet*, *Macbeth*, *A Midsummer Night's Dream*, *Julius Caesar* and *Othello*). Further popular stories, including Dickens' *Oliver Twist* and *A Christmas Carol*, have been remade many times, as have Lewis Carroll's *Alice in Wonderland*, Defoe's *Robinson Crusoe* and Dumas's *The Three Musketeers*. The original stories of Stevenson's *Dr Jekyll and Mister Hyde*, Mary Shelley's *Frankenstein* and Bram Stoker's *Dracula* have all been retold on many occasions and the characters have also appeared in further stories by other authors. There is an extensive range of heroes and villains who have similarly been represented in innumerable films, among them Robin Hood, William Tell, Tarzan, Bulldog Drummond, James Bond, Sherlock Holmes and Dr Fu Manchu.

THE FIRST 10 TO WIN THE 'BEST ACTOR' OSCAR

	Actor	Film	Year
1	Emil Jannings	*The Last Command; The Way of All Flesh*	1928
2	Warner Baxter	*In Old Arizona*	1929
3	George Arliss	*Disraeli*	1930
4	Lionel Barrymore	*A Free Soul*	1931
5	Wallace Beery	*The Champ*	1932
6	Charles Laughton	*The Private Life of Henry VIII*	1933
7	Clark Gable	*It Happened One Night*	1934
8	Victor McLaglen	*The Informer*	1935
9	Paul Muni	*The Story of Louis Pasteur*	1936
10	Spencer Tracy	*Captains Courageous*	1937

THE FIRST 10 TO WIN THE 'BEST ACTRESS' OSCAR

	Actress	Film	Year
1	Janet Gaynor	*Seventh Heaven*	1928
2	Mary Pickford	*Coquette*	1929
3	Norma Shearer	*The Divorcée*	1930
4	Marie Dressler	*Min and Bill*	1931
5	Helen Hayes	*The Sin of Madelon Claudet*	1932
6	Katharine Hepburn	*Morning Glory*	1933
7	Claudette Colbert	*It Happened One Night*	1934
8	Bette Davis	*Dangerous*	1935
9	Luise Rainer	*The Great Ziegfeld*	1936
10	Alice Brady	*In Old Chicago*	1937

LEFT Emil Jannings in *The Last Command*, winner of the first-ever 'Best Actor' Oscar.

BELOW LEFT Norma Shearer receives her 'Best Actress' Oscar, 1930.

THE STORY OF 'OSCAR'

The Hollywood-based Academy of Motion Picture Arts and Sciences, the brain-child of Louis B. Mayer of Metro-Goldwyn-Mayer, was founded on 4 May 1927. One of its aims was to improve the image of the film industry by issuing 'awards for merit or distinction', and under its first president, the actor Douglas Fairbanks Sr, a system of voting and award categories was devised. At the first ceremony, held on 19 May 1929, awards were presented for films released during 1927–28. The award itself takes the form of a 13½-inch statuette designed by Cedric Gibbons and originally modelled and cast in tin and copper by a young artist, George Stanley. The gold-plated naked male figure clutches a sword and stands on a reel of film with five holes, each representing a branch of the Academy. It was simply called 'the statuette' until 1931 when Academy librarian Margaret Herrick commented, 'It looks like Uncle Oscar!' (identified by some authorities as a Texan wheat and fruit grower, Oscar Pierce). The name stuck, but it was used informally until 1934 when Walt Disney referred to it by this name in his acceptance speech (for Best Cartoon, *The Tortoise and the Hare*; Disney was later to become the record-holder for the greatest number of Oscars – 20 statuettes plus 12 other awards). Thereafter 'Oscar' became the award's accepted name, and a universally recognized symbol of excellence in film-making.

THE FIRST 10 TO WIN THE 'BEST PICTURE' OSCAR

	Film	Studio	Year
1	Wings	Paramount	1928
2	The Broadway Melody	MGM	1929
3	All Quiet on the Western Front	Universal	1930
4	Cimarron	RKO Radio	1931
5	Grand Hotel	MGM	1932
6	Cavalcade	Fox	1933
7	It Happened One Night	Columbia	1934
8	Mutiny on the Bounty	MGM	1935
9	The Great Ziegfeld	MGM	1936
10	The Life of Emile Zola	Warner Bros	1937

THE 10 FILMS TO WIN MOST OSCARS

	Film	Year	Awards
1	Ben Hur	1959	11
2=	Gone With the Wind	1939	10
2=	West Side Story	1961	10
4=	Gandhi	1982	9
4=	The Last Emperor	1987	9
6=	Gigi	1958	8
6=	From Here to Eternity	1953	8
6=	On the Waterfront	1954	8
6=	Cabaret	1972	8
6=	Amadeus	1984	8

Six other films have won seven Oscars each: *The Bridge on the River Kwai* (1957), *Lawrence of Arabia* (1962), *My Fair Lady* (1964), *Patton* (1970), *The Sting* (1973) and *Out of Africa* (1985). *All About Eve* (1950) was nominated for 14 awards and won six while *The Turning Point* (1977) had 11 nominations and did not win any.

ABOVE Epic success: *Ben Hur's* tally of 11 Oscar wins has never been beaten.

Katharine Hepburn, nominated for a record 12 Oscars.

THE 10 ACTORS AND ACTRESSES WITH MOST OSCAR NOMINATIONS

Actor/actress/nomination years	Nominations
1 Katharine Hepburn 1932–33*; 1935; 1940; 1942; 1951; 1955; 1956; 1959; 1962; 1967*; 1968*(shared); 1981*	12
2= Bette Davis 1935*; 1938*; 1939; 1940; 1941; 1942; 1944; 1950; 1952; 1962	10
2= Laurence Olivier 1939; 1940; 1946; 1948*; 1956; 1960; 1965; 1972; 1976†; 1978	10
4 Spencer Tracy 1936; 1937*; 1938*; 1950; 1955; 1958; 1960; 1961; 1967	9
5= Geraldine Page 1953†; 1961; 1962; 1966; 1972; 1978; 1984; 1985*	8
5= Jack Lemmon 1955†; 1959; 1960; 1962; 1973*; 1979; 1980; 1982	8
7= Greer Garson 1939; 1941; 1942; 1943; 1944; 1945; 1960	7
7= Ingrid Bergman 1943; 1944*; 1945; 1948; 1956*; 1974†*; 1978	7
7= Marlon Brando 1951; 1952; 1953; 1954*; 1957; 1972*; 1973	7
7= Richard Burton 1952†; 1953; 1964; 1965; 1966; 1969; 1977	7
7= Peter O'Toole 1962; 1964; 1968; 1969; 1972; 1980; 1982	7

*Won Academy Award.
†Nomination for Best Supporting Actor or Actress.

THE 10* STUDIOS WITH MOST 'BEST PICTURE' OSCARS

	Studio	Awards
1	United Artists	13
2	Columbia	12
3	MGM	9
4	Paramount	8
5	Twentieth Century Fox	7
6	Warner Bros	5
7	Universal	4
8=	RKO	2
8=	Orion	2

*In fact, in the 63 years of the Academy Awards, only nine studios have won 'Best Picture' Oscars.

A Bridge Too Far, one of the most successful films in which Michael Caine (left) appeared.

THE TOP 10 MICHAEL CAINE FILMS

	Film	Year
1	California Suite	1978
2	A Bridge Too Far	1977
3	Dirty Rotten Scoundrels	1988
4	Hannah and Her Sisters	1986
5	Dressed to Kill	1980
6	Jaws – The Revenge	1987
7	Blame it on Rio	1984
8	Deathtrap	1982
9	Alfie	1966
10	The Swarm	1978

THE TOP 10 JACK NICHOLSON FILMS

	Film	Year
1	Batman	1989
2	One Flew Over the Cuckoo's Nest	1975
3	Terms of Endearment	1983
4	The Witches of Eastwick	1987
5	The Shining	1980
6	Reds	1981
7	Easy Rider	1969
8	Tommy	1974
9	Carnal Knowledge	1971
10	Prizzi's Honor	1985

THE TOP 10 SEAN CONNERY FILMS

	Film	Year
1	Indiana Jones and the Last Crusade	1989
2	The Hunt for Red October	1990
3	The Untouchables	1987
4	Thunderball	1965
5	Never Say Never Again	1983
6	Goldfinger	1964
7	Time Bandits	1981
8	A Bridge Too Far	1977
9	Diamonds Are Forever	1971
10	You Only Live Twice	1967

THE TOP 10 CLINT EASTWOOD FILMS

	Film	Year
1	Every Which Way But Loose	1978
2	Any Which Way You Can	1980
3	Sudden Impact	1983
4	Firefox	1982
5	The Enforcer	1976
6	Tightrope	1984
7	Heartbreak Ridge	1986
8	Escape from Alcatraz	1979
9	City Heat	1984
10	Pale Rider	1985

THE TOP 10 HARRISON FORD FILMS

	Film	Year
1	Star Wars	1977
2	Return of the Jedi	1983
3	The Empire Strikes Back	1980
4	Raiders of the Lost Ark	1981
5	Indiana Jones and the Last Crusade	1989
6	Indiana Jones and the Temple of Doom	1984
7	American Graffiti	1973
8	Presumed Innocent	1990
9	Apocalypse Now	1979
10	Witness	1985

LEFT Monkey business is good business: Clint Eastwood and co-star in *Every Which Way But Loose*.

ABOVE *Indiana Jones and the Last Crusade*, Sean Connery's top and Harrison Ford's fifth most successful film.

THE 10 MOST EXPENSIVE FILMS EVER MADE*

	Film	Year	Production cost ($)
1	Total Recall	1990	85,000,000
2=	Die Hard 2	1990	70,000,000
2=	Who Framed Roger Rabbit?	1988	70,000,000
4	The Godfather Part III	1990	65,000,000
5	Rambo III	1988	58,000,000
6=	Superman	1978	55,000,000
6=	Ishtar	1987	55,000,000
6=	Tango and Cash	1989	55,000,000
6=	Days of Thunder	1990	55,000,000
10	Superman II	1981	54,000,000

*To end of 1990.

Although four films made in 1990 are new to this list since last year, there are indications that Hollywood's appetite for mega-budget movies may have been sated for a while, in which case the listing could remain stable for the next few years.

How much?! *Total Recall* is the most expensive film of all time.

THE 10 BIGGEST FILM FLOPS OF ALL TIME

	Film	Year	Loss ($)
1	The Adventures of Baron Munchausen	1988	48,100,000
2	Ishtar	1987	47,300,000
3	Inchon	1981	44,100,000
4	The Cotton Club	1984	38,100,000
5	Santa Claus – The Movie	1985	37,000,000
6	Heaven's Gate	1980	34,200,000
7	Pirates	1986	30,300,000
8	Rambo III	1988	30,000,000
9	Raise the Titanic	1980	29,200,000
10	Lion of the Desert	1981	28,500,000

Based on North American (USA and Canada) rental receipts balanced against production cost. *Baron Munchausen* emerges as the all-time greatest flop, although it and other major loss-making films are slowly recovering some of their deficits through worldwide distribution, video and television showings – with the exception of *Inchon*. Financed by the Moonies religious sect, it portrays Laurence Olivier as General MacArthur receiving divine guidance during the Korean War, and was described by Jack Kroll of *Newsweek* as 'The worst film ever made, a turkey the size of Godzilla'.

QUIZ

BRITISH FILM STARS

Identify the following British-born Hollywood film stars:

1 The star of *The Great Dictator*.
2 Co-star of several 'Road' films (*Road to Morocco*, etc).
3 The chief villain in *Marathon Man*.
4 Indiana Jones's father in *Indiana Jones and the Last Crusade*.
5 Took the title role in *Mary Poppins*.
6 Took the title role in *Arthur*.
7 The dinosaur expert in *Bringing up Baby*.
8 The 'I' of the film *The King and I*.
9 Title-role star of the unfinished film *I, Claudius*.
10 The author of *The Moon's a Balloon*.

THE 10 ALL-TIME FILM RENTAL BLOCKBUSTERS

	Film	Year	Total rental ($)
1	E.T.	1982	228,600,000
2	Star Wars	1977	193,500,000
3	Return of the Jedi	1983	168,000,000
4	Batman	1989	150,500,000
5	The Empire Strikes Back	1980	141,500,000
6	Ghostbusters	1984	132,000,000
7	Jaws	1975	129,500,000
8	Raiders of the Lost Ark	1981	115,600,000
9	Indiana Jones and the Last Crusade	1989	115,500,000
10	Indiana Jones and the Temple of Doom	1984	109,000,000

Since many of the most recently released films are also among the highest earners, this list is almost identical to The Top 10 Films Released in the 1980s, with the exception of *Star Wars* and *Jaws*, the two most successful films of the 1970s that have also earned a place in the all-time list.

Two men, Steven Spielberg (born 1946) and George Lucas (born 1945), continue to dominate this list. Steven Spielberg directed Nos. 1, 7, 8, 9 and 10 and co-produced 1, and George Lucas directed No. 2 and co-produced 3, 5, 8, 9 and 10. The actor Harrison Ford (born 1942) also appeared in all of the Lucas films (*see* separate list for The Top 10 Harrison Ford Films).

Hard on the heels of these films are *Beverly Hills Cop* and *Back to the Future*, the only other films that have earned more than $100,000,000 in rentals. *Ghost*, *Pretty Woman* and *Home Alone*, all of which were released in 1990, had each earned more than $80,000,000 before the end of the year, making them strong contenders for future appearance in this list.

ABOVE *Ghost* was the No. 1 1990 box office hit in the UK.

ABOVE RIGHT *Return of the Jedi*, the third most successful film ever made.

THE TOP 10 FILMS AT THE UK BOX OFFICE IN 1990

	Film	Box office gross (£)
1	Ghost	17,269,748
2	Pretty Woman	11,990,862
3	Look Who's Talking	10,117,000
4	Honey, I Shrunk the Kids	9,395,091
5	Total Recall	8,508,181
6	Ghostbusters II	8,301,000
7	Back to the Future, Part III	7,996,334
8	Gremlins 2: The New Batch	7,419,354
9	Back to the Future, Part II	7,252,133
10	Shirley Valentine	6,417,864

THE 10 MOST SUCCESSFUL CHILDREN'S FILMS* OF ALL TIME

	Film	Year
1	Honey, I Shrunk the Kids	1989
2	Teenage Mutant Ninja Turtles	1990
3	The Karate Kid Part II	1986
4	Mary Poppins	1964
5	The Karate Kid	1984
6	WarGames	1983
7	The Muppet Movie	1979
8	The Goonies	1985
9	Willow	1988
10	The Bad News Bears	1976

*Excluding animated films.

The two *Beverly Hills Cop* films are regarded by some authorities as 'action thrillers' rather than comedies. If they are excluded, Nos. 9 and 10 become *Look Who's Talking* (1989) and *Coming to America* (1988). If the two newcomers, *Ghost* and *Pretty Woman* (both released in 1990 and arguably either comedies or romances with comedy elements), are also excluded, the next two on this list are *Nine to Five* (1980) and *Smokey and the Bandit* (1977) – followed very closely by *Stir Crazy* (1980) and *Crocodile Dundee II* (1988). All these films are high earners, each having made more than $55,000,000 in North American rentals alone.

THE 10 MOST SUCCESSFUL COMEDY FILMS OF ALL TIME

	Film	Year
1	Beverly Hills Cop	1984
2	Tootsie	1982
3	Ghost	1990
4	Pretty Woman	1990
5	Three Men and a Baby	1987
6	Beverly Hills Cop II	1987
7	Home Alone	1990
8	The Sting	1973
9	National Lampoon's Animal House	1978
10	Crocodile Dundee	1986

THE 10 MOST SUCCESSFUL HORROR FILMS OF ALL TIME

	Film	Year
1	The Exorcist	1973
2	Poltergeist	1982
3	King Kong	1976
4	The Amityville Horror	1979
5	Arachnophobia	1990
6	Predator	1987
7	The Shining	1980
8	The Abyss	1988
9	The Omen	1976
10	Pet Sematary	1989

THE 10 LEAST DISASTROUS DISASTER FILMS OF ALL TIME

	Film	Year
1	The Towering Inferno	1975
2	Airport	1970
3	The Poseidon Adventure	1972
4	Earthquake	1974
5	Airport 1975	1974
6	Airport '77	1977
7	The Hindenburg	1975
8	Black Sunday	1977
9	Rollercoaster	1977
10	Two-Minute Warning	1976

THE 10 MOST SUCCESSFUL WESTERNS OF ALL TIME

	Film	Year
1	Butch Cassidy and the Sundance Kid	1969
2	Jeremiah Johnson	1972
3	How the West Was Won	1962
4	Pale Rider	1985
5	Young Guns	1988
6	Young Guns II	1990
7=	Little Big Man	1970
7=	Bronco Billy	1980
9	True Grit	1969
10	The Outlaw Josey Wales	1976

THE 10 MOST SUCCESSFUL WAR FILMS OF ALL TIME

	Film	Year
1	Platoon	1986
2	Good Morning, Vietnam	1987
3	Apocalypse Now	1979
4	M*A*S*H	1970
5	Patton	1970
6	The Deer Hunter	1978
7	Full Metal Jacket	1987
8	Midway	1976
9	The Dirty Dozen	1967
10	A Bridge Too Far	1977

LEFT Dustin Hoffman (in drag), with Jessica Lange, stars of comedy classic *Tootsie*.

OPPOSITE TOP Well, what *do* you say to a naked lady? Allen Funt's 1971 production is the seventh most successful performance and documentary film of all time.

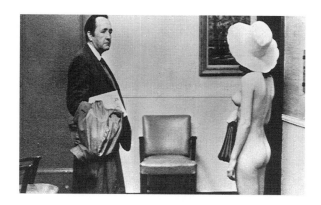

THE TOP 10 PERFORMANCE AND DOCUMENTARY FILMS OF ALL TIME

	Film	Year
1	Eddie Murphy Raw	1987
2	Richard Pryor Live on the Sunset Strip	1982
3	Woodstock	1970
4	Richard Pryor Here and Now	1983
5	Richard Pryor Live in Concert	1979
6	The Song Remains the Same	1976
7	What Do You Say to a Naked Lady?	1971
8	Dirt	1979
9	U2 Rattle and Hum	1988
10	Stop Making Sense	1984

In addition to those in the Top 10, further successful films in this category include those of rock concerts by such groups as Abba, the Rolling Stones and Pink Floyd, the comedy revue *The Secret Policeman's Other Ball* and documentaries on subjects as diverse as sharks (*Blue Water, White Death*) and bodybuilding (*Pumping Iron*).

THE 10 MOST SUCCESSFUL MUSICAL FILMS OF ALL TIME

	Film	Year
1	Grease	1978
2	The Sound of Music	1965
3	Saturday Night Fever	1977
4	American Graffiti	1973
5	The Best Little Whorehouse in Texas	1982
6	Mary Poppins	1964
7	Fiddler on the Roof	1971
8	Annie	1982
9	A Star is Born	1976
10	Flashdance	1983

Traditional musicals (films in which the cast actually sing) and films in which a musical soundtrack is a major component of the film are included. Several other musical films have also each earned in excess of $30,000,000 in North American rentals, among them *Coalminer's Daughter* (1980), *The Rocky Horror Picture Show* (1975), *Footloose* (1984), *The Blues Brothers* (1980) and *Purple Rain* (1984), but it would appear that the era of the blockbuster musical film is over.

THE 10 MOST SUCCESSFUL ANIMATED FILMS OF ALL TIME

	Film	Year
1	Who Framed Roger Rabbit?	1988
2	Snow White and the Seven Dwarfs	1937
3	Jungle Book	1967
4	Bambi	1942
5	Fantasia	1940
6	Cinderella	1949
7	Lady and the Tramp	1955
8	The Little Mermaid	1989
9	One Hundred and One Dalmatians	1961
10	Pinocchio	1940

All except No. 1 (which is part animation, part live action) and No. 8 were made by the Disney studio.

Martin Sheen in *Apocalypse Now*, one of the Top 10 war films.

THE 10 MOST SUCCESSFUL SCIENCE-FICTION AND FANTASY FILMS OF ALL TIME

	Film	Year
1	E.T.	1982
2	Star Wars	1977
3	Return of the Jedi	1983
4	Batman	1989
5	The Empire Strikes Back	1980
6	Ghostbusters	1984
7	Back to the Future	1985
8	Ghost	1990
9	Superman	1978
10	Close Encounters of the Third Kind	1977/80

Reflecting our taste for escapist fantasy adventures, the first six in this list also appear in the All-Time Top 10, and all 10 are among the 27 most successful films of all time. Five further contenders just outside the Top 10 also achieved North American rentals in excess of $60,000,000: *Gremlins*, *Honey, I Shrunk the Kids*, *Back to the Future, Part II*, *Total Recall* and *Ghostbusters II*.

THE FIRST 10 'CARRY ON' FILMS

	Film	Year
1	*Carry On Sergeant*	1958
2	*Carry On Nurse*	1959
3	*Carry On Teacher*	1959
4	*Carry On Constable*	1960
5	*Carry On Regardless*	1960
6	*Carry On Cruising*	1962
7	*Carry On Cabby*	1963
8	*Carry On Jack*	1964
9	*Carry On Spying*	1964
10	*Carry On Cleo*	1964

This hugely successful series of British comedy films spanned 20 years. The first 10 were followed by *Carry On Cowboy, Carry On Screaming, Carry On – Don't Lose Your Head, Carry On – Follow That Camel, Carry On Doctor, Carry On Up the Khyber, Carry On Again Doctor, Carry On Camping, Carry On Up the Jungle, Carry On Loving, Carry On Henry, Carry On at Your Convenience, Carry On Abroad, Carry On Matron, Carry On Girls, Carry On Dick, Carry On Behind, Carry On England* and *Carry On Emanuelle*, the last of the series released in 1978.

THE 10 MOST EXPENSIVE ITEMS OF FILM MEMORABILIA SOLD AT AUCTION

	Item	Price (£)*
1	James Bond's Aston Martin from *Goldfinger* Sotheby's, New York, 28 June 1986 ($275,000)	179,793
2	Herman J. Mankiewicz's scripts for *Citizen Kane* and *The American* Christie's, New York, 21 June 1989 ($231,000)	139,157
3	Judy Garland's ruby slippers from *The Wizard of Oz* Christie's, New York, 21 June 1988 ($165,000)	104,430
4	Piano from the Paris scene in *Casablanca* Sotheby's, New York, 16 December 1988 ($154,000)	97,469
5	Charlie Chaplin's hat and cane Christie's, London, 11 December 1987	82,500
6	Clark Gable's script from *Gone With the Wind* Sotheby's, New York, 16 December 1988 ($77,000)	48,734
7	Charlie Chaplin's boots Christie's, London, 11 December 1987	38,500
8	A special effects painting of the Emerald City from *The Wizard of Oz* Camden House, Los Angeles, 1 April 1991 ($44,000)	29,944
9	16-mm film of the only meeting between Danny Kaye and George Bernard Shaw Christie's, London, 27 April 1989	20,900
10	The Witch's hat from *The Wizard of Oz* Sotheby's, New York, 16 December 1988 ($33,000)	20,886

*$/£ conversion at rate then prevailing.

If memorabilia relating to film stars rather than films is included, Orson Welles' annotated script from the radio production of *The War of the Worlds* ($143,000/£90,500 in 1988) would qualify for the Top 10, while among near-misses are Marilyn Monroe's 'shimmy' dress from *Some Like it Hot*, sold at Christie's, London, on 5 May 1988 for £19,800, and the stand-in model of Boris Karloff as Frankenstein's monster from the 1935 film *The Bride of Frankenstein* (£16,500 in 1988).

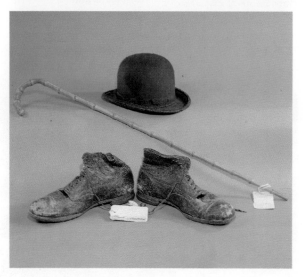

LEFT Expensive outfit: Charlie Chaplin's hat, cane and boots fetched a total of £121,000.

ABOVE LEFT An arresting scene from *Carry On Constable*, one of the long-running 'Carry On' series.

RADIO, TV & VIDEO

THE 10 LONGEST-RUNNING PROGRAMMES ON BBC RADIO

	Programme	First broadcast
1	*The Week's Good Cause*	24 January 1926
2	*Choral Evensong*	7 October 1926
3	*Daily Service*	2 January 1928*
4	*The Week in Westminster*	6 November 1929
5	*Sunday Half Hour*	14 July 1940
6	*Desert Island Discs*	29 January 1942
7	*Saturday Night Theatre*	3 April 1943
8	*This Week's Composer*	2 August 1943
9	*Letter From America* (originally *American Letter*)	24 March 1946
10	*From Our Own Correspondent*	4 October 1946

Experimental broadcast; national transmission began December 1929.

In addition to these 10 long-running programmes, a further six that started in the 1950s are still on the air: *Woman's Hour* (first broadcast 7 October 1946), *Down Your Way* (29 December 1946), *Round Britain Quiz* (2 November 1947), *Any Questions?* (12 October 1948), *Book at Bedtime* (6 August 1949) and *Morning Story* (17 October 1949). A pilot for *The Archers* was broadcast in 1950, but the serial began its run on 1 January 1951.

THE TOP 10 BBC 1 AUDIENCES, 1990

	Programme	Day	Date	Audience
1	*Neighbours*	Mon	26 February	21,160,000
2	*EastEnders*	Thu	4 January	20,300,000
3	*Only Fools and Horses*	Tue	25 December	17,970,000
4	Film: *E.T.*	Tue	25 December	17,500,000
5	*Christmas Generation Game*	Tue	25 December	16,730,000
6	World Cup Semi-Final	Wed	4 July	16,690,000
7	*Bergerac*	Sun	4 February	14,250,000
8	*'Allo 'Allo*	Mon	22 October	14,240,000
9	*Antiques Roadshow*	Sun	4 March	14,070,000
10	Film: *Appointment With Death*	Sun	30 December	13,920,000

QUIZ
RADIO

1   In what year were radio programmes first broadcast regularly in the USA and UK – 1920, 1925 or 1930?

2   What 1938 radio broadcast by Orson Welles terrified its audience into believing that Martians had landed?

3   What were Radio 2, 3 and 4 called before 1967?

4   Who played the parts of Neddie Seagoon, Major Bloodnok and Eccles in *The Goon Show*?

5   In what year did the pirate radio station Radio Caroline begin broadcasting – 1960, 1964 or 1968?

6   What radio series is subtitled 'An everyday story of country-folk'?

7   In what year was the *Radio Times* first published?

8   What was the popular nickname of the Second World War pro-Nazi radio propagandist William Joyce?

9   Who was the first British monarch to speak on the radio?

10   On 30 September 1967 disc jockey Tony Blackburn played the first record on BBC Radio 1. Was it Engelbert Humperdinck's *The Last Waltz*, Scott McKenzie's *San Francisco* or the Move's *Flowers in the Rain*?

ABOVE Rita Tushingham performs in a 1974 *Saturday Night Theatre*, one of the BBC's longest-running radio programmes.

OPPOSITE LEFT *Only Fools and Horses*, BBC1's 1990 Christmas hit.

THE TOP 10 BBC 2 AUDIENCES, 1990

	Programme	Day	Date	Audience
1	World Cup Grandstand	Tue	12 June	8,910,000
2	Film: *Handgun*	Mon	5 December	8,600,000
3	*Twin Peaks*	Tue Sat	23 October/ 27 October	8,150,000*
4	Film: *Right to Kill*	Mon	19 February	8,080,000
5	Wimbledon Men's Final	Sun	8 July	7,760,000
6	World Championship Snooker Final	Sun	29 April	7,550,000
7	Film: *Assault on Precinct 13*	Sun	6 May	6,690,000
8	Film: *Mosquito Coast*	Sun	7 January	6,660,000
9	Film: *Terminator*	Sun	24 June	6,300,000
10	*Close Relations*	Sun	4 February	5,900,000

Aggregates two screenings of the same programme.

ABOVE Central TV's *Inspector Morse* achieved two entries in ITV's Top 10 audiences of 1990.

TOP The 12 June World Cup Grandstand attracted BBC 2's largest audience of 1990.

THE TOP 10 ITV AUDIENCES, 1990

	Programme	Day	Date	Audience
1	*Coronation Street*	Mon	1 January	22,830,000
2	*It'll Be Alright on the Night*	Sun	2 December	17,920,000
3	Film: *View to a Kill*	Wed	31 January	16,930,000
4	*Inspector Morse*	Wed	24 January	16,160,000
5	ITV World Cup	Mon	11 June	15,960,000
6	Film: *Octopussy*	Sat	20 January	15,860,000
7	*Blind Date*	Sat	3 February	15,800,000
8	*This Is Your Life*	Wed	10 January	15,650,000
9	*Inspector Morse*	Wed	17 January	15,600,000
10	*Blind Date*	Sat	27 January	15,540,000

THE TOP 10 CHANNEL 4 AUDIENCES, 1990

	Programme	Day	Date	Audience
1	*Wish You Were Here*	Thu	15 February	6,670,000
2	*Castaway*	Mon	26 November	6,630,000
3	*Rita, Sue and Bob Too*	Thu	10 May	5,760,000
4	*Inspector Morse*	Thu	11 October	5,600,000
5	*Cosby Show*	Sun	28 October	5,220,000
6	*Land of the Giants*	Sun	4 February	5,070,000
7	*Golden Girls*	Fri	31 August	5,060,000
8	*Roseanne*	Fri	20 July	5,030,000
9	*Desmonds*	Mon	26 February	4,980,000
10	*Brookside*	Wed	11 April	4,580,000

THE TOP 10 BBC 1 AUDIENCES, 1981–90

	Programme	Date	Audience
1	*EastEnders*	25/28 December 1986	30,100,000*
2	Film: *Crocodile Dundee*	25 December 1989	21,770,000
3	*Neighbours*	26 February 1990	21,160,000
4	*Bread*	11 December 1988	21,000,000
5	*Just Good Friends*	25 December 1986	20,800,000
6	*Royal Variety Performance*	25 November 1984	20,550,000
7	*Only Fools and Horses*	25 December 1989	20,120,000
8	*Porridge*	27 December 1984	19,350,000
9	*A Question of Sport*	5 February 1987	19,050,000
10=	Film: *Indiana Jones and the Temple of Doom*	25 December 1987	18,950,000
10=	*Open All Hours*	6 October 1986	18,950,000

Aggregates two screenings of the same programme. This is EastEnders' highest audience figure, but the programme has also achieved audiences of over 20,000,000 on many occasions.

The method of evaluating BBC audiences came into effect in August 1981. These lists encompass programmes since then and up to December 1990.

THE TOP 10 BBC 2 AUDIENCES, 1981–90

	Programme	Date	Audience
1	World Championship Snooker Final	18 April 1985	14,400,000
2	*Fawlty Towers*	10 November 1985	12,750,000
3	*Cliff!*	23 November 1981	12,200,000
4=	Wimbledon Men's Final	7 July 1985	11,900,000
4=	*Des O'Connor Tonight*	16 November 1981	11,900,000
6	*The Two Ronnies*	18 August 1985	11,700,000
7	*Blott on the Landscape*	6/9 February 1985	11,500,000*
8	*Lame Ducks*	22 October 1984	11,000,000
9=	International Snooker	31 January 1982	10,900,000
9=	*Dave Allen*	12 January 1987	10,900,000

Aggregates two screenings of the same programme.

ABOVE RIGHT Christopher Trace and Valerie Singleton, with Petra the dog and Jason the cat, in a 1966 edition of the long-running *Blue Peter*.

THE 10 LONGEST-RUNNING PROGRAMMES ON BRITISH TELEVISION

	Programme	Channel	First shown
1	*Come Dancing*	BBC	29 September 1950
2	*Panorama*	BBC	11 November 1953
3	*This Week*	ITV	6 January 1956
4	*What the Papers Say*	ITV	5 November 1956
5	*The Sky at Night*	BBC	24 April 1957
6	*Grandstand*	BBC	11 October 1958
7	*Blue Peter*	BBC	16 October 1958
8	*Coronation Street*	ITV	9 December 1960
9	*Songs of Praise*	BBC	1 October 1961
10	*Dr Who*	BBC	23 November 1963

Only programmes appearing every year since their first screenings are listed. Several other BBC programmes, such as *The Good Old Days* (1953–83), ran for many years but are now defunct. *The Sky at Night* has the additional distinction of having had the same presenter, Patrick Moore, since its first programme. Although *The Sooty Show* has been screened intermittently, Sooty is the longest-serving TV personality. The puppet's show, started by Harry Corbett in 1952, was transferred to Thames in 1968 where it has been presented since 1975 by its creator's son, Matthew Corbett. *This Is Your Life* was started by the BBC in 1953 and, after a break, was taken over by Thames in 1973. ITV has also presented a number of long-running programmes that are no longer with us, among them *Opportunity Knocks* (1956–77), *University Challenge* (1962–87) and *Crossroads* (1964–88).

THE 10 BESTSELLING BBC TV PROGRAMMES

	Programme	Countries
1	*The Living Planet*	74
2	*Flight of the Condor*	73
3=	*The Six Wives of Henry VIII*	66
3=	*Animal Olympians*	66
5=	*Ascent of Man*	62
5=	*The Impossible Bird*	62
7	*The Onedin Line* (first series)	61
8=	*Civilisation*	59
8=	*Fawlty Towers* (first series)	59
8=	*War and Peace*	59
8=	*Tender is the Night*	59
8=	*Supersense*	59

BBC Enterprises is responsible for selling BBC TV programmes to TV stations around the world. Although drama, comedy, documentary and educational programmes all feature strongly among their bestsellers, as the list of the Top 10 suggests, the international appeal of high quality natural history programmes makes them particularly saleable overseas. *Rhino Rescue* and *At Home with Badgers* have also been sold in more than 50 countries, while within the year of its first screening in 1990, David Attenborough's *The Trials of Life* had already been sold in 12 countries, as had *Land of the Eagle*.

THE 10 COUNTRIES WITH MOST TVs

	Country	Households with TV
1	USSR	94,000,000
2	USA	91,500,000
3	China	85,000,000
4	Japan	38,600,000
5	Brazil	38,500,000
6	Germany	31,180,000
7	UK	21,375,000
8	France	20,102,000
9=	Indonesia	20,000,000
9=	Italy	20,000,000
	World total	658,453,000

According to research conducted by *Screen Digest*, of the world total of TVs 140,286,000 are in Western Europe, 119,139,000 in Eastern Europe, 107,315,000 in Asia, 101,718,000 in North America, 81,670,000 in the Far East, 60,525,000 in South America, 16,375,000 in Africa, 15,461,000 in Central America, 9,784,000 in the Middle East and 6,180,000 in Australasia.

BELOW LEFT *Fawlty Towers* is one of the BBC's most internationally exported TV programmes of all time.

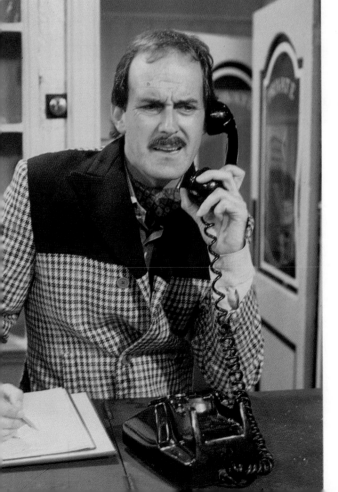

THE 10 COUNTRIES WITH MOST VCRs

	Country	As % of homes with TV	VCRs
1	USA	67.5	61,740,000
2	Japan	67.8	26,169,000
3	Germany	51.4	16,024,000
4	UK	67.0	14,324,000
5	France	46.6	9,372,000
6	Canada	71.4	6,639,000
7	Brazil	13.5	5,195,000
8	Italy	25.7	5,138,000
9	Spain	44.9	4,485,000
10	Australia	69.8	3,583,000
	World total	31.3	206,061,000

In 1990 *Screen Digest* published data revealing that there are eight countries in the world where more than two-thirds of homes with TVs also have video cassette recorders – Nos. 1, 2, 4, 6 and 10 in the Top 10, plus Bahrein, Bermuda and Kuwait (which, prior to the invasion by Iraq in August 1990, had VCRs in 87.2 per cent of TV households, the world's highest proportion). Western Europe has 65,666,000 VCRs (46.8 per cent of TV households) compared with North America's 68,760,000 (67.6 per cent). The percentage is much smaller in certain countries – 2.2 per cent in the USSR and 1.4 in China.

THE WORLD'S TOP 10 VIDEO CONSUMERS

	Country	Spending per video household (US$)		
		rental	purchase	total*
1	Norway	174.11	1.18	175.28
2	Australia	164.13	10.61	174.74
3	USA	125.53	48.59	174.12
4	Iceland	149.02	21.29	170.30
5	Canada	128.80	27.05	155.85
6	Japan	83.08	63.24	146.32
7	Sweden	102.77	18.14	120.90
8	New Zealand	96.58	12.88	109.45
9	UK	66.32	38.40	104.72
10	Ireland	77.57	22.30	99.88

*May not precisely equal rental plus purchase figures due to rounding-off.

Based on figures prepared by *Screen Digest* for 1990 (except Canada, which are for 1989). Total spending per *head* of population, rather than per *household* with video, produces a somewhat different picture:

	Country	Total (US$)
1	USA	43.43
2	Canada	37.59
3	Australia	37.35
4	Norway	35.31
5	Iceland	31.87
6	Japan	31.08
7	UK	26.23
8	Sweden	23.68
9	New Zealand	20.48
10	Denmark	14.59

ABOVE RIGHT *Lethal Weapon 2*, the most rented video of 1990 in the UK.

RIGHT *Pretty Woman*, a bestselling and much rented video.

THE 10 MOST-RENTED VIDEOS OF ALL TIME IN THE UK*

1 *Crocodile Dundee*

2 *Dirty Dancing*

3 *A Fish Called Wanda*

4 *Robocop*

5 *Back to the Future*

6 *Police Academy*

7 *Beverly Hills Cop*

8 *Lethal Weapon*

9 *E.T.*

10 *Three Men and a Baby*

*To 28 February 1991.

THE TOP 10 VIDEO RENTALS OF 1990 IN THE UK

1 *Lethal Weapon 2*

2 *Pretty Woman*

3 *Indiana Jones and the Last Crusade*

4 *The Naked Gun*

5 *Turner and Hooch*

6 *Tango and Cash*

7 *Road House*

8 *See No Evil, Hear No Evil*

9 *K-9*

10 *Honey, I Shrunk the Kids*

THE 10 BESTSELLING VIDEOS OF ALL TIME IN THE UK

1 *Lady and the Tramp*

2 *Dirty Dancing*

3 *Pretty Woman*

4 *Callanetics*

5 *Watch With Mother*

6 *Sleeping Beauty*

7 *Jane Fonda's New Workout*

8 *Pinocchio*

9 *Crocodile Dundee*

10 *The Videos* (Kylie Minogue)

The under-£10 video sales market has boomed in the UK from a business worth some £15,000,000 in 1985 to more than £300,000,000 by 1990. Walt Disney's *Lady and the Tramp* sold over 1,700,000 copies in the UK between its release on 1 October 1990 and withdrawal from the market on 28 February 1991. *Dirty Dancing* and *Pretty Woman* have both sold over 1,000,000 copies.

THE 10 BESTSELLING CHILDREN'S VIDEOS OF ALL TIME IN THE UK

1 *Lady and the Tramp*

2 *Watch With Mother*

3 *Sleeping Beauty*

4 *Pinocchio*

5 *Teenage Mutant Hero Turtles: How it All Began*

6 *Thomas the Tank Engine: The Deputation*

7 *Postman Pat 1*

8 *Rupert and the Frog Song*

9 *Teenage Mutant Hero Turtles: Case of the Killer Pizzas*

10 *Robin Hood*

Four of the Top 10 are Walt Disney cartoon animations. As with the company's cinema release policy, the videos were available for a limited period and will not be released again for several years, when they will reappear for the next 'Disney generation'. It seems likely that the hugely successful BBC *Watch With Mother* video, containing vintage episodes of *Bill and Ben*, *The Woodentops* and other favourites from the 1950s, was bought more by and for nostalgic adults than their offspring.

THE 10 BESTSELLING FOOTBALL VIDEOS OF ALL TIME IN THE UK

1 *Arsenal: Official Review of Division One Game by Game, 1988–89*

2 *Liverpool FC: The Mighty Reds*

3 *Italia '90: Gascoigne's Glory*

4 *Genius: The George Best Story*

5 *Gazza: The Real Me*

6 *Liverpool: Team of the Decade*

7 *Liverpool: Official Review of Division One Game by Game, 1989–90*

8 *Gunning for Glory: Arsenal League Champions, 1988–89*

9 *25 Years of Match of the Day: The 60s*

10 *Italia '90: England's World Cup Heroes*

In recent years, soccer has become the largest slice of the sports video sale market in the UK, dominated by the major teams and leading personalities.

THE 10 BESTSELLING AEROBICS AND KEEP-FIT VIDEOS OF ALL TIME IN THE UK

1 *Callanetics*

2 *Jane Fonda's New Workout*

3 *Beginning Callanetics*

4 *Lizzie Webb's Body Programme*

5 *Seven Pounds in Seven Days*

6 *The Y Plan*

7 *Super Callanetics*

8 *3 Stages to Fitness with Lizzie Webb*

9 *Jane Fonda's Low Impact Workout*

10 *Rosemary Conley's Whole Body Programme*

Keep fit is now a major area in the video market, most programmes being aimed at women. *Callanetics*, said to have worked for the Duchess of York, is the fourth bestselling video of all time in the UK and its sequels clearly benefited from its exceptional success.

THE 10 MOST-RENTED COMEDY VIDEOS OF ALL TIME IN THE UK

1 *Crocodile Dundee*

2 *A Fish Called Wanda*

3 *Police Academy*

4 *Beverly Hills Cop*

5 *Three Men and a Baby*

6 *Twins*

7 *Pretty Woman*

8 *Beverly Hills Cop II*

9 *The Naked Gun*

10 *Coming to America*

This category poses problems of definition: are the *Beverly Hills Cop* films comedies or 'action thrillers' containing comedy elements? We have included them here (and in The 10 Most Successful Comedy Films of All Time), but if they are excluded, the next two on the list are *Porky's* and *See No Evil, Hear No Evil*, and if *Three Men and a Baby* and *Pretty Woman* are discounted as 'romances', the next two become *Honey, I Shrunk the Kids* and *Look Who's Talking*.

Bill and Ben and Little Weed feature in the bestselling *Watch With Mother* video.

Robocop, the UK's all-time most-rented science-fiction video.

Making Michael Jackson's 'Thriller' was the first music video to sell in large numbers, and continues to achieve volume sales years after its release. Most of the other Top 10 bestsellers date from 1988–89 and reflect the huge expansion of the video sales market during those years. The appearance of a classical concert at No. 3 indicates the widening boundaries of the music video field.

THE 10 BESTSELLING MUSIC VIDEOS OF ALL TIME IN THE UK

	Title	Artist
1	The Videos	Kylie Minogue
2	Making Michael Jackson's 'Thriller'	Michael Jackson
3	The Three Tenors Concert	Pavarotti, Domingo, Carreras
4	The Immaculate Collection	Madonna
5	Rattle and Hum	U2
6	Hangin' Tough Live	New Kids on the Block
7	The Legend Continues	Michael Jackson
8	Private Collection	Cliff Richard
9	The Videos, Vol.2	Kylie Minogue
10	The Singles Collection	Phil Collins

THE 10 MOST-RENTED SCIENCE-FICTION VIDEOS OF ALL TIME IN THE UK

1	Robocop
2	Back to the Future
3	E.T.
4	Aliens
5	The Terminator
6	Return of the Jedi
7	Inner Space
8	Back to the Future, Part II
9	Mad Max – Beyond Thunderdome
10	Cocoon

Since *E.T.* was viewed by so many people on illegal pirate videos in the years before its release, it should top this list. However, along with other lists, the rankings are based on legal rentals only.

THE 10 BESTSELLING MUSICALS ON VIDEO IN THE UK

	Film	Year film released
1	Dirty Dancing	1987
2	The Blues Brothers	1980
3	The Sound of Music	1965
4	Grease	1978
5	Mary Poppins	1964
6	The King and I	1956
7	South Pacific	1958
8	The Wizard of Oz	1939
9	Annie	1982
10	Saturday Night Fever	1977

Musicals (*Dirty Dancing* excepted) have never been important to the video rental business in the UK, but with the establishment of the low-price sales market, they have recently achieved consistent success, owing much to the 'repeatability factor' of their high song content.

THE 10 MOST-RENTED HORROR VIDEOS OF ALL TIME IN THE UK

1	The Evil Dead
2	Poltergeist
3	A Nightmare on Elm Street
4	The Fly
5	A Nightmare on Elm Street 2: Freddy's Revenge
6	Poltergeist 2
7	The Entity
8	The Thing
9	Christine
10	An American Werewolf in London

Sam Raimi's low-budget horror movie *The Evil Dead* was the most popular rental title of 1983, despite attempts through the courts to ban its distribution on the basis of its being a 'video nasty'.

THE 10 MOST-RENTED VIETNAM VIDEOS OF ALL TIME IN THE UK

1	Good Morning, Vietnam
2	Rambo: First Blood 2
3	Full Metal Jacket
4	Platoon
5	Born on the Fourth of July
6	The Deer Hunter
7	Hamburger Hill
8	Bat 21
9	Uncommon Valour
10	Casualties of War

Perhaps the oddest aspect of this list is that only the top film actually contains the word 'Vietnam' in its title – an apparent taboo which would also apply if the list were extended to a Top 20 (with the marginal exception of the video of the Australian mini-series, *Nam*).

INDUSTRY, COMMERCE & COMMUNICATIONS

THE TOP 10 RETAILERS IN THE UK

	Retailer	Annual sales (£)*
1	J. Sainsbury	5,932,000,000
2	Tesco	5,402,000,000
3	Marks & Spencer	4,725,000,000
4	Argyll Group	3,920,000,000
5	Asda Group	3,519,000,000
6	The Boots Company	3,002,000,000
7	Kingfisher	2,910,000,000
8	Isosceles	2,370,000,000
9	John Lewis Partnership	1,873,000,000
10	Sears	1,820,000,000

*1989–90, excluding VAT.

Based on The Retail Rankings (1991) published by The Corporate Intelligence Group Ltd.

THE 10 RETAILERS WITH THE MOST OUTLETS IN THE UK

	Retailer	Outlets*
1	Sears (including Selfridges, Freeman Hardy & Willis, Dolcis, Fosters, Adams, Olympus, etc)	3,668
2	Burton Group (including Top Shop, Dorothy Perkins, Debenhams, Principles, Evans, etc)	2,465
3	The Boots Company (including Halfords, Fads, etc)	2,378
4	Kingfisher (including Woolworths, Comet, Superdrug, B & Q, etc)	2,173
5	Gallaher (including Dollond & Aitchison, Forbuoys, NSS, Tobacco Kiosks, etc)	2,145
6	Thorn EMI (including Rumbelows, HMV, DER, Radio Rentals, etc)	1,639
7	Dixons (including Currys, Supasnaps, etc)	1,263
8	Dewhurst butchers	1,250
9	Ratners (including H. Samuel, Ernest Jones, Salisburys, Watches of Switzerland, etc)	1,150
10	Argyll Group (including Safeway, Presto, Lo-Cost, Liquorsave, etc)	1,134

*Includes concessions (shops within stores, etc).

Based on The Retail Rankings (1991) published by The Corporate Intelligence Group Ltd.

THE TOP 10 SUPERMARKET GROUPS* IN THE UK

	Group	Annual sales (£)**
1	J. Sainsbury	5,415,000,000†
2	Tesco	5,402,000,000
3	Argyll Group	3,784,000,000
4	Asda Group	3,300,000,000
5	Isosceles (Gateway, etc)	2,370,000,000
6	Kwik Save	1,446,000,000
7	Waitrose (John Lewis)	923,000,000
8	William Morrison	776,000,000
9	Iceland (including Bejam)	672,000,000
10	William Low	354,000,000

*Excluding Co-ops.
**1989–90, excluding VAT.
†Excluding Savacentre.

Based on The Retail Rankings (1991) published by The Corporate Intelligence Group Ltd.

THE TOP 10 GROCERY SUPPLIERS IN THE UK

	Grocer	% of shoppers using*
1	Sainsbury's	27.0
2	Tesco	20.9
3	Gateway	14.2
4	Asda	13.0
5	Co-op	12.4
6	Safeway	11.1
7	Kwik Save	10.3
8	Marks & Spencer	9.8
9	Milk delivery roundsman	7.3
10	Morrisons	3.5

*For regular major shopping.

Tesco, a close second as one of the UK's top retailers and supermarket groups.

THE TOP 10 CLOTHING RETAILERS IN THE UK

	Retailer	Annual sales (£)*
1	Burton Group	987,000,000
2	C & A/Brenninkmeyer	660,000,000
3	Sears (including Fosters, Adams, Miss Selfridge, Wallis, Warehouse, etc)	418,000,000
4	Storehouse (including Mothercare, Richards, Blazer, etc)	345,000,000
5	Next	302,000,000
6	Etam	181,000,000
7	Lewis Trust Group (including River Island, Concept Man, etc)	179,000,000
8	Alexon	108,000,000
9=	Coats Viyella (including Jaeger, Thrifty, Viyella)	85,000,000
9=	Benetton	85,000,000

*1989–90, excluding VAT.

Based on The Retail Rankings (1991) published by The Corporate Intelligence Group Ltd.

Note: The annual sales figures for certain retailers that are specialist components of larger groups will be different from those of the group as a whole.

THE TOP 10 DEPARTMENT STORE GROUPS IN THE UK

	Group	Annual sales (£)*
1	House of Fraser	1,110,000,000**
2	John Lewis Partnership	950,000,000
3	Burton Group (Debenhams, Harvey Nichols, etc)	759,000,000
4	Allders	274,000,000
5	Sears (Selfridges)	190,000,000
6	Lewis's Retail†	170,000,000
7	Fenwicks	162,000,000
8	London & Edinburgh Trust (Owen Owen)	99,000,000
9	Bentalls	72,000,000
10	James Beattie	64,000,000

*1989–90, excluding VAT.
**Pro rata estimate based on 39 week financial 'year'.
†Placed in receivership, January 1991.

Based on The Retail Rankings (1991) published by The Corporate Intelligence Group Ltd.

The John Lewis Partnership is the UK's No. 2 department store group.

QUIZ
SHOPS

1 How did William Whitely, the founder of the first London department store, die?
2 What chain of stores was originally called 'The Great Five Cent Store'?
3 What was the original nationality of Harry Gordon Selfridge, the founder of Selfridges department store?
4 What was the name of the London shop started by Barbara Hulanicki that came to symbolize the 'Swinging Sixties'?
5 What is the world's largest department store?
6 The founder of which chain of British shops was created First Baron Trent in 1929?
7 What was the name of the fictitious department store in the BBC Television comedy series, Are You Being Served??
8 In what city would you find the famous shopping street Rodeo Drive?
9 What well-known chain of British stores started in Leeds market in 1884 as the 'Penny Bazaar'?
10 The founder of what British chain of shops became First Lord of the Admiralty?

THE TOP 10 GROCERY BRANDS IN THE UK

	Brand (product)	Manufacturer	Annual sales (£)*
1	Ariel (washing powder)	Procter & Gamble	188,000,000
2	Persil (washing powder)	Lever Brothers	187,200,000
3	Nescafé (instant coffee)	Nestlé	186,500,000
4	Whiskas (catfood)	Pedigree Petfoods	178,200,000
5	Andrex (toilet paper)	Scott	177,100,000
6	Coca-Cola (soft drink)	Coca-Cola	175,600,000
7	Silver Spoon (sugar)	British Sugar	139,200,000
8	PG Tips (tea)	Brooke Bond Foods (Unilever)	133,600,000
9	Flora (margarine)	Van den Berghs & Jurgens (Unilever)	110,000,000
10	Heinz Baked Beans	H. J. Heinz	104,600,000

Through grocery outlets only; total brand sales may be higher.

Procter & Gamble, Britain's largest advertisers, now have Britain's bestselling grocery brand, Ariel having overtaken Persil since the 1989 introduction of Ariel Ultra. Persil, the first-ever household detergent, first went on the market in Germany on 6 June 1907. Its name may derive either from the parsley trademark of a French inventor ('persil' is French for parsley), or from two ingredients, *per*borate and *sil*icate, used by Professor Hermann Geissler and Dr Hermann Bauer, the German inventors of dry soap powder. The product has been made in Great Britain since 1909. Nescafé was the original instant coffee, first sold in 1938 by the Swiss firm, Nestlé. Whiskas is now the bestselling petfood brand in the world. The name Andrex stems from the location of the factory where it was first made in 1945: St Andrews Road, Walthamstow, London. It was originally called 'Androll' and changed to Andrex in 1954. Coca-Cola, invented in 1886, is today regarded as the most widely-known and powerful brand name in the world. Silver Spoon claims 55 per cent of the white granulated sugar market – a total of 300,000 tonnes a year. 'PG Tips' comes from the abbreviation of its earlier name, *Pre-gestee*, referring to its supposed 'before digestion' medicinal properties: the tips are the best parts of tea leaves. Launched in 1964, some 64,500 tonnes of Flora were sold in 1989. Heinz Baked Beans were introduced from the USA in 1901 and now 3,000,000 tins are consumed in the UK every day. Only one other grocery brand – Pedigree Chum – has sales of over £100,000,000 a year (£103,700,000, to be precise).

The UK's bestselling grocery brand: annual sales of Ariel now top £188,000,000.

ABOVE Duty-free Cognac ranks fifth in the bestselling league.

OPPOSITE Firefighting is rated as the most stressful job in the USA.

THE TOP 10 DUTY-FREE PRODUCTS

	Product	Sales (US$)
1	Women's fragrances	1,700,000,000
2	Cigarettes	1,640,000,000
3	Scotch whisky	1,200,000,000
4	Women's cosmetics and toiletries	940,000,000
5	Cognac	800,000,000
6	Leather goods	760,000,000
7	Men's fragrances and toiletries	640,000,000
8	Confectionery	560,000,000
9	Accessories	540,000,000
10	Jewellery and pearls	460,000,000

Total world sales of duty-free goods in 1989 were estimated to have reached $13,500,000,000.

THE 10 LARGEST RETAILERS IN THE USA

	Company	Annual sales ($)
1	Sears, Roebuck	30,332,100,000
2	K Mart	16,652,200,000
3	Wal-Mart Stores	14,553,500,000
4	American Stores	12,407,200,000
5	Kroger	10,771,700,000
6	J. C. Penney	9,079,800,000
7	Safeway Stores	8,077,000,000
8	Dayton Hudson Corporation	7,693,300,000
9	Great Atlantic and Pacific Tea Company	6,285,900,000
10	Supa Valu Stores	6,279,100,000

THE TOP 10 ACQUISITIONS AND MERGERS IN UK RETAILING, 1980–90

	Purchaser	Acquisition	Year	Value (£)
1	Isosceles	Gateway	1989	2,200,000,000
2	Habitat Mothercare	British Home Stores	1985	1,520,000,000
3	The Boots Company	Ward White	1989	900,000,000
4	Asda Group	61 Gateway stores	1989	705,000,000
5	Dee Corporation	Fine Fare/ Shoppers Paradise	1986	686,000,000
6	Argyll Group	Safeway	1987	681,000,000
7	Management buy-out	Magnet	1989	629,000,000
8=	Alfayed Investment Trust	House of Fraser (Harrods, etc)	1987	615,000,000
8=	Associated Dairies Group	MFI	1985	615,000,000
10	Burton Group plc	Debenhams	1985	566,000,000

Based on The Retail Rankings *(1991) published by The Corporate Intelligence Group Ltd.*

THE 10 MOST STRESSFUL JOBS IN THE USA

1. Firefighter
2. Racing car driver
3. Astronaut
4. Surgeon
5. National Football League player
6. Police officer
7. Osteopath
8. State police officer
9. Air traffic controller
10. Mayor

THE 10 MOST DANGEROUS JOBS IN THE UK

1. Asbestos worker
2. Crews of boats, ships, railway trains and aircraft
3. Demolition contractor
4. Diver
5. Fireman
6. Miner
7. Oil/gas-rig worker
8. Steeplejack
9. Tunneller
10. Steel erector

Life assurance companies carefully base their premiums on actuarial statistics that take into account the likelihood of people in each job being injured or killed at work. This does not mean that assurance companies will not provide cover for such professions, but the more risky the job, the higher the premium.

At least 240 people die every working day in the USA as a result of accidents at work or from diseases caused by their jobs. All the 10 riskiest jobs (except for pilots) are so-called 'blue-collar' or manual jobs. Other dangerous jobs that do not quite make the Top 10 are miners, taxi drivers and policemen. The risk attached to most 'white-collar' jobs is under 10 per 100,000, with some being placed extremely low – the chance of death at work among embalmers and librarians, for example, is put at zero.

THE 10 MOST DANGEROUS JOBS IN THE USA

	Job	Deaths per 100,000
1	Timber-cutters and loggers	129.0
2	Aircraft pilots	97.0
3	Asbestos and insulation workers	78.7
4	Structural metal workers	72.0
5	Electric power line and cable installers and repairers	50.7
6	Firefighters	48.8
7	Garbage collectors	40.0
8	Truck drivers	39.6
9	Bulldozer operators	39.3
10	Earth drillers	38.8

THE 10 BRITISH COMPANIES WITH THE MOST EMPLOYEES

	Company	Employees
1	British Telecom	247,912
2	Post Office	204,627
3	BAT Industries	188,492
4	Unilever	154,000
5	Grand Metropolitan	152,157
6	BET	137,101
7	British Rail	135,243
8	ICI	133,800
9	Electricity Council	131,179
10	British Aerospace	127,500

In 1972 the zip manufacturer YKK became one of the first Japanese manufacturing companies to establish a factory in the UK. Since then, more than 150 wholly or partly Japanese-owned plants have been opened. Japanese companies have also acquired or merged with a number of well-known British firms in a wide range of activities, including Lucas (now Lucas Yuasa Batteries Ltd), Thermos Ltd, Aquascutum and Freed of London, the ballet-shoe makers.

THE 10 JAPANESE COMPANIES WITH MOST EMPLOYEES IN THE UK

	Company/products	Location	Employees
1	Sony (UK) Ltd Colour TVs, TV tubes and components	Bridgend	2,400
2	SP Tyres (UK) Ltd Tyres	Birmingham/ Eccles	2,372
3	Matsushita Electric (UK) Ltd Colour TVs, TV monitors, microwave ovens	Cardiff/ Treforest	1,608
4	AVX Ltd Capacitators	Coleraine/ Larne/Paignton	1,600
5	Sharp Manufacturing Co VCRs, CD players, microwave ovens, electric typewriters, photocopiers	Wrexham	1,439
6	Mitsubishi Electric (UK) Ltd Colour TVs, VCRs, microwave ovens	Haddington/ Livingston	1,434
7	Nissan Motor Manufacturing Ltd Bluebird and Micra cars	Sunderland	1,300
8	Toshiba Products (UK) Ltd Colour TVs, VCRs, microwave ovens	Plymouth	1,079
9	Brother Industries (UK) Ltd Electronic typewriters, computer printers, microwave ovens	Wrexham	1,057
10	Epson Telford Ltd Computer printers	Telford	1,000

THE TOP 10 FUND-RAISING CHARITIES IN THE UK

	Charity	Voluntary income (£)
1	Oxfam	49,266,000
2	National Trust	43,418,000
3	Royal National Lifeboat Institution	40,487,000
4	Imperial Cancer Research Fund	40,295,000
5	Save the Children Fund	36,502,000
6	Cancer Research Campaign	31,689,000
7	Salvation Army	29,657,000
8	Charity Projects Ltd	27,559,000
9	Barnardos	25,778,000
10	National Society for the Prevention of Cruelty to Children	22,868,000

There are over 165,000 registered charities in England and Wales alone. The order of the Top 10 is for *voluntary* income only. Most charities also receive income from other sources, such as rents and interest on investments.

THE TOP 10 CHILDREN'S CHARITIES* IN THE UK

	Charity	Voluntary income (£)
1	Save the Children Fund	36,502,000
2	Barnardos	25,778,000
3	National Society for the Prevention of Cruelty to Children	22,868,000
4	Spastics Society	22,349,000
5	Action Aid	14,230,000
6	Church of England Children's Society	11,713,000
7	National Children's Home	9,000,000
8	Masonic Trust for Girls and Boys	6,961,000
9	Action Research	3,846,000
10	Childline Charitable Trust	2,241,000

Includes some charities that aid adults as well as children.

ABOVE RIGHT An oiled seabird is cared for by an official of the RSPCA, the UK's foremost animal charity.

THE TOP 10 ANIMAL CHARITIES IN THE UK

	Charity	Voluntary income (£)
1	Royal Society for the Prevention of Cruelty to Animals	20,457,000
2	World Wide Fund for Nature	18,898,000
3	People's Dispensary for Sick Animals	12,568,000
4	Royal Society for the Protection of Birds	11,097,000
5	Donkey Sanctuary	3,434,000
6	Blue Cross Animals Hospital	2,991,000
7	National Canine Defence League	2,608,000
8	Cats Protection League	1,866,000
9	Wood Green Animal Shelters	1,541,000
10	Wildfowl & Wetlands Trust	1,520,000

OPPOSITE Tree-cutting is reckoned to be the USA's most dangerous job.

THE TOP 10 CARBON DIOXIDE EMITTERS IN THE WORLD

	Country	CO_2 emissions (in tonnes of carbon) per capita	total
1	USA	5.339	1,310,250,000
2	USSR	3.828	1,086,000,000
3	China	0.562	609,858,000
4	Japan	2.204	269,766,000
5	West Germany	3.009	182,703,000
6	India	0.200	163,757,000
7	UK	2.666	152,520,000
8	Poland	3.300	125,342,000
9	Canada	4.575	119,388,000
10	Italy	1.712	98,105,000

Gregg Marland and the Carbon Dioxide Information Analysis Center at Oak Ridge, Tennessee, calculate CO_2 emissions from three principal sources – fossil fuel burning, cement manufacturing and gas flaring. Their findings show that between 1950 and 1988 increasing industrialization in many countries resulted in huge increases in carbon output: in the USSR it went up sixfold, while Japan, India and Brazil experienced increases of between nine and 10 times. That of China multiplied 28 times and of Korea 93-fold, from 610,000 to 55,837,000 tonnes. From peaks in 1979, the UK and France have both reduced their emissions. The USA, although still the worst offender, reduced its output from over 40 per cent of the world's total to just over 20 per cent. Its per capita emission of 5.339 tonnes of carbon was exceeded in 1988 only by East Germany's 5.362 tonnes per inhabitant.

THE TOP 10 SULPHUR DIOXIDE EMITTERS IN THE EC

	Country	Annual SO_2 emissions (tonnes)
1	UK	3,863,000
2	Spain	2,543,000
3	West Germany	2,223,000
4	Italy	2,075,000
5	France	1,517,000
6	Belgium	610,000
7	Greece	546,000
8	Portugal	286,000
9	Netherlands	274,000
10	Denmark	248,000

Based on the most recent statistics available for emissions of sulphur dioxide – the principal cause of acid rain – from fuel combustion in EC factories and power stations during the 1980s. During the decade, emissions by all countries declined: the UK's production was estimated at 5,310,000 tonnes in 1975 and further reductions are planned so that the level in the year 2003 will be 60 per cent less than that in 1980. At present, 71 per cent of the UK's SO_2 emissions are from power stations.

THE TOP 10 ENVIRONMENTAL CONCERNS

	Environmental problem	Total % worried
1	Chemicals put into rivers and the sea	91
2	Sewage contamination of beaches and bathing water	89
3	Oil spills at sea and oil on beaches	86
4	Destruction of the ozone layer	83
5	Loss of wildlife and habitats, destruction of species	82
6	Radioactive waste	81
7	Insecticides, fertilizers and chemical sprays	80
8	Destruction of tropical forests	76
9	Acid rain	75
10=	Traffic exhaust fumes	74
10=	Litter and rubbish	74

Based on a 1989 Department of the Environment Survey of Public Attitudes to the Environment conducted in England and Wales in which people were asked how worried they were about environmental problems. Interviewees were asked whether they were 'very worried' or 'quite worried', and the list combines the two degrees of concern.

THE 10 COMMONEST TYPES OF LITTER

1 Cigarette ends

2 Paper items

3 Matchsticks

4 Ring pulls

5 Plastic cups

6 Sweet wrappers

7 Glass bottles

8 Bottle tops

9 Tickets and stickers

10 Metal cans

Based on a survey conducted by the Tidy Britain Group, which counted the number of items in each category in typical samplings of litter deposited on Britain's streets.

THE TOP 10 PERSONAL ENVIRONMENTAL IMPROVEMENT ACTIVITIES

	Activity	% already undertaking
1	Use of ozone-friendly aerosols	64
2	Picking up other people's litter	52
3	Avoiding use of pesticides in the garden	42
4	Taking bottles to a bottle bank	40
5=	Cutting down on the use of electricity	38
5=	Collecting old newspapers for recycling	38
7	Using alternative transport to the car	28
8=	Using recycled paper	25
8=	Making compost out of kitchen waste	25
10	Using unleaded petrol	22

Based on a 1989 Department of the Environment Survey of Public Attitudes to the Environment conducted in England and Wales in which people were asked what environment-improving activities they already undertake. When interviewees were also asked what activities they would consider, the largest number, 59 per cent, claimed they would use recycled paper and the same number would buy phosphate-free washing powder, although only nine per cent said they already used it.

THE 10 COMMONEST COMPLAINTS ABOUT NOISE

1 Noisy neighbours

2 Barking dogs

3 Parties

4 Radio-playing in the street

5 Roadworks

6 Traffic

7 Construction sites

8 Aircraft and helicopter noise

9 Personal stereos

10 Factories and industrial noise

Based on data supplied by The Institution of Environmental Health Officers.

BACKGROUND Coal-fired power stations are the leading contributors to both SO_2 and CO_2 pollution.

OPPOSITE Oil spills have become a major environmental concern.

RIGHT Roadworks account for a large number of noise complaints.

BRITAIN'S TOP 10 COMPANIES

	Company	Annual sales (£)
1	British Petroleum (petroleum products, oil and gas exploration)	29,641,032,000
2	ICI (chemicals, plastics, paints)	13,171,014,000
3	Electricity Council (electricity)	12,373,800,000
4	British Telecom (telecommunications)	12,315,014,000
5	BAT Industries (tobacco, financial services, paper and pulp, retailing)	9,301,010,000
6	Grand Metropolitan (hotels, food, drinks, leisure)	9,298,010,000
7	British Aerospace (aerospace, vehicles)	9,085,010,000
8	British Gas (gas supply)	7,983,010,000
9	Unilever (consumer products, food)	7,419,009,000
10	BTR (consumer products, building and industrial projects)	7,025,009,000

THE TOP 10 COMPUTER COMPANIES IN THE WORLD

	Company	Country	Annual sales ($)
1	IBM	USA	63,438,000,000
2	Fujitsu	Japan	18,734,000,000
3	Digital Equipment	USA	12,866,000,000
4	Hewlett-Packard	USA	11,899,000,000
5	Unisys	USA	10,097,000,000
6	Canon	Japan	10,024,000,000
7	Olivetti	Italy	6,586,000,000
8	NCR	USA	5,956,000,000
9	Ricoh	Japan	5,780,000,000
10	Apple	USA	5,284,000,000

THE TOP 10 BUILDING SOCIETIES IN THE UK

	Building Society	Assets (£)
1	Halifax	47,986,700,000,000
2	Nationwide Anglia	24,415,300,000,000
3	Woolwich	15,120,400,000,000
4	Alliance and Leicester	13,545,200,000,000
5	Leeds Permanent	12,917,400,000,000
6	National and Provincial	8,465,100,000,000
7	Cheltenham and Gloucester	7,270,100,000,000
8	Bradford and Bingley	7,155,200,000,000
9	Britannia	6,301,800,000,000
10	Bristol and West	4,685,200,000,000

THE 10 HOTEL GROUPS IN THE UK WITH MOST BEDROOMS

	Hotel group	Hotels	Bedrooms
1	Trusthouse Forte	323	29,363
2	Thistle Hotels	105	14,000
3	Queens Moat Houses	102	10,411
4	Hilton International	35	7,137
5	Holiday Inns	33	5,913
6	Rank and Mecca	26	4,331
7	Swallow Hotels	32	4,070
8	Stakis Hotels	30	3,800
9	Jarvis Hotels	41	3,150
10	De Vere Hotels	25	2,771

Trusthouse Forte provide the largest number of hotel bedrooms in the UK.

THE TOP 10 CATEGORIES OF GOVERNMENT EXPENDITURE

	Category	Expenditure (£)
1	Social Security	57,300,000,000
2	Health	25,300,000,000
3	Education	24,400,000,000
4	Defence	21,000,000,000
5	Police, prisons, safety, etc	9,500,000,000
6	Public services	9,100,000,000
7	Housing and community amenities	7,700,000,000
8	Transport and communication	7,200,000,000
9	Recreational and cultural affairs	3,100,000,000
10	Agriculture, forestry and fishing	2,100,000,000

Out of a total annual budget of some £196,000,000,000, a further £1,700,000,000 is spent on mining and other industries. Two nebulous categories, 'Other expenditure' and 'Other economic affairs and services', account for a further £24,500,000,000 and £5,300,000,000 respectively. The Government receives a net income of £2,000,000,000 from 'Fuel and energy' – principally oil revenue.

THE TOP 10 COAL PRODUCERS IN THE WORLD

	Country	Annual production (tonnes)
1	China	956,443,000
2	USA	862,069,000
3	USSR	784,936,000
4	East Germany*	316,697,000
5	Poland	284,029,000
6	India	196,007,000
7	West Germany*	187,840,000
8	South Africa	176,044,000
9	Australia	167,761,000
10	Czechoslovakia	127,042,000
	UK	*98,300,000*

Figure for united country not yet available.

THE TOP 10 ENERGY CONSUMERS IN THE WORLD

	Country	Annual consumption coal equivalent (tonnes)
1	USA	2,327,580,000
2	USSR	1,878,085,000
3	China	815,339,000
4	Japan	456,739,000
5	West Germany*	344,020,000
6	UK	290,742,000
7	Canada	254,022,000
8	India	214,877,000
9	France	206,944,000
10	Italy	204,704,000

Figure for united country not yet available.

THE TOP 10 OIL PRODUCERS IN THE WORLD

	Country	Production (barrels)*
1	USSR	4,352,625,000
2	USA	2,724,360,000
3	Saudi Arabia	2,007,500,000
4	Iraq	1,113,615,000
5	Iran	1,072,005,000
6	China	1,004,845,000
7	Mexico	954,840,000
8	United Arab Emirates	753,360,000
9	Venezuela	735,110,000
10	UK	685,835,000
	World total	*22,354,425,000*

A barrel contains 42 US gallons/34.97 UK gallons.

Despite its huge output, the USA produces only 43 per cent of the 6,300,000,000-plus barrels of oil it consumes every year – equivalent to more than 25 barrels per capita. The average US citizen thus uses one barrel of oil every 14 days. This compares with the UK's consumption of 634,000,000 barrels per annum – 11 per capita, or one barrel every 33 days.

ABOVE The USA is ranked second among the world's oil producers.

THE TOP 10 ELECTRICITY SURGES OF ALL TIME IN THE UK

	TV programme	Channel	Date	Time	Pick-up (MW)
1	World Cup Semi-final: West Germany *v* England	BBC1 ITV	4 Jul 90	21.38 21.48	2,800
2	*The Thornbirds*	BBC1	22 Jan 84	21.07	2,600
3=	*The Thornbirds*	BBC1	16 Jan 84	21.30	2,200
3=	*Dallas* *This is Your Life*	BBC1 ITV	8 May 85	20.56 21.00	2,200
5=	*Dallas* *This is Your Life*	BBC1 ITV	1 May 85	20.56 21.00	2,100
5=	*The Colbys*	BBC1	19 Feb 86	21.00	2,100
7=	*Coronation Street* *Blue Thunder*	ITV BBC1	2 Apr 84	19.57 20.00	2,000
7=	*Dallas*	BBC1	15 May 84	20.50	2,000
7=	*EastEnders*	BBC1	1 Apr 86	20.00	2,000
7=	*Coronation Street* *A Song for Europe*	ITV BBC1	2 Apr 86	19.57 20.00	2,000
7=	*Dallas* *Minder*	BBC1 ITV	30 Apr 86	20.57 21.00	2,000
7=	*EastEnders*	BBC1	4 Sep 86	20.00	2,000
7=	World Cup Semi-final: Italy *v* Argentina	BBC1 ITV	3 Jul 90	21.51 21.57	2,000

'TV pick-ups' are monitored in a National Grid control room.

Demand for electricity in the UK varies gradually during the day: as it gets dark, progressively more lights are switched on, or, during the winter, heating comes on at varying times during the morning, and the National Grid responds to such increases by steadily increasing the supply. The effect of television programmes is far more dramatic, however. It is not the programmes themselves but when they end that causes surges in demand (known as 'TV pick-ups'), as millions of viewers get up and switch on electric kettles and other appliances (even the action of flushing lavatories has an effect, as demand for electricity from water pumping stations increases). Because barely a few minutes separates the ends of certain programmes on BBC1 and ITV, it is not possible to differentiate between them, but all those listed contributed to national TV pick-ups of 2,000 megawatts or more. With the increasing spread of viewing across BBC, ITV, satellite and cable channels and the use of video recorders, such notable TV pick-ups will probably be less evident in the future.

Sellafield, Cumbria: more than a fifth of the UK's electricity comes from nuclear energy.

THE 10 COUNTRIES PRODUCING THE MOST ELECTRICITY FROM NUCLEAR SOURCES

	Country	Nuclear power stations in operation	Nuclear % of total	Output (megawatt-hours)
1	USA	110	19.1	98,321
2	France	55	74.6	52,588
3	USSR	46	12.3	34,230
4	Japan	39	27.8	29,300
5	West Germany	24	34.3	22,716
6	Canada	18	15.6	12,185
7	UK	39	21.7	11,242
8	Sweden	12	45.1	9,817
9	Spain	10	38.4	7,544
10	South Korea	9	50.2	7,220

THE 10 COUNTRIES WITH THE LARGEST OIL RESERVES

	Country	Reserves (barrels)*
1	Saudi Arabia	255,000,000,000
2	Iraq	100,000,000,000
3	United Arab Emirates	98,100,000,000
4	Kuwait	94,500,000,000**
5	Iran	92,900,000,000
6	Venezuela	58,500,000,000
7	USSR	58,400,000,000
8	Mexico	56,400,000,000
9	USA	25,900,000,000
10	China	24,000,000,000

*A barrel contains 42 US gallons/34.97 UK gallons.
**Pre-1991 Gulf War estimate.

THE TOP 10 PETROL STATIONS IN THE UK*

	Brand	Outlets
1	Shell	2,653
2	Esso	2,520
3	BP/National	1,992
4	Burmah/Major	1,374
5	Texaco	1,268
6	Jet	1,112
7	Mobil	890
8	Q8/Pace	876
9	Fina	844
10	UK	668

*Including shared sites on motorways, at supermarkets etc.

There are 19,465 petrol stations in the UK. Of these, 11,043 are self-service, 6,847 are owned by the major companies, 112 are sited on motorways and 443 at hypermarkets and supermarkets.

THE TOP 10 URANIUM PRODUCERS IN THE WORLD

	Country	Annual production (tonnes)
1	Canada	11,720
2	USA	5,200
3	South Africa	4,600
4	Australia	4,154
5	Namibia	3,300
6	France	3,247
7	Niger	3,110
8	Gabon	900
9	Spain	215
10	India	200

The amount of uranium produced in the USSR is a closely-guarded secret, but is assumed to be several thousand tonnes per annum. It is estimated that Australia has the greatest reserves of uranium – some 463,000 tonnes.

THE TOP 10 SALT PRODUCERS IN THE WORLD

	Country	Annual production (tonnes)
1	USA	31,284,000
2	USSR	16,200,000
3	China	15,875,000
4	West Germany*	11,266,000
5	India	10,000,000
6	Canada	7,542,000
7	France	6,579,000
8	UK	6,130,000
9	Australia	6,000,000
10	Mexico	5,500,000
	World total	165,000,000

*Figure for united country not yet available.

ABOVE RIGHT Esso has 2,520 petrol stations in the UK.

RIGHT Salt extraction in China, the world's No. 3 producer.

THE TOP 10 COMPLAINTS TO THE CONSUMERS' ASSOCIATION

1   *Problems with faulty goods or services*
Includes shops and problems in getting refunds for goods returned. The item most complained about is washing machines.

2   *Cars and garages*
Cars that go wrong and garages that fail to put them right.

3   *Commercial services*
Includes complaints about builders, plumbers, double-glazers and roofers.

4   *Financial services*
Banks, building societies, insurance and investment. Insurance, particularly motor insurance, gets most complaints.

5   *Junk mail*
An area dominated by timeshare promotional offers.

6   *Holiday problems*
Including missed flights and building sites where there should be hotels.

7   *Public utilities*
Gas, water, electric, and Telecom.

8   *Credit rating*

9   *Transport*
Mainly British Rail.

10   *Food*
Especially misleading labelling of food, foreign bodies and goods past their sell-by date.

THE TOP 10 ADVERTISING COMPLAINTS

	Product category	Advertisements reported
1	Cars	40
2	Financial services	33
3	Computers	29
4	Property and estate agents	28
5	Recruitment	26
6=	Radio, TV and video equipment	24
6=	Travel	24
8	Telephones	21
9	Holidays and hotels	19
10	Clothing	18

Based on complaints to the Advertising Standards Authority, 1989–90.

A Mars a day.

Mars is one of the leading TV advertisers in the UK.

WHAT'S IN A BRAND NAME?

The more international businesses become, the more value is placed on the asset of a widely-recognized brand. Interbrand, an international organization that advises companies on maximizing the potential of their brands, recently conducted a survey in which it analysed various attributes of well-known brands, evaluating them on a variety of qualities, including such factors as their stability in the marketplace, their internationality, vulnerability to changes in fashion and degree of protection against potential infringement of their trademarks. Derived from their researches, Interbrand has produced a list of the world's Top 10 brand names. The first seven companies in the list are American. Although no British brand appears in the Top 10, Marks & Spencer is regarded as the strongest home brand, followed by internationally famous British brands as diverse as Kit Kat, Schweppes, Land Rover and the BBC.

1	Coca-Cola	5	Marlboro	8	Sony
2	Kellogg's	6	IBM	9	Mercedes-Benz
3	McDonald's	7	American Express		
4	Kodak			10	Nescafé

THE TOP 10 TV ADVERTISERS IN THE UK

	Advertiser/products	TV advertising expenditure 1990 (£)
1	Procter & Gamble (domestic products) Fairy Liquid, Ariel, Daz, etc	53,561,000
2	Lever Brothers Persil, Radion, etc	47,882,000
3	Kellogg's Cornflakes, Rice Krispies, etc	45,307,000
4	Mars Mars bars, Snickers, Bounty, etc	33,666,000
5	Procter & Gamble (health and beauty products) Vidal Sassoon, Crest toothpaste, Old Spice, etc	31,423,000
6	Kraft General Foods Maxwell House coffee, Philadelphia cheese, etc	29,777,000
7	Birds Eye Walls Fish fingers, etc	28,639,000
8	British Telecom	27,701,000
9	Rowntree Mackintosh Aero, Smarties, Kit Kat, etc	27,421,000
10	Cadbury Dairy Milk, Whole Nut, Milk Tray, Roses, etc	26,017,000

THE 10 COUNTRIES THAT SPEND THE MOST ON ADVERTISING

	Country	Total annual expenditure ($)
1	USA	110,272,000,000
2	Japan	23,392,000,000
3	UK	9,474,000,000
4	West Germany*	8,201,000,000
5	France	6,647,000,000
6	Canada	5,480,000,000
7	Italy	4,432,000,000
8	Spain	3,345,000,000
9	Australia	2,720,000,000
10	Netherlands	2,408,000,000

Figure for united country not yet available.

THE 10 COUNTRIES THAT SPEND THE MOST ON TV ADVERTISING

	Country	Total annual expenditure ($)
1	USA	24,150,000,000
2	Japan	8,257,000,000
3	UK	3,070,000,000
4	Italy	2,189,000,000
5	France	1,708,000,000
6	Brazil	1,058,000,000
7	Spain	1,050,000,000
8	Australia	933,000,000
9	West Germany*	902,000,000
10	Canada	888,000,000

Figure for united country not yet available.

Mail order catalogues dominate the direct mail business.

THE TOP 10 SENDERS OF DIRECT MAIL IN THE UK

	Sender	% of total volume
1	Mail order companies	24.5
2	Insurance companies	8.9
3	Banks and Girobank	7.5
4	Retailers	6.7
5	Magazines	6.3
6	Travel agencies	6.0
7	Credit card companies	5.3
8	Manufacturers	4.6
9	Charities	4.4
10	Book clubs	3.8

THE 10 EUROPEAN COUNTRIES RECEIVING THE MOST DIRECT MAIL

	Country	Average no. of items per head per annum
1	Switzerland	102
2	Belgium	76
3	Sweden	73
4	West Germany	60
5	Netherlands	58
6	France	50
7	Finland	48
8	Denmark	47
9	Norway	46
10	UK	38

The amount of direct mail (sometimes known as 'junk mail') advertising a wide range of goods and services has been inexorably increasing in recent years. Of items that are received through the average UK consumer's letterbox, about 18 per cent is direct mail (the balance comprises personally addressed mail: 47 per cent; free newspapers: 18.4 per cent; leaflets and coupons: 16.6 per cent). By the end of the 1980s, over 2,000,000,000 direct mail items were sent to homes and businesses every year – more than double the amount at the beginning of the decade – at a cost of £758,000,000. Of these, 80 per cent are opened and over 60 per cent opened and read. The direct mail industry employs some 25,000 people and the business it generates is said to be worth over £7,000,000,000 a year. Despite such apparent benefits, however, many people regard direct mail as an unwarranted intrusion into their lives and an environmentally unsound activity that consumes vast quantities of paper and energy in producing and disposing of the material. Nevertheless, when people in the USA were interviewed about their views on the subject, most said they would prefer to receive *more* rather than *less* junk mail. If Europeans follow this attitude, they seem likely to have their wish granted: as the European Single Market becomes a reality in 1992, the signs are that trans-European direct mail marketing is on the increase.

THE 10 COUNTRIES THAT MAKE THE MOST INTERNATIONAL PHONE CALLS

	Country	Calls per head	Total calls
1	USA	3.7	835,248,000
2	West Germany	11.2	694,301,000
3	UK	6.3	360,000,000*
4	Canada	9.5	240,000,000*
5	Italy	4.2	239,589,000
6	Switzerland	34.6	229,240,000
7	Netherlands	14.9	222,500,000
8	Japan	1.4	166,800,000
9	Belgium	16.6	164,877,000
10	Spain	3.5	135,095,000

Estimated.

All figures are for 1989, except Italy (1988) and Japan (12 months to 31 March 1990).

After Switzerland, Denmark, which does not even appear in the Top 10, makes the second highest number of international calls per person (20.9).

THE 10 MOST-DIALLED UK TELEPHONE SERVICES

	Service	Provider
1	123 ('Speaking Clock')	British Telecom
2	Rapid Raceline (horse racing results)	William Hill Leisure
3	Rapid Cricketline	William Hill Leisure
4	Turfcall (horse racing results)	British Telecom Supercall
5	Racecall (horse racing results)	Telephone Information Services
6	F.I.S.T. (Fantasy Interactive Scenarios by Telephone – fantasy game)	Computerdial
7	F.T. Cityline (financial data)	*Financial Times*
8	Russell Grant Horoscope	Computerdial
9	*The Sun* Justin Toper Horoscope	Legion Telecommunications
10	Weathercall	Telephone Information Services

The Top 10 covers charged services only, not those to the operator and other (as yet) free facilities. British Telecom will not reveal how many people dial 123 (formerly 'TIM'), but it is estimated that some of the leading services generate up to 50,000,000 calls each per annum. The total value of the telephone information market, some 225,000,000 calls a year, is reckoned to be in excess of £130,000,000.

THE TOP 10 CELLULAR MOBILE PHONE USERS

	Country	Mobile phones
1	USA	3,500,000
2	UK	870,000
3	Japan	490,000
4	Canada	370,000
5	Sweden	350,000
6	France	180,000
7	Norway	170,000
8	West Germany	165,000
9	Finland	160,000
10	Australia	150,000

THE TOP 10 FAX COUNTRIES

	Country	Fax machines
1	Japan	5,400,000
2	USA	4,100,000
3	Germany	940,000
4	Italy	820,000
5	UK	770,000
6	Canada	710,000
7	France	600,000
8	Spain	390,000
9	Australia	380,000
10	Netherlands	260,000

Facsimile transmission from one point to another was suggested in the early nineteenth century and developed in a primitive form soon after the invention of the telephone. The first practical machines came into use after the Second World War and were employed by the police and newspapers for transmitting photographs via telephone lines or radio. The technology was slow and the machines cumbersome until the Japanese pioneered their development as a quick means of sending handwritten documents, Japanese typewriters being notoriously slow and unwieldy. Their international proliferation during the 1980s made considerable inroads into such long-established forms of communication as post and telex, and now in the 1990s the ubiquitous 'fax' is being put to imaginative new uses, from faxed copies of works of art to ordering food from faxed menus. The so-called 'junk fax' (an unsolicited faxed version of direct mail) is becoming an increasing nuisance, consuming the subscriber's fax paper and occupying his fax line, thereby blocking legitimate incoming and outgoing faxes. Among the more audacious of these is one that asks, 'Are you bothered by junk faxes?'

WEALTH

THE 10 HIGHEST-EARNING ACTORS IN THE WORLD

	Actor	1989–90 income ($)
1	William H. Cosby Jr	115,000,000
2	Sylvester Stallone	63,000,000
3	Arnold Schwarzenegger	55,000,000
4	Jack Nicholson	50,000,000
5	Eddie Murphy	48,000,000
6	Bruce Willis	36,000,000
7	Sean Connery	35,000,000
8	Michael J. Fox	33,000,000
9	Tom Cruise	26,000,000
10	Michael Douglas	24,000,000

Used by permission of Forbes Magazine.

In the 1989–90 period, Bill Murray, Jane Fonda, Tom Selleck, Steve Martin and Mel Gibson all dropped out of the Top 10. Harrison Ford ($22,000,000) and Mel Gibson ($20,000,000) were the only other actors reckoned by *Forbes* to have made $20,000,000 or more.

THE 10 HIGHEST-EARNING POP STARS IN THE WORLD

	Artist(s)	1989–90 income ($)
1	Michael Jackson	100,000,000
2	Rolling Stones	88,000,000
3	New Kids on the Block	78,000,000
4	Madonna	62,000,000
5	Paul McCartney	45,000,000
6	Julio Iglesias	44,000,000
7=	The Who	35,000,000
7=	Bon Jovi	35,000,000
7=	Prince	35,000,000
10	Billy Joel	32,000,000

Used by permission of Forbes Magazine.

Forbes Magazine's survey of top entertainers' income covers a two-year period in order to iron out fluctuations, especially those caused by successful tours – the Who, for example, earned $30,000,000 in 1989, when they had their 25th anniversary tour, but this dipped to $5,000,000 in 1990. In the same period several other super-groups had substantial earnings, among them Aerosmith ($31,000,000), Pink Floyd ($30,000,000), Grateful Dead ($30,000,000), U2 ($25,000,000) and Guns 'n' Roses ($17,000,000), while among solo singers were Janet Jackson ($30,000,000), Frank Sinatra ($27,000,000), Paula Abdul ($23,000,000) and George Michael ($18,000,000).

Ayrton Senna's ship came in – to the tune of $10,000,000 in 1989–90.

THE 10 HIGHEST-EARNING SPORTSMEN IN THE WORLD

	Name	Sport	1989–90 income ($)
1	Mike Tyson	Boxing	28,600,000
2	Buster Douglas	Boxing	26,000,000
3	Sugar Ray Leonard	Boxing	13,000,000
4	Ayrton Senna	Motor racing	10,000,000
5	Alain Prost	Motor racing	9,000,000
6	Jack Nicklaus	Golf	8,600,000
7	Greg Norman	Golf	8,500,000
8=	Michael Jordan	Basketball	8,100,000
8=	Arnold Palmer	Golf	8,100,000
8=	Evander Holyfield	Boxing°	8,100,000

Used by permission of Forbes Magazine.

The ratio between earnings from salary and winnings and from 'other sources', as surveyed by *Forbes*, varies enormously: some $27,000,000 of Mike Tyson's income was reckoned to have come from winnings, whereas as much as $8,000,000 of Jack Nicklaus' total, and $6,000,000 of Michael Jordan's, was believed to have been derived from such sources as sponsorship and royalty income from endorsed sporting products. Among other sports stars earning in excess of $5,000,000 in the 1989–90 period were British motor racing driver Nigel Mansell, tennis players Steffi Graf, Boris Becker, Stefan Edberg and Ivan Lendl, and footballer Diego Maradona.

THE 10 RICHEST PEOPLE IN THE USA

In 1990 *Forbes Magazine*, which annually surveys the 400 wealthiest people in the USA, ranked some 66 Americans as dollar billionaires – that is, with assets in excess of $1,000,000,000. The *Forbes 400* includes both the inheritors of great family fortunes and self-made individuals. A placing in the list is extremely volatile, however, particularly during recent times, when many who made vast fortunes in a short period lost them with even greater rapidity, while stock market falls have led to a decline in the assets of many members of this élite club. Even the Top 10 changes from year to year, and now stands as:

	Name(s)	Assets ($)
1	John Werner Kluge	5,600,000,000+

Founder of the Metromedia Company of Charlottesville, Virginia. The family of German-born Kluge settled in Detroit in 1922, where he worked on the Ford assembly line. He won a scholarship to Columbia University and

gained a degree in economics. He started a radio station and in 1959, with partners, acquired the Metropolitan Broadcasting Company, developing it into Metromedia, a corporation that owns TV and radio stations and cellular telephone franchises but with other properties as varied as the Chock Full O'Nuts Corporation and, formerly, the Harlem Globetrotters basketball team. Kluge has diversified his interests into such areas as films, printing and a chain of steak houses. He also owns a 78,000-acre estate in Scotland.

2	Warren Edward Buffett	3,300,000,000

Buffett was born and still lives in Omaha, Nebraska. His professional career started as a pinball service engineer, after which he published a horse race tip sheet. His diverse business interests include the major New England textile company, Berkshire Hathaway. He is reported to have left his fortune in trust to aid such causes as population control and nuclear disarmament.

3	Ronald Owen Perelman	2,870,000,000

Perelman is a wide-ranging entrepreneur who acquired Revlon, Max Factor and other cosmetics businesses, was the former owner of Technicolor and has professional interests that encompass firms from Marvel Comics to a camping goods company.

4	Henry Lea Hillman	2,650,000,000

Son of the coal, gas and steel magnate John Hartwell Hillman Jr, Hillman is an industrialist and property developer who was a pioneer investor in computer technology in the 1970s and is now moving his portfolio into new industries based on biotechnology.

5=	Barbara Cox Anthony and sister Anne Cox Chambers	5,200,000,000+ (shared)

Daughters of a former schoolteacher who bought the *Dayton Daily News* (for $26,000) in 1898. The family business grew into a media empire encompassing newspapers, magazines, TV and radio stations and many other interests. During the Carter administration, Anne Cox Chambers was US Ambassador to Belgium.

5=	Samuel Irving Newhouse Jr and brother Donald Edward Newhouse	5,200,000,000+ (shared)

The New York City-based Newhouse brothers are owners of America's largest privately-owned chain of newspapers, with interests that include cable television and book publishing. Samuel ('Si') Newhouse runs book publishers Random House and magazine publishers Condé Nast, the publishers of *Vogue,* bought by their father in 1959 as an anniversary gift for his wife ('She asked for a fashion magazine and I went out and got her *Vogue*'). Donald controls their newspaper group.

7	Jay Arthur Pritzker and Robert Alan Pritzker	5,000,000,000+ (shared)

Of Russian ancestry, the Pritzker brothers are Chicago financiers, the owners of Hyatt Hotels (run by Jay Pritzker's son Thomas), real estate and other interests.

8=	Samuel Moore Walton, S. Robson Walton, John T. Walton, Jim C. Walton and Alice L. Walton	12,500,000,000 (shared)

Samuel Moore Walton headed the list of America's richest people for several years, but has latterly been relegated to joint 8th position since he shared his wealth equally with his children. President of Wal-Mart Stores, based in Bentonville, Arkansas, he attended the University of Missouri, paying for his tuition himself by doing a paper round. In 1940, he worked for the J. C. Penney store in Arkansas as a shirt salesman, earning $85 per month. With his brother James he developed a chain of discount retail outlets serving predominantly rural areas, building it up until it became the third largest chain of retail stores in the USA, his 1,400 Wal-Mart Stores achieving annual sales of $25,000,000,000.

8=	William Henry Gates III	2,500,000,000

In 1975, aged 19, Gates left law college to co-found (with Paul G. Allen) the Microsoft Corporation of Seattle, now one of the world's leading computer software companies.

10	Henry Ross Perot	2,200,000,000+

Son of a Texan horse-trader, Perot once sold saddles and served in the US Navy before becoming IBM's star salesman. In 1962, with $1,000, he founded Electronic Data Systems of Dallas. It crashed in 1970, losing a record $600,000,000 in a single day's trading, but Perot got the firm back on its feet and in 1984 sold it to General Motors for $991,000,000. A subsequent management dispute led to his being bought out in 1986 for $742,000,000. He now runs an investment company which has backed other high-tech entrepreneurs such as Steve Jobs (the founder of Apple Computers) in the launch of NeXT, Inc – to the tune of $20,000,000 – and owns Alliance Airport, Dallas.

ABOVE LEFT John Werner Kluge, top of the Top 10 richest in the USA.

THE 10 RICHEST BRITISH PEOPLE

This list is based on round-figure estimates of 'realisable' wealth – assets that their owner could dispose of if he so wished. The list includes only British citizens (though not necessarily residents), although there are several very wealthy foreigners living in the UK who would rank in the Top 10, among them Gad and Hans Rausing (Swedish – shared £2,000,000,000+) and John Paul Getty III (American – £1,500,000,000).

Name(s)	Assets (£)
1 Her Majesty Queen Elizabeth II	6,700,000,000

Much of her wealth derives from assets such as the Crown Estates and the royal art collection, components of the British national heritage that she manages but will ultimately pass on to her successor and which it is inconceivable would ever be sold. However, recent assessments have indicated that based solely on the Queen's privately-owned assets – unlikely though it may be that she would ever liquidate them – she ranks as the wealthiest British person and the richest woman in the world. The Queen's private fortune is held in jewellery, art, racehorses, land, property in the UK (including Balmoral Castle and Sandringham), Europe and the USA, and shares worth an estimated £3,300,000,000.

2 The Duke of Westminster	3,700,000,000

Gerald Grosvenor owns 300 acres in Mayfair and Belgravia (part of which was once a cabbage-patch, acquired in 1677 as the dowry of the 12-year-old bride of Sir Thomas Grosvenor), Eaton Hall near Chester and its 13,000-acre estate, and 100,000 acres of Scottish forest, as well as property around the world. His fortune has actually declined recently with the general dip in the value of land.

3 The Sainsbury Family	1,850,000,000

Founded in 1869 and expanded as high-street grocers, Sainsbury's were among the first to develop American-style supermarkets in the UK. Today Lord (Alan) Sainsbury, Sir Robert Sainsbury, Sir John Sainsbury and David Sainsbury own the majority of the shares in the chain which has an annual turnover in excess of £5,000,000,000. The family has financed the extension to the National Gallery, London, known as the Sainsbury Wing.

4 Garfield Weston	1,750,000,000

Weston's family emigrated to Canada over a century ago and made a fortune in the bakery business. Galen Weston runs the Canadian company, while his elder brother Garfield is today Chairman of the British arm of the firm, Associated British Foods, bakers of Sunblest bread and owners of other well-known brands, including the British Sugar Company.

5 Lord Samuel and Edmund Vestey	1,300,000,000

Running a business built up during the nineteenth century from a cattle-ranching and meat-shipping business, cousins Lord Samuel and Edmund Vestey's company, Union International plc, is today the world's largest retail butcher.

6= Robert Maxwell	1,200,000,000

The son of a poor Czechoslovakian labourer, Robert Maxwell (whose name was originally Jan Ludwig Hoch) distinguished himself in the British army during the Second World War and went on to found a global printing and publishing empire which today, as Maxwell Communications Corporation, includes Mirror Group Newspapers (recently publicly quoted), publishers of the *Daily Mirror*, *Sunday Mirror* and *The European* among other newspapers; Macdonald Publishers in the UK; and the New York *Daily News* and Macmillan in the USA.

6= Sir John Moores	1,200,000,000

Originally a post office messenger, Sir John Moores was in 1923 founder and remains the owner of Littlewoods, Britain's largest private company, which operates Littlewoods Football Pools and the Littlewoods retail and mail-order stores group.

| 8 | Charles Feeney | 940,000,000 |

Duty Free Shoppers, the world's largest duty-free business, is the principal source of Feeney's income.

| 9 | Sir James Goldsmith | 875,000,000 |

Principally a financier, Sir James was the one-time owner of a diverse group of businesses ranging from food companies to the French newspaper, *L'Express*, and of 2,500,000 acres of American forests, much of which he has disposed of in order to finance ecological causes, an area of interest he shares with his brother, Teddy Goldsmith.

| 10 | Sir Adrian and Sir John Swire | 700,000,000 |

The Swire brothers inherited a business started in the early nineteenth century and based on shipping. Today the John Swire Group includes Cathay Pacific Airline and extensive interests, especially in Hong Kong, in areas as diverse as Coca-Cola bottling and property.

THE 10 RICHEST COUNTRIES IN THE WORLD

	Country	GNP per capita (US$)
1	Switzerland	30,270
2	Japan	23,730
3	Finland	22,060
4	Norway	21,850
5	Sweden	21,710
6	USA	21,100
7	West Germany*	20,750
8	Denmark	20,510
9	Canada	19,020
10	United Arab Emirates	18,430
17	UK	14,570

Up-to-date figure for united Germany not yet available.

Gross National Product (GNP) is the total value of all the goods and services produced annually by the country. Dividing it by the country's population produces GNP per capita, which is often used as a measure of how 'rich' a country is. A total of 21 industrialized nations (excluding Soviet countries for which figures are not available) have GNPs in excess of $10,000, while a number of Third World countries, particularly in Africa, have per capita GNPs of less than $200.

OPPOSITE The publisher Robert Maxwell, one of Britain's 10 richest people.

BELOW Sierra Leone produces 600,000 carats of diamonds a year.

QUIZ

MILLIONAIRES

1 Name one of the three female stars of the 1953 film, *How to Marry a Millionaire.*
2 Who wrote the play on which the 1960 Peter Sellers and Sophia Loren film *The Millionairess* was based?
3 Who was the first actress to become a millionairess before the age of 10?
4 In what year was the word 'millionaire' first recorded in written English – 1826, 1876 or 1926?
5 Said to be the world's richest man, he died at Sutton Place in 1976. What was his name?
6 Name the American millionaire who in 1947 piloted the aeroplane with the largest wing span of all time.
7 What Dunfermline-born iron and steel millionaire endowed innumerable educational and other institutions in Great Britain and the USA?
8 What was the first name of the millionaire Gatsby in F. Scott Fitzgerald's novel, *The Great Gatsby*?
9 With what product was British millionaire philanthropist Lord Nuffield associated?
10 What 1956 film contained the Cole Porter song, *Who Wants to Be a Millionaire*?

THE TOP 10 DIAMOND PRODUCERS IN THE WORLD

	Country	Production (carats per annum)
1	Australia	37,000,000
2	Zaïre	20,000,000
3	Botswana	15,200,000
4	USSR	12,000,000
5	South Africa	9,000,000
6	Angola	1,200,000
7	Namibia	900,000
8=	Central African Republic	600,000
8=	Sierra Leone	600,000
10	Liberia	300,000
	World total	98,500,000

THE 10 LARGEST UNCUT DIAMONDS IN THE WORLD

The weight of diamonds is measured in carats (the word derives from the carob bean which grows on the *Ceratonia siliqua* tree and which is remarkable for its consistent weight of 0.2 of a gram). There are approximately 142 carats to the ounce.

The value of large diamonds is truly astonishing: at Sotheby's, New York on 19 April 1988, the London firm of Graff Diamonds paid a record $9,310,000 for an 85.91-carat diamond, ending the eight-year reign of the 41.28-carat *Polar Star* which had been sold in Geneva on 21 November 1980 for £2,100,000. On 20 April 1988 at Christie's, New York a 52.59-carat stone made $7,980,000, a record $151,740 per carat. Just eight days later, a tiny rare red diamond weighing just 0.95 of a carat made £500,000, equivalent to £526,316 per carat.

Fewer than 100 uncut diamonds weighing more than 100 carats have ever been found. The 10 largest of these are:

Diamond	Carats
1 *Cullinan*	3,106.00

The largest diamond ever found, the *Cullinan* was named after Thomas Cullinan, President of De Beers, the diamond mining corporation. Measuring approximately 10 x 6.5 x 5 cm/4 x 2½ x 2 in and weighing almost 6,237 g/1 lb 6 oz, it was unearthed in 1905 at the Premier Mine in South Africa. Bought by the Transvaal Government for £150,000, it was presented to King Edward VII on the occasion of his 66th birthday on 9 November 1907. The King decided to have it cut and called upon Dutch expert Joseph Asscher who spent weeks making meticulous calculations before commencing his task. At 2.45 pm on 10 February 1908, surrounded by assistants in his Amsterdam workshop, Asscher started work, knowing that the slightest mistake could cause the world's largest diamond to shatter into fragments. His first blade immediately snapped, but on his second attempt the diamond was cleft in two – precisely along the plane Asscher intended. Further cutting resulted in 105 separate gems, the most important of which are now among the British Crown Jewels. The largest of them are:

The *Great Star of Africa* – a pearshape of 530.20 carats, mounted in the Queen's Sceptre. This is the largest cut diamond in the world.

The *Second Star of Africa* – a square-shaped gem of 317.40 carats, it is set in the Imperial State Crown beneath the Black Prince's Ruby.

The *Third Star of Africa* – a 94.40-carat pearshape – and the *Fourth Star of Africa* – a heartshape of 63.60 carats, both originally set in Queen Mary's Crown, but now set in a brooch which, along with other lesser gems cut from the *Cullinan*, are worn by Queen Elizabeth II.

2 *Braganza*	1,680.00

All trace of this enormous stone has been lost. Found in Brazil in the eighteenth century, there is much dispute about whether it was really a diamond at all, some authorities believing it was a giant white sapphire, a topaz or an aquamarine. Its position in the Top 10 is thus somewhat dubious. (If the *Braganza* is disqualified from the list, the 10th largest uncut diamond becomes a 620.14-carat stone which has not yet been finally named.)

3 *Excelsior*	995.20

The native worker who found this diamond (in 1893 – in a shovelful of gravel at the Jagersfontein Mine in South Africa) hid it and took it directly to the mine manager, who rewarded him with a horse, a saddle and £500. Cut by the celebrated Amsterdam firm of Asscher in 1903, it produced 21 superb stones, which were sold mainly through Tiffany's of New York and entered private hands. The largest, *Excelsior I*, weighing 69.68 carats, has since reappeared and was sold in London in 1984.

4 *Star of Sierra Leone*	968.80

Found in Sierra Leone on St Valentine's Day, 1972, the uncut diamond weighed 225 g/8 oz and measured 6.5 x 4 cm/2½ x 1½ in. Acquired by the famous New York diamond dealer Harry Winston (who is celebrated in the song, *Diamonds are a Girl's Best Friend*), it was cut into 11 individual stones, the largest weighing 143.20 carats. This in turn was cut into seven, and all but the largest set in the magnificent *Star of Sierra Leone Brooch*.

5 *Zale Corporation/'Golden Giant'*	890.00

Its origin is so shrouded in mystery that it is not even known which country it came from. Bought uncut in 1984, it took three years to cut it to a 407-carat, 65-facet yellow stone, after the *Great Star of Africa* the second largest cut stone of all time. On 19 October 1988, it came up for auction at Christie's, New York, with press speculation that it might smash all previous records by fetching $30,000,000 (£16,666,666). However, although the bidding went up to $12,000,000, which would have broken the

The *Star of Sierra Leone*, the fourth largest uncut diamond ever found.

world record, it failed to reach its unknown but clearly much higher reserve price, and will presumably come onto the market again at some future date – unless it finds a private buyer willing to spend more than $12,000,000.

6	*Great Mogul*	787.50

When found in 1650 in the Gani Mine, India, this diamond was presented to Shah Jehan, the builder of the Taj Mahal. It is said that when his son Aurangzeb gave it to the cutter, Hortensio Borgio, he reduced its size so much (to 280 carats) that Aurangzeb flew into a rage and fined him 10,000 rupees. After Nadir Shah conquered Delhi in 1739, it entered the Persian treasury and apparently vanished from history, but it has been claimed that it merely changed its name and is the *Orlov* diamond, one of the Russian Imperial diamonds which are held in the Soviet Union by the USSR Diamond Fund.

7	*Woyie River*	770.00

Found in 1945 beside the river in Sierra Leone whose name it now bears, it was cut into 30 stones. The largest of these, known as *Victory* and weighing 31.35 carats, was auctioned at Christie's, New York in 1984 for $880,000.

8	*Presidente Vargas*	726.60

Discovered in the Antonio River, Brazil, in 1938, it was named after the then President, Getulio Vargas. Harry Winston paid a reputed $700,000 for it in 1939 and had it cut into no fewer than 29 gems, the whereabouts of most of which are now unknown.

9	*Jonker*	726.00

In 1934 Jacobus Jonker, a previously unsuccessful diamond prospector, found this massive diamond after it had been exposed by a heavy storm. Acquired by Harry Winston, it was exhibited in the American Museum of Natural History and attracted enormous crowds. It was cut into 13 gems, the largest of which, bearing the name *Jonker* and said to be the most perfect cut diamond in the world, was sold to King Farouk of Egypt. After he was deposed in 1952, it disappeared. It then resurfaced in the Queen of Nepal's collection and was finally sold in Hong Kong in 1977 for a reputed £1,300,000.

10	*Reitz*	650.80

Like the *Excelsior*, the *Reitz* was found in the Jagersfontein Mine in South Africa in 1895 and was named after the President of the Orange Free State, Francis William Reitz. Two years later, it was cut and the principal gem renamed the *Jubilee* to celebrate Queen Victoria's Diamond Jubilee. At 245.35 carats one of the largest cut diamonds in the world, the *Jubilee* is also said to be the most precisely cut, capable of being balanced on one of its facets measuring only two millimetres across. It was first acquired by an Indian industrialist and later by Paul-Louis Weiller, a French millionaire.

The *Hope* diamond has undergone a turbulent history.

THE CURSE OF THE *HOPE* DIAMOND

It is said that the *Hope*, America's most famous diamond, is cursed and has caused at least 20 deaths. This blue gem was first acquired by the French traveller and jeweller Jean Baptiste Tavernier who sold it to Louis XIV in 1669, when it became known as the *Tavernier Blue*. Although Tavernier himself lived to a ripe old age, Louis XVI, who later owned it, and Marie Antoinette, who may have worn it, were both guillotined in 1793. The diamond had been stolen the previous year, but it later reappeared and was bought by Irish banker Henry Hope, after whom it was named. He survived, as did his nephew who exhibited the *Hope* at the Crystal Palace in 1851, but another owner, a mysterious Russian prince called Ivan Kanitowsky, was alleged to have given it to his French mistress, Mlle Ladre, whom he then shot, while he himself was stabbed to death during the Russian Revolution. After further disasters – few of which stand up to investigation – supposedly befell subsequent owners, American newspaper magnate Edward McClean bought the *Hope* for his wife Evalyn. He became an alcoholic and died in a mental institution, their son was killed in a motoring accident and their daughter committed suicide in 1946. After Evalyn McClean's own death, the *Hope* was bought by diamond dealer Harry Winston, who succeeded in avoiding the 'curse' by presenting it in 1958 to the Smithsonian Institution in Washington, DC, where it remains on public display.

THE TOP 10 COINS AND NOTES IN CIRCULATION IN THE UK

	Unit	Units in circulation	Value in circulation (£)
1	£10	586,000,000	5,860,000,000
2	£20	219,000,000	4,380,000,000
3	£50	45,000,000	2,250,000,000
4	£5	307,000,000	1,535,000,000
5	£1 coins	974,000,000	974,000,000
6	50p	670,000,000	335,000,000
7	10p	1,498,000,000	149,800,000
8	5p (new)	1,524,000,000	76,200,000
9	2p	3,585,000,000	71,700,000
10	£1 notes	62,000,000	62,000,000

Surprising though it may seem, although they were last issued on 31 December 1984 and ceased to be legal tender on 11 March 1988, the value of £1 notes still in circulation is greater than that of 1p coins (5,921,000,000 units worth £59,210,000), which are hence not in the Top 10. One may well speculate as to the whereabouts of £62,000,000 of unspendable banknotes.

The total weight of 1p coins in circulation is 21,102 tonnes and that of 2p coins 25,584 tonnes. Notes in circulation reached a peak total of £17,564,000,000 at Christmas 1989 – the equivalent of a pile of £5 notes 279 km/174 miles high.

The Royal Mint adds to the vast number of coins in circulation.

THE 10 COUNTRIES WITH THE HIGHEST INFLATION

	Country	Currency unit	Annual inflation rate (%)
1	Peru	Inti	3,399
2	Argentina	Austral	3,080
3	Brazil	Cruzeiro	1,340
4	Yugoslavia	Dinar	1,287
5	Poland	Zloty	251
6	Zaïre	Zaïre	104
7	Uganda	Shilling	90
8	Venezuela	Bolivar	84
9	Uruguay	Peso	80
10	Afghanistan	Afghani	77

These figures are for 1989, the latest year for which complete statistics exist (although it is apparent that in 1990 certain countries 'improved' their rates – those of Venezuela and Afghanistan, for example, to 41 and 49 per cent respectively, although Uruguay's position worsened with inflation escalating to 113 per cent).

Inflation rates of these levels of magnitude, however, seem almost insignificant when compared with the multi-million per cent hyper-inflation experienced by Germany in 1923, or Hungary in 1946, and have been far exceeded in recent times by that of Bolivia which was over 24,000 per cent in 1985. Britain's highest annual rate of inflation was in 1974–75 when it reached almost 27 per cent.

FOOD & DRINK

THE TOP 10 CHOCOLATE-CONSUMING NATIONS IN THE WORLD

	Country	Total cocoa consumption (tonnes)
1	USA	489,500
2	USSR	245,300
3	West Germany	199,600
4	UK	156,100
5	France	131,100
6	Japan	113,400
7	Italy	66,100
8	Spain	52,600
9	Canada	51,500
10	Brazil	44,500

THE TOP 10 SWEETS ADVERTISED IN THE UK

	Sweet	Annual advertising expenditure (£)
1	Mars Twix	5,162,500
2	Rowntree's Kit Kat	3,945,100
3	Mars Bar	3,627,900
4	Wrigley's Spearmint Gum	3,458,400
5	Mars Snickers	3,454,500
6	Mars M & Ms	3,070,200
7	Mars Bounty	3,010,500
8	Rowntree's Quality Street	2,703,900
9	Suchard Milka	2,463,700
10	Mars Milky Way	2,260,900

Cocoa is the principal ingredient of chocolate, and its consumption is therefore closely linked to the production of chocolate in each consuming country. Like coffee, the consumption of chocolate tends to occur mainly in the Western world and in more affluent countries. Since some of the Top 10 consuming nations also have large populations, the figures for cocoa consumption *per head* present a somewhat different picture, led by those countries with a long-established tradition of manufacturing high-quality chocolate products:

CADBURY'S TOP 10 CHOCOLATE PRODUCTS

1	Dairy Milk
2	Roses
3	Milk Tray
4	Wispa
5	Creme Eggs
6	Flake
7	Crunchie
8	Fruit & Nut
9	Whole Nut
10	Double Decker

	Country	Consumption per head		
		kg	lb	oz
1	Switzerland	5.071	11	3
2	Belgium/Luxembourg	3.761	8	5
3	Austria	3.241	7	2
4	West Germany	3.219	7	2
5	Norway	2.738	6	1
6	UK	2.729	6	0
7	France	2.332	5	2
8	USA	1.968	4	5
9	Canada	1.964	4	5
10	Denmark	1.921	4	4

The firms of Fry's and Cadbury's were founded in the early eighteenth and nineteenth centuries respectively by Quakers (who viewed drinking chocolate as a healthy alternative to alcohol) and merged in 1919. Many of their best-known products date back longer than one might suppose: Dairy Milk, famed for its 'glass-and-a-half of full cream milk in every half pound' (the slogan of a campaign started in 1928) has been around since 1905, and Milk Tray since 1915. Flake, Fruit & Nut and Crunchie bars all date from the 1920s and Roses and Whole Nut from the 1930s. Wispas are made by machines that are capable of producing 1,680 bars per minute, yet with such precision that the size of the tiny air bubbles in the chocolate is controlled to within 0.2–0.3 mm. Creme Eggs (last year No. 10 but now at 5th position in the list) are made at the rate of 1,100 a minute on machines that cost £14,000,000 and have the capacity to produce an astonishing 370,000,000 a year, equivalent to 6½ for every inhabitant of the United Kingdom!

Chocomania – Cadbury's 10 bestsellers.

THE 10 BESTSELLING SWEETS IN THE UK

	Product	Manufacturer	Sales per annum (£)
1	Kit Kat	Rowntree	165,000,000
2	Mars Bar	Mars	150,000,000
3	Twix	Mars	97,000,000
4	Dairy Milk	Cadbury	86,000,000
5	Quality Street	Rowntree	56,000,000
6=	Maltesers	Mars	54,000,000
6=	Roses	Cadbury	54,000,000
8=	Wispa	Cadbury	50,000,000
8=	Flake	Cadbury	50,000,000
10	Milk Tray	Cadbury	46,000,000

It is estimated that there are over 1,000 different confectionery brands available in the UK, but a relatively small number account for a major proportion of sales. The Top 30 brands had a market value of some £1,400,000,000 in 1988, or around 43 per cent of the total, including imports. The two largest firms, Cadbury/Nestlé and Rowntree, each have approximately 22 per cent of this market; Mars is in third place with 18 per cent, followed by Terry's at 4 per cent and all the other companies, each with a very small percentage of the total.

The Kit Kat bar – for several years Britain's bestselling confectionery item – is also the 5th bestselling chocolate bar in both the USA and Japan.

QUIZ

SWEETS

1 What 1938 novel by Graham Greene has a well-known south coast sweet as its title?
2 Were Rowntree's Smarties introduced in 1937, 1947 or 1957?
3 What group had a Number One hit in 1963 with the song *Sweets For My Sweet*?
4 What sweet was advertised with the slogan, 'Melts in your mouth, not in your hand'?
5 Which TV detective was in the habit of sucking lollipops?
6 What sweet was originally made from chicle, the dried sap of a Mexican jungle tree?
7 Name the boy hero of the Roald Dahl novel on which the film *Willie Wonka and the Chocolate Factory* is based.
8 What was a Mars Snicker bar originally called in the UK?
9 What is the origin of the name of the confectionery company, Trebor?
10 What chocolate filling was named after a seventeenth-century French Field Marshal?

THE TOP 10 MEAT-EATING NATIONS IN THE WORLD

	Country	Consumption per head per annum kg	lb	oz
1	USA	115.2	254	0
2	Uruguay	103.1	227	5
3	Australia	101.4	223	9
4	Canada	99.4	219	2
5	Czechoslovakia	99.3	218	15
6	Hungary	98.5	217	3
7	Denmark	96.3	212	5
8	New Zealand	95.8	211	3
9	Argentina	94.6	208	9
10	Germany	93.9	207	0

Figures compiled by the Meat and Livestock Commission show a huge range of meat consumption in developed countries around the world, from those featured in the Top 10 to Turkey where they eat 16.2 kg/36 lb of meat per head per year, while some estimates suggest that in very poor countries, such as India, meat consumption may be as little as 1.5 kg/3 lb per annum.

Meat-eating is a reflection of various factors: wealth – in general, the richer the country, the more meat is eaten, although in recent years 'healthy eating' concerns of many Western countries have resulted in a deliberate decline in consumption. Availability is also significant – New Zealand's consumption of lamb is the world's highest at 30.2 kg/67 lb per head, while Argentineans eat 68.0 kg/150 lb and Uruguayans 63.6 kg/140 lb of beef per head. Culture also plays a role – as a result of dietary prohibitions, very little pork is eaten in the Middle East, and the Japanese eat only 41.2 kg/91 lb of meat, but larger quantities of fish than many other nations. Figures for Eastern European countries are from official sources, and those who have seen customers there queuing for small rationed quantities of meat may well question them. If Czechoslovakia and Hungary are excluded altogether from the Top 10, the 9th and 10th places are occupied by France (93.8 kg/207 lb) and Argentina (88.2 kg/194 lb). The United Kingdom's meat consumption (56.9 kg/125 lb) is the second lowest in the EC, just beating that of Portugal (51.8 kg/114 lb).

THE TOP 10 CALORIE-CONSUMING NATIONS IN THE WORLD

	Country	Average daily consumption
1	Belgium/Luxembourg	3,901
2	East Germany	3,855
3	Greece	3,702
4	Ireland	3,688
5	Bulgaria	3,650
6	USA	3,644
7	Hungary	3,635
8	Switzerland	3,623
9	Denmark	3,605
10	Italy	3,571
	UK	*3,259*

The Calorie requirement of the average man is 2,700 and of a woman 2,500. Inactive people need less, while those engaged in heavy labour might require to increase, perhaps even to double these figures. Calories that are not consumed as energy turn to fat – which is why Calorie-counting is one of the key aspects of most diets. The high Calorie intake of certain countries, such as those in Eastern Europe and Italy, is a reflection of the high proportion of starchy foods, such as potatoes, bread and pasta, in the national diet. Yugoslavia and Czechoslovakia are in 11th and 12th places, both with average consumption figures of more than 3,500. In many Western countries the high figures simply reflect over-eating – especially since these figures are averages that include men, women and children, suggesting that large numbers in each country are greatly exceeding them. While weight-watchers of the West guzzle their way through 30 per cent more than they need, every country in Europe consuming more than 3,000 Calories per head, the Calorie consumption in Bangladesh, Haiti and some of the poorest African nations falls below 2,000, while in Mozambique it drops to as little as 1,604.

No. 11 on the US list is cheese (10.8 kg/23 lb 11 oz), followed by low-calorie sweeteners, the consumption per head of which (9.1 kg/20 lb) is greater than that of fish (7.1 kg/15 lb 11 oz). Also high on the list come the great American staple foodstuff, ice cream (7.3 kg/16 lb), and coffee (4.6 kg/10 lb 3 oz).

ABOVE RIGHT Meat, No. 1 on the US list of foods consumed, but a lowly seventh on the comparative UK list.

THE TOP 10 FOOD AND DRINK ITEMS CONSUMED IN THE USA

	Product	Average consumption per head per annum kg	lb	oz
1	Meat	115.2	254	0
2	Milk and cream	104.6	230	8
3	Vegetables	91.6	201	14
4	Beer	89.3	196	14
5	Grain products (bread, breakfast cereals, etc)	68.6	151	3
6	Sugar, honey and glucose	60.5	133	5
7	Potatoes	55.9	123	5
8	Fruit	49.9	109	14
9	Oils and fats	27.5	60	11
10	Eggs	13.5	29	11

THE TOP 10 FOOD AND DRINK ITEMS CONSUMED IN THE UK

	Product	Average consumption per head per annum kg	lb	oz
1	Milk and cream	133.1	293	7
2	Potatoes and potato products	113.1	249	5
3	Beer	109.0	240	0
4	Fruit	94.2	207	11
5	Vegetables	86.5	190	1
6	Grain products (bread, breakfast cereals, etc)	71.8	158	5
7	Meat	56.9	125	7
8	Sugar, honey and glucose	43.9	96	12
9	Oils and fats	22.7	50	1
10	Eggs	13.7	30	0

HARRODS FOOD HALLS' 10 BESTSELLING LINES

1 Smoked salmon

2 Christmas puddings

3 Traditional cheeses

4 Aberdeen Angus beef

5 Harrods chocolates

6 Shortbread and cookies

7 Turkeys, geese and pheasants

8 Nuts

9 Fruit baskets

10 York hams

THE 10 MOST-ADVERTISED FOOD PRODUCTS IN THE UK

	Product	Annual advertising expenditure (£)
1	Chocolate confectionery	76,465,000
2	Breakfast cereals	63,287,000
3	Coffee	46,222,000
4	Margarine	30,154,000
5	Sauces, pickles and salad cream	24,585,000
6	Crisps and snacks	23,192,000
7	Sugar confectionery	22,539,000
8	Tea	21,903,000
9	Biscuits	18,458,000
10	Milk and milk products	17,356,000

FORTNUM & MASON'S 10 BESTSELLING LINES

1 Speciality tea (loose)

2 Jams and marmalades

3 Biscuits

4 Christmas puddings

5 Smoked Scottish salmon

6 Blue Stilton cheese

7 Russian caviar

8 Hand-made English chocolates

9 Champagne

10 Claret

Fortnum & Mason Ltd of Piccadilly dates from the eighteenth century when William Fortnum, a former footman in Queen Anne's household, joined forces with Hugh Mason to form a grocery store that soon became one of the most famous in the world. It was the first to stock the products of H. J. Heinz and has a long-standing reputation for producing food hampers, including, in 1985, the world's largest, a 2.7 cu m / 96 cu ft wicker basket of food and drink costing £20,000 – although it came complete with the services of a butler for one day!

Super snack: the giant Fortnum & Mason hamper (with butler).

MARKS & SPENCER'S 10 BESTSELLING FOOD LINES

	Food type	Bestselling items
1	Fresh chicken	Whole and portions
2	Delicatessen	Roast chicken and ham
3	Sandwiches	Prawn mayonnaise
4	Fruit	Bananas, strawberries, peaches
5	Quiches	Quiche Lorraine
6	Pies	Cottage pies, pork pies
7	Ready-prepared recipe dishes	Chicken Kiev, lasagne
8	Salads	Tomato, crispheart lettuce
9	Fish	Prawns, smoked salmon
10	Orange juice	Freshly squeezed, Jaffa orange

Though Britain's best-known retailers of clothing, Marks & Spencer is, perhaps surprisingly, also the country's largest fishmonger, while their overall bestselling line for many years has not been knickers, but chickens! The firm pioneered a number of food developments: iceberg lettuces, for example, were previously grown in California until Marks & Spencer encouraged British growers to produce them, and cherry tomatoes were strictly a garden variety until the company arranged for them to be grown commercially.

THE TOP 10 IMPORTERS OF FOOD AND DRINK FROM THE UK

	Importer	Value 1990 (£)
1	France	864,000,000
2	Eire	535,000,000
3	USA	512,000,000
4	Holland	386,000,000
5	Germany	385,000,000
6	Spain	358,000,000
7	Belgium/ Luxembourg	284,000,000
8	Italy	280,000,000
9	Japan	254,000,000
10	USSR	158,000,000

THE TOP 10 EXPORTERS OF FOOD AND DRINK TO THE UK

	Exporter	Value 1990 (£)
1	France	1,627,000,000
2	Holland	1,404,000,000
3	Eire	1,089,000,000
4	Denmark	806,000,000
5	Germany	699,000,000
6	Italy	574,000,000
7	Spain	485,000,000
8	Belgium/ Luxembourg	382,000,000
9	New Zealand	358,000,000
10	USA	300,000,000

THE TOP 10 FOOD AND DRINK PRODUCTS IMPORTED TO THE UK

	Product	Value 1990 (£)
1	Alcoholic drinks	1,437,000,000
2	Fruit and nuts	1,286,000,000
3	Vegetables	807,000,000
4	Sugar, molasses and honey	554,000,000
5	Salted and smoked meat (bacon, ham, etc)	538,000,000
6	Fish	477,000,000
7	Cheese and curd	459,000,000
8	Prepared and preserved meat (sausages, etc)	441,000,000
9	Edible products and prepared food (sauces, pasta, etc)	389,000,000
10	Prepared and preserved vegetables	383,000,000

THE TOP 10 FOOD AND DRINK PRODUCTS EXPORTED FROM THE UK

	Product	Value 1990 (£)
1	Alcoholic drinks	2,065,000,000
2	Wheat	426,000,000
3	Cereal products (biscuits, etc)	402,000,000
4	Edible products and prepared food (sauces, pasta, etc)	256,000,000
5	Beef	232,000,000
6	Milk and cream	223,000,000
7	Barley	186,000,000
8	Fish	182,000,000
9	Sheep and goat meat	178,000,000
10	Shellfish	176,000,000

THE TOP 10 ALCOHOL-CONSUMING NATIONS IN THE WORLD

	Country	Annual consumption per head (100% alcohol) litres	pints
1	France	13.3	23.4
2	Luxembourg	13.0	22.9
3	Spain	12.1	21.3
4=	Switzerland	11.0	19.4
4=	East Germany*	11.0	19.4
6	Hungary	10.5	18.5
7=	West Germany*	10.4	18.3
7=	Portugal	10.4	18.3
9	Belgium	10.0	17.6
10	Austria	9.9	17.4
21	USA	7.5	13.2
22	UK	7.4	13.0

Figures for united country not yet available.

Even though its total consumption has declined from its peak of 17.4 litres/30.6 pints per head, France has held its lead in this list for many years.

THE TOP 10 BEER-DRINKING NATIONS IN THE WORLD

	Country	Annual consumption per head litres	pints
1	Germany	143.0	251.6
2	Czechoslovakia	130.0	228.7
3	Denmark	119.9	211.0
4	Belgium	118.6	208.7
5	Austria	117.8	207.3
6	Luxembourg	115.8	203.8
7	New Zealand	115.2	202.7
8	Australia	113.1	199.0
9	UK	111.2	195.7
10	Hungary	101.0	177.7

THE TOP 10 BEER-PRODUCING COUNTRIES IN THE WORLD

	Country	Annual production	
		litres	pints
1	USA	23,226,500,000	40,872,900,000
2	Germany	11,704,300,000	20,596,700,000
3	UK	6,016,500,000	10,587,500,000
4	Japan	5,789,400,000	10,187,900,000
5	USSR	5,580,000,000	9,819,400,000
6	China	5,500,000,000	9,678,600,000
7	Brazil	4,780,000,000	8,411,600,000
8	Mexico	3,453,400,000	6,077,100,000
9	Spain	2,657,900,000	4,677,200,000
10	Canada	2,314,900,000	4,073,600,000
	World total	*107,700,000,000*	*189,525,400,000*

World beer production is almost sufficient to allow every person on the planet to drink 0.57 litres/1 pint every ten days of the year. That of the UK is adequate to provide every UK inhabitant with the same quantity every two days.

THE TOP 10 COUNTRIES OF ORIGIN OF BEER IMPORTS TO THE UK

	Country	Annual importation	
		litres	pints
1	Ireland	185,900,000	327,138,083
2	West Germany	120,200,000	211,522,311
3	Netherlands	66,700,000	117,375,525
4	Belgium/Luxembourg	9,100,000	16,013,752
5	Australia	7,600,000	13,374,123
6	Denmark	4,200,000	7,390,963
7	Spain	3,900,000	6,863,037
8	France	3,500,000	6,159,136
9=	USA	3,200,000	5,631,210
9=	East Germany	3,200,000	5,631,210

A total of 420,300,000 litres/739,624,186 pints of imported beer entered the UK in 1988 – equivalent to almost 13 pints for every person in the country.

Only Herr for the beer: German beer-drinkers lead the world.

THE TOP 10 WINE-DRINKING NATIONS IN THE WORLD

	Country	Litres per head per annum	Equiv. 75 cl bottles
1	France	74.0	98.7
2	Italy	62.1	82.8
3	Luxembourg	58.3	77.7
4	Portugal	58.0	77.3
5	Argentina	55.8	74.4
6	Switzerland	49.9	66.5
7	Spain	47.4	63.2
8	Chile	35.0	46.7
9	Austria	32.9	43.9
10	Greece	32.0	42.7
26	*UK*	*11.4*	*15.2*
29	*USA*	*8.6*	*11.5*

THE TOP 10 WINE-DRINKING NATIONS IN EUROPE

	Country	% who have drunk wine in the last seven days	
		1969	1990
1	France	74	61
2	Italy	82	59
3	Switzerland	54	54
4	Denmark	17	53
5	Austria	49	51
6	Portugal	73	46
7	Luxembourg	65	41
8	West Germany	42	40
9	Belgium	21	35
10=	Netherlands	18	32
10=	Spain	69	32
10=	Sweden	18	32
	UK	*9*	*28*

Reader's Digest's *Eurodata Report*, a survey of the lifestyles, consumer spending habits and attitudes of people in 17 European countries (12 EC and five EFTA), drew comparisons with a similar survey undertaken by the same organization in 1969. The Top 10 is based on interviewees' responses to the question 'Have you drunk any wine in the last seven days?' It is a revealing measure of changing habits that in the intervening 21 years, the number in the UK who answered 'yes' more than trebled, while other countries showed smaller increases or even reductions.

THE 10 MOST EXPENSIVE BOTTLES OF WINE EVER SOLD AT AUCTION

	Wine	Price (£)
1	Château Lafite 1787 Christie's, London, 5 December 1985	105,000

The highest price ever paid for a bottle of red wine resulted from the bottle having been initialled by the third US President, Thomas Jefferson. It was purchased by Christopher Forbes and is now on display in the Forbes Magazine Galleries, New York.

	Wine	Price (£)
2	Château d'Yquem 1784 Christie's, London, 4 December 1986	39,600

The highest price ever paid for a bottle of white wine.

	Wine	Price (£)
3	Château Lafite Rothschild 1832 (double magnum) International Wine Auctions, London, 9 April 1988	24,000
4	Château Lafite 1806 Sotheby's, Geneva, 13 November 1988 (SF 57,200)	21,700
5	Château Lafite 1811 (tappit-hen – equivalent to three bottles) Christie's, London, 23 June 1988	20,000
6	Château Margaux 1784 (half-bottle) Christie's, at Vin Expo, Bordeaux, France, 26 June 1987	18,000

The highest price ever paid for a half-bottle.

	Wine	Price (£)
7	Château d'Yquem 1811 Christie's, London, 1 December 1988	15,000
8	Château Lafite Rothschild 1806 Sold at a Heublein Auction, San Francisco, 24 May 1979 ($28,000)	14,000
9	Château Lafite 1822 Sold at a Heublein Auction, San Francisco, 28 May 1980 ($31,000)	13,400
10	Château Lafite Rothschild 1811 International Wine Auctions, London, 26 June 1985	12,000

On 25 April 1989, No. 6, also initialled by Thomas Jefferson and now with an asking price of $500,000/£304,878, was smashed by a waiter's tray while on display at a tasting in the Four Seasons restaurant, New York. A small quantity of the wine was salvaged, but was declared virtually undrinkable.

As well as these high prices paid at auction, rare bottles of wine have also been sold privately for sums in excess of £25,000 – a jeroboam (equivalent to four bottles) of 1870 Mouton Rothschild, for example, changed hands for £26,500 in 1984.

LEFT Spain produces 2,266,500,000 litres of wine a year.

THE TOP 10 WINE-PRODUCING COUNTRIES IN THE WORLD

	Country	Annual production (litres)
1	Italy	6,180,000,000
2	France	5,713,700,000
3	Spain	2,266,500,000
4	Argentina	1,925,500,000
5	USSR	1,890,000,000
6	USA	1,823,700,000
7	South Africa	996,200,000
8	West Germany	931,500,000
9	Portugal	883,600,000
10	Romania	870,000,000
	World total	32,000,000,000

BELOW A good year: the 1784 Château d'Yquem sold for a record £39,600.

THE TOP 10 COUNTRIES OF ORIGIN OF WINE* IMPORTS TO THE UK

	Country	Litres per annum
1	France	210,400,000
2	West Germany	148,600,000
3	Italy	49,300,000
4	Spain	24,500,000
5	Bulgaria	15,000,000
6	Yugoslavia	14,800,000
7	Portugal	7,700,000
8	Australia	6,400,000
9=	USA	3,400,000
9=	Cyprus	3,400,000
	Total	491,400,000

*Table wine, excluding sparkling and fortified wine.

Total imports are equivalent to approximately 11½ bottles per head of the population per annum.

THE TOP 10 SPIRIT BRANDS IN THE WORLD

	Brand	Type	Annual sales (litres)
1	Bacardi	Rum	205,200,000
2	Smirnoff	Vodka	134,100,000
3	Ricard	Anis/pastis	67,500,000
4	Johnnie Walker Red	Scotch whisky	59,400,000
5	Gordon's Gin	Gin	56,700,000
6	J & B Rare	Scotch whisky	51,300,000
7	Ballantine's	Scotch whisky	48,600,000
8	Jim Beam	Bourbon	45,000,000
9	Presidente	Brandy	42,300,000
10	Bell's	Scotch whisky	38,700,000

THE TOP 10 WINE BRANDS IN THE WORLD

	Brand	Country	Type	Annual sales (litres)
1	Martini & Rossi	Italy	Vermouth	157,500,000
2	Carlo Rossi	USA	Table	120,600,000
3	Gallo Label	USA	Table	105,300,000
4	Almaden	USA	Table	78,300,000
5	Reserve Cellars of E & J Gallo	USA	Table	68,400,000
6	Inglenook	USA	Table	63,000,000
7	Richards Wild Irish Rose	USA	Fortified	55,800,000
8=	Paul Masson	USA	Table	51,300,000
8=	La Villageoise	France	Table	51,300,000
10	Cinzano Vermouth	Italy	Vermouth	50,400,000

GUINNESS FOR STRENGTH

THE 10 MOST-ADVERTISED BEER BRANDS IN THE UK

	Product	Annual advertising expenditure (£)
1	Tennents	8,088,000
2	Guinness	6,926,000
3	Carlsberg	6,540,000
4	Carling	5,581,000
5	Heineken	4,049,000
6	Fosters	4,030,000
7	Miller	3,969,000
8	Holsten	3,510,000
9	Castlemaine	2,503,000
10	Labatt	2,346,000

THE 10 MOST-ADVERTISED WINE BRANDS IN THE UK

	Product	Annual advertising expenditure (£)
1	Le Piat d'Or	1,660,000
2	Asti Spumante	1,413,000
3	Stowells	854,000
4=	Rougemont	798,000
4=	Appellation Contrôlée/ French Wine	798,000
6	Veuve du Vernay	726,000
7	Concorde	693,000
8	Eisberg	686,000
9	Stones Ginger Wine	660,000
10	Black Tower	531,000

ABOVE RIGHT John Gilroy's famous 1934 poster for Guinness, the second most-advertised beer in the UK.

THE TOP 10 SPIRITS-CONSUMING NATIONS IN THE WORLD

	Country	Annual consumption per head (100% alcohol) litres	pints
1	West Germany*	5.2	9.2
2	Poland	4.6	8.1
3	Hungary	4.5	7.9
4	Czechoslovakia	3.3	5.8
5	Finland	3.1	5.5
6	Spain	3.0	5.3
7	Bulgaria	2.8	4.9
8=	Luxembourg	2.5	4.4
8=	Canada	2.5	4.4
8=	Cyprus	2.5	4.4
13	USA	2.4	4.2
20	UK	1.8	3.2

Figures for united country not yet available.

THE TOP 10 SCOTCH WHISKY IMPORTERS IN THE WORLD

	Country	Value (£)	Volume (equivalent in litres of pure alcohol)
1	USA	274,000,000	46,200,000
2	France	195,000,000	27,400,000
3	Japan	176,000,000	21,000,000
4	Spain	123,000,000	16,900,000
5	Greece	66,000,000	9,100,000
6	Italy	72,000,000	9,000,000
7	South Africa	45,000,000	7,400,000
8	Australia	34,000,000	6,900,000
9	Germany	52,000,000	6,700,000
10	Thailand	61,000,000	6,000,000
	World total	1,712,000,000	238,300,000

THE TOP 10 CHAMPAGNE IMPORTERS IN THE WORLD

	Country	Bottles imported
1	UK	21,291,532
2	Germany	14,237,831
3	USA	11,669,222
4	Italy	9,626,094
5	Switzerland	8,599,632
6	Belgium	5,866,197
7	Netherlands	1,652,889
8	Japan	1,509,123
9	Australia	1,231,529
10	Spain	983,956

In 1990 an estimated total of 232,365,682 bottles of champagne were produced, a 6.6 per cent decline on the previous year's record production of 248,913,509 bottles. As usual, the French kept most of it for themselves and continued to lead the world as the leading champagne consumers, with 147,578,584 bottles drunk – equivalent to an annual consumption of 2.6 bottles for every man, woman and child in the country. A total of 84,787,098 bottles were exported and for many years the UK has led the world as the principal importer of champagne – although in 1990 its consumption fell, as did that of the USA, Switzerland, the Netherlands and Australia. The consumption of the other five countries in the Top 10 increased – that of Japan, in 1989 a newcomer to the list, by over 17 per cent. Canada, No. 9 in 1989, fell to 11th place in 1990 (982,901 bottles), a 33.25 per cent decline, which has been attributed to economic recession and a nationalistic trend towards home-produced sparkling wines.

Champagne by the barrel for the world's thirsty consumers.

THE 10 BRITISH PUBS WITH THE LONGEST NAMES

	Pub	Letters
1	Henry J Bean's But His Friends, Some of Whom Live Down This Way, All Call Him Hank Bar And Grill Fulham Road, London SW6	74

This establishment was given its long name solely in order to appear at the top of lists such as this.

2	The Old Thirteenth Cheshire Astley Volunteer Rifleman Corps Inn Astley Street, Stalybridge, Manchester	55

In order to maintain its pre-eminence, it was renamed from its former 39-letter version, 'The Thirteenth Mounted Cheshire Rifleman Inn', and was the longest pub name until Henry J Bean etc, came on the scene.

3	The Fellows, Moreton And Clayton Brewhouse Company Canal Street, Nottingham	43
4	The Ferret And Firkin In The Balloon Up The Creek Lots Road, London SW10	40
5=	The London Chatham And Dover Railway Tavern Cabul Road, London SW11	37
5=	The Footballers And Cricketers Public Arms Linlithgow, Lothian	37
7	The Argyll And Sutherland Highlander Inn Eastham, Cheshire	35
8=	The Shoulder Of Mutton And Cucumbers Inn Yapton, West Sussex	34
8=	The Green Man And Black's Head Royal Hotel Ashbourne, Derbyshire	34
10=	The Nightingale Theatre Public House Brighton, East Sussex	32
10=	The Queen Victoria and Railway Tavern Paddington, London W2	32
10=	The Worcestershire Brine Baths Hotel Droitwich, Worcestershire	32
10=	The Royal Gloucestershire Hussar Inn Frocester, Gloucestershire	32
10=	The Sir Gawain and the Green Knight Inn Connah's Quay, Clwyd	32

The 24-letter I Am The Only Running Footman, Charles Street, London W1, was for many years London's longest-named pub. The shortest-named public house in Britain was the now defunct X at Westcott, two miles south of Collumpton, Devon, but there have also been several with two letters, including the GI, Hastings, East Sussex, the XL Bar, Edinburgh and the CB Hotel, Arkengarthdale, North Yorkshire.

THE 10 COMMONEST PUB NAMES IN THE UK

1	The Red Lion*
2	The Crown
3	The Royal Oak
4	The White Hart
5	The King's Head
6	The Bull
7	The Coach and Horses
8	The George
9	The Plough
10	The Swan

*There are over 600 Red Lions in Britain.

Red Lions and White Harts abound among UK pub names.

THE 10 BESTSELLING SOFT DRINKS IN THE USA

	Brand	% of market
1	Coca-Cola	20.0
2	Pepsi-Cola	18.3
3	Diet Coke	8.9
4	Diet Pepsi	5.7
5	Dr Pepper	4.6
6	Sprite	3.6
7	Mountain Dew	3.5
8	7-Up	2.9
9	CF Diet Coke	2.4
10	CF Diet Pepsi	1.5

CF – Caffeine Free.

THE 10 MOST-ADVERTISED SOFT DRINKS* IN THE UK

	Brand	Annual advertising expenditure (£)
1	Coca-Cola	8,332,000
2	Pepsi-Cola	6,671,000
3	7-Up	2,717,000
4	Schweppes	2,268,000
5	Tango	1,772,000
6	Perrier	1,566,000
7	Lilt	1,444,000
8	Fanta	1,235,000
9	Spa	1,133,000
10	Orangina	1,127,000

*Excluding low-alcohol beer.

CRIME & PUNISHMENT

THE 10 LARGEST PRISONS IN SCOTLAND

	Prison	Inmates
1	Barlinnie, Glasgow	899
2	Edinburgh	488
3	Glenochil, near Alloa	441
4	Schotts, Lanarkshire	381
5	Perth	370
6	Polmont, near Falkirk*	367
7	Low Moss, near Glasgow	329
8	Greenock	206
9	Longriggend, Airdrie**	189
10	Glenochil, near Alloa*	167

*Young Offenders' Institution.
**Remand Institution.

THE 10 COMMONEST MOTORING OFFENCES IN THE UK

	Offence	% of motoring offences
1	Driving while uninsured	13.53
2	Speeding	10.78
3	Failing to pay road tax	9.38
4	Drink-driving	6.41
5	Careless driving	5.38
6	Driving without a licence	3.58
7	Defective tyres	3.42
8	Driving without L-plates	3.26
9	Unaccompanied L-driver	2.52
10	Driving while disqualified	2.22

THE 10 LARGEST PRISONS IN ENGLAND AND WALES

	Prison	Inmates
1	Wandsworth, London	1,395
2	Walton, Liverpool	991
3	Brixton, London	944
4	Wormwood Scrubs, London	919
5	Armley, Leeds	898
6	Durham*	876
7	Winson Green, Birmingham	872
8	Pentonville, London	825
9	Highpoint, Newmarket	775
10	Lindholme, Doncaster	746

*Male and female.

Figures are for total prison populations as at 31 December 1990. Strangeways, Manchester, formerly England's largest prison, was wrecked during a prisoners' riot in April 1990 and had not been fully re-opened.

QUIZ

MURDERERS

1 What was unusual about the execution of William Kemmler at Auburn Prison, New York, on 6 August 1890?
2 In the Edgar Allan Poe novel, who was discovered to have committed the murders in the rue Morgue?
3 Who was the last murderess to be hanged in England?
4 The wife and victim of which murderer was called Kunigunde Mackamotzki, Cora Turner and Belle Elmore?
5 Of what murderer were Mary Ann Nicholls and Mary Kelly believed to be the first and the last victims?
6 John Lee, a murderer who in 1885 survived three attempts to hang him, was the subject of a 1971 album by which British group?
7 What Russian revolutionary was murdered in Mexico by Ramón Mercader in 1940?
8 What was the name of the man convicted for the murder of Beatle John Lennon?
9 Who killed the man who is believed to have killed President Kennedy?
10 How many British prime ministers have been murdered?

Pentonville Prison, England and Wales's eighth largest with 825 inmates.

THE 10 MOST PROLIFIC MURDERERS IN THE UK

1 Mary Ann Cotton

Cotton (b.1832), a former nurse, is generally held to be Britain's worst mass murderer. Over a 20-year period, it seems probable that she disposed of 14–20 victims, including her husband, children and stepchildren by arsenic poisoning. She was hanged at Durham on 24 March 1873.

2 Dr William Palmer

Known as the 'Rugeley Poisoner', Palmer (b.1824) may have killed at least 13 and possibly as many as 16, including his wife, brother and children in order to claim insurance, and various men whom he robbed to pay off his gambling debts. He was hanged at Stafford on 14 June 1856. The true number of his victims remains uncertain.

3= William Burke and William Hare

Two Irishmen living in Edinburgh, Burke and Hare murdered at least 15 people in order to sell their bodies (for £8 to £14 each) to anatomists in the period before human dissection was legal. Burke was hanged on 28 January 1829 while Hare, having turned king's evidence against him, was released a week later and allegedly died a blind beggar in London in the 1860s.

3= Bruce Lee

In 1981 Lee was convicted of arson that resulted in the deaths of 26 residents of an old people's home. He was later cleared by the Court of Appeal of 11 of the deaths. He is currently in a mental hospital.

3= Dennis Andrew Nilsen

Nilsen (b.1948) admitted to murdering 15 men between 1978 and 1983. On 4 November 1983 he was sentenced to life imprisonment on six charges of murder and two attempted murders.

3= Michael Ryan

On 19 August 1987 in Hungerford, Berkshire, Ryan (b.1960) shot 15 dead and wounded 15 others before shooting himself.

7 Peter Sutcliffe

Known as the 'Yorkshire Ripper', Sutcliffe (b.1946) was caught on 2 January 1981 and on 22 May 1981 found guilty of murdering 13 women and seven attempted murders between 1975 and 1980. He was sentenced to life imprisonment on each charge and is currently in Parkhurst Prison.

Bruce Lee's original conviction for 26 murders was reduced to 15 on appeal.

8 Peter Thomas Anthony Manuel

Found guilty of murdering seven people, it is likely that Manuel killed as many as 12. He was hanged at Barlinnie Prison on 11 July 1958.

9 John George Haigh

The so-called 'Acid Bath Murderer' may have killed up to nine victims. He was hanged at Wandsworth Prison on 10 August 1949.

10 'Jack the Ripper'

In 1888 in Whitechapel, London, 'Jack the Ripper' killed and mutilated six women. His true identity and dates are unknown.

Other multiple murderers in British history include John Reginald Halliday Christie who may have killed as many as six women at 10 Rillington Place, London, and was hanged at Pentonville Prison on 15 July 1953. On 7 May 1981 John Thompson was found guilty on one specimen charge of murder by arson during an incident in which a total of 37 died at the Spanish Club, Denmark Street, London.

THE 10 MOST PROLIFIC MURDERERS IN THE WORLD*

1 Behram

The leader of the Thug cult in India, in the period 1790–1840 he was reputed to have committed over 931 ritual strangulations.

2 Countess Erszebet Bathory

In the period up to 1610 in Hungary, Bathory (1560–1614), known as 'Countess Dracula', murdered 300–650 girls in the belief that drinking their blood would prevent her from ageing. She was eventually arrested in 1611. Tried and found guilty, she died on 21 August 1614 walled up in her own castle at Csejthe.

3 William Estel Brown

On 17 July 1961 Brown admitted that on 18 March 1937 he had deliberately loosened the gas pipes in his school basement in New London, Texas, thereby causing an explosion that killed 282 children and 24 teachers.

4 Pedro Alonso López

Known as the 'Colombian Monster' and the 'Monster of the Andes', up to his 1980 capture he murdered at least 300 young girls in Colombia, Ecuador and Peru. He was caught by Ayacucho Indians in Peru, whose children he had been abducting, and escorted to Ecuador by a female missionary. He was arrested and led police to 53 graves; further bodies were revealed when a river flooded, but others were devoured by wild animals or buried under roads and on construction sites and were never discovered. López was convicted and sentenced to life imprisonment.

5 Gilles de Rais

A fabulously wealthy French aristocrat, de Rais (b.1404) was accused of having kidnapped and killed between 60 and 200 children. He was strangled and his body burnt at Nantes on 25 October 1440.

6 Herman Webster Mudgett

Also known as 'H.H. Holmes', Mudgett (b.1860) was believed to have lured over 150 women to his 63rd Street, Chicago, 'Castle', which was fully equipped for torturing and murdering them and disposing of the bodies. Arrested in 1894 and found guilty of murder, he confessed to killing 27. Mudgett, regarded as America's first mass murderer, was hanged on 7 May 1896.

7 Julio Gonzalez

On the morning of Sunday 25 March 1990, Gonzalez, a Cuban refugee who had lived in the USA for 10 years, allegedly firebombed Happy Land, a discotheque in The

Bronx, New York (ordered closed in 1988 because it lacked basic fire safety measures), killing 87.

8 Bruno Lüdke

Lüdke (b.1909) was a German who confessed to murdering 85 women between 1928 and 29 January 1943. Declared insane, he was incarcerated in a Vienna hospital where he was subjected to medical experiments, apparently dying on 8 April 1944 after a lethal injection.

9 Wou Bom-Kon

An off-duty policeman, on 26–27 April 1982 in South Korea he went on a drunken rampage with guns and grenades, killing 57 and injuring 35 before blowing himself up with a grenade.

10 John Gilbert Graham

Graham placed a time bomb in his mother's luggage as she boarded an airliner in Denver, Colorado, on 1 November 1955. En route for San Francisco, it blew up killing all 44 on board. Graham was executed in the gas chamber of Colorado State Penitentiary.

*Includes only individual murderers; excludes murders by bandits, those carried out by groups, such as political atrocities, and gangland slayings.

Other possible contenders for this unenviable list include Ted Bundy who, after spending nine years on death row, was executed at Florida State Prison on 24 January 1989 for the murder of 12-year-old Kimberley Leach. During his last hours he confessed to 23 murders. Police linked him conclusively to the murders of 36 girls and he once admitted that he might have killed as many as 100 times.

On 13 March 1980 John Wayne Gacy (b.1943) was sentenced to death by electrocution for the Chicago murders of 33 men. The sentence was never carried out and he is currently in prison (in the USA there are currently over 2,200 convicted murderers on death row).

At the end of the First World War Fritz Haarman of Hanover, West Germany, may have murdered as many as 40 refugees in order to steal their clothes and sell their bodies as meat. He was charged with 27 murders and executed in 1924.

Dr Marcel Petiot is known to have killed at least 27 but admitted to 63 murders at his Paris house during the Second World War. He claimed that they were Nazi collaborators, but it is probable that they were wealthy Jews whom he robbed and killed after pretending to help them escape from occupied France. He was guillotined on 26 May 1946.

Bella Gunness (née Grunt) (1859–1908) is said to have lured 16–28 suitors through 'Lonely Hearts' advertisements, as well as numerous others, to her La Porte, Indiana, farm, where – along with her two husbands – she murdered them. On 28 April 1908 she burned the farm down and either committed suicide or, according to some reports, faked her own death and disappeared.

The worst gun massacre in the USA took place on 19 July 1984 when 41-year-old James Huberty opened fire in a McDonald's restaurant in San Ysidro, California, killing 21 before being shot dead by police. A 22nd victim died from wounds the following day. In recent years several other incidents of this nature in the USA and Canada have resulted in the deaths of up to 16 people.

THE 10 DIPLOMATIC MISSIONS WITH THE MOST UNPAID PARKING FINES

| | Mission | Total unpaid fines | |
		1989	1990
1	Poland	244	531
2	Saudi Arabia	287	346
3	USSR	599	308
4	Pakistan	243	220
5	Kuwait	113	218
6	Sudan	238	193
7	Cameroon	261	191
8	United Arab Emirates	231	185
9	Ivory Coast	272	183
10	Morocco	135	156

For many years diplomats used their immunity from prosecution to avoid paying parking fines. In 1984 they managed to clock up a record 108,845 unpaid tickets. Since 1985, however, this practice has been challenged and pressure brought to bear on the offending embassies and international organizations to make their staffs behave responsibly. The total in 1990 was 6,551, a 16 per cent reduction on the 1989 figure of 7,831.

THE 10 COMMONEST REPORTED CRIMINAL OFFENCES IN ENGLAND AND WALES

| | Offence | Number | |
		1980	1989
1	Criminal damage	349,500	630,100
2	Theft from a vehicle	294,400	628,900
3	Burglary in a dwelling	294,900	437,700
4	Theft or unauthorized taking of a motor vehicle	324,400	393,400
5	Burglary in other buildings	323,500	388,200
6	Theft from a shop	206,200	223,000
7	Violence against the person	97,200	177,000
8=	Fraud and forgery	105,200	134,500
8=	Theft of a pedal cycle	99,900	134,500
10	Handling stolen goods	38,800	44,900

Although the year-on-year increases of all the commonest criminal offences during the 1980s were relatively small – some even showing occasional annual decreases – over the decade as a whole, all the Top 10 offences recorded by the police underwent increases ranging from under 16 per cent for handling stolen goods to 80 per cent for criminal damage, 82 per cent for crimes of violence against the person and a staggering 114 per cent for theft from a vehicle.

OPPOSITE Julio Gonzalez, indicted for 87 murders in New York.

RIGHT Thefts from motor vehicles more than doubled in the 1980s.

MILITARY

THE 10 LARGEST ARMED FORCES OF WORLD WAR I

	Country	Personnel*
1	Russia	12,000,000
2	Germany	11,000,000
3	British Empire	8,904,467
4	France	8,410,000
5	Austria–Hungary	7,800,000
6	Italy	5,615,000
7	USA	4,355,000
8	Turkey	2,850,000
9	Bulgaria	1,200,000
10	Japan	800,000

*Total at peak strength.

THE 10 LARGEST ARMED FORCES OF WORLD WAR II

	Country	Personnel*
1	USSR	12,500,000
2	USA	12,364,000
3	Germany	10,000,000
4	Japan	6,095,000
5	France	5,700,000
6	UK	4,683,000
7	Italy	4,500,000
8	China	3,800,000
9	India	2,150,000
10	Poland	1,000,000

*Total at peak strength.

THE 10 SMALLEST ARMED FORCES OF WORLD WAR II

	Country	Personnel*
1	Costa Rica	400
2	Liberia	1,000
3=	Honduras	3,000
3=	Nicaragua	3,000
3=	El Salvador	3,000
6	Haiti	3,500
7	Dominican Republic	4,000
8	Guatemala	5,000
9=	Bolivia	8,000
9=	Uruguay	8,000
9=	Paraguay	8,000

*Total at peak strength.

As well as mobilizing very small armed forces, several South American countries entered the Second World War at a very late stage: Argentina, for example, did not declare war on Germany and Japan until 27 March 1945 – six weeks before Germany was defeated. The smallest European armed force was that of Denmark, with a maximum strength of 15,000.

ABOVE First World War British Empire troops totalled almost nine million.

THE 10 CITIES MOST BOMBED BY THE RAF AND USAF, 1939–45

	City	Estimated civilian fatalities
1	Dresden	100,000+
2	Hamburg	55,000
3	Berlin	49,000
4	Cologne	20,000
5	Magdeburg	15,000
6	Kassel	13,000
7	Darmstadt	12,300
8=	Heilbronn	7,500
8=	Essen	7,500
10=	Wuppertal	6,000
10=	Dortmund	6,000

A Boeing 'Flying Fortress' in a raid on Berlin, third most bombed German city during the Second World War.

THE TOP 10 FILMS SHOWN IN LONDON DURING WORLD WAR II

1 *Pimpernel Smith*

2 *49th Parallel*

3 *Dangerous Moonlight*

4 *A Yank in the RAF*

5 *One of Our Aircraft is Missing*

6 *Pardon My Sarong*

7 *Beyond the Blue Horizon*

8 *The Road to Morocco*

9 *The Life and Death of Colonel Blimp*

10 *The Sullivans*

Of the 10 most successful films shown in Granada group cinemas during the period 1939–45, eight were war films.

THE TOP 10 RANKS OF THE ROYAL NAVY, ARMY AND ROYAL AIR FORCE

	Navy	Army	Royal Air Force
1	Admiral of the Fleet	Field Marshal	Marshal of the Royal Air Force
2	Admiral	General	Air Chief Marshal
3	Vice-Admiral	Lieutenant-General	Air Marshal
4	Rear-Admiral	Major-General	Air Vice-Marshal
5	Commodore	Brigadier	Air Commodore
6	Captain	Colonel	Group Captain
7	Commander	Lieutenant-Colonel	Wing Commander
8	Lieutenant Commander	Major	Squadron Leader
9	Lieutenant	Captain	Flight Lieutenant
10	Sub-Lieutenant	Lieutenant	Flying Officer

THE TOP 10 REGIMENTS OF THE BRITISH ARMY*

1 The Royal Scots

2 The Queen's Regiment

3 The King's Own Royal Border Regiment

4 The Royal Regiment of Fusiliers

5 The King's Regiment

6 The Royal Anglian Regiment

7 The Devonshire and Dorset Regiment

8 The Light Infantry

9 The Prince of Wales's Own Regiment of Yorkshire

10 The Green Howards (Alexandra, Princess of Wales's Own Yorkshire Regiment)

Based on order of precedence.

THE TOP 10 CORPS OF THE BRITISH ARMY*

1 The Life Guards and The Blues and Royals

2 The Royal Horse Artillery

3 The Royal Armoured Corps

4 The Royal Regiment of Artillery

5 The Corps of Royal Engineers

6 The Royal Corps of Signals

7 The Foot Guards

8 Infantry Regiments

9 The Special Air Service Regiment

10 The Army Air Corps

Based on order of precedence.

THE TOP 10 REGIMENTS OF THE ROYAL ARMOURED CORPS*

1 The Queen's Dragoon Guards

2 The Royal Scots Dragoon Guards (Carabiniers and Greys)

3 4th/7th Dragoon Guards

4 5th Royal Inniskilling Dragoon Guards

5 The Queen's Own Hussars

6 The Queen's Royal Irish Hussars

7 9th/12th Royal Lancers (Prince of Wales's)

8 The Royal Hussars (Prince of Wales's Own)

9 13th/18th Royal Hussars (Queen Mary's Own)

10 14th/20th King's Hussars

Based on order of precedence.

THE TOP 10 COLONELS-IN-CHIEF OF THE BRITISH ARMY

	Colonel-in-Chief	No. of regiments/ corps
1	Queen Elizabeth II	19
2	The Queen Mother	9
3	The Prince of Wales	6
4	Prince Philip	5
5	The Princess Royal	4
6=	Princess Margaret	3
6=	Princess Alice, Duchess of Gloucester	3
6=	The Duchess of Kent	3
9=	Princess Alexandra	2
9=	The Princess of Wales	2
9=	The Duke of Kent	2
9=	The Duke of Gloucester	2
9=	The Duchess of Gloucester	2

HM The Queen is Colonel-in-Chief of 19 regiments.

QUIZ

BATTLES

1   By what name is the Battle of Senlac better known?
2   Which two British generals commanded the British 8th Army during the 1942 battles at El Alamein?
3   Which battle is preceded by Henry V's 'Crispin Crispian' speech in Shakespeare's play?
4   What vessels were used for the last time in a major naval battle at Lepanto in 1571?
5   What Second World War battle is the subject of the film *A Bridge Too Far*?
6   At what battle was the 7th US Cavalry under General Custer defeated by the Sioux under Chief Sitting Bull?
7   Who was the last British king to die in battle?
8   What famous battle took place in Belgium on 18 June 1815?
9   At which battle did the Charge of the Light Brigade take place?
10 What was the last battle on English soil?

THE 10 CAMPAIGNS IN WHICH THE MOST VICTORIA CROSSES HAVE BEEN WON

RIGHT A total of 111 VCs were won during the Crimean War.

Campaign	VCs
1 First World War (1914–18)	634
2= Indian Mutiny (1857–58)	182
2= Second World War (1939–45)	182
4 Crimean War (1854–56)	111
5 Second Boer War (1899–1902)	78
6 Zulu War (1879)	23
7 Second Afghan War (1878–80)	16
8 Maori War (1863–66)	13
9= Basuto War (1879–82)	6
9= First Boer War (1880–81)	6

THE 10 YOUNGEST WINNERS OF THE VICTORIA CROSS

	Name	Campaign/action date	Age yrs	mths
1	Andrew Fitzgibbon	Taku Forts, China, 21 Aug 1860	15	3
2	Thomas Flinn	Indian Mutiny, 28 Nov 1857	15	3
3	John Travers Cornwall	Battle of Jutland, 31 May 1916	16	4
4	Arthur Mayo	Indian Mutiny, 22 Nov 1857	17	6
5	George Monger	Indian Mutiny, 18 Nov 1857	17	8
6	Thomas Ricketts	Belgium, 14 Oct 1918	17	9
7	Edward St John Daniel	Crimean War, 5 Nov 1854; 18 Jun 1855*	17	10
8	William McWheeny	Crimean War, 20 Oct 1854; 5 Dec 1854; 18 Jun 1855*	17	?†
9	Basil John Douglas Guy	Boxer Rebellion, 13 Jul 1900	18	2
10	Wilfred St Aubyn Malleson	Gallipoli, 25 Apr 1915	18	7

VC awarded for actions on more than one date; age based on first date.
†Precise date of birth unknown; said to have been 'aged 17' at the time of his award.

Andrew Fitzgibbon beats Thomas Flinn into second place by being just 10 days younger at the time of the action for which he received his VC.

The supremely prestigious VC, won by soldiers as young as 15.

THE TOP 10 US MEDAL OF HONOR CAMPAIGNS

	Campaign	Years	Medals awarded
1	Civil War	1861–65	1,520
2	Second World War	1941–45	433
3	Indian Wars	1861–98	428
4	Vietnam War	1965–73	238
5	Korean War	1950–53	131
6	First World War	1917–18	123
7	Spanish-American War	1898	109
8	Philippines/Samoa	1899–1913	91
9	Boxer Rebellion	1900	59
10	Mexico	1914	55

The Congressional Medal of Honor, the USA's highest military award, was first issued in 1863. In addition to the medal itself, recipients receive such benefits as a $200 per month pension for life, free air travel and the right to be buried in the Arlington National Cemetery.

THE TOP 10 BRITISH ORDERS, DECORATIONS AND MEDALS*

1   Victoria Cross (VC)

2   George Cross (GC)

3   Order of the Garter (KG)

4   Order of the Thistle (KT)

5   Order of St Patrick (KP)

6   Order of the Bath (GCB, KCB, CB)

7   Order of Merit (OM)

8   Order of the Star of India (GCSI, KCSI, CSI)

9   Order of St Michael and St George (GCMG, KCMG, CMG)

10   Order of the Indian Empire (GCIE, KCIE, CIE)

*In order of precedence.

THE TOP 10 BRITISH GALLANTRY AWARDS*

1   Victoria Cross (VC)

2   George Cross (GC)

3   Distinguished Service Order (DSO)

4   Distinguished Service Cross (DSC)

5   Military Cross (MC)

6   Distinguished Flying Cross (DFC)

7   Air Force Cross (AFC)

8   Distinguished Conduct Medal (DCM)

9   Conspicuous Gallantry Medal (CGM)

10   George Medal (GM)

*In order of precedence, excluding defunct awards.

THE 10 COUNTIES RECEIVING THE MOST V1 HITS*

	County	V1s
1	Kent	1,444
2	Sussex	880
3	Essex	412
4	Surrey	295
5	Suffolk	93
6	Hertfordshire	82
7	Hampshire	80
8	Buckinghamshire	27
9	Norfolk	13
10	Berkshire	12

Excluding London.

The V1 was notoriously inaccurate: although most were targeted on London, one of them landed near Hitler's headquarters at Soissons, France, while others came down as far afield as Northampton.

THE 10 COUNTIES RECEIVING THE MOST V2 HITS

	County	V2s
1	London	517
2	Essex	378
3	Kent	64
4	Hertfordshire	34
5	Norfolk	29
6	Suffolk	13
7	Surrey	8
8	Sussex	4
9	Bedfordshire	3
10	Buckinghamshire	2

The last V2 to hit England exploded on Court Road, Orpington, Kent at 4.54 pm on 27 March 1945, killing one man – the last British civilian casualty of the Second World War.

THE 10 LONDON BOROUGHS RECEIVING THE MOST V1 HITS

	Borough	V1s
1	Croydon	141
2	Wandsworth	122
3	Lewisham	114
4	Camberwell	80
5	Woolwich	77
6	Lambeth	71
7	Beckenham	70
8	Orpington	63
9	West Ham	58
10	Coulsdon	54

During 1944, V1 flying bombs destroyed approximately 24,000 houses in London and damaged a further 800,000 – particularly in the southern suburbs, which were the nearest to the V1 launch sites on the Channel coast of France. Casualty figures were also very high: in one incident, on Sunday 18 June, 121 members of the congregation were killed when a V1 hit the Guards Chapel at the Wellington Barracks during a service.

THE 10 LONDON BOROUGHS RECEIVING THE MOST V2 HITS

	Borough	V2s
1	Woolwich	33
2	West Ham	27
3	Greenwich	22
4	Barking	21
5	Dagenham	19
6=	Erith	17
6=	Chislehurst	17
8	Waltham	15
9=	Wanstead	14
9=	East Ham	14

Masterminded by Wernher von Braun, later leader of the US space programme, the 14.3 m/ 47 ft long V2 rocket was more accurate and more powerful than the V1, while its speed of 5,633 kph/3,500 mph made it virtually impossible to combat with anti-aircraft fire or to intercept with fighter aircraft. The first two were launched from Holland against Paris on 6 September 1944, and on 8 September the first two fell on London, followed by more than 1,000 over the next seven months, resulting in a total of 2,855 fatalities (an even larger number was directed at Belgium with 4,483 killed). On 25 November 1944 a V2 hit Woolworth's in Deptford, killing 160 shoppers, and on 8 March 1945 one hit Smithfield Market, killing 110. On 27 March one of the last V2s – and the last explosive of the war in London – hit a block of flats in Stepney, killing 134.

LEFT Smithfield after the 8 March 1945 V2 rocket that killed 110.

OPPOSITE Cannon Street and St Paul's Cathedral after the Blitz.

THE 10 MOST HEAVILY BLITZED CITIES IN THE UK

	City	Major raids	Tonnage of high explosive dropped
1	London	85	23,949
2	Liverpool/Birkenhead	8	1,957
3	Birmingham	8	1,852
4	Glasgow/Clydeside	5	1,329
5	Plymouth/Devonport	8	1,228
6	Bristol/Avonmouth	6	919
7	Coventry	2	818
8	Portsmouth	3	687
9	Southampton	4	647
10	Hull	3	593

THE 10 MOST HEAVILY BOMBED LONDON BOROUGHS

	Borough	High-explosive bombs per 100 acres
1	Holborn	39.75
2	City	29.53
3	Westminster	28.85
4	Shoreditch	23.56
5	Southwark	23.35
6	Stepney	20.02
7	Finsbury	19.11
8	Chelsea	18.51
9	Bethnal Green	17.26
10	Bermondsey	17.16

During the Blitz, German bombing was concentrated on the centre of London and the Docks, but also caused enormous damage in adjacent boroughs, including the densely populated East End, and to a lesser extent, in the outer suburbs. About 15,000 people were killed and some 3,500,000 houses in London were bombed during the Second World War. The worst period was between 7 September 1940 and 11 May 1941 when an estimated 18,800 tons of high-explosive bombs were dropped. The last major raid, but one of the heaviest, occurred on Saturday 10 May 1941 when, in addition to 1,436 fatalities, many important buildings were gutted, including the churches of St Clement Danes, St Olave, Hart Street and All Hallows, Barking, the House of Commons, Lambeth Palace library, the Deanery of Westminster Abbey and the British Museum library, destroying 150,000 books.

THE TOP 10 LUFTWAFFE AIRCRAFT OF WORLD WAR II

	Model	Type	No. produced
1	Messerschmitt Me 109	Fighter	30,480
2	Focke Wulf Fw 190	Fighter	20,000
3	Junkers Ju 88	Bomber	15,000
4	Messerschmitt Me 110	Fighter-bomber	5,762
5	Heinkel He 111	Bomber	5,656
6	Junkers Ju 87	Dive bomber	4,881
7	Junkers Ju 52	Transport	2,804
8	Fieseler Fi 156	Communications	2,549
9	Dornier Do 217	Bomber	1,730
10	Heinkel He 177	Bomber	1,446

THE TOP 10 U-BOAT COMMANDERS OF WORLD WAR II

	Commander	U-boats commanded	Ships sunk
1	Otto Kretschmer	U23, U99	45
2	Wolfgang Luth	U9, U138, U43, U181	44
3	Joachim Schepko	U3, U19, U100	39
4	Erich Topp	U57, U552	35
5	Victor Schutze	U25, U103	34
6	Heinrich Leibe	U38	30
7=	Karl F. Merten	U68	29
7=	Günther Prien	U47	29
7=	Johann Mohr	U124	29
10	Georg Lassen	U160	28

THE TOP 10 LUFTWAFFE ACES OF WORLD WAR II

	Pilot	Kills claimed
1	Eric Hartmann	352
2	Gerhard Barkhorn	301
3	Günther Rall	275
4	Otto Kittel	267
5	Walther Nowotny	255
6	Wilhelm Batz	237
7	Erich Rudorffer	222
8	Heinrich Baer	220
9	Herman Graf	212
10	Heinrich Ehrler	209

Luftwaffe ace Walther Nowotny claimed a total of 255 kills.

Although these apparently high claims have been dismissed by some military historians as inflated for propaganda purposes, it is worth noting that many of them relate to kills on the Eastern Front, where the Luftwaffe was undoubtedly superior to its Soviet opponents.

ABOVE LEFT The Messerschmitt Me 109 was the top Luftwaffe aircraft of the Second World War.

LEFT The Top 10 U-boat commanders sunk a total of 342 ships.

THE 10 SMALLEST ARMED FORCES IN THE WORLD*

	Country	Estimated total active forces (1990)
1	Belize	700
2	The Bahamas	750
3	Luxembourg	800
4	The Gambia	900
5	Cape Verde	1,200
6	The Seychelles	1,300
7	Equatorial Guinea	1,400
8	Malta	1,500
9	Trinidad and Tobago	2,650
10	Jamaica	2,800

*Excluding countries not declaring a defence budget.

THE 10 LARGEST ARMED FORCES IN THE WORLD

	Country	Estimated total active forces (1990)
1	USSR	4,258,000
2	China	3,030,000
3	USA	2,124,900
4	India	1,260,000
5	Vietnam	1,249,000
6	North Korea	1,040,000
7	Iraq	1,000,000*
8	Turkey	650,900
9	South Korea	650,000
10	Iran	604,000
	UK	311,650

*Pre-Gulf War approximation; postwar level not yet officially confirmed.

THE TOP 10 NAVIES IN THE WORLD

	Country	Manpower	Combat tonnage (1990)
1	USA	584,000	3,208,000
2	USSR	437,000	2,585,000
3	UK	57,000	336,000
4	China	227,000	325,000
5	Japan	44,000	242,000
6	France	63,000	229,000
7	India	46,000	170,000
8	Taiwan	35,000	121,000
9	Italy	51,000	113,000
10	Turkey	51,000	99,000

ABOVE RIGHT Vastly enlarged under Chairman Mao, China's army remains the world's second largest.

THE TOP 10 ARMS MANUFACTURERS IN THE WESTERN WORLD

	Manufacturer	Country	Arms sales per annum (£)
1	McDonnell Douglas	USA	4,760,000,000
2	Lockheed	USA	4,704,000,000
3	General Dynamics	USA	4,480,000,000
4	General Electric	USA	3,500,000,000
5	General Motors	USA	3,360,000,000
6	Raytheon	USA	3,080,000,000
7	British Aerospace	UK	3,063,200,000
8	Rockwell International	USA	2,800,000,000
9=	Boeing	USA	2,520,000,000
9=	Northrop	USA	2,520,000,000
9=	United Technologies	USA	2,520,000,000

RELIGION

THE TOP 10 ORGANIZED RELIGIONS IN THE WORLD

	Religion	Followers
1	Christianity	1,711,897,440
2	Islam	924,611,500
3	Hinduism	689,205,100
4	Buddhism	311,438,000
5	Sikhism	17,735,100
6	Judaism	17,357,000
7	Confucianism	5,821,400
8	Baha'ism	5,072,000
9	Jainism	3,581,500
10	Shintoism	3,205,300

This list excludes the followers of various tribal and folk religions, new religions and shamanism, which together total almost 400,000,000. There are also perhaps more than 850,000,000 people who may be classified as 'non-religious', including large proportions of the populations of China and the USSR.

THE 10 LARGEST JEWISH POPULATIONS IN THE WORLD

	Country	Total Jewish population
1	USA	5,834,650
2	Israel	3,575,000
3	USSR	2,200,000
4	France	700,000
5	UK	385,000
6	Canada	304,000
7	Argentina	300,000
8	Brazil	175,000
9	South Africa	118,000
10	Australia	88,000

The Diaspora or scattering of Jewish people has been in progress for nearly 2,000 years, and as a result Jewish communities are found in virtually every country in the world. In 1939 it was estimated that the total world Jewish population was 17,000,000. Some 6,000,000 fell victim to Nazi persecution, reducing it to about 11,000,000. In 1990 it was estimated to be over 17,000,000 again.

ABOVE LEFT With over 300 million adherents, Buddhism is the world's fourth largest religion.

LEFT The Jewish population of Israel is actually less than that of the United States.

THE TOP 10 CHRISTIAN DENOMINATIONS IN THE WORLD

	Denomination	Adherents
1	Roman Catholic	872,104,646
2	Slavonic Orthodox	92,523,987
3	United (including Lutheran/Reformed)	65,402,685
4	Pentecostal	58,999,862
5	Anglican	52,499,051
6	Baptist	50,321,923
7	Lutheran (excluding United)	44,899,837
8	Reformed (Presbyterian)	43,445,520
9	Methodist	31,718,508
10	Disciples (Restorationists)	8,783,192

The Top 10 is based on 1985 estimates supplied by MARC Europe, a Christian research and information organization. The Vatican's 1987 estimate increased the figure for Roman Catholics to 911,000,000 while retaining the 52,000,000 figure for Anglicans – which indicates something of the problem of arriving even at 'guesstimates' when it comes to global memberships.

THE TOP 10 RELIGIOUS AFFILIATIONS IN THE USA

	Religion/organization	Membership
1	Roman Catholic Church	54,918,949
2	Southern Baptist Convention	14,812,844
3	United Methodist Church	9,055,575
4	Muslim	6,000,000*
5	National Baptist Convention, USA, Inc.	5,500,000*
6	Evangelical Lutheran Church in America	5,251,534
7	Jews	4,300,000**
8	Church of Jesus Christ of Latter-day Saints (Mormons)	4,193,936**
9	Presbyterian Church	2,929,608
10	National Baptist Convention of America	2,668,799

*Estimated.
**Combined membership of several groups.

The Roman Catholic Church has more registered members in the UK than the Church of England.

THE 10 LARGEST CHRISTIAN POPULATIONS IN THE WORLD

	Country	Total Christian population
1	USA	197,344,000
2	Brazil	118,856,000
3	USSR	96,726,500
4	Mexico	67,866,900
5	West Germany	57,557,300
6	UK	49,964,000
7	Philippines	49,201,700
8	Italy	47,104,500
9	France	44,110,800
10	Spain	35,932,700

Although Christian communities are found in almost every country in the world, it is more difficult to put a precise figure on nominal membership than on active participation. David Barrett's *World Christian Encyclopaedia* (1982) contained one of the most recent attempts to estimate global Christian populations, and the Top 10 is based on his findings.

THE 10 LARGEST MUSLIM POPULATIONS IN THE WORLD

	Country	Total Muslim population
1	India	80,540,000
2	Pakistan	80,320,350
3	Bangladesh	72,848,640
4	Indonesia	67,213,000
5	Turkey	45,018,800
6	Iran	37,694,300
7	Egypt	34,648,360
8	Nigeria	32,668,000
9	USSR	30,297,000
10	Afghanistan	21,885,280

The phenomenal growth of Islam in recent years suggests that these figures, last compiled in the early 1980s, are already out of date, although the order of the Top 10 is probably unchanged. At the time they were prepared, the global Muslim population was said to be under 600,000,000; by 1990 a total figure of 924,611,500 was claimed by one authoritative source.

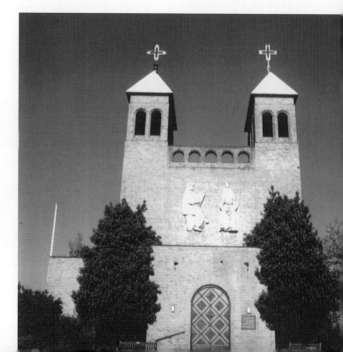

THE TOP 10 RELIGIONS IN THE UK

	Religion	Membership
1	Roman Catholicism	2,530,000
2	Anglicanism	2,270,000
3	Presbyterianism	1,650,000
4	Islam	1,000,000
5	Methodism	510,000
6	Baptist	240,000
7	Sikhism	220,000
8	Hinduism	170,000
9	Mormonism	150,000
10	Judaism	110,000

This list is based on figures for adult *membership*, as recorded in, for example, the electoral rolls of the Church of England. Adherents are thus held to be practising rather than nominal members of each religion – although they are not necessarily all regular attenders of their respective places of worship.

THE 10 SHORTEST-SERVING POPES

	Pope	Year in office	Duration (days)
1	Urban VII	1590	12
2=	Valentine	827	c14
2=	Boniface VI	896	c14
4	Celestine IV	1241	16
5	Sisinnius	708	20
6	Sylvester III	1045	21
7	Theodore II	897	c21
8	Marcellus II	1555	22
9	Damasus II	1048	23
10=	Pius III	1503	26
10=	Leo XI	1605	26

Eleven popes have reigned for less than a month. Some authorities give Stephen's two- or three-day reign in March 757 as the shortest, but although he was elected, he died before he was enthroned and is therefore not included in the official list of popes; in fact, his successor was given his title, Stephen II, and reigned for five years – although some call the uncrowned Stephen 'Stephen II' and his successors are confusingly known as 'Stephen II(III)', and so on. The life of a pope is not always tranquil: Boniface VI, the equal second shortest-serving, was deposed, and Damasus II probably poisoned. Pope Johns have been particularly unfortunate: John XXI lasted nine months but was killed in 1277 when a ceiling collapsed on him, while John XII was beaten to death by the husband of a woman with whom he was having an affair. In modern times, John Paul I was pontiff for just 33 days in 1978, and was succeeded by the present Pope John Paul II.

Pope Pius VI's 24 years in office rank him as fourth longest serving.

THE 10 LONGEST-SERVING POPES

	Pope	Period in office	Years
1	Pius IX	16 Jun 1846–7 Feb 1878	31
2	Leo XIII	20 Feb 1878–20 Jul 1903	25
3	Peter	c42–67	c25
4	Pius VI	15 Feb 1775–29 Aug 1799	24
5	Adrian I	1 Feb 772–25 Dec 795	23
6	Pius VII	14 Mar 1800–20 Aug 1823	23
7	Alexander III	7 Sep 1159–30 Aug 1181	21
8	Sylvester	31 Jan 314–31 Dec 335	21
9	Leo I	29 Sep 440–10 Nov 461	21
10	Urban VIII	6 Aug 1623–29 Jul 1644	20

Popes are usually chosen from the ranks of cardinals, who are customarily men of mature years (although Pope Benedict IX, elected in 1033, is believed to have been about 15). As a result, it is unusual for a pope to remain in office for more than 20 years. Although St Peter is regarded as the first Pope, some authorities doubt the historical accuracy of his reign. If he is omitted as unhistorical, Nos. 4–10 all move up one place and 10th becomes Clement XI (23 Sep 1700– 19 Mar 1721, a reign of 20 years). Pius IX, the longest-serving pope, was 85 years old at the time of his death. The longest-lived in the Top 10 was Leo XIII at 93. Although he served for less than two years, it is said (with little evidence) that Pope Agatho died in 681 at the age of 106. If he is still in office, the present pope, John Paul II, will enter the Top 10 in 1999 and could top it in 2010, when he would be 90 years old.

SPORTS, GAMES & PASTIMES

THE TOP 10 WINTER OLYMPICS GOLD MEDAL WINNERS, 1924–1988

	Country	Gold medals
1	USSR	79
2	Norway	54
3	USA	42
4	East Germany	39
5	Sweden	36
6	Finland	33
7	Austria	28
8	West Germany	26
9	Switzerland	23
10=	Canada	14
10=	Italy	14

There have been 15 Winter Olympics since the 1924 Games in Chamonix, France.

Middle-distance runners Sebastian Coe and Steve Cram add two medals to Great Britain's Olympic tally.

THE TOP 10 SUMMER OLYMPICS GOLD MEDAL WINNERS, 1896–1988

	Country	Gold medals
1	USA	756
2	USSR	395
3	Great Britain	173
4	West Germany	157
5=	France	153
5=	East Germany	153
7	Italy	147
8	Sweden	131
9	Hungary	124
10	Finland	97

There have been 22 Summer Olympics since the 1896 Games in Athens (including the 1906 intercalatary Games, also held in Athens). The USSR first entered the Olympic Games in 1952, but boycotted the 1984 Games. The United States boycotted the 1980 Games.

QUIZ

THE OLYMPICS

1. Who was the first British woman to win a track and field gold medal?
2. Five of the six gold medals won by the USA in 1980 went to the same man. What is his name?
3. Which star of numerous *Tarzan* films won the 100 metres freestyle swimming gold medal in 1924 and 1928?
4. When lawn tennis made its return to the Olympics programme in 1988, which woman gained the ladies' singles title?
5. In which team sport did Great Britain become the surprise champions in 1936 by winning the gold medal for the first and only time?
6. Which 1968 Olympic gold medallist's biography was entitled *The Perfect Jump*?
7. How is Eddie Eagan of the USA unique in Olympic history?
8. Which two Olympic heavyweight boxing champions went on to capture the world heavyweight title?
9. Who outraged Adolf Hitler by winning four track and field gold medals at the 1936 Berlin Olympics?
10. What is the name of the girl who at the 1976 Games became the first gymnast to register a perfect score of 10 points?

THE 10 SPORTS TO WIN MOST OLYMPIC GOLD MEDALS FOR GREAT BRITAIN

	Sport	Gold medals
1	Athletics	46
2=	Lawn tennis	16
2=	Rowing	16
4	Yachting	15
5	Swimming/diving	14
6	Shooting	13
7	Boxing	12
8	Cycling	8
9	Equestrianism	5
10	Water polo	4

THE 10 SPORTS TO WIN MOST OLYMPIC MEDALS FOR GREAT BRITAIN

	Sport	Medals
1	Athletics	173
2	Swimming/diving	64
3	Shooting	46
4	Lawn tennis	44
5	Cycling	43
6	Boxing	42
7	Rowing	37
8	Yachting	31
9	Equestrianism	21
10	Wrestling	17

THE TOP 10 INDIVIDUAL OLYMPIC GOLD MEDAL WINNERS

	Medal winner	Total gold medals
1	Ray C. Ewry (USA) – Athletics 1900, 1904, 1906, 1908	10
2=	Larissa Latynina (USSR) – Gymnastics 1956, 1960, 1964 (also 5 silver and 4 bronze medals)	9
2=	Paavo Nurmi (Finland) – Athletics 1920, 1924, 1928 (also 3 silver)	9
2=	Mark Spitz (USA) – Swimming 1968, 1972 (also 1 silver and 1 bronze)	9
5	Sawao Kato (Japan) – Gymnastics 1968, 1972, 1976 (also 3 silver and 1 bronze)	8
6=	Nikolai Andrianov (USSR) – Gymnastics 1972, 1976, 1980 (also 5 silver and 3 bronze)	7
6=	Boris Shakhlin (USSR) – Gymnastics 1956, 1960, 1964 (also 4 silver and 2 bronze)	7
6=	Vera Čáslavská (Czechoslovakia) – Gymnastics 1960, 1964, 1968 (also 4 silver)	7
6=	Viktor Chukarin (USSR) – Gymnastics 1952, 1956 (also 4 silver and 2 bronze)	7
6=	Aladár Gerevich (Hungary) – Fencing 1932, 1936, 1948, 1952, 1956, 1960 (also 1 silver and 2 bronze)	7

The only British Olympic Games competitor to have won four gold medals is Henry Taylor (1885–1951), for swimming. He competed in 1906, 1908, 1912 and 1920, and also won one silver and three bronze medals. Gerevich is the only competitor to win medals at six consecutive Games.

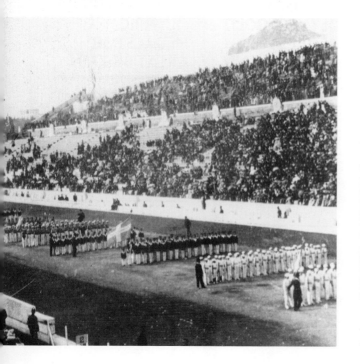

THE 10 SPORTS TO WIN MOST GOLD MEDALS AT THE OLYMPIC GAMES

	Sport	Gold medals
1	Athletics	685
2	Swimming/diving	411
3	Wrestling	284
4	Gymnastics	242
5	Shooting	184
6	Boxing	168
7	Rowing	161
8	Fencing	151
9	Nordic skiing	135
10	Cycling	125

Paavo Nurmi, winner of nine Olympic golds, photographed at the 1920 Games in Antwerp.

THE 10 SUMMER OLYMPICS ATTENDED BY THE MOST COMPETITORS

	City	Year	Countries represented	Competitors
1	Seoul	1988	159	9,101
2	Munich	1972	122	7,156
3	Los Angeles	1984	141	7,058
4	Montreal	1976	92	6,085
5	Mexico City	1968	112	5,530
6	Rome	1960	83	5,346
7	Moscow	1980	81	5,326
8	Tokyo	1964	93	5,140
9	Helsinki	1952	69	4,925
10	London	1948	59	4,099

The first Games in 1896 were attended by just 311 competitors, all men, representing 13 countries. Women took part for the first time four years later at the Paris Games. At the XXIV Olympiad in Seoul, 6,760 competitors were men and 2,341 women.

The first modern Olympics, at Athens in 1896, was attended by just 311 competitors.

THE TOP 10 CRICKET BATTING AVERAGES*

	Player	Season	Runs	Average
1	Don Bradman	1938	2,429	115.66
2	Geoff Boycott	1979	1,538	102.53
3	William Johnston	1953	102	102.00
4	Graham Gooch	1990	2,746	101.70
5	Geoff Boycott	1971	2,503	100.12
6	Don Bradman	1930	2,960	98.66
7	Herbert Sutcliffe	1931	3,006	96.96
8	Robert Poore	1899	1,551	91.23
9	Douglas Jardine	1927	1,002	91.09
10	Denis Compton	1947	3,816	90.85

Minimum qualification 12 innings.

While Johnston scored only 102 runs, he batted 17 times and was not out on 16 occasions, which explains his high average.

THE 10 OLDEST TEST CRICKETERS

	Player	Country	Final season	Age at final match yrs	days
1	Wilfred Rhodes	England	1929–30	52	165
2	Herbert Ironmonger	Australia	1932–33	50	327
3	W. G. Grace	England	1899	50	320
4	George Gunn	England	1929–30	50	303
5	James Southerton	England	1876–77	49	139
6	Miran Bux	Pakistan	1954–55	47	302
7	Jack Hobbs	England	1930	47	249
8	Frank Woolley	England	1934	47	87
9	Donald Blackie	Australia	1928–29	46	309
10	Dudley Nourse	South Africa	1924	46	206

James Southerton's only Test match was the very first Test at Melbourne in 1876–77. He was thus the oldest player to make his Test debut.

THE 10 YOUNGEST TEST CRICKETERS

	Player	Country	Season	Age at debut yrs	days
1	Mushtaq Mohammad	Pakistan	1958–59	15	124
2	Aaqib Javed	Pakistan	1988–89	16	189
3	Sachin Tendulkar	India	1989–90	16	205
4	Aftab Baloch	Pakistan	1969–70	16	221
5	Nasim-ul-Ghani	Pakistan	1957–58	16	248
6	Khalid Hassan	Pakistan	1954	16	352
7	Laxman Sivaramakrishnan	India	1982–83	17	118
8	James Sealy	West Indies	1929–30	17	122
9	Sanjeeva Weerasinghe	Sri Lanka	1985–86	17	189
10	Maninder Singh	India	1982–83	17	193

England's youngest Test cricketer was Brian Close, who was aged 18 years 149 days when he made his debut against New Zealand at Manchester in 1949.

Geoff Boycott's batting average is exceeded only by Don Bradman's.

THE 10 ENGLISH LEAGUE FOOTBALLERS SCORING THE MOST GOALS IN A SEASON (SINCE 1946–47)

	Name	Club	Season	Goals
1	Terry Bly	Peterborough United	1960–61	52
2	Derek Dooley	Sheffield Wednesday	1951–52	46
3=	Kevin Hector	Bradford Park Avenue	1965–66	44
3=	Arthur Rowley	Leicester City	1956–57	44
5	Tommy Johnston	Leyton Orient and Blackburn Rovers	1957–58	43
6=	John Charles	Leeds United	1953–54	42
6=	Brian Clough	Middlesbrough	1958–59	42
6=	Edward MacDougall	Bournemouth	1970–71	42
6=	Clarrie Jordan	Doncaster Rovers	1946–47	42
6=	Cliff Holton	Watford	1959–60	42

THE TOP 10 GOAL-SCORERS IN 1989–90 FOOTBALL LEAGUE* MATCHES

	Name	Club	Goals
1	Mike Quinn	Newcastle United	32
2	Bob Taylor	Bristol City	27
3	Dean Holdsworth	Brentford and Watford	25
4=	Steve Bull	Wolverhampton Wanderers	24
4=	Gary Lineker	Tottenham Hotspur	24
6=	Guy Whittingham	Portsmouth	23
6=	Ian Muir	Tranmere Rovers	23
6=	Brett Angell	Stockport County	23
9=	John Barnes	Liverpool	22
9=	John McGinlay	Shrewsbury Town	22

English and Scottish.

Steve Bull was at the top of this list with 37 goals in the 1988–89 season, and is the only player to appear in the Top 10 for both that season and for 1989–90. Lineker and Barnes are the only First Division players in the Top 10.

ABOVE Derek Dooley scored 46 goals in the 1951–52 football season.

RIGHT Mike Quinn, top goal-scorer of the 1989–90 season.

THE 10 COMMONEST REASONS FOR CAUTIONS IN FOOTBALL LEAGUE MATCHES

	Offence	Total
1	Foul tackle	1,609
2	Showing dissent	435
3	Tripping	368
4	Persistent infringement of the laws of the game	318
5	Adopting an aggressive attitude	189
6	Ungentlemanly conduct	136
7	Dangerous play	132
8	Time wasting	131
9	Shirt pulling	120
10	Foul play	61

In addition to these cautions (recorded during league matches in the 1989–90 season) there were smaller numbers of sendings-off for a variety of reasons, led by 'Persistent misconduct' (56 instances), 'Striking' (35), 'Serious foul play' (29) and 'Foul language' (17), followed by a variety of examples of 'Violent conduct' including elbowing, kicking and butting.

Tripping is the third commonest reason for cautions.

THE 10 HIGHEST FOOTBALL CLUB GROUND ATTENDANCES

	Club/ground	Match	Date	Crowd
1	Manchester City/Maine Road	v Stoke City, FA Cup 6th Round	3 Mar 1934	84,569
2	Chelsea/Stamford Bridge	v Arsenal, First Division	12 Oct 1935	82,905
3	Everton/Goodison Park	v Liverpool, First Division	18 Sep 1948	78,299
4	Manchester United/Old Trafford	Wolverhampton Wanderers v Grimsby Town, FA Cup Semi-final	25 Mar 1939	76,962
5	Aston Villa/Villa Park	v Derby County, FA Cup 6th Round	2 Mar 1946	76,588
6	Sunderland/Roker Park	v Derby County, FA Cup 6th Round replay	8 Mar 1933	75,118
7	Tottenham Hotspur/White Hart Lane	v Sunderland, FA Cup 6th Round	5 Mar 1938	75,038
8	Charlton Athletic/The Valley	v Aston Villa, FA Cup 5th Round	12 Feb 1938	75,031
9	Arsenal/Highbury	v Sunderland, First Division	9 Mar 1935	73,295
10	Sheffield Wednesday/Hillsborough	v Manchester City, FA Cup 5th Round	17 Feb 1934	72,841

These figures are the highest recorded attendances at English football club grounds only (Wembley Cup Final attendances, such as that at the 1923 Bolton Wanderers versus West Ham United game, were estimated to have been almost double the highest of these). However, with increasingly stringent safety regulations – especially since the Hillsborough disaster – it is unlikely that such enormous crowds will ever be seen again at an English football match. If Scottish clubs were included, Rangers, Celtic and Queen's Park would appear on the list. Rangers' top attendance at their Ibrox ground is 118,567, which would put them at the top of the list. Celtic's top crowd at Celtic Park is 92,000, while the largest for a club match at Queen's Park's Hampden Park ground is 95,772 – although the ground also housed the official British record of 149,547 for the Scotland versus England international in 1937.

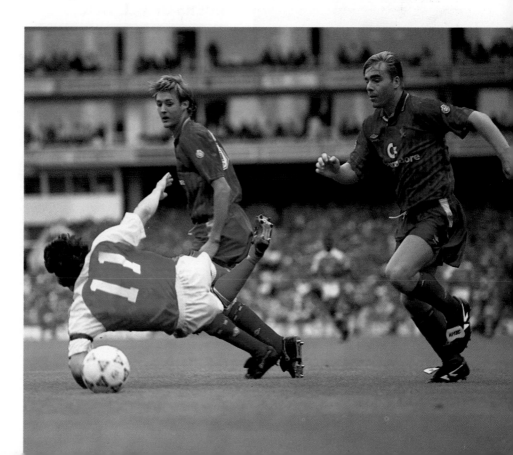

THE 10 MOST UNSUCCESSFUL* FOOTBALL LEAGUE CLUBS

	Club	Matches played
1	Crewe Alexandra	2,908
2	Halifax Town	2,800
3=	Hartlepool United	2,798
3=	Rochdale	2,798
5	Torquay United	2,558
6	Chester	2,386
7	Aldershot	2,346
8	Barrow	1,924
9	Colchester United	1,838
10	Accrington Stanley	1,542

Up to the end of the 1990–91 season, none had won a Football League title since entering the League (in the case of Crewe Alexandra, 66 years ago).

THE 10 HIGHEST-SCORING GAMES IN SENIOR BRITISH FOOTBALL

	Teams (winners first)	Competition	Date	Score
1	Arbroath *v* Bon Accord	Scottish Cup	12 Sep 1885	36–0
2	Dundee Harp *v* Aberdeen Rovers	Scottish Cup	12 Sep 1885	35–0
3	Preston North End *v* Hyde United	FA Cup	15 Oct 1887	26–0
4	Cowlairs *v* Victoria	Scottish Cup	7 Sep 1889	21–0
5=	Arbroath *v* Orion	Scottish Cup	3 Sep 1887	20–0
5=	Johnstone *v* Greenock Abstainers	Scottish Cup	5 Sep 1891	20–0
5=	Cowlairs *v* Temperance Athletic	Scottish Cup	1 Sep 1888	18–2
8	Preston North End *v* Reading	FA Cup	27 Jan 1894	18–0
9=	Camelon *v* Redding Athletic	Scottish Cup	24 Sep 1887	17–0*
9=	Mid-Annandale *v* Rising Thistle	Scottish Cup	6 Sep 1890	16–1
9=	Tranmere Rovers *v* Oldham Athletic	Third Division North	26 Dec 1935	13–4

Highest-scoring away win.

Coincidentally, the two highest-scoring matches were both played on 12 September 1885.

Ingemar Stenmark, the most successful skier of all time.

THE 10 MOST SUCCESSFUL SKIERS OF ALL TIME

	Skier	Country	World Cup titles
1	Ingemar Stenmark	Sweden	18
2	Annemarie Moser-Pröll	Austria	16
3=	Gustavo Thoeni	Italy	9
3=	Pirmin Zurbriggen	Switzerland	9
3=	Marc Girardelli	Luxembourg	9
6	Michela Figini	Switzerland	8
7=	Erika Hess	Switzerland	7
7=	Lise-Marie Morerod	Sweden	7
7=	Vreni Schneider	Switzerland	7
10=	Jean-Claude Killy	France	6
10=	Phil Mahre	USA	6
10=	Maria Walliser	Switzerland	6

THE 10 MOST SUCCESSFUL SUPERBOWL TEAMS

	Team	Wins
1=	Pittsburgh Steelers	4
1=	San Francisco 49ers	4
3	Oakland/Los Angeles Raiders	3
4=	Dallas Cowboys	2
4=	Green Bay Packers	2
4=	Miami Dolphins	2
4=	New York Giants	2
4=	Washington Redskins	2
9=	Baltimore Colts	1
9=	Chicago Bears	1
9=	Kansas City Chiefs	1
9=	New York Jets	1

All these were world championship contests under the Marquess of Queensberry rules (first published in 1866) which stipulate the length of a round at three minutes. Prior to the rules, a round ended when a fighter was knocked down, and consequently many fights in the bare-knuckle days consisted of many rounds, the longest being the 276-round contest between Jack Jones and Patsy Tunney in Cheshire in 1825. The fight lasted 4 hours 30 minutes. The longest heavyweight contest under Queensberry rules was the Jess Willard *v* Jack Johnson contest on 5 April 1915, which lasted 26 rounds.

THE 10 LONGEST WORLD CHAMPIONSHIP BOXING CONTESTS

	Fighters	Weight	Date	Rounds
1	Ike Weir *v* Frank Murphy	Featherweight	31 Mar 1889	80
2	Jack McAuliffe *v* Jem Carney	Lightweight	16 Nov 1887	74
3	Paddy Duffy *v* Tom Meadows	Welterweight	29 Mar 1889	45
4	Joe Gans *v* Battling Nelson	Lightweight	3 Sep 1906	42
5=	George Dixon *v* Johnny Murphy	Bantamweight	23 Oct 1890	40
5=	Ad Wolgast.*v* Battling Nelson	Lightweight	22 Feb 1910	40
7=	George LaBlanche *v* Jack Dempsey	Middleweight	27 Aug 1889	32
7=	Stanley Ketchel *v* Joe Thomas	Middleweight	2 Sep 1907	32
9	Jack Dempsey *v* Billy McCarthy	Middleweight	18 Feb 1890	28
10	Jack Dempsey *v* Jack Fogarty	Middleweight	3 Feb 1886	27

THE 10 HEAVIEST WORLD BOXING CHAMPIONS

	Boxer	Year	Weight kg	lb
1	Primo Carnera	1934	122.5	270
2	James Douglas	1990	111.5	246
3	Jess Willard	1919	111.0	245
4	Tony Tubbs	1986	110.5	244
5	John Tate	1979	109.0	240
6	Greg Page	1984	108.5	239½
7	Tim Witherspoon	1986	106.5	235
8	Mike Weaver	1980	105.0	232
9	Muhammad Ali	1976	104.5	230
10	George Foreman	1974	102.0	224¾

All these fighters were from the USA except Primo Carnera, who was Italian.

Primo Carnera, heaviest of all heavyweight boxing champions.

THE 10 FASTEST WINNING TIMES FOR THE OXFORD AND CAMBRIDGE BOAT RACE

	Crew	Year	Lengths	Time min	sec
1	Oxford	1984	3¾	16	45
2	Oxford	1976	6½	16	58
3	Oxford	1991	4¼	16	59
4	Oxford	1985	4¾	17	11
5	Oxford	1990	2¼	17	15
6=	Oxford	1974	5½	17	35
6=	Oxford	1988	5½	17	35
8	Cambridge	1948	5	17	50
9=	Cambridge	1971	10	17	58
9=	Cambridge	1986	7	17	58

The Boat Race was first rowed at Henley in 1829, but the course from Putney to Mortlake (6.78 km/4 miles 374 yards) has been used since 1843 (Mortlake to Putney in 1846, 1856 and 1863). The course time has steadily improved from the 25 minutes or more of the early years to the record-breaking times of the postwar period. Cambridge has won 69 times, Oxford 67 and there has been one dead-heat (1877). The largest margin was the 20 lengths by which Cambridge won in 1900. Cambridge sank in 1859 and 1978 and Oxford in 1925; both crews sank in 1912 and Oxford won when the race was re-rowed a week later; Oxford sank near the start in 1951 and the race took place two days later, with Cambridge the winner.

THE 10 MOST SUCCESSFUL GRAND PRIX TEAMS

	Manufacturer	Years	Wins
1	Ferrari	1951–90	103
2	McLaren	1968–90	86
3	Lotus	1960–87	79
4	Williams	1979–90	44
5	Brabham	1964–85	35
6	Tyrrell	1971–83	23
7	BRM	1959–72	17
8	Cooper	1958–67	16
9	Renault	1979–83	15
10	Alfa Romeo	1950–51	10

THE 10 MOST SUCCESSFUL GOLFERS OF ALL TIME

	Golfer	Country	Majors
1	Jack Nicklaus	USA	18
2	Walter Hagen	USA	11
3=	Ben Hogan	USA	9
3=	Gary Player	South Africa	9
5	Tom Watson	USA	8
6=	Bobby Jones	USA	7
6=	Arnold Palmer	USA	7
6=	Gene Sarazen	USA	7
6=	Sam Snead	USA	7
6=	Harry Vardon	UK	7

THE 10 HIGHEST EARNERS IN GOLF IN 1990

US TOUR*		
	Player	Winnings ($)
1	Greg Norman	1,165,477
2	Wayne Levi	1,024,647
3	Payne Stewart	976,281
4	Paul Azinger	944,731
5	Jodie Mudd	911,746
6	Hale Irwin	838,249
7	Mark Calcavecchia	834,281
8	Tim Simpson	809,772
9	Fred Couples	747,999
10	Mark O'Meara	707,175

All 10 golfers are from the USA, except Greg Norman, who is Australian.

EUROPEAN PGA TOUR		
	Player	Country	Winnings (£)
1	Ian Woosnam	Wales	574,166.30
2	Mark McNulty	Zimbabwe	507,540.95
3	José Maria Olazabal	Spain	434,765.85
4	Bernhard Langer	Germany	320,449.65
5	Ronan Rafferty	Northern Ireland	309,851.08
6	Mike Harwood	Australia	280,084.43
7	Sam Torrance	Scotland	248,203.32
8	David Feherty	Northern Ireland	237,830.16
9	Roger Davis	Australia	233,841.87
10	Mark James	England	229,742.39

OPPOSITE TOP Mr Frisk, fastest-ever winner of the Grand National.

LEFT Jack Nicklaus is the most successful golfer in the world.

THE 10 FASTEST WINNING TIMES FOR THE GRAND NATIONAL

	Horse	Year	Time min	sec
1	Mr Frisk	1990	8	47.8
2	Red Rum	1973	9	1.9
3	Grittar	1982	9	12.6
4	Maori Venture	1987	9	19.0
5	Reynoldstown	1935	9	20.2
6	Red Rum	1974	9	20.3
7	Golden Miller	1934	9	20.4
8	Bogskar	1940	9	20.6
9	Rag Trade	1956	9	20.9
10=	ESB	1956	9	21.4
10=	Hallo Dandy	1984	9	21.4

THE 10 MOST SUCCESSFUL JOCKEYS IN GREAT BRITAIN

	Jockey	Years	Wins
1	Gordon Richards	1921–54	4,870
2	Lester Piggott	1948–90	4,352
3	Willie Carson	1962–90	3,154
4	Doug Smith	1931–67	3,111
5	Pat Eddery	1969–90	2,908
6	Joe Mercer	1950–85	2,810
7	Fred Archer	1870–86	2,748
8	Edward Hide	1951–85	2,591
9	George Fordham	1850–84	2,587
10	Eph Smith	1930–65	2,313

Jockey Willie Carson achieved 3,154 wins up to 1990.

THE 10 MOST POPULAR PARTICIPATION SPORTS IN THE UK

	MEN			WOMEN	
	Sport	%		Sport	%
1	Snooker, pool, billiards	27	1	Swimming, diving	13
2	Darts	14	2	Keep fit, yoga, aerobics, dance exercise	12
3	Swimming, diving	13	3	Cycling	7
4=	Soccer	10	4	Snooker, pool, billiards	5
4=	Cycling	10	5	Darts	4
6	Jogging, running	8	6=	Jogging, running	3
7=	Golf	7	6=	Badminton	3
7=	Weight training, lifting	7	8	Weight training, lifting	2
9	Keep fit, yoga, aerobics	5	9=	Bowls	1
10=	Fishing	4	9=	Equestrian sports	1
10=	Badminton	4	9=	Golf	1
10=	Squash	4	9=	Ice skating	1
10=	Table tennis	4	9=	Netball	1
			9=	Squash	1
			9=	Table tennis	1
			9=	Tennis	1
			9=	Tenpin bowling	1
			9=	Watersports	1

The Office of Populations Censuses and Surveys conducted interviews of some 9,000 men and 10,000 women to assess the numbers participating in a wide range of sporting activities. The percentages listed refer to those interviewed who had participated in one or more of these sports during the four weeks prior to the interview, and cover all interviewees aged 16 to 60. As might be expected, in younger age groups certain sports predominate, the highest percentage participating being 62 for snooker, pool and billiards among 16 to 19-year-olds, followed by 40 per cent in the same age group playing soccer. Among women aged 16 to 19, keep fit, yoga, aerobics and dance exercise activities and swimming and diving both attracted 24 per cent, closely followed by snooker, pool and billiards (23 per cent).

THE 10 BESTSELLING TOYS OF 1990

1	Barbie
2	Ghostbusters
3	Matchbox vehicles
4	Sylvanian Families
5	Legoland Town
6	Fisher Price preschool ranges
7	Teenage Mutant Hero Turtles
8	Tomytime preschool toys
9	Micromachines
10	Duplo

THE 10 BESTSELLING COMPUTER GAMES IN THE UK

1	Teenage Mutant Hero Turtles
2	Double Dragon
3	Robocop 2
4	Paperboy
5	Kwik Snax
6	Golden Axe
7	Target Renegade
8	Out Run
9	Hollywood Collection
10	Quattro Adventure

HAMLEYS' 10 BESTSELLING TOYS AND GAMES OF 1990

1	Hamleys bears
2	Mr Friendly Frog
3	Guk
4	Jet Hopper remote controlled car
5	Dance Magic Barbie
6	Spectrangle board game
7	Diving Dolphin bath toy
8	Mini Paddington Bear in a bag
9	Pictionary
10	Hornby train set

W. H. SMITH'S 10 BESTSELLING GAMES

1	Pictionary
2	Trivial Pursuit – Genus Edition
3	Scrabble
4	Trivial Pursuit – Family Edition
5	Hero Quest
6	Space Crusade
7	Advance Hero Quest
8	Whack Attack
9	Trivial Pursuit – Genus II
10	Twenty Questions

Mr Friendly Frog, swimming to success among Hamleys' top toys.

THE 10 MOST EXPENSIVE TEDDY BEARS SOLD AT AUCTION IN THE UK

	Bear	Price (£)
1	Dual-plush Steiff Teddy bear, c1920 Sotheby's, London, 19 September 1989	55,000

Although estimated at £700–£900, competitive bidding by several people pushed the price up to £40,000, with two battling for it up to the world record price.

	Bear	Price (£)
2	Black Steiff Teddy bear, c1912 Sotheby's, London, 18 May 1990	24,200
3	Alfonzo, a red Steiff Teddy bear, c1906–09, once owned by Russian Princess Xenia Christie's, London, 18 May 1989	12,100
4	Black Steiff Teddy bear, c1912 Phillips, London, 19 October 1990	8,800
5	Apricot-coloured Steiff Teddy bear, c1904 Sotheby's, London, 31 January 1990	7,700
6=	White plush Steiff Teddy bear, c1904 Sotheby's, London, 31 January 1990	6,050
6=	White plush Steiff Teddy bear, c1905 Sotheby's, London, 18 May 1990	6,050
8	White plush Steiff Teddy bear, c1920 Sotheby's, London, 22 January 1991	4,620
9	Brown plush Steiff Teddy bear, c1908 Sotheby's, London, 4 September 1990	4,400
10=	Central seam Steiff Teddy bear, c1907 Christie's, London, 23 November 1989	4,180
10=	Dark cinnamon plush Steiff Teddy bear, 1907 Christie's, London, 17 May 1990	4,180

It is said that, while on a hunting trip, US President Theodore ('Teddy') Roosevelt refused to shoot a young bear. This became the subject of a famous cartoon by Clifford K. Berryman, published in the *Washington Post* on 16 November 1902. Immediately afterwards, Morris Michtom, a New York shopkeeper (and later founder of the Ideal Toy and Novelty Company) made stuffed bears and – with Roosevelt's permission – began advertising them as 'Teddy's Bears'. At about the same time, Margarete Steiff, a German toymaker, began making her first toy bears, exporting them to the USA to meet the demand 'Teddy's Bears' had created. In 1903 Steiff's factory produced 12,000 bears; by 1907, the figure had risen to 974,000. Steiff bears, recognizable by their distinctive ear tags, are still made and are sold internationally, but it is the early examples that are most prized among collectors, with the result that all the Top 10 are Steiffs.

Alfonzo in Russian costume, sold for £12,100 in 1989.

THE 10 MOST EXPENSIVE TOYS SOLD AT SOTHEBY'S, LONDON

	Toy	Year sold	Price (£)
1	Kämmer and Reinhardt bisque character doll, German, c1909	1989	90,200
2	William and Mary wooden doll, English, c1690	1987	67,000
3	Dual-plush Steiff Teddy bear, German, c1920 (*see also* The 10 Most Expensive Teddy Bears)	1989	55,000
4	Tinplate clockwork battleship, *Maine*, by Märklin, German, c1904	1989	39,600
5	Tinplate clockwork paddleboat, *Emily*, by Märklin, German, c1902	1989	28,600
6	Tinplate Gauge I train, *Rocket*, by Märklin, German, c1909	1984	28,050
7	Gauge I armoured train set by Märklin, German, c1902	1988	26,400
8=	Charles II oak baby house on stand, English, c1675	1988	25,300
8=	Tinplate live steam riverboat, *25 de Mayo*, by Märklin, German, c1912	1990	25,300
10=	Kämmer and Reinhardt bisque character doll, German, c1909	1986	24,200
10=	Clockwork riverboat, *Shamrock II*, by Märklin, German, c1909	1990	24,200
10=	Black Steiff Teddy bear, German, c1912	1990	24,200

The William and Mary doll held the world record price for a doll for just two years until toppled by the £90,200 Kämmer and Reinhardt doll. Models by the German tinplate maker Märklin are regarded by collectors as the Rolls-Royce of toys, and similarly feature among the record prices of most of the world's auction houses.

AIR & SPACE

THE FIRST 10 MANNED BALLOON FLIGHTS*

1   The first 10 flights of the ballooning pioneers all took place within a year. The Montgolfier Brothers, Joseph and Etienne, tested their first unmanned hot-air balloon in the French town of Annonay on 5 June 1783. They were then invited to demonstrate it to Louis XVI at Versailles. On 19 September 1783 it took off with the first-ever airborne passengers – a sheep, a rooster and a duck. On 21 November 1783 François Laurent, Marquis d'Arlandes, and Jean-François Pilâtre de Rozier took off from the Bois de Boulogne, Paris, in a Montgolfier hot-air balloon. This first-ever manned flight covered a distance of about 9 km/5½ miles in 23 minutes, landing safely near Gentilly. (On 15 June 1785 de Rozier and his passenger were killed near Boulogne when their hydrogen balloon burst into flames during an attempted Channel crossing, making them the first air fatalities.)

2   On 1 December 1783, watched by a crowd of 400,000, Jacques Alexandre César Charles and Nicholas-Louis Robert made the first-ever flight in a hydrogen balloon. They took off from the Tuileries, Paris, and travelled about 43 km/27 miles north to Nesle in a time of about two hours. Charles then took off again alone, thus becoming the first solo flier.

3   On 19 January 1784 *La Flesselle*, a gigantic 40 m/131 ft high Montgolfier hot-air balloon named after its sponsor, the local Governor, ascended from Lyons piloted by Pilâtre de Rozier with Joseph Montgolfier, Prince Charles de Ligne and the Comtes de La Porte d'Anglefort, de Dampierre and de Laurencin – as well as the first-ever aerial stowaway, a young man called Fontaine, who leaped in as it was taking off.

4   On 25 February 1784 the Chevalier Paolo Andreani and the brothers Augustino and Carlo Giuseppi Gerli (the builders of the balloon) made the first-ever flight outside France, at Moncuco near Milan, Italy.

5   On 2 March 1784 Jean-Pierre François Blanchard made his first flight in a hydrogen balloon from the Champ de Mars, Paris, after experimental hops during the preceding months.

6   On 14 April 1784 a Mr Rousseau and an unnamed 10-year-old drummer boy flew from Navan to Ratoath in Ireland, the first ascent in the British Isles.

7   On 25 April 1784 Guyton de Morveau, a French chemist, and L'Abbé Bertrand flew at Dijon.

8   On 8 May 1784 Bremond and Maret flew at Marseilles.

9   On 12 May 1784 Brun ascended at Chambéry.

10 On 15 May 1784 Adorne and an unnamed passenger took off but crash-landed near Strasbourg.

Several of the balloonists listed also made subsequent flights, but in each instance only their first flights are included.

After the first 10 flights, the pace of ballooning accelerated rapidly. On 4 June 1784 a Monsieur Fleurand took as his passenger in a flight at Lyons a Mme Thiblé, an opera singer, who was thus the first woman to fly (the Marchioness de Montalembert and other aristocratic ladies had ascended on 20 May 1784, but in a tethered balloon). On 27 August James Tytler (known as 'Balloon Tytler'), a doctor and newspaper editor, took off from

The 10th manned balloon ascent was that of Adorne at Strasbourg on 15 May 1784.

Comely Gardens, Edinburgh, achieving an altitude of 107 m/350 ft in a 0.8 km/½-mile hop in a homemade balloon – the first (and until Smeath in 1837, the only) hot-air balloon flight in Great Britain. On 15 September, watched by a crowd of 200,000, Vincenzo Lunardi ascended from the Artillery Company Ground, Moorfields, London, flying to Standon near Ware in Hertfordshire, the first balloon flight in England. (An attempt the previous month by a Dr Moret ended with the balloon catching fire and the crowd rioting.) Lunardi went on to make further flights in Edinburgh and Glasgow. On 4 October 1784 James Sadler flew a Montgolfier balloon at Oxford, thereby becoming the first English pilot.

On 7 January 1785 Jean-Pierre Blanchard achieved the first Channel crossing with Dr John Jeffries (the first American to fly). They also carried the first airmail letter. As they lost height, they had to reduce weight, so they threw almost everything overboard, including their clothes. On 23 March of the same year Rear-Admiral (later Admiral) Sir Edward Vernon flew with Count Francesco Zambeccari from Tottenham Court Road, London, to Horsham, Sussex. On 29 June a certain George Biggin, piloting Lunardi's balloon, took Letitia Sage, the first Englishwoman to fly, from St George's Fields, London to Harrow, Middlesex – despite some apparent concern that Miss Sage was rather overweight and that the balloon might not get airborne. On 9 January 1793 in Philadelphia, Blanchard made the first flight in America, watched by George Washington.

THE FIRST 10 PEOPLE TO FLY IN HEAVIER-THAN-AIR AIRCRAFT

1 Orville Wright (1871–1948; American)

On 17 December 1903 at Kitty Hawk, North Carolina, Wright made the first-ever manned flight in his *Wright Flyer I*. It lasted 12 seconds and covered a distance of 37 m/120 ft.

2 Wilbur Wright (1867–1912; American)

On the same day, Orville Wright's brother made his first flight in the *Wright Flyer I* (59 sec; 260 m/852 ft).

3 Alberto Santos-Dumont (1873–1932; Brazilian)

On 12 November 1906 at Bagatelle, France, in his *Santos-Dumont 14-bis* (21.2 sec; 220 m/722 ft).

4 Léon Delagrange (1873–1910; French)

On 5 November 1907 at Issy, France, in his *Voisin-Delagrange I* (40 sec; 500 m/1,640 ft).

5 Robert Esnault-Pelterie (1881–1957; French)

On 16 November 1907 at Buc, France, in his *REP 1* (55 sec; 600 m/1,969 ft).

6 Henri Farman (1874–1958; British – later French)

On 11 January 1908 at Issy, France, in his *Voisin-Farman I* (1 min 45 sec; distance not recorded). This was the first European flight of more than one minute; on 13 January Farman flew the first circle in Europe in the same aircraft.

7 Charles W. Furnas (1880–1941; American)

On 14 May 1908 at Dayton, Ohio, Wilbur Wright took Furnas, his mechanic, for a spin in the *Wright Flyer III* (29 sec; 600 m/1,968 ft). He was thus the first aeroplane passenger.

8 Louis Blériot (1872–1936; French)

On 29 June 1908 at Issy, France, in his *Blériot VIII* (50 sec; 700 m/2,297 ft). By 6 July 1908, Blériot had made a flight of 8 min 25 sec (distance not recorded); he flew across the English Channel on 25 July 1909.

9 Glenn Hammond Curtiss (1878–1930; American)

On 4 July 1908 at Hammondsport, New York, in an *AEA June Bug* (1 min 42.5 sec; 1,551 m/5,090 ft), the first official public flight in the USA.

10 Thérèse Peltier (French)

On 8 July 1908 at Turin, Italy, in a *Voisin* piloted by Delagrange. This short hop of 152 m/500 ft made her the first female aeroplane passenger.

While most of the fliers listed flew on numerous subsequent occasions and broke their first-time records, most other 'flights' of the 1906–08 period, other than those of the Wright Brothers, were no more than short hops of a few seconds' duration; meanwhile, the Wrights were so far in advance of their competitors that they were flying under full control for more than an hour and over distances of 80 km/50 miles.

The first flight in Britain was by an American, Samuel Franklin Cody, at Farnborough on 16 October 1908; it lasted barely 27 seconds and covered just 424 m/1,390 ft.

THE 10 BUSIEST AIRPORTS IN THE WORLD

	Airport	City/country	Passengers per annum
1	O'Hare	Chicago, USA	59,130,007
2	DFW International	Dallas-Fort Worth, USA	47,579,046
3	LA International	Los Angeles, USA	44,967,221
4	Hartsfield Atlanta International	Atlanta, USA	43,312,285
5	London Heathrow	London, England	39,905,200
6	Tokyo-Haneda International	Tokyo, Japan	36,567,738
7	J.F. Kennedy International	New York, USA	30,323,077
8	San Francisco International	San Francisco, USA	29,939,835
9	Stapleton International	Denver, USA	27,568,033
10	Frankfurt	Frankfurt, Germany	26,006,900

Wilbur Wright (standing) witnesses Orville Wright's historic first flight as he takes off at Kitty Hawk.

THE 10 BUSIEST AIRPORTS IN EUROPE

	Airport	City/country	Passengers per annum
1	London Heathrow	London, England	39,905,200
2	Frankfurt	Frankfurt, Germany	26,006,900
3	Orly	Paris, France	24,288,440
4	London Gatwick	London, England	21,293,200
5	Charles de Gaulle	Paris, France	20,669,542
6	Fiumicino	Rome, Italy	16,117,277
7	Schiphol	Amsterdam, Netherlands	15,998,174
8	Arlanda	Stockholm, Sweden	14,278,156
9	Copenhagen	Copenhagen, Denmark	12,436,654
10	Zurich	Zurich, Switzerland	12,150,558

Three further European airports, Athens, Munich and Manchester, each handle over 10,000,000 passengers a year.

THE FIRST WOMEN FLIERS

After the first women had taken to the air in balloons other intrepid lady balloonists followed, among them Mme Blanchard who was wont to let off fireworks during her ascents – a dangerous pursuit in a hydrogen balloon, which resulted in her plunging to her death over Paris on 7 July 1819 after setting her balloon on fire.

Following French sculptor Thérèse Peltier's flight as the first female aeroplane passenger, on 7 October 1908 Wilbur Wright took up the first American woman to fly, Mrs Hart O. Berg, tying her full skirt down with string to prevent it billowing over her head. Another American woman, the wife of pilot Samuel Franklin Cody, became the first woman air passenger in England on 14 August 1909, followed by the first British woman, a Mrs Capper, on 27 September 1909. Mrs Van Deman made a four-minute flight with Wilbur Wright on 27 October 1909 at College Park, Maryland, becoming the first woman to fly in the USA.

The world's first solo woman pilot was the Baronne de la Roche, on 22 October 1909. She gained her licence the following year, but was killed in a plane crash in 1919. In England, Edith Maude Cook was killed in a parachute jump shortly before gaining her licence, so the first British female pilot became Hilda Hewlett. Harriet Quimby, an American, was the first woman to fly the English Channel, on 16 April 1912.

The first woman transatlantic passenger was Amelia Earhart, on 17 June 1928. She went on to make the first solo female transatlantic flight on 21 May 1932, and in January 1935 became the first woman to fly the Pacific, from Honolulu to California. With her husband James Mollinson, Amy Johnson made the first east–west crossing by a woman, from Wales to the USA, on 22–23 July 1933.

The first woman to be married in mid-air was Ann Hayward, to Arno Rudolphi, on 25 August 1940 at the World's Fair in New York: the ceremony was conducted with the bride, groom, vicar, bridesmaid, best man and musicians all descending by parachute.

Jacqueline Cochran was the first woman to break the sound barrier, on 18 May 1953 in California, and Valentina Tereshkova of the USSR became the first woman astronaut, orbiting the Earth in *Vostok VI* from 16–19 June 1963. There were no more women astronauts until the 1980s, Sally Ride becoming the youngest American in space at the age of 32 on 18 June 1983. In 1984 Kathryn Sullivan became the first woman to walk in space, and on 19 May 1991 Helen Sharman became Britain's first cosmonaut.

THE 10 BUSIEST AIRPORTS IN THE UK

	Airport	Passengers per annum
1	London Heathrow	39,905,200
2	London Gatwick	21,293,200
3	Manchester	10,100,000
4	Glasgow	3,900,000
5	Birmingham	3,300,000
6	Luton	2,800,000
7	Edinburgh	2,400,000
8	Belfast Aldergrove	2,200,000
9	Jersey	1,900,000
10	Aberdeen	1,700,000

ABOVE Frankfurt airport is beaten into second place in Europe by Heathrow.

THE FIRST 10 MOONWALKERS

	Astronaut	Birthdate	Mission	Total EVA* hr:min	Mission dates
1	Neil A. Armstrong	5 Aug 30	Apollo 11	2:32	16–24 Jul 69
2	Edwin E. Aldrin	20 Jan 30	Apollo 11	2:15	16–24 Jul 69
3	Charles Conrad Jr	2 Jun 30	Apollo 12	7:45	14–24 Nov 69
4	Alan L. Bean	15 Mar 32	Apollo 12	7:45	14–24 Nov 69
5	Alan B. Shepard	18 Nov 23	Apollo 14	9:23	31 Jan–9 Feb 71
6	Edgar D. Mitchell	17 Sep 30	Apollo 14	9:23	31 Jan–9 Feb 71
7	David R. Scott	6 Jun 32	Apollo 15	19:08	26 Jul–7 Aug 71
8	James B. Irwin	17 Mar 30	Apollo 15	18:35	26 Jul–7 Aug 71
9	John W. Young	24 Sep 30	Apollo 16	20:14	16–27 Apr 72
10	Charles M. Duke	3 Oct 35	Apollo 16	20:14	16–27 Apr 72

*Extravehicular activity (i.e. time spent out of the lunar module on the Moon's surface).

Eugene A. Cernan (b.14 March 1934) and Harrison H. Schmitt (b.3 July 1935) in Apollo 17 (7–19 Dec 1972) were the last and only other astronauts to date who have walked on the Moon; both spent a total of 22:04 in EVA. No further Moon landings are planned, but Soviet scientists have proposed sending a series of unmanned probes to land on Mars, which, if successful, would lead to a follow-up manned mission between 2005 and 2010.

THE FIRST 10 PEOPLE IN SPACE

	Name	Age	Orbits	Duration hr:min	Spacecraft/ country	Date
1	Fl Major Yuri Alekseyivich Gagarin	27	1	1:48	*Vostok I* USSR	12 Apr 1961
2	Major Gherman Stepanovich Titov	25	17	25:18	*Vostok II* USSR	6–7 Aug 1961
3	Lt-Col John Herschel Glenn	40	3	4:56	*Friendship 7* USA	20 Feb 1962
4	Lt-Col Malcolm Scott Carpenter	37	3	4:56	*Aurora 7* USA	24 May 1962
5	Major Andrian Grigoryevich Nikolayev	32	64	94:22	*Vostok III* USSR	11–15 Aug 1962
6	Col Pavel Romanovich Popovich	31	48	70:57	*Vostok IV* USSR	12–15 Aug 1962
7	Cdr Walter Marty Schirra	39	6	9:13	*Sigma 7* USA	3 Oct 1962
8	Major Leroy Gordon Cooper	36	22	34:19	*Faith 7* USA	15–16 May 1963
9	Lt-Col Valeri Fyodorovich Bykovsky	28	81	119:6	*Vostok V* USSR	14–19 Jun 1963
10	Jr Lt Valentina Vladimirovna Tereshkova	26	48	70:50	*Vostok VI* USSR	16–19 Jun 1963

No. 2 was the youngest-ever astronaut, aged 25 years 329 days. No. 10 was the first woman in space. Among early pioneering flights, neither Alan Shepard (5 May 1961: *Freedom 7*) nor Gus Grissom (21 July 1961: *Liberty Bell 7*) actually entered space, achieving altitudes of only 185 km/115 miles and 190 km/118 miles respectively, and neither flight lasted more than 15 minutes. Glenn was the first American to orbit.

ABOVE 'Buzz' Aldrin, the second man to set foot on the Moon.

OPPOSITE Sally Ride, the first American woman in space, and her fellow astronauts on the *STS-7 Challenger* Space Shuttle.

THE FIRST 10 WOMEN IN SPACE

1 Valentina Vladimirovna Tereshkova (USSR)
16–19 June 1963 *Vostok VI*

Tereshkova was the first and youngest (26) woman in space.

2 Svetlana Savitskaya (USSR)
19 August 1982 *Soyuz T7*

On 25 July 1984 Savitskaya also became the first woman to walk in space.

3 Sally Ride (USA)
18–24 June 1983 *STS-7 Challenger Shuttle*

Ride was the first American woman and the youngest (32) American in space. She also flew in the *STS-41-G Challenger Shuttle* (5–13 October 1984).

4 Judith A. Resnik (USA)
30 August–5 September 1984 *STS-41-D Discovery Shuttle*

Resnik was killed in the *STS-51-L Challenger Shuttle* disaster of 28 January 1986.

5 Kathryn D. Sullivan (USA)
5–13 October 1984 *STS-41-G Challenger Shuttle*

Sullivan was the first American woman to walk in space. She also flew in *Discovery* (24–29 April 1990).

6 Anna L. Fisher (USA)
8–16 November 1984 *STS-51-A Discovery Shuttle*

7 Margaret Rhea Seddon (USA)
12–19 April 1985 *STS-51-D Discovery Shuttle*

8 Shannon W. Lucid (USA)
17–24 June 1985 *STS-51-G Discovery Shuttle*

Lucid is the oldest (42) woman in space. She also flew in *Atlantis* (18–23 October 1989).

9 Bonnie J. Dunbar (USA)
30 October–6 November 1985 *STS-61-A Challenger Shuttle*

Dunbar also flew in *Columbia* (9–20 January 1990).

10 Mary L. Cleave (USA)
26 November–3 December 1985 *STS-61-B Atlantis Shuttle*

Cleave also flew in *Atlantis* (4–8 April 1989).

Other female Space Shuttle astronauts to date include Ellen S. Baker (*Atlantis*, 18–23 October 1989), Kathryn C. Thornton (*Discovery*, 22–27 November 1989) and Marsha S. Ivins (*Columbia*, 9–20 January 1990). In May 1991 Helen Sharman, a 27-year-old chemist, became Britain's first astronaut.

The acronym *STS* has been used throughout the Shuttle programme. The first nine flights were simply numbered *STS-1* to *STS-9*. Thereafter a more complex system was employed: the first of the double-digit numbers shows the fiscal year (1 October to the following 30 September) in which the launch took place; the number *1* indicates that it was made from the Kennedy Space Center, and the letter the order in which the flights were scheduled, starting with A, though the alphabetical designation does not necessarily show the actual sequence in which the mission occurred, due to occasional delays.

ACCIDENTS & DISASTERS

THE 10 WORST VOLCANIC ERUPTIONS IN THE WORLD

	Location	Year	Estimated no. killed
1	Tambora, Indonesia	1815	92,000*
2	Mt Pelée, Martinique	1902	40,000
3	Krakatoa, Sumatra/Java	1883	36,380**
4	Nevado del Ruiz, Colombia	1985	22,940†
5	Mt Etna, Sicily	1669	20,000
6	Pompeii, Italy	79	16–20,000
7	Mt Etna, Sicily	1169	15,000
8	Mt Unzen-Dake, Japan	1792	10,400
9	Mt Laki, Iceland	1783	10,000
10	Kelut, Java	1919	5,110

*Many killed by subsequent famine resulting from crops being destroyed.
**Most killed by subsequent tidal wave.
†Most killed by resultant mud river that engulfed Armero.

The 1902 eruption of Mt Pelée, Martinique, devastated St Pierre and left 40,000 dead.

THE 10 WORST EARTHQUAKES IN THE WORLD

	Location	Date	No. killed
1	Near East/Mediterranean	cJuly 1201	1,100,000
2	Shaanxi, China	24 January 1556	830,000
3	Calcutta, India	11 October 1737	300,000
4	Antioch, Syria	20 May 526	250,000
5	Tangshan, China	28 July 1976	242,000*
6	Nan-Shan, China	22 May 1927	200,000
7	Yeddo, Japan	1703	190,000
8	Kansu, China	16 December 1920	180,000
9	Tokyo/Yokohama, Japan	1 September 1923	142,807
10	Hokkaido, Japan	30 December 1730	137,000

*Official figure; the total could have been as high as 750,000.

Some authorities have suggested a death toll of up to 160,000 for the earthquake that devastated Messina, Italy, on 28 December 1908, but the true figure seems closer to 83,000. Several other earthquakes in China and Turkey resulted in deaths of 100,000 or more. In recent times, the Armenian earthquake of 7 December 1988 and that which struck northwest Iran on 21 June 1990 resulted in the deaths of more than 55,000 and 40,000 respectively. One of the most famous earthquakes, that which destroyed San Francisco on 18 April 1906, killed between 500 and 1,000 – mostly in the fire that followed the shock.

THE 10 WORST DISASTERS AT SPORTS AND ENTERTAINMENT VENUES

	Location	Date	No. killed
1	Canton, China (theatre fire)	May 1845	1,670
2	Ring Theatre, Vienna (fire)	8 December 1881	620
3	Hong Kong Jockey Club (stand collapse and fire)	26 February 1918	604
4	Iroquois Theatre, Chicago (fire)	30 December 1903	602
5	Cocoanut Grove Night Club, Boston (fire)	28 November 1942	491
6	Abadan, Iran (arson in theatre)	20 August 1978	400
7	Lenin Stadium, Moscow (crush)	20 October 1982	340
8	Niteroi, Brazil (circus fire)	7 December 1961	323
9	Lima, Peru (football stadium riot)	24 May 1964	300
10	Sinceljo, Colombia (bullring collapse)	20 January 1980	222

In addition to these disasters, a further 188 died in a fire at the Theatre Royal, Exeter, on 5 September 1887, and 183 during a panic caused by a fire at the Victoria Hall, Sunderland, on 16 June 1883. The USA's worst circus fire occurred at Ringling Brothers' Circus, Hartford, Connecticut, on 6 July 1944 when 168 lives were lost. The worst at a motor-racing circuit was at Le Mans on 11 June 1955, when a car hurtled into the crowd, killing 82.

A number of large-scale disasters have occurred at football stadiums, among them the stand collapse at Burnden Park, Bolton, on 9 March 1946, leaving 33 dead; the fire at Bradford on 11 May 1985 (56 deaths); an incident on 12 March 1988 at Katmandu, Nepal, when 80 football fans were trampled to death; and crushes at Ibrox Park, Glasgow, on 2 January 1971 (66), at the Heysel Stadium, Brussels, on 29 May 1985 (39), and at Hillsborough, Sheffield, on 15 April 1989 (95). As a result of the latter tragedies, football ground attendances have been considerably reduced and safety measures introduced that will make such events less likely to happen in the future.

THE 10 WORST RAIL DISASTERS IN THE WORLD

	Incident	No. killed
1	6 June 1981, Bagmati River, India: A train travelling from Samastipur to Banmukhi in Bihar plunged off a bridge over the river Bagmati. Although the official death toll was said to have been 268, many authorities have claimed that the train was so massively overcrowded that the actual figure was in excess of 800, making it the worst rail disaster of all time.	c800
2	4 June 1989, Chelyabinsk, USSR: Two passenger trains travelling on the Trans Siberian railway, one of them laden with holidaymakers heading for Black Sea resorts, were destroyed by exploding liquid gas from a nearby pipeline.	600–800
3	12 December 1917, Modane, France: A troop-carrying train ran out of control and was derailed.	543+
4	2 March 1944, Balvano, Italy: A train stalled in the Armi Tunnel, and many passengers were suffocated.	521
5	3 January 1944, Torre, Spain: A collision and fire in a tunnel resulted in many deaths.	500–800
6	3 April 1955, near Guadalajara, Mexico: A train plunged into a ravine.	c300
7	29 September 1957, Montgomery, Pakistan: A collision between an express and an oil train.	250–300
8	4 February 1970, near Buenos Aires, Argentina: A collision between an express and a standing commuter train.	236
9	23 December 1933, Lagny-Pomponne, France: France's second-worst rail disaster.	230
10	22 May 1915, Quintinshill, Scotland: Britain's worst rail disaster (see The 10 Worst Rail Disasters in the UK).	227

THE 10 WORST RAIL DISASTERS IN THE UK

	Incident	No. killed
1	22 May 1915, Quintinshill near Gretna Green: A troop train carrying 500 members of the 7th Royal Scots Regiment from Larbert to Liverpool collided head-on with a local passenger train. The 15 coaches of the troop train, 195 m/ 213 yards long, were so crushed that they ended up just 61 m/ 67 yards long. Barely a minute later, the Scottish express, drawn by two engines and weighing a total of 600 tons, ploughed into the wreckage. The gas-lit troop train then caught fire. Since their records were destroyed in the blaze, the actual number of soldiers killed was never established, but was probably 215, as well as two members of the train's crew, eight in the express and two in the local train – a total of 227 killed and 246 injured, many very seriously. An enquiry established that the accident was caused by the negligence of the signalmen, George Meakin and James Tinsley, who were convicted of manslaughter and jailed.	227
2	8 October 1952, Harrow and Wealdstone Station: In patchy fog, Robert Jones, the relief driver of the Perth to Euston sleeping-car express, pulled by the *City of Glasgow*, failed to see a series of signal lights warning him of danger and at 8.19 a.m. collided with the waiting Watford to Euston train. Seconds later, the Euston to Liverpool and Manchester express (with two locomotives, *Windward Islands* and *Princess Anne*), hit the wreckage of the two trains. The casualties were 112 killed instantly, 10 who died later, and 349 injured.	122

3   4 December 1957, Lewisham, South London:
A steam and an electric train were in collision in fog, the disaster made worse by the collapse of a bridge onto the wreckage, leaving 90 dead and 109 seriously injured.   90

4   28 December 1879, Tay Bridge, Scotland:
As the North British mail train passed over it during a storm, the bridge collapsed killing all 75 passengers and the crew of five. The bridge – the longest in the world at that time – had only been opened on 31 May the previous year, and Queen Victoria had crossed it in a train soon afterwards. The locomotive was salvaged from the bed of the Tay several months later. Surprisingly little-damaged, it was repaired and continued in service until 1919.   80

5   12 June 1889, Armagh, Northern Ireland:
A Sunday school excursion train with 940 passengers stalled on a hill. When 10 carriages were uncoupled, they ran backwards and collided with a passenger train, leaving 250 injured. Railway officials were charged with negligence.   78

6   5 November 1967, Hither Green, South London:
The Hastings to Charing Cross train was derailed by a broken track. As well as those killed, 78 were injured, 27 of them very seriously.   49

7   28 February 1975, Moorgate Station, London:
The Drayton Park to Moorgate tube ran into the wall at the end of the tunnel, killing 43 and injuring 74 in London Transport's worst rail disaster.   43

8   10 December 1937, Castlecary, Scotland:
In heavy snow the Edinburgh to Glasgow train ran into a stationary Dundee to Glasgow train and rode over the top of it, leaving 179 injured.   35

9= 12 December 1988, Clapham Junction, London:
The 7.18 Basingstoke to Waterloo train, carrying 906 passengers, stopped at signals outside Clapham Junction; the 6.30 train from Bournemouth ran into its rear and an empty train from Waterloo hit the wreckage, leaving 33 dead (and one who died later) and 111 injured.   34

9= 24 December 1874, Shipton near Oxford:
The Paddington to Birkenhead train plunged over the embankment after a carriage wheel broke, killing 34 and badly injuring 65.   34

The 1988 Clapham rail disaster.

THE 10 WORST AIR DISASTERS IN THE WORLD

Incident	No. killed
1 27 March 1977, Tenerife, Canary Islands: Two Boeing 747s (KLM and Pan Am) collided on the runway.	583
2 12 August 1985, Mt Ogura, Japan: A JAL Boeing 747 on an internal flight from Tokyo to Osaka crashed, killing all but four on board in the worst-ever disaster involving only one aircraft.	520
3 3 March 1974, Paris, France: A Turkish Airlines DC-10 crashed at Ermenonville immediately after take-off.	346
4 23 June 1985, off the Irish coast: An Air India Boeing 747 on a flight from Vancouver to Delhi exploded in mid-air.	329
5 19 August 1980, Riyadh, Saudi Arabia: A Saudi Arabian Airlines Lockheed Tristar caught fire during an emergency landing.	301
6 3 July 1988, off the Iranian coast: An Iran Air A300 airbus was shot down in error by a missile fired by the *USS Vincennes*.	290
7 25 May 1979, Chicago, USA: An American Airlines DC-10 crashed on take-off.	275
8 21 December 1988, Lockerbie, Scotland: Pan Am Flight 103 from London Heathrow to New York exploded in mid-air as a result of a terrorist bomb, killing 243 passengers, 16 crew and 11 on the ground in the UK's worst-ever air disaster.	270
9 1 September 1983, off the Siberian coast: A South Korean Boeing 747 that had strayed into Soviet airspace was shot down by a Soviet fighter.	269
10 28 November 1979, Mt Erebus, Antarctica: An Air New Zealand DC-10 crashed while on a sightseeing trip.	257

One further disaster misses the Top 10 by a single victim: on 12 December 1985 an Arrow Air DC-8 crashed on take-off at Gander, Newfoundland, killing all 256 on board, including 248 members of the US 101st Airborne Division.

THE 10 WORST AIR DISASTERS IN THE UK

	Incident	No. killed
1	21 December 1988, Lockerbie, Scotland (*see* World List, No. 8)	270
2	18 June 1972, Staines, Middlesex: A BEA Trident crashed after take-off.	118
3	12 March 1950, Siginstone, Glamorgan: An Avro Tudor V crashed while attempting to land at Llandow; two saved.	81
4	23 August 1944, Freckelton, Lancashire: A US Air Force B-24 crashed onto a school.	76
5	4 June 1967, Stockport, Cheshire: An Argonaut airliner carrying holidaymakers returning from Majorca crashed, killing all but 12 on board.	72
6	24 August 1921, off the coast near Hull: Airship R38, sold by the British Government to the USA, broke in two on a training and test flight.	62
7	22 August 1985, Manchester: A British Airtours Boeing 737 caught fire on the ground.	55
8	5 January 1969, near Gatwick Airport: An Ariana Afghan Airlines Boeing 727 crash-landed; the deaths include two on the ground.	50
9	8 January 1989, M1 Motorway: A British Midland Boeing 737 attempting to land without engine power crashed on the M1 Motorway embankment near East Midlands Airport.	47
10=	6 November 1986, off Sumburgh, Shetland Islands: A Chinook helicopter ferrying oil rig workers ditched in the sea.	45
10=	15 November 1957, Isle of Wight: Following an engine fire, an Aquila Airlines Solent flying boat struck a cliff.	45

In addition to disasters within the UK, a number of major air crashes involving British aircraft have occurred overseas. One of the earliest was that of British airship R101 which crashed near Beauvais, France, on 5 October 1930, killing 47. The biplane *City of Liverpool* crashed in Belgium on 28 March 1933, killing 13 (one passenger fell out before the crash, and sabotage was suspected). On 4 March 1962 a chartered Caledonian DC-7C crashed near Douala, Cameroon, with the loss of 111 lives; at the time, this was the worst disaster involving a British airliner and the worst in Africa. A BOAC Boeing 707 crashed on Mount Fuji, Japan, on 5 March 1966, killing 124, but the worst on record was the crash of a Dan-Air Boeing 727 at Santa Cruz de Tenerife, Canary Islands, on 25 April 1980 in which all 146 on board perished.

ABOVE RIGHT The 1972 Staines BEA Trident air crash killed 118.

RIGHT Rescue workers at Senghenydd, scene in 1913 of the UK's worst mining disaster.

THE 10 WORST MINING DISASTERS IN THE WORLD

	Location	Date	No. killed
1	Hinkeiko, China	26 April 1942	1,572
2	Courrières, France	10 March 1906	1,060
3	Omuta, Japan	9 November 1963	447
4	Senghenydd, Wales	14 October 1913	439
5	Coalbrook, South Africa	21 January 1960	437
6	Wankie, Rhodesia	6 June 1972	427
7	Bihar, India	28 May 1965	375
8	Chasnala, India	27 December 1975	372
9=	Barnsley, Yorkshire	12 December 1866	361*
9=	Monongah, West Virginia, USA	6 December 1907	361

A further 28 were killed the following day while searching for survivors.

THE 10 COUNTRIES WITH THE HIGHEST NUMBER OF ROAD DEATHS

	Country	Total deaths
1	USA	48,900
2	France	10,548
3	Japan	10,344
4	West Germany	8,205
5	Spain	7,296
6	Italy	6,939
7	Great Britain	5,373
8	Poland	4,667
9	Yugoslavia	4,414
10	Canada	4,017

This comparison of international road deaths for the latest years for which statistics are available shows that the USA remains well ahead of the rest of the world – although in proportion to the number of vehicle miles travelled, the USA's road deaths are actually lower than Great Britain's (2.5 deaths per 100,000,000 miles compared with Great Britain's 2.7). Sweden's fatality rate is the lowest at 2.2. Portugal emerges as the most dangerous country based on the ratio of road deaths to population (26.4 deaths per 100,000, compared with Great Britain's 9.8) and based on the ratio of road deaths to cars (10.7 per 10,000 vehicles) is second only to Yugoslavia (11.8), compared with Great Britain's 2.5.

THE 10 WORST EXPLOSIONS IN THE WORLD*

	Location	Date	No. killed
1	Halifax, Nova Scotia (ammunition ship *Mont Blanc*)	6 December 1917	1,654
2	Salang Tunnel, Afghanistan (petrol tanker)	23 November 1982	1,100+
3	Cali, Colombia (ammunition trucks)	7 August 1956	1,100
4	Bombay Harbour	14 April 1944	700
5	Chelyabinsk, USSR (liquid gas destroyed train)**	4 June 1989	600–800
6=	Texas City, Texas (ammonium nitrate on *Grandcamp* freighter)	16 April 1947	561
6=	Oppau, Germany (chemical plant)	21 September 1921	561
8	Invergordon, Scotland (cruiser *Natal*)	30 December 1915	428
9	Mexico City (gas)	19 November 1984	334
10	Port Chicago, California (ammunition ships)	17 July 1944	322

Excluding mining disasters, terrorist and military bombs.
**See also *The 10 Worst Rail Disasters in the World*.*

THE 10 WORST FIRES IN THE WORLD*

	Location	Date	No. killed
1	Kwanto, Japan (following earthquake)	1 September 1923	60,000
2	Cairo	1824	4,000
3	London Bridge	July 1212	3,000**
4	Santiago, Chile (church of La Compañía)	8 December 1863	1,800
5	Chungking, China (docks)	2 September 1949	1,700
6	Peshtigo, Wisconsin (forest)	8 October 1871	1,182
7	Minnesota (forest)	1 September 1894	480
8	Cloquet, Minnesota (forest)	12 October 1918	400
9	Hoboken, New Jersey (docks)	30 June 1900	326
10	Brussels (department store)	22 May 1967	322

Excluding sports and entertainment venues, mining disasters and as a result of military action.
**Burned, crushed and drowned in ensuing panic.*

The crater left by the 1921 Oppau chemical plant explosion that resulted in 561 deaths.

TRANSPORT & TOURISM

THE 10 COUNTRIES PRODUCING THE MOST CARS

	Country	Total production (1989)
1	Japan	9,052,406
2	USA	6,823,097
3	West Germany	4,563,673
4	France	3,409,017
5	Italy	1,971,969
6	Spain	1,638,615
7	UK	1,299,082
8	USSR	1,200,000
9	Canada	1,001,588
10	South Korea	871,898
	World total	*35,455,838*

THE 10 COUNTRIES WITH THE HIGHEST RATIO OF CARS TO PEOPLE

	Country	Cars per 1,000 pop.
1	USA	570
2	West Germany	485
3	Canada	469
4	New Zealand	457
5	Luxembourg	456
6	Australia	450
7	Switzerland	426
8	Sweden	416
9	Guam	413
10	Italy	409
	UK	*369*
	World average	*82*

The high ratios of cars per 1,000 people in the Top 10 contrast markedly with the figures for such countries as India (two cars per 1,000) and China (fewer than one car per 1,000) – or the equivalent, respectively, of 482 and 1,188 people per car.

The Ford Fiesta is the UK's bestselling car.

THE 10 BESTSELLING CARS IN THE UK

	Make	Model	Total sold (1990)
1	Ford	Fiesta	151,475
2	Ford	Escort	141,985
3	Vauxhall	Cavalier	138,357
4	Ford	Sierra	128,705
5	Vauxhall	Astra	101,087
6	Rover	Metro	81,064
7	Rover	200 series	62,487
8	Vauxhall	Nova	54,786
9	Ford	Orion	51,404
10	Peugeot	205	50,205

Total sales of new cars in 1990 were 2,008,934 – a 12.69 per cent decrease on 1989's all-time record of 2,300,944. Although Ford, Vauxhall and Rover (some of whose models are made overseas) dominate the Top 10, imported cars are hard on their heels in the rest of the Top 20, with the Nissan Micra at No. 11 and Volkswagen Golf at No. 12. The total sales of imported cars accounted for 56.74 per cent of the market. Sales by manufacturer were:

	Manufacturer/country	UK-built	Total sold
1	Ford (UK/Germany/Belgium/Spain/USA)	301,233	507,260
2	GM-Vauxhall (UK/Germany/Belgium/Spain/USA)	210,971	323,054
3	Rover (UK)	281,385	281,385
4	Peugeot-Talbot (UK/France)	30,067	123,671
5	Audi-Volkswagen (Germany/Belgium/Spain)	0	115,740
6	Nissan (UK/Japan/Spain)	24,337	106,783
7	Renault (France)	0	67,578
8	Volvo (Sweden/Netherlands/Belgium)	0	66,017
9	Citroën (France/Spain)	0	60,899
10	Fiat (Italy/Portugal)	0	54,945

All the other companies achieving 1990 sales in excess of 20,000 are foreign-owned and (with the exception of about one-quarter of Honda's total UK sales) assembled abroad. They were: BMW (Germany), Toyota (Japan), Honda (UK/Japan), Mercedes-Benz (Germany), Mazda (Japan) and Lada (USSR). 'Prestige' British-made cars such as Jaguar-Daimler and Rolls-Royce/Bentley accounted for relatively small numbers of new registrations in 1990 (10,664 and 1,007 respectively), while two other British companies, Lotus and Reliant, sold just 1,017 and 41 cars each in the UK.

THE TOP 10 CAR MANUFACTURERS IN THE USA

	Manufacturer	Domestic sales (1989)
1	Ford	1,433,550
2	Chevrolet	1,232,761
3	Lincoln-Mercury	666,223
4	Pontiac	634,327
5	Oldsmobile	600,037
6	Buick	542,917
7	Dodge	410,995
8	Honda	389,472
9	Plymouth	271,645
10	Toyota	212,388

In the USA total sales of domestically-manufactured cars declined in 1989 to 7,072,902, well below the 1986 peak of 8,214,897. Imports accounted for a further 2,825,165 vehicles, making the overall total 9,898,067 (11,459,518 in 1986).

Eight of the Top 10 companies are components of gigantic US car-making conglomerates: Dodge and Plymouth (as well as Chrysler-Plymouth and Eagle, which do not feature in the Top 10) are part of the Chrysler Corporation; Lincoln-Mercury is owned by the Ford Motor Company; and Chevrolet, Pontiac, Oldsmobile and Buick belong to General Motors (as does Cadillac). If sales by all the Ford companies are amalgamated, the total is 2,099,773, while those of General Motors' companies is 3,276,941 – almost half the total number of home-produced cars sold in the year. Two Japanese-owned companies that build cars in the USA feature increasingly strongly in this list – Honda, which entered the Top 10 for the first time in 1987 and is now in 8th place, and Toyota, which ousted Chrysler-Plymouth in 1989, when it more than trebled its previous year's output.

THE TOP 10 CAR MANUFACTURERS IN THE UK

	Company	Total car production (1990)
1	Rover Group	464,612
2	Ford Motor Company	329,597
3	General Motors	256,293
4	Peugeot-Talbot	116,548
5	Nissan	76,190
6	Jaguar	41,891
7	Carbodies*	3,700
8	Rolls-Royce	3,274
9	Lotus Group	2,142
10	TVR	748

THE TOP 10 CAR MANUFACTURERS IN THE WORLD

	Company	Country	Total car production
1	General Motors	USA	5,662,843
2	Ford Motor Company	USA	4,234,583
3	Toyota	Japan	3,093,692
4	Volkswagen	West Germany	2,748,152
5	Peugeot-Citroën	France	2,227,528
6	Nissan	Japan	2,016,626
7	Fiat	Italy	1,790,631
8	Renault	France	1,767,516
9	Honda	Japan	1,489,185
10	Chrysler	USA	1,209,156
	World total		34,258,842

Robots at work on the Ford production line, Dagenham.

Carbodies manufacture the traditional 'black cab' taxi.

Figures are for 1988 production, amalgamating worldwide production in all companies owned by the manufacturers. The Top 10 car manufacturers (plus Mazda of Japan, which produced 1,043,420 cars) are the only firms in the world that produce more than 1,000,000 cars a year, although all of them also produce commercial vehicles, General Motors making just over and Ford just under 2,000,000. VAZ of the USSR, which makes only cars, is in 12th position with 731,455. The British Rover Group is in 15th place in the world league, just beating both BMW and Volvo.

THE TOP 10 CAR-OWNING COUNTRIES IN THE WORLD

	Country	Total cars registered
1	USA	141,251,695
2	Japan	30,776,243
3	West Germany	29,190,322
4	Italy	23,500,000
5	France	22,370,000
6	UK	20,923,423
7	USSR	15,874,700
8	Canada	11,900,000
9	Brazil	11,760,459
10	Spain	10,787,424
	World total	*412,907,178*

THE TOP 10 FORD CAR COLOURS

1	Diamond white
2	Radiant red
3	Mercury grey
4	Moondust silver
5	Black
6=	Tasmin blue
6=	Galaxy blue
8	Burgundy red
9	Maritime blue
10	Magenta

It was, of course, Henry Ford (1863–1947), the company's founder, who was quoted as saying (of the Model T Ford car), 'People can have it in any colour – so long as it's black.'

THE TOP 10 CAR ADVERTISERS IN THE UK

	Manufacturer	Advertising expenditure 1989 (£)
1=	Ford	38,000,000
1=	Rover Group	38,000,000
3	VW-Audi	29,000,000
4	Vauxhall	25,000,000
5	Renault	23,000,000
6=	Citroën	22,000,000
6=	Fiat	22,000,000
6=	Peugeot	22,000,000
9	Volvo	15,000,000
10	Nissan	14,000,000

THE 10 COMMONEST CAUSES OF CAR BREAKDOWN

1	Battery
2	Carburettor
3	Alternator
4	Puncture
5	Lock-out
6	Contact-breaker points
7	Timing belts
8	Distributor
9	Clutch cable
10	Fuel pump

Based on calls to the Automobile Association in 1990.

THE 10 MOST EXPENSIVE CARS SOLD AT AUCTION

	Car	Price (£)
1	1962 Ferrari 250 Gran Turismo Berlinetta Competition GTO Sotheby's, Monte Carlo, 1990	6,410,000
2	1931 Bugatti Royale Type 41 Chassis '41.141' Christie's, London, 1987	5,575,000
3	1929 Bugatti Royale, Chassis '41.150' William F. Harrah Collection Sale, Reno, USA, 1986	4,300,000
4	1960 Ferrari Dino Christie's, Monaco, 1990	2,574,591
5	1957 Aston-Martin DBR2 Christie's, Monaco, 1989	2,178,000
6	1934 Alfa Romeo Tipo B Monoposto Christie's, Monaco, 1989	1,971,000
7	1934 Mercedes-Benz 500K Special Roadster Sotheby's, Monaco, 1989	1,956,237
8	John Lennon's 1965 Rolls-Royce Phantom V Sotheby's, New York, 1985	1,768,462
9	Alfa Romeo Tipo 8C 2300 Christie's, Monaco, 1989	1,763,000
10	1907 Rolls-Royce Silver Ghost 40/50 Tourer Sotheby's, Florida, 1990	1,733,332

Although these are the highest prices ever paid at public auction, it was reported in 1989 that the only surviving 1967 original ex-factory team Ferrari 330P4 sports prototype had been purchased privately by a Swiss collector for £5,800,000 and in November of the same year that another 1962 Ferrari 250 GTO, one of only 36 made, had been purchased from a British businessman by a Japanese collector for in excess of £8,500,000 – a figure as high as £10,000,000 was rumoured for this vehicle and for a 1929 Bentley Speed Six sold privately in 1990. Although three cars entered the Top 10 in 1990, one breaking the world record, the classic car market experienced a substantial downturn in that year, and it seems unlikely that such exceptional prices will be repeated in the foreseeable future.

The 1931 Bugatti Royale, sold in 1987 for £5,575,000.

THE 10 MOST-VISITED NATIONAL TRUST PROPERTIES

	Property	Annual visitors
1	Fountains Abbey and Studley Royal, North Yorkshire	300,067
2	Stourhead Garden, Wiltshire	228,399
3	St Michael's Mount, Cornwall	194,973
4	Polesden Lacey House and Garden, Surrey	192,738
5	Styal, Quarry Bank Mill, Cheshire	187,841
6	Chartwell, Kent	181,983
7	Bodnant Castle, Gwynedd	170,105
8	Sissinghurst Castle Garden, Kent	170,075
9	Wakehurst Place, West Sussex	168,541
10	Bodiam Castle, East Sussex	164,304

Over 10,000,000 people a year visit properties administered by the National Trust in England and Wales and Northern Ireland (the National Trust for Scotland is a separate organization). Of the more than 300 properties under the Trust's aegis, 77 are visited by 50,000 or more people a year.

ABOVE Registration number 1A comes under the hammer, attaining the auction record of £176,000.

RIGHT St Michael's Mount, Cornwall, one of the National Trust's most visited properties.

THE 10 MOST EXPENSIVE CAR REGISTRATION NUMBERS SOLD AT AUCTION IN THE UK

	Number	Sale	Price (£)
1	1A	Christie's, 14 December 1989	176,000
2	1S	Christie's, 7 December 1990	88,000
3	G1 LLY	Central Motor Auctions, 12–13 March 1990	75,250
4	MUS 1C	Christie's, 14 December 1989	71,500
5	ELV 1S	Christie's, 7 December 1990	66,000
6	IT	Christie's, 14 December 1990	61,600
7	1 PM	Central Motor Auctions, 12–13 March 1990	60,200
8	1 BR	Christie's, 7 December 1990	55,000
9	1 AM	Central Motor Auctions, 12–13 March 1990	53,750
10	APR 1L	Central Motor Auctions, 12–13 March 1990	49,990

Prices include buyer's premium.

Glasgow's Museum of Transport attracts over 500,000 visitors a year.

THE TOP 10 TOURIST ATTRACTIONS CHARGING ADMISSION IN SCOTLAND

	Attraction	Annual visitors
1	Edinburgh Castle	1,078,120
2	Magnum Leisure Centre, Irvine	800,253
3	Perth Leisure Pool	704,000
4	Edinburgh Zoo	542,020*
5	The Aquatec Ice and Water Complex, Motherwell	499,500
6	Culzean Castle and Country Park, Ayrshire	365,679
7	Loch Ness Monster Exhibition, Drumnadrochit, Highland	350,000*
8	Palace of Holyroodhouse, Edinburgh	316,679
9	The Old Blacksmith's Shop Visitor Centre, Gretna Green	300,000*
10	Stirling Castle	264,734

*Estimated.

THE TOP 10 FREE TOURIST ATTRACTIONS IN SCOTLAND*

	Attraction	Annual visitors
1	Glasgow Museum and Art Gallery	1,008,180
2	Burrell Collection, Glasgow	878,772
3	Royal Botanical Gardens, Edinburgh	785,591
4	Museum of Transport, Glasgow	535,938
5	Royal Museum of Scotland, Edinburgh	508,299
6	City Art Centre, Edinburgh	484,697
7	People's Palace Museum, Glasgow	466,695
8	Glasgow Botanic Gardens	350,000**
9	Aberdeen Art Gallery	346,757
10	Scottish United Services Museum, Edinburgh	309,940

*Excluding country parks.
**Estimated.

THE TOP 10 TOURIST ATTRACTIONS IN WALES*

	Attraction	Annual visitors
1	Ocean Beach Amusement Park, Rhyl	500,000**
2	James Pringle Weavers, Llanfair	433,977
3	Pembrey Country Park	413,000
4	Barry Island Log Flume	392,671
5	Padarn Country Park, Llanberis	380,000**
6	Oakwood Leisure Park, Nr Narberth	372,000
7	Rhyl Suncentre	330,300
8	Penscynor Wildlife Park, Neath	285,000
9	Caernarfon Castle	282,000
10	Portmeirion, Penrhyndeudraeth	275,329

*Excluding leisure centres.
**Estimated.

THE TOP 10 HISTORIC PROPERTIES IN THE UK

	Property	Annual visitors
1	Tower of London	2,298,193
2	Edinburgh Castle	1,078,120
3	Roman Baths and Pump Room, Bath	950,472
4	Windsor Castle, State Apartments	855,239
5	Stonehenge, Wiltshire	703,221
6	Warwick Castle	685,000
7	Leeds Castle, Kent	540,483
8	Tower Bridge, London	527,766
9	Hampton Court Palace	524,627
10	Blenheim Palace, Oxfordshire	516,630

Caernarfon Castle, ranked ninth among Welsh tourist attractions.

THE TOP 10 TOURIST ATTRACTIONS IN THE UK*

	Attraction	Annual visitors
1	Blackpool Pleasure Beach	6,500,000**†
2	Albert Dock, Liverpool	5,100,000**†
3	Strathclyde Country Park, Motherwell	4,200,000**†
4	Palace Pier, Brighton	3,500,000**†
5	Great Yarmouth Pleasure Beach	2,600,000**†
6	Madame Tussaud's, London	2,547,447
7	Alton Towers, Staffordshire	2,070,000
8	Chessington World of Adventures	1,500,000**
9	Pleasureland, Southport	1,426,000
10=	Blackpool Tower	1,300,000**
10=	Bradgate Park, Leicestershire	1,300,000**†

Excluding historic properties, cathedrals, museums and galleries.
**Estimated.*
†*Free admission.*

THE 10 MOST-VISITED GARDENS IN THE UK

	Garden	Annual visitors
1	Kew Gardens, London	1,196,346
2	Royal Botanical Gardens, Edinburgh	785,591*
3	Walsall Arboretum Illuminations, West Midlands	450,000*
4	University of Oxford Botanic Gardens	400,000*
5=	Belfast Botanic Gardens	350,000*
5=	Glasgow Botanic Gardens	350,000*
7	Sir Thomas and Lady Dixon Park, Belfast	300,000*
8	Stourhead Garden, Wiltshire	228,399
9	Bodnant Garden, Gwynedd	170,105
10	Sissinghurst Castle Garden, Kent	170,075

Free admission.

Water-lilies at Kew, the UK's most popular gardens.

THE 10 MOST-VISITED WILDLIFE ATTRACTIONS IN THE UK

	Attraction	Annual visitors
1	London (Regent's Park) Zoo	1,250,000
2	Windsor Safari Park	1,050,000
3	Chester Zoo	1,000,000*
4	Tropical World, Leeds	863,024
5	Edinburgh Zoo	542,020*
6	Whipsnade Park Zoo, Bedfordshire	530,000
7	Lotherton Hall Bird Garden, West Yorkshire	490,000*
8	Twycross Zoo, Atherstone	462,383
9	Bristol Zoo	450,000*
10	Cotswold Wildlife Park, Burford	376,412

Estimated.

THE TOP 10 MUSEUMS AND GALLERIES IN THE UK

	Museum/gallery	Annual visitors
1	British Museum, London	4,769,439*
2	National Gallery, London	3,682,233*
3	Tate Gallery, London	1,562,431*
4	Natural History Museum, London	1,534,298
5	Royal Academy of Arts, London	1,308,500
6	Science Museum, London	1,303,345
7	Glasgow Museum and Art Gallery	1,008,180*
8	Victoria & Albert Museum, London	962,235*
9	Burrell Collection, Glasgow	878,772*
10	Jorvik Viking Centre, York	846,228

Free admission.

THE TOP 10 EUROPEAN CITY BREAK HOLIDAY DESTINATIONS IN 1990

1	Paris
2	Amsterdam
3	Rome
4	Florence
5	Venice
6	Berlin
7	Vienna
8	Madrid
9	Budapest
10	Reykjavik

Based on bookings through Thomas Cook.

THE TOP 10 SKI HOLIDAY DESTINATIONS IN 1990

1	Andorra
2	Mayrhofen
3	Val d'Isère
4	Obergurgl
5	Livigno
6	Tignes
7	Meribel Les Allues
8	Zell Am See
9	Val Thorens
10	Les Deux Alpes

Based on bookings through Thomas Cook.

LEFT One of the attractions of Amsterdam as a tourist city.

BELOW Bournemouth station has the longest platform in the UK and fifth longest in the world.

THE 10 LONGEST RAIL PLATFORMS IN THE WORLD

	Station	Platform length m	ft
1	State Street Center Subway, Chicago, Illinois, USA	1,067	3,500
2	Khargpur, India	833	2,733
3	Perth, Australia	762	2,500
4	Sonepur, India	736	2,415
5	Bournemouth, England	720	2,362
6	Bulawayo, Zimbabwe	702	2,302
7	New Lucknow, India	686	2,250
8	Bezwada, India	640	2,100
9	Gloucester, England	624	2,047
10	Jhansi, India	617	2,025

THE 10 LONGEST RAIL PLATFORMS IN THE UK

	Station	Platform length m	ft
1	Bournemouth	720	2,362
2	Gloucester	624	2,047
3	Colchester	604	1,920
4	York	535	1,755
5	Perth	517	1,696
6	Crewe	510	1,672
7	Cambridge	503	1,650
8	Edinburgh Waverley	486	1,596
9	York	475	1,558
10=	Manchester Victoria	457	1,500
10=	London Victoria	457	1,500
10=	York	457	1,500

ABOVE Victoria is the London Underground's busiest station.

OPPOSITE (background) The Forth Road Bridge, second longest in the UK and 10th longest in the world.

THE 10 BUSIEST LONDON UNDERGROUND STATIONS

	Station	Total passengers
1	Victoria	72,000,000
2	King's Cross	69,000,000
3	Oxford Circus	55,700,000
4	Liverpool Street	43,300,000
5	Waterloo	37,900,000
6	Piccadilly Circus	34,500,000
7	Tottenham Court Road	28,700,000
8	Charing Cross	28,400,000
9	Green Park	26,700,000
10	Paddington	26,200,000

The 10 busiest stations in the morning rush-hour (07.00–10.00):

	Station	Average daily passengers
1	King's Cross	34,502
2	Victoria	32,361
3	Liverpool Street	24,167
4	Waterloo	23,629
5	Brixton	14,760
6	Charing Cross	13,804
7	Paddington	13,426
8	Finsbury Park	13,187
9	Seven Sisters	10,995
10	Euston	10,068

The 10 busiest stations in the evening rush-hour (16.00–19.00):

	Station	Average daily passengers
1	Oxford Circus	44,539
2	Green Park	29,195
3	Victoria	28,892
4	King's Cross	26,414
5	Piccadilly Circus	21,058
6	Tottenham Court Road	19,703
7	Bank	19,242
8	Moorgate	18,495
9	Liverpool Street	18,101
10	Holborn	15,361

Based on passenger figures for 1989. A total of over 800,000,000 people a year travel on the London Underground, with an average (Monday–Friday) of 2,500,000 a day.

QUIZ

TRAINS

1 Where does the Blue Train run?
2 Was the holder of the record speed for a steam train in England (a) *The Mallard*, (b) *The Swan* or (c) *The Kingfisher*?
3 Who narrates the children's videos of the Rev W. Awdry's *Thomas the Tank Engine* stories?
4 The first person to be killed by a train was William Huskisson, a Member of Parliament. What was the name of the train?
5 What was the fate of the disused Paris railway station, the Gare d'Orsay?
6 What group had a 1967 hit record with *Last Train to Clarksville*?
7 In what British county would you find the Bluebell Railway?
8 In the film of Agatha Christie's *Murder on the Orient Express*, who played the part of the detective, Hercule Poirot?
9 In what year did the Great Train Robbery take place – 1953, 1963 or 1973?
10 What is the most southerly British Rail station?

THE 10 FASTEST PRODUCTION MOTORCYCLES AVAILABLE IN THE UK

	Make	Model	Speed kph	mph
1	Kawasaki	ZX1100–C1 (ZZ-R1100)	278.4	173.0
2	Kawasaki	ZX1000B2 (ZX-10)	262.0	162.8
3	Yamaha	FZR1000R	259.8	161.4
4	Suzuki	GSX-R1100L	258.1	160.4
5	Honda	VF750R (RC30)	254.3	158.0
6	Honda	CBR1000F-L	252.5	156.9
7	Kawasaki	ZX750-H2	244.6	152.0
8	Suzuki	GSX-R750L	242.2	150.5
9	Kawasaki	ZX600D1 (ZZ-R600)	240.6	149.5
10	Honda	VFR750F-L	238.2	148.0

Based on figures obtained for 1989–90 production bikes by *Performance Bikes* magazine, using radar timing equipment and highest prone speeds (i.e. with riders lying on the tanks to reduce wind resistance, rather than sitting upright).

THE 10 LONGEST BRIDGES IN THE WORLD

	Bridge	Completed	Length of main span m	Length of main span ft
1	Messina Bridge, Sicily to Calabria, Italy	Under construction	3,320	10,892
2	Akashi-Kaikyo, Japan	Under construction	1,780	5,839
3	Humber Estuary, UK	1980	1,410	4,626
4	Verrazano Narrows, New York, USA	1964	1,298	4,260
5	Golden Gate, San Francisco, USA	1937	1,280	4,200
6	Mackinac Straits, Michigan, USA	1957	1,158	3,800
7	Bosphorus, Istanbul, Turkey	1973	1,074	3,524
8	George Washington, New York, USA	1931	1,067	3,500
9	Ponte 25 Abril (Ponte Salazar), Lisbon, Portugal	1966	1,013	3,323
10	Forth Road Bridge, UK	1964	1,006	3,300

If only completed bridges are included, the Humber Estuary Bridge heads the list, No. 9 is another British structure, the Severn Bridge (completed 1966; 988 m/3,240 ft), and No. 10 the Tacoma Narrows II, Washington (completed 1950; 853 m/2,800 ft).

THE 10 LONGEST BRIDGES IN THE UK

	Bridge	Completed	Length of main span m	Length of main span ft
1	Humber Estuary	1980	1,410	4,626
2	Forth Road Bridge	1964	1,006	3,300
3	Severn Bridge	1966	988	3,240
4	Firth of Forth	1890	521	1,710
5	Tamar, Saltash	1961	335	1,100
6	Runcorn–Widnes	1961	330	1,082
7	Clifton Suspension	1864	214	702
8	Menai Straits	1834	176	579
9	Tyne Bridge, Newcastle	1930	162	531
10=	Medway (M2 Motorway)	1963	152	500
10=	George Street, Newport	1964	152	500

THE FIRST 10 THAMES CROSSINGS IN LONDON

	Crossing	Years in operation
1	London Bridge	1st century AD–1014
2	Kingston Bridge	Medieval
3	Putney Bridge	1729–1886
4	Westminster Bridge	1750–1857
5	Kew Bridge	1759–89
6	Blackfriars Bridge	1769–1860
7	Battersea Bridge	1772–1890
8	Vauxhall Bridge	1816–98
9	Waterloo Bridge	1817–1934
10	Southwark Bridge	1819–1913

None of the first 10 crossings still exists, all having been replaced with new bridges on the same sites and with the same names (there have been at least five London Bridges). The 10 oldest crossings that are still operational – though some have changed their function and several have been widened or otherwise modified – are:

	Crossing	Opened
1	Richmond Bridge	1777
2	Kingston Bridge	1828
3	Thames Tunnel*	1843
4	Westminster Bridge	1862
5	Battersea Railway Bridge	1863
6	Hungerford Bridge	1864
7	Alexandra Bridge	1866
8	Kew Railway Bridge	1869
9	Blackfriars Bridge	1869
10	Tower Subway**	1870

*Built as foot tunnel; rebuilt for London Underground's Metropolitan Line.
**Built for pedestrian traffic; now used for water mains.

THE 10 LONGEST ROADS IN THE UK

	Road	Length km	miles
1	A1*	655	407
2=	A9	465	289
2=	A6	465	289
4	A38	451	280
5	A30	440	273
6	A40	434	270
7	A5	400	249
8	M6	393	244
9	A39	344	214
10	A41	326	203

*Including A1(M).

Book end: London Transport's commonest lost property items.

THE 10 COUNTRIES WITH THE LONGEST ROAD NETWORKS

	Country	Total roads km	miles
1	USA	6,233,308	3,873,197
2	Brazil	1,673,733	1,040,009
3	USSR	1,609,900	1,000,345
4	India	1,554,200	965,735
5	Japan	1,109,981	689,710
6	China	982,200	610,311
7	Australia	852,986	530,021
8	Canada	844,386	524,677
9	France	805,450	500,483
10	West Germany	496,652	308,605
11	UK	370,970	230,510
	World total	24,300,000	15,099,317

At a constant 80 kph/50 mph it would take 34 years 173 days to cover every road in the world, 8 years 308 days to drive over every road in the USA and a mere 192 days to traverse the entire United Kingdom road network. Unfortunately, in doing so you would be breaking the speed limit on a large proportion of them and would therefore probably lose your licence before completing your marathon rally.

THE 10 COMMONEST TYPES OF LOST PROPERTY ON LONDON TRANSPORT

	Type	Number 1986–87	1987–88	1988–89	1989–90
1	Books	19,013	19,329	19,148	20,006
2	'Value items' (handbags, purses, wallets, etc)	21,940	19,868	18,628	18,397
3	Clothing	16,497	15,211	14,954	15,088
4	Umbrellas	21,080	23,250	17,129	13,889
5	Cases and bags	9,222	9,317	9,155	9,272
6	Keys	9,923	9,265	8,793	8,595
7	Spectacles	5,975	5,754	5,756	5,985
8	Cameras, electronic articles and jewellery	5,550	5,304	5,493	5,352
9	Gloves (pairs)	5,625	4,402	3,770	3,428
10	Gloves (odd)	844	701	576	577

As we noted in previous editions, there is an inexplicable consistency in the numbers of articles handed in to London Transport's Lost Property Office in Baker Street from year to year. Books remain in the No. 1 position but changes in fashion have meant that hats, once one of the commonest lost items, no longer even warrant a separate category while expensive electronic calculators and cameras are now lost in large numbers. Among the stranger items that have been lost in recent years are sets of false teeth, a box of glass eyes, an artificial leg, a Yamaha outboard motor, part of a jump from the Horse of the Year Show, television sets, a complete double bed, a stuffed gorilla and an urn containing human ashes – the latter was never claimed and the ashes were eventually scattered in a Regent's Park flowerbed.

INDEX

ACKNOWLEDGEMENTS

I would like to thank the following organizations and individuals who kindly supplied
me with information to enable me to compile many of the lists in
THE TOP 10 OF EVERYTHING:

Academy of Motion Picture Arts
  and Sciences
Advertising Standards
  Authority
AGB Group
Airport Operators Council
Allergy International Ltd
Alpine Club
American Forestry Association
American Kennel Club
Amusement and Music
  Operators' Association
Arbiter Group plc
The Art Group Ltd
Art Sales Index
The Arts Council
ASH
Association of Comics
  Enthusiasts
Audiotex Briefing
Audit Bureau of Circulations Ltd
Automobile Association
Banking Information Service
BBC Enterprises
Beefeater Gin, Sponsors of the
  Oxford & Cambridge Boat
  Race
BIS Mackintosh
BLMS
The Bookseller
Bookwatch Ltd
The Brewers Society
British Airports Services Ltd
British Antarctic Survey
British Broadcasting
  Corporation
British Cave Research
  Association
The British Council
British National Space Centre
The British Olympic Association
British Rail
British Rate & Data
British Tourist Authority
Building Societies Association
Business Magazine
Cadbury Schweppes Group
Capital Radio plc
Carbon Dioxide Information
  Analysis Center
The Cat Fanciers' Association of
  the USA
The Governing Council of the
  Cat Fancy
Catfax
Central Car Auctions
Central Statistical Office
The Champagne Bureau
Channel Four Television
Channel Swimming Association

Charities Aid Foundation
Chicago Sound Co
Christie's East
Christie's London
Christie's South Kensington
Consumers' Association
Thomas Cook
The Corporate Intelligence
  Group Ltd
Department of the Environment
Department of Transport
The Diamond Information
  Centre
The Direct Mail Sales Bureau
Electoral Reform Society
Employment Conditions Abroad
Euromonitor Ltd
Flight International
Food and Agriculture
  Organization of the United
  Nations
Food from Britain
Football Association
Football League
Forbes Magazine
Ford Motor Company
Foreign and Commonwealth
  Office
The Forestry Commission
Fortnum & Mason Ltd
Fortune
Gallup
Noel Gay Organization
Generation AB
Hallmark Cards Ltd
Hamleys Ltd
Harrods Ltd
Home Office
Independent Broadcasting
  Authority
Institution of Environmental
  Health Officers
Interbrand Group plc
Interflora Ltd
International Cocoa
  Organization
International Dental Federation
International Monetary Fund
International Road Federation
Jukebox Journal
Keep Britain Tidy
The Kennel Club
Keynote Publications
Kiss 100 FM
Kissagrams Ltd
Law Society
London Regional Transport
London Underground
MARC Europe
Marks & Spencer plc

MEAL
Meat & Livestock Commission
MORI
Motor Vehicle Manufacturers
  Association of the United
  States, Inc
MRIB
National Aeronautics and Space
  Administration
National Alliance of Women's
  Organizations
National Canine Defence League
The National Grid Company plc
The National Pier Society
National Portrait Gallery
The National Trust
A. C. Nielsen Co Ltd
Nielsen Media Research
Office of Population Censuses
  and Surveys
The Open University
The Oxford English Dictionary
Penguin Books Ltd
Performance Bikes
Pet Health Council
Petroleum Review
Phillips
The Phobics' Society
The Polytechnic of Central
  London
Produktschap voor
  Gedistilleerde Dranken
Proprietory Association of Great
  Britain
Public Information Office, House
  of Commons
The Really Useful Group plc
The Royal Aeronautical Society
The Royal College of General
  Practitioners
Royal College of Surgeons of
  England
The Royal Greenwich
  Observatory
The Royal Mint
The Royal Opera House
Scotch Whisky Association
Scottish Tourist Board
Screen Digest
SGL Corporate
Shanken International
Siemens AG
Smålands Turistråd
W. H. Smith & Son Ltd
Smithsonian Institution Libraries
Society of Authors
The Society of Motor Vehicle
  Manufacturers and Traders Ltd
Sotheby's London
Sotheby's New York City

Sports Council
Swedish Embassy
Theatre Record
D. C. Thomson & Co Ltd
The Times
Trades Union Congress
The Tree Register of the British
  Isles
United Nations
United Nations Educational,
  Scientific and Cultural
  Organization
US Department of Commerce –
  Bureau of the Census
Variety
WEC International
Welsh Tourist Board
World Bank
World Health Organization

John Amos
D'Este Bond
Charles Brice
Ian Brown
Terry Charman
David Chesterman
Robert Clark
Nick Clee
Ludo Craddock
Luke Crampton
Paul Dickson
Christopher Forbes
Bill Forse
Philippe Garner
Denis Gifford
Claudia Gropper
Max Hanna
Peter Harland
Barry Lazell
John Lloyd
Dr Benjamin Lucas
Hugh Meller
Ian Morrison
Dr Keith Mumby
Adrian Room
Rob Southwood
Eric Syddique
Carey Wallace
Tony Waltham
Beth Gates Warren
Margaret Willes

Thanks also to the book's picture
researcher, Linda Silverman, and
especially its editor, Lorraine
Jerram.

PICTURE CREDITS

Ace Photo Agency: 23, 81, 84
Allsport: 218, 219, 222, 224, 225B
Associated Press: 179, 200
Baiser, Hôtel de Ville, available
    from the Art Group: 100
Barnabys Picture Library: 29T,
    67, 88, 105, 247, 248
Barts Medical Picture Library: 47
BBC: 86, 113, 154, 155TL, 155TR,
    156, 157, 159
British Dental Association
    Museum: 46
British Film Institute: 144
Ian Brown: 129
Cadbury Ltd: 186
Camera Press (UK) Ltd: 210BL
J. A. Cash: 16, 72, 76, 106, 169,
    172, 196, 214, 232, 249
Central Independent Television
    plc: 155BR
Christie's Colour Library: 93, 95,
    96, 152, 193, 227, 243, 244
Bruce Coleman Limited: 42
Colorsport: 178, 217, 220, 221
Rod Davies: 78
De Beers: 182, 183
Zoë Dominic: 134
Environmental Picture Library: 168

Esso UK plc: 173
Mary Evans Picture Library: 64
    inset, 215
Ford Motor Company: 241, 242
Forestry Commission: 27
Fortnum & Mason: 189
Freemans plc: 175
Girl Guides Association: 58
Ronald Grant: 57
Hamleys: 226
Robert Harding Picture Library:
    20, 22, 35, 91, 166; 168–69, 173
Heathrow Airport Ltd 1990: 164
Michael Holford: 14
Hulton Picture Company: 19, 62,
    208
Hutchison Library: 17
Illustrated London News: 37,
    238BR, 239
Image Bank: 79, 191
Alex Imrie: 210BR
Interflora: 32
Kobal Collection: 50, 141, 142,
    143, 144, 145, 146, 147, 148,
    149, 150, 151, 158, 160
John Lewis Partnership: 163
London Transport Museum: 70,
    71

P. Morris Photographics: 37, 39
Mountain Camera: 21, 22
National Grid Company: 172
National Portrait Gallery: 56, 111
National Trust: 90
Peter Newark's Western
    Americana: 83
NHPA: 40, 43, 44
Robert Opie: 174, 194
Oxford English Dictionary: 109
Oxford Scientific Films: 41
Photo Co-op: 59
Photostage: 137, 138, 139
Pinewood Studios: 152T
Polytechnic of Central London:
    107
Popperfoto: 55, 60, 203, 204, 206,
    207, 209, 211, 230, 233, 235,
    238TR
Procter & Gamble: 164
Professional Sport: 223
Quadrant Picture Library: 210TL
Radio Times: 118
Betty Rawlings: 246
Redferns: 121, 122, 123T, 124,
    125T, 126, 127, 128, 131, 132,
    133
Reed Farmers Publishing Group:

188
Rex Features: 12–13, 30, 74, 75,
    80, 102, 103, 104, 117, 125B,
    180, 181, 198, 201
Royal Mint: 184
RSPCA: 167
Science Photo Library: 10, 12, 13
SmithKline Beecham: 48
Sotheby's: 123B
Sotheby's New York: 98
Sport & General: 199
Stockphotos: 231
Syndication International: 29B,
    63, 64, 65, 69, 205, 244, 245, 247
Telegraph Colour Library: 24, 34,
    52, 82
Tesco: 162
Bob Thomas Sports
    Photography: 220, 225T
Topham Picture Library: 250
Trusthouse Forte: 170
Universal Pictorial Press: 112,
    113T, 115
Vintage Magazines: 118, 119
John Watney: 48
ZEFA: 36, 49, 51, 89, 165, 171,
    192, 195, 213, 237

Quiz

ANSWERS

Stars (p. 10)   **1** (c) – the Big Bang Theory.   **2** Pulsars.   **3** *Paint Your Wagon* (1969).   **4** 13.   **5** (b) – an astrolabe.   **6** The Royal Air Force.   **7** (b) – Edward the Confessor. It was at its most visible in 1054.   **8** The whale.   **9** Kiki Dee.   **10** It comes from *gala*, the Greek for milk (hence the 'Milky Way').

Rivers (p. 18)   **1** The Mississippi.   **2** The Isis.   **3** Because Ossining Correctional Facility (formerly Sing Sing Prison) is up the Hudson River from New York.   **4** They all have their mouths in the Wash.   **5** The Severn, Seine and Loire.   **6** The Moskva.   **7** Johann Strauss.   **8** In Greek mythology, in Hades, the home of dead spirits.   **9** The Thames.   **10** Ohio, USA.

Crops (p. 29)   **1** They are all varieties of apple.   **2** Rice and oats.   **3** Poland (268,898 tonnes in 1989).   **4** Hampton Court Palace.   **5** The mechanical reaper.   **6** *Bananas*.   **7** Twice – in *Merry Wives of Windsor* and *Troilus and Cressida*.   **8** Wheat found in the tombs of ancient Egypt (some people believe – erroneously – that it will still grow if planted).   **9** The tomato.   **10** Avocado, courgette, chicory and aubergine.

Famous Animals (p. 35)   **1** Tintin, the Belgian boy detective (Snowy is called 'Milou' in Hergé's original stories).   **2** The Duke of Wellington (he rode him at the Battle of Waterloo).   **3** Lord Emsworth, in various P. G. Wodehouse novels.   **4** Nonsense poet and artist Edward Lear.   **5** The Lone Ranger.   **6** The poet Elizabeth Barrett Browning.   **7** Long John Silver in *Treasure Island*.   **8** Queen Victoria.   **9** Alexander the Great.   **10** Dorothy Gale in *The Wizard of Oz*.

Top Docs (p. 47)   **1**–E.   **2**–D.   **3**–H.   **4**–J.   **5**–G.   **6**–A.   **7**–F.   **8**–C.   **9**–B.   **10**–I.

Names (p. 57)   **1**–C.   **2**–A.   **3**–J.   **4**–I.   **5**–B.   **6**–G.   **7**–F.   **8**–E.   **9**–D.   **10**–H.

Capital Cities (p. 72)   **1** 1960.   **2** Fiji.   **3** Valletta, Malta.   **4** Buenos Aires, the capital of Argentina.   **5** Ankara, the capital of Turkey (called Angora before 1930).   **6** Ulan Bator.   **7** Wellington, the capital of New Zealand, named after the Duke of Wellington.   **8** (Lord) Salisbury.   **9** Spain – Madrid is in the centre of the country.   **10** It was given the name in 1882 by the explorer Henry Morton Stanley, after King Léopold of the Belgians, who had financed his expedition to the Congo.

London Buildings (p. 88)   **1** The Tower of London – it is a tiny cell in the White Tower.   **2** The British Museum, built to house King George III's library.   **3** The National Gallery.   **4** St Paul's Cathedral.   **5** Westminster Abbey.   **6** The Museum of London – it is brought out annually for the Lord Mayor's Show.   **7** Lloyds of London, the insurance market; it is rung on ceremonial occasions and when announcements are being made – but not, as is popularly believed, whenever a shipwreck is reported.   **8** The Public Record Office, Chancery Lane.   **9** The Royal Observatory, Greenwich – a line through it defines the Prime Meridian of the world, from which longitude and Standard Time are measured.   **10** Euston Station.

Famous Paintings (p. 95)   **1** *The Mona Lisa*.   **2** At the Courtauld Institute Galleries in Somerset House, London.   **3** *A Bigger Splash*.   **4** Fording a river.   **5** A Great Western train travelling over Maidenhead Bridge.   **6** William Hogarth.   **7** *The Monarch of the Glen*.   **8** The water-lilies in his garden in Giverny.   **9** *Guernica* – Picasso refused to allow his painting depicting the bombing of the city on 26 April 1937, during the Spanish Civil War, to be hung in Spain until democracy was restored.   **10** *Ophelia*.

Books (p. 114)   **1** One that has extra illustrations added, named after James Granger (1723-76), the English vicar who pioneered the fashion.   **2** Incunabula – which literally means 'swaddling clothes,' hence the 'birth' of the book.   **3** They were all pseudonyms used by Jonathan Swift, the author of *Gulliver's Travels*.   **4** One in which any word or phrase that might be regarded as offensive is removed, named after Dr Thomas Bowdler (1754-1825), or possibly his twin sister, Harriet.   **5** 1935.   **6** Bibliophile.   **7** It might eat his books – it is the common booklouse, or bookworm.   **8** Crown octavo.   **9** Their original manuscripts were all lost – the first two were burned (the first accidentally, the second deliberately) and the third left at Reading station.   **10** They stand for 'top edge gilt' – the pages have been trimmed and gold leaf added to the top edge.

Pop Groups (p. 122)   **1**–F.   **2**–G.   **3**–D.   **4**–A.   **5**–H.   **6**–J.   **7**–I.   **8**–C.   **9**–B.   **10**–E.

British Film Stars (p. 148)   **1** Charlie Chaplin.   **2** Bob Hope.   **3** Laurence Olivier.   **4** Sean Connery.   **5** Julie Andrews.   **6** Dudley Moore.   **7** Cary Grant.   **8** Deborah Kerr.   **9** Charles Laughton.   **10** David Niven.

Radio (p. 154)   **1** 1920.   **2** *The War of the Worlds*, a radio adaptation of H. G. Wells's novel.   **3** The Light Programme, the Third Programme and the Home Service.   **4** Harry Secombe, Peter Sellers and Spike Milligan.   **5** 1964.   **6** *The Archers*.   **7** 1923.   **8** 'Lord Haw-Haw'. Found guilty of treason, he was executed in 1946.   **9** King George V, at the opening of the Empire Exhibition, Wembley, 23 April 1924.   **10** *Flowers in the Rain*.

Shops (p. 163)   **1** He was shot in his office on 24 January 1907 by Horace Rayner, who claimed to be his son.   **2** Woolworth's.   **3** American (he became a British citizen in 1937).   **4** Biba – after the nickname for Hulanicki's sister Biruta.   **5** Macy's, New York.   **6** Sir Jesse Boot (1850-1931), founder of Boots the Chemists.   **7** Grace Brothers.   **8** Los Angeles.   **9** Marks & Spencer.   **10** W. H. (William Henry) Smith.

Millionaires (p. 181)   **1** Lauren Bacall, Marilyn Monroe, Betty Grable.   **2** George Bernard Shaw.   **3** Shirley Temple.   **4** 1826 (by Benjamin Disraeli, later British prime minister, in his novel *Vivian Grey*).   **5** J. Paul Getty.   **6** Howard Hughes.   **7** Andrew Carnegie.   **8** Jay.   **9** Morris cars (named after himself – William Richard Morris).   **10** *High Society*.

Sweets (p. 187)   **1** *Brighton Rock*.   **2** 1937.   **3** Searchers (their next two hits in 1963 were *Sweet Nothins* [sic] and *Sugar and Spice*).   **4** Treets (and, later, Minstrels).   **5** Kojak.   **6** Chewing gum.   **7** Charlie Bucket (the novel's title is *Charlie and the Chocolate Factory*).   **8** A Marathon bar.   **9** The firm's original premises were Trebor Villas in East London (the fact that 'Trebor' is Robert spelled backwards, and one of the founders of the firm was called Robert Robertson, was regarded as an auspicious coincidence).   **10** Praline, after Maréchal Duplessis-Praslin (1598-1675).

Murderers (p. 198)   **1** He was the first murderer to be electrocuted.   **2** An orang-utan.   **3** Ruth Ellis, on 13 July 1955.   **4** Doctor Crippen.   **5** Jack the Ripper.   **6** Fairport Convention (the album was called 'Babbacombe' Lee).   **7** Leon Trotsky.   **8** Mark David Chapman.   **9** Jack Ruby, who shot Lee Harvey Oswald on 24 November 1963.   **10** One – Spencer Percival, in 1812.

Battles (p. 206)   **1** The Battle of Hastings, 1066.   **2** Auchinleck and Montgomery.   **3** Agincourt, 1415.   **4** Oar-driven ships.   **5** The Battle of Arnhem (September 1944).   **6** Little Big Horn (25 June 1876).   **7** Richard III (at Bosworth, 21 August 1485).   **8** Waterloo.   **9** Balaclava (25 October 1854).   **10** Sedgemoor (6 July 1685).

The Olympics (p. 217)   **1** Mary Rand, for the long jump, 1964.   **2** Eric Heiden, speed skater at the Lake Placid Winter Games (the USA boycotted the Summer Games in Moscow).   **3** Johnny Weissmuller.   **4** Steffi Graf (West Germany; tennis was previously included in the Games until 1924).   **5** Ice hockey.   **6** Bob Beamon's (USA).   **7** He is the only competitor to win gold medals at the Summer and Winter Olympics (he won a gold medal for boxing in 1920 and 12 years later was in the successful US 4-man bobsleigh team).   **8** Joe Frazier and George Foreman (Cassius Clay, later Muhammad Ali, and Floyd Patterson also won Olympic golds and went on to become world champions, but their Olympic achievements were at light-heavyweight and middleweight respectively).   **9** Jesse Owens (Hitler was preaching white racial supremacy at the time, and Owens was black).   **10** Nadia Comaneci (Romania).

Trains (p. 248)   **1** Between Pretoria and Cape Town, South Africa.   **2** (a) - *The Mallard*.   **3** Ringo Starr.   **4** Stephenson's *Rocket* (at the opening ceremony of the Liverpool and Manchester Railway, 15 September 1830).   **5** It was converted into a museum, the Musée d'Orsay.   **6** The Monkees.   **7** Sussex (it actually crosses both West and East Sussex).   **8** Albert Finney.   **9** 1963 (on 8 August).   **10** Penzance, Cornwall.